Systems Engine Demystified

A practitioner's handbook for developing complex systems using a model-based approach

Jon Holt

BIRMINGHAM—MUMBAI

Systems Engineering Demystified

Group Product Manager: Aaron Lazar
Publishing Product Manager: Alok Dhuri
Senior Editor: Storm Mann
Content Development Editor: Tiksha Lad
Technical Editor: Gaurav Gala
Copy Editor: Safis Editing
Language Support Editor: Safis Editing
Project Coordinator: Deeksha Thakkar
Proofreader: Safis Editing
Indexer: Tejal Daruwale Soni
Production Designer: Shankar Kalbhor

First published: January 2021

Production reference: 1270121

Published by Packt Publishing Ltd.
Livery Place
35 Livery Street
Birmingham
B3 2PB, UK.

ISBN 978-1-83898-580-6

www.packt.com

For Min Dejlide Skildpadde.

– Jon Holt

Packt.com

Subscribe to our online digital library for full access to over 7,000 books and videos, as well as industry leading tools to help you plan your personal development and advance your career. For more information, please visit our website.

Why subscribe?

- Spend less time learning and more time coding with practical eBooks and Videos from over 4,000 industry professionals

- Improve your learning with Skill Plans built especially for you

- Get a free eBook or video every month

- Fully searchable for easy access to vital information

- Copy and paste, print, and bookmark content

Did you know that Packt offers eBook versions of every book published, with PDF and ePub files available? You can upgrade to the eBook version at packt.com and as a print book customer, you are entitled to a discount on the eBook copy. Get in touch with us at customercare@packtpub.com for more details.

At www.packt.com, you can also read a collection of free technical articles, sign up for a range of free newsletters, and receive exclusive discounts and offers on Packt books and eBooks.

Contributors

About the author

Jon Holt is an internationally-recognized expert in the field of model-based systems engineering. He is an international award-winning author and public speaker and has authored 17 books on systems engineering, including a children's STEM book.

Jon currently works for Scarecrow Consultants, holds a Chair in systems engineering at Cranfield University, and is a Fellow of both the IET and the BCS. He is currently the technical director of INCOSE UK and, in 2015, was identified as one of the 25 most-influential systems engineers in the last 25 years by INCOSE.

He is also actively involved in the promotion of STEM where he uses magic, mind-reading, and occasional escapology to promote systems engineering at various festivals.

About the reviewers

Dr Mike Rodd obtained his BSc (Eng), MSc, and PhD from the University of Cape Town. After acquiring some industrial experience, he was appointed professor at the University of the Witwatersrand and then at the University of Wales, Swansea.

His research focuses on industrial applications of real-time distributed computer systems, including the theoretical fundamentals, industrial networking, use of AI techniques, system specification, and machine vision. He has produced 12 books and over 100 papers and has supervised 45 PhD candidates. He was awarded a senior doctorate from the University of Wales.

He has served as an external examiner for many UK and international universities, and as honorary professor at the Universities of Cardiff, Warwick, Penn State, and Cranfield.

Simon Perry holds BSc degrees from both the University of Leeds and the Open University. Since gaining his mathematics degree in 1986, he has spent over 30 years working in all aspects of software and systems engineering. Since 2014, he has been a director and principal consultant for Scarecrow Consultants. He often speaks at systems engineering conferences and is the author of 11 books on systems engineering and related topics. Such public-speaking events, book writing, and the delivery and facilitation of courses and workshops have given Simon great experience in communicating technical concepts to non-domain experts and non-technical audiences.

Packt is searching for authors like you

If you're interested in becoming an author for Packt, please visit `authors.packtpub.com` and apply today. We have worked with thousands of developers and tech professionals, just like you, to help them share their insight with the global tech community. You can make a general application, apply for a specific hot topic that we are recruiting an author for, or submit your own idea.

Table of Contents

Section 2: Systems Engineering Concepts

3

Systems and Interfaces

4

Life Cycles

5

Systems Engineering Processes

Section 3:
Systems Engineering Techniques

6
Needs and Requirements

7
Modeling the Design

8
Verification and Validation

9
Methodologies

10

Systems Engineering Management

Section 4: Next steps

11
Best Practices

Other Books You May Enjoy

Index

Preface

Systems engineering allows us to develop successful systems while managing complexity. This brings together all aspects of systems engineering in a concise, clear, and consistent way.

This book is a comprehensive introduction for those who are new to systems engineering as well as experienced practitioners. Complete with examples and self-assessment questions, this easy-to-follow guide will teach you all the concepts and techniques required for modern systems engineering.

It provides you with an overview of systems engineering and describes why we need such an approach in our complex world. It covers the essential aspects of model-based systems engineering, systems, life cycles, and processes, along with techniques to realize systems engineering successfully.

By the end of the book, you will be in a position to start applying a systems engineering approach in your organization.

Who this book is for

This book is aimed at aspiring systems engineers, systems managers, systems modelers, and anyone with an interest in systems engineering or modeling.

The book is also suitable for those who are complete newcomers to systems engineering. However, experienced systems engineers may also benefit from reading this book.

What this book covers

Chapter 1, Introduction to Systems Engineering, provides a brief history of systems engineering, then provides an overview of exactly what we mean by systems engineering and what differentiates it from other disciplines of engineering. The real-world, pragmatic need for systems engineering is explored by considering the increased complexity of today's systems, the need for effective and efficient communication, and the need for a clear, context-based understanding of different stakeholders' views of our systems. The practical issues with implementing systems engineering successfully in an organization are also discussed.

Chapter 2, Model-Based Systems Engineering, introduces the most effective and efficient way to realize systems engineering in the form of **Model-Based Systems Engineering** (**MBSE**). MBSE allows systems engineers to understand systems by developing a model to represent the single source of truth and how to use this as the basis for all systems engineering activities.

The system and its model are discussed, along with the importance of a framework that provides the blueprint for the model and various visualization techniques, such as SysML. This is then expanded to include tools and best practices to ensure that the model is as effective as possible.

Chapter 3, Systems and Interfaces, describes exactly what we mean by a system and the different types of systems that exist, including systems of systems. The structure of systems and their system elements – subsystems, assemblies, and components – are discussed as well as how they are arranged in hierarchies. The importance of understanding the relationships between these system elements is explained and how this impacts the system behavior. Behavioral concepts such as states, modes, and interactions are then defined. The key concept of the interfaces that connect a system together and to other systems is explained and the requirements for such interfaces are defined.

Chapter 4, Life Cycles, introduces the concept of life cycles and how they control the evolution of a system. Different types of life cycles are introduced and the importance of understanding the potentially complex relationships between them is stressed. The basic construct of a life cycle, the stage, is introduced and an example system life cycle based on best practice is defined. The behavior of life cycles is then described by considering life cycle models and some of the different types of execution of models. The international best practice model of ISO 15288 and its processes are used as a reference for these life cycle stages.

Chapter 5, *Systems Engineering Processes*, introduces the concepts of processes and their related elements, such as activities, artifacts, stakeholders, and resources. The importance of effective processes that define the overall approach to systems engineering is emphasized. The four different categorizations of processes are introduced and then a description of each of these four categories and their associated processes is provided. The international best practice model of ISO 15288 and its processes are used as a reference for these processes.

Chapter 6, *Needs and Requirements*, explains the importance of needs along with different types, specifically requirements. The whole area of stakeholder needs identification and analysis is described, along with the views necessary to understand the different aspects of needs. Describing needs using text is introduced, and then how to define contexts that may be used for the basis of use cases, as well as how these use cases may be validated by describing scenarios. There is then a discussion of how needs fit into the systems life cycle, which processes are relevant, and how to comply with them.

Chapter 7, *Modeling the Design*, discusses how solutions may be defined by developing effective designs. Various levels of abstraction of design are discussed, such as architectural design and detailed design. Also, different aspects of design, such as logical, functional, and physical designs, are introduced and the relationships between them are defined. There is then a discussion of how design fits into the systems life cycle, which processes are relevant, and how to comply with them.

Chapter 8, *Verification and Validation*, introduces how the system may be demonstrated to be fit for purpose by introducing the concepts of verification (the system works) and validation (the system does what it is supposed to do). A number of techniques are introduced and described that show how verification and validation may be applied at different levels of abstraction of the system and an overview of other techniques that may be used is provided. There is then a discussion of how verification and validation fit into the systems life cycle, which processes are relevant, and how to comply with them.

Chapter 9, *Methodologies*, describes some of the most widely used methodologies for systems engineering that are used in modern industry. Some of these use specific techniques while others are variations on the standard life cycle model. Each is described at a high level, examples are given, and a summary of the methodology's effective use is provided. There is then a discussion of how methodologies fit into the systems life cycle, which processes are relevant, and how to comply with them.

Chapter 10, Systems Engineering *Management*, provides an overview of some of the key management processes and associated techniques that need to be considered and how they can be implemented. The relationship between management techniques and technical techniques is also discussed. There is then a discussion of how design fits into the systems life cycle, which processes are relevant, and how to comply with them.

Chapter 11, Best Practices, is a short chapter that provides a set of information that can be used to continue systems engineering in your own organizations. This includes modern standards and other best practice sources, such as guidelines and also a list of organizations who actively promote systems engineering and provide valuable resources.

To get the most out of this book

This book assumes no prior knowledge of systems engineering or modeling and, therefore is suitable for beginners in the field.

Download the color images

We also provide a PDF file that has color images of the screenshots/diagrams used in this book. You can download it here: `https://static.packt-cdn.com/downloads/9781838985806_ColorImages.pdf`.

Get in touch

Feedback from our readers is always welcome.

General feedback: If you have questions about any aspect of this book, mention the book title in the subject of your message and email us at `customercare@packtpub.com`.

Errata: Although we have taken every care to ensure the accuracy of our content, mistakes do happen. If you have found a mistake in this book, we would be grateful if you would report this to us. Please visit `www.packtpub.com/support/errata`, selecting your book, clicking on the Errata Submission Form link, and entering the details.

Piracy: If you come across any illegal copies of our works in any form on the Internet, we would be grateful if you would provide us with the location address or website name. Please contact us at `copyright@packt.com` with a link to the material.

If you are interested in becoming an author: If there is a topic that you have expertise in and you are interested in either writing or contributing to a book, please visit `authors.packtpub.com`.

Reviews

Please leave a review. Once you have read and used this book, why not leave a review on the site that you purchased it from? Potential readers can then see and use your unbiased opinion to make purchase decisions, we at Packt can understand what you think about our products, and our authors can see your feedback on their book. Thank you!

For more information about Packt, please visit `packt.com`.

Section 1:
Introduction to
Systems Engineering

In this section, we will understand what Systems Engineering is and why there is a growing need for such an approach with today's increasingly complex systems.

This section has the following chapters:

- *Chapter 1, Introduction to Systems Engineering*
- *Chapter 2, Model-Based Systems Engineering*

1
Introduction to Systems Engineering

This chapter focuses on the background of systems engineering, considering the history of the subject and why it is needed. This chapter will also provide an understanding of the main concepts associated with systems engineering and the terminology that will be adopted throughout this book, thus aiding our understanding of the topic as we progress. To do this, we will look at the following topics:

- A brief history of systems engineering
- Defining systems engineering
- The need for systems engineering

A brief history of systems engineering

It may be argued that systems engineering has been being employed ever since mankind started building and developing complex systems. It could also be said that the pyramids in ancient Egypt are examples of complex systems, along with simple stone structures, such as henges, which may actually form part of a larger astrological system. Furthermore, mankind has been observing complex systems such as the solar system since the ancient Greeks first observed the motion of the planets and created the model of the geocentric universe.

In more recent times, the term **systems engineering** may be traced back to the early part of the 20th century in Bell Laboratories in the USA (Fagen 1978). Examples of systems engineering may be observed in the Second World War and the first attempt to teach systems engineering is claimed to have been in 1950 at MIT (Hall 1962).

The 1960s saw the formulation of the field of study known as systems theory, which was first postulated by Ludwig von Bertalanffy (Bertalanffy 1968) as "general systems theory."

The main tenet of systems theory is that it *is a conceptual framework based on the principle that the component parts of a system can best be understood in the context of the relationships with each other and with other systems, rather than in isolation* (Wilkinson 2011). This is essential for all systems engineering as it means that elements in a system, or the systems themselves, are never considered by themselves but in relation to other elements or systems.

As systems became more complex, the need for a new approach to developing systems became more prevalent. Throughout the latter part of the 20th century, this need grew until it reached the point, in 1990, that the **National Council on Systems Engineering (NCOSE)** was founded in the USA. Since then, this organization has evolved into the **International Council on Systems Engineering (INCOSE)**, in 1995, which is the world's foremost authority on systems engineering and has over 70 chapters throughout the world.

Today, as the complexity of the world that we live in and the systems that are being developed are increasing at an ever-expanding rate, there is an increased need for approaches that are rigorous and robust and can cope with these high levels of complexity. Systems engineering is such an approach.

Defining systems engineering

When considering systems engineering as a topic, it is important to understand exactly what is meant by the key terms that are being used. One aspect of all engineering (and all other professions for that matter) that will emerge from this book very quickly is that there is seldom a single, definitive definition for any term. This creates a potential problem as communication, as will be discussed later in this chapter, is key to successful systems engineering.

In order to address this potential problem, this chapter will introduce, discuss, and define specific concepts and their associated terminology that will be used throughout the book. This will enable a domain-specific language to be built up that will then be used consistently throughout this book. Wherever possible and appropriate, the terminology adopted will be based on international best practices, such as standards such as ISO 15288 (ISO 2015), to ensure the provenance of the information presented here.

Defining a system

The first concept that will be discussed is that of a **system**. A system will be defined in different ways by different people, depending on the nature of the system. So, first of all, some types of systems will be identified to illustrate some of the typical types of systems that may be encountered in systems engineering.

There are many different classifications, or taxonomies, of systems and one of the more widely accepted classifications is the one defined by Peter Checkland (Checkland, 1999), which is illustrated in the following diagram:

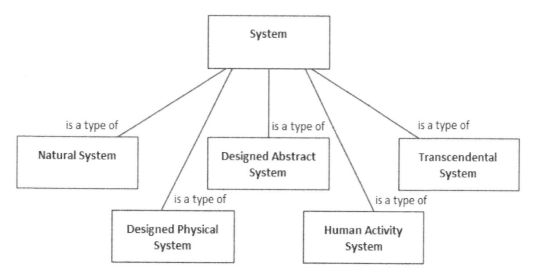

Figure 1.1 – Checkland's five types of system

The diagram in *Figure 1.1* shows Checkland's five types of generic systems, which are as follows:

- **Natural systems**, which represent open systems whose characteristics are beyond the control of humans. Such systems include weather systems, nature, the environment, time, and so on.

- **Designed physical systems**, which represent what most people would immediately think of when considering a system, such as smartphones, tablets, helicopters, cars, trains, planes, spaceships, boats, TVs, cameras, bridges, computer games, satellites, and even domestic appliances. The list is almost endless. The systems will typically consist of physical artifacts that represent the real-world manifestation of the system.

- **Designed abstract systems**, which represent systems that have no physical artifacts but that are used by people to understand or explain an idea or concept. Examples of such systems include models, equations, thought experiments, and so on.

- **Human activity systems**, which are people-based systems that can be seen or observed in the real world. These systems will typically consist of different sets of people interacting to achieve a common goal or purpose. Examples of such systems include a political system, social groups, people-based services, and so on.

- **Transcendental systems**, which are systems that go beyond our current understanding. Examples of such systems include deities, unknown problems, and Numberwang.

This is a good set of classifications that will be the one that is used as a reference in this book. These classifications are a good way to think about different types of systems, but the important point to understand here is that we can apply systems engineering to all five of these different categories of systems.

Also, it should be kept in mind that it is possible to have systems that actually fit into more than one of these categories. Imagine, for example, a transport system that would have to take into account: vehicles (designed physical systems), operating models (designed abstract systems), the environment (a natural system), and the governing political system (a human activity system). In real life, the complexity of systems is such that it is typical, rather than unusual, to encounter examples of these systems that can fit into multiple categories.

Characteristics of a system

The five different broad types of systems have been introduced, but there is also a common set of characteristics that may be associated with all of these types of systems. These characteristics allow the systems to be understood and developed. Let's explore these in the following sections.

System elements – characterizing system structure

Any system will have its own natural structure and may be thought of as a set of interacting **system elements**, as shown in the following diagram:

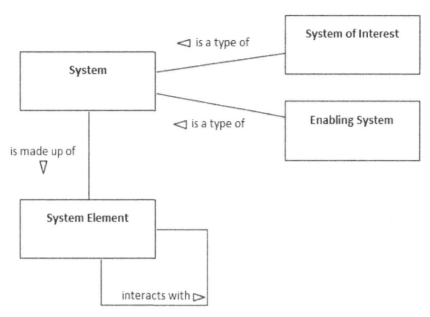

Figure 1.2 – Basic structure of a system – system elements

The diagram in *Figure 1.2* shows that a system is made up of a set of system elements and that there are two types of systems: a **system of interest** and an **enabling system**. System of interest refers to a system that is under development, whereas enabling system refers to any system that has an interest in, or interacts with, a system of interest.

One point to note here is that the structure of the system is actually more complex than this as a system element itself may be broken down into lower-level system elements, which will lead to a system hierarchy of several levels being identified for a specific system. For the purposes of this initial discussion, the number of levels will be kept low in order to keep the explanations simple. Later in this book, when systems are discussed in more detail, examples of hierarchies that span multiple levels will be considered.

The next key point for discussion here is that system elements interact with other system elements. This is a key concept in understanding true systems and applying systems engineering. When considering any system, or system element, it is important to understand that they will interact with other system elements, rather than existing in isolation. In systems engineering, everything is connected to something else and so understanding the relationships between system elements, which form the basis of the interactions between them, is just as important as understanding the system elements themselves.

The interactions between system elements also allow interfaces to be identified and defined between them. Understanding interfaces between system elements is crucial to be able to specify and define all types of systems. As part of understanding interfaces, it is also necessary to understand the information or the material (anything that is not information) that flows across the interfaces.

System structures and interfaces will be discussed in far more detail in *Chapter 3, Systems and Interfaces*.

Stakeholders – characterizing who or what has an interest in the system

One of the key aspects of a system that it is essential to understand as part of any systems engineering endeavor is the **stakeholders** that are associated with the system, as shown in the following diagram:

Figure 1.3 – Defining who or what has an interest in the system – stakeholders

The diagram in *Figure 1.3* shows that a stakeholder has an interest in the system. Understanding stakeholders is key to successful systems engineering, and the definition of a stakeholder is the role of any person, organization, or thing that has an interest in the system.

There are a number of subtleties associated with understanding stakeholders:

- When considering stakeholders, it is the role of the stakeholder that is of interest, not the name of the person, organization, or thing that is associated with it. For example, consider a person, named Jon, who owns a car. The person, Jon, is not a stakeholder associated with the car, rather, the stakeholder is the role that Jon plays when interacting with the car. So, in this example, Jon will play a number of stakeholder roles, such as *owner, driver, passenger, sponsor, maintainer*, and so on. Each of these stakeholder roles will view the system of the car in different ways. It is important, therefore, that rather than thinking about Jon the person, that it is the stakeholder roles that Jon plays that are considered.

- Stakeholders are not necessarily people and can be many other things, such as organizations or just about anything. For example, when considering the system of the car, the stakeholder role of *owner* could be taken on by the person, Jon, but it may be a company car that is owned by a business, in which case it is the organization that takes on the stakeholder role, rather than the person. Equally, the law has an interest in the car, which means that the law is also a stakeholder.

- There is not a one-to-one correlation between stakeholders and the person, organization, or thing that takes on the role. For example, it has already been shown that a single person, Jon, may take on multiple stakeholder roles but, equally, it is possible for many people to take on the same stakeholder role. Consider the passengers that travel in the vehicle along with the driver. In this situation, we may have several people all taking on the same stakeholder role of passenger.

- Stakeholders lie outside the boundary of the system, as do enabling systems. With the definition of stakeholder being anything that has an interest in the system, then it follows that an enabling system is actually just a special type of stakeholder, as the basic definition is the same.

Identifying stakeholders is an essential part of systems engineering as stakeholders will each look at the same system in different ways, depending on the stakeholder role that they play. This leads to an important concept of context, which will be discussed in more detail later in this chapter.

Attributes – characterizing system properties

It is possible to describe the high-level properties of any given system by identifying a set of **attributes**, as shown in the following diagram:

Figure 1.4 – Describing properties of a system – attributes

The diagram in *Figure 1.4* shows that attributes describe a system. Attributes are shown here as relating to the concept of the system but, bearing in mind that a system comprises a number of system elements, these attributes may also apply to the system elements.

These attributes will typically be represented as nouns that may take on a number of different values and be of a specific, pre-defined type, and may also have specific units. Examples of simple types of attributes could be as follows:

- **Dimensions**, such as length, width, and height, which would be typed as real numbers and may have units of millimeters associated with them.

- **Weight**, which would be typed as a real number and have the unit of kilograms associated with it.

- **Element number**, which may be of type integer and may not have a unit associated with it.

- **Name**, which may be of type character or text and may not have a unit associated with it.

Attributes may also take on more complex types; for example:

- **Timestamp**, which may be a set of simple types brought together to provide a more complex type. In this case, the timestamp may be a combination of day (an integer between 1 and 31), month (an integer between 1 and 12), year (an integer ranging from 0000 upwards), hour (an integer between 1 and 24), minute (an integer between 0 and 59), and second (an integer between 0 and 59).

- **Data structures**, which may represent an entire audio or video file that complies with a specific protocol, such as MP3, MP4, and so on.

The full set of possible attributes is almost limitless so the list provided here is intended to provide food for thought rather than be any sort of comprehensive list.

Boundaries – defining the scope of a system

Each system will have at least one **boundary** associated with it, which helps to explain the scope of the system, as shown in the following diagram:

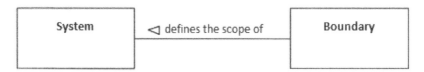

Figure 1.5 – Defining the scope of a system – boundary

The diagram in *Figure 1.5* shows that the boundary defines the scope of the system.

There are many types of boundary that may exist, including the following:

- **Physical boundary**: This may be some sort of enclosure that surrounds the system and separates it from the outside world. This could be a cabinet that houses a number of system elements, such as the body of a car, a barrier that surrounds a piece of land, a wall and doors that define a room, and so on.

- **Conceptual boundary**: This is a non-physical boundary that can be imagined but not necessarily observed. An example of this is the boundary between a car and the GPS satellite that it interacts with. In this case, where is the boundary of the system considered to be? Is it the transmitter and receiver in the car, the transmitter and receiver on the satellite, or is it the waves that are transmitted or the protocols that are used as part of the transmission?

- **Stakeholder Boundary**: Different stakeholders may look at the same system in different ways and, therefore, where they perceive the boundary of the system to be may change depending on the stakeholder. Consider again two different stakeholders for a car. A passenger may consider the boundary of the car as being the physical body, or the shell of the car, whereas the maintainer of the car may also consider the conceptual boundary of the link between the car and the satellite as the boundary.

The boundary of a system allows a number of key aspects of the system to be understood:

- **What is inside the boundary**: It is important to understand which system elements are considered to be inside the boundary of the system and which are considered to be outside the boundary of the system. System elements that are considered inside the boundary of the system will help to define exactly what the scope of the system is.

- **What is outside the boundary**: In the same way that understanding what is inside the boundary is important, in terms of system elements, it is also important to understand what lies outside the boundary of the system. Things that exist outside the boundary of the system are considered to be either stakeholders or enabling systems, or as was discussed previously, both.

- **Where key interfaces exist**: Every time an interaction occurs across the boundary of a system, it identifies an interface to that system. Identifying interfaces is an important part of systems engineering and a boundary can be used to identify all interfaces between a system and the outside world.

Bearing in mind these discussion points, defining the boundary of a given system may not be as simple as it first appears as different stakeholders may identify different boundaries. This is not necessarily a problem but it is important to bear this in mind and to ensure that no conflicts occur because of these differences.

Needs: the purpose of the system

Each system must have a purpose and this purpose is expressed by defining a set of **needs**, as shown in the following diagram:

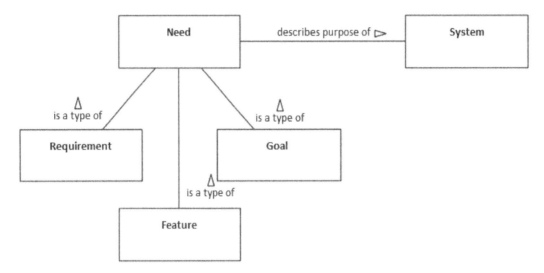

Figure 1.6 – Defining the purpose of the system – needs

The diagram in *Figure 1.6* shows that needs describe the purpose of the system. A need describes the concept of something that is described about the System. The diagram also shows that there are different types of needs, three of which are listed here:

- **Requirement**: A requirement represents a statement of something that it is desirable for the system to do. These are often related to the desired specific functionality of the system. For example, a requirement for a car may be that the driver must be able to slow the car down using the brake pedal, the car must have seat belts, or the car must travel at a top speed of at least 1,000 miles per hour.

- **Feature**: A feature represents a higher-level need of the system that does not necessarily relate to a specific function but may relate to a collection of functions. An example of a feature may be that the car must have adaptive cruise control, the car must self-park, or the car must have crash prevention capabilities.

- **Goal**: A goal is a very high-level need that represents a need of the overall system. An example of this may be to transport a driver and three passengers over a distance of 300 miles on a single charge.

It should be stressed here that there are many different terms used for all aspects of needs that differ vastly from organization to organization and from industry to industry. For example, the term "capability" is often used in the aerospace and defense industries whereas the term "feature" is more typically used in transport industries, such as automotive and rail. In a way, it does not matter which terminology is adopted, providing that it is adopted consistently.

Constraints: limiting the realization of the system

All systems will be limited in some way in terms of how they can be realized and these limitations are referred to as **constraints**, as shown in the following diagram:

Figure 1.7 – Defining limitations on the realization of the system – constraints

The diagram in *Figure 1.7* shows that constraints limit the realization of the system. All systems will have constraints associated with them that will limit how the system may be realized and these are often grouped into a number of categories, examples of which are as follows:

- **Quality constraints**: In almost all systems, there will be constraints that relate to best practice sources, such as standards. It is typical for a number of standards to be identified that the development approach used to deliver the system must comply with. These standards will typically relate to the development processes used to describe the overall systems engineering approach. For example, a standard that is often used for cars in the automotive industry is ISO 26262.

- **Implementation constraints**: These constraints will limit the way that the system can be built. This may limit the materials that are used; for example, a car may be limited to being made out of aluminum rather than steel.

- **Environmental constraints**: All systems must be deployed somewhere and many systems will be defined in a natural environment, which may lead to certain constraints coming into play. For example, a car may be limited in its emissions in order to minimize the impact on the environment.

- **Safety constraints**: Almost all systems will have constraints placed on them that ensure that the system can operate in a safe manner, particularly if things go wrong. For example, a car may be required to have functions in place that will protect the driver and passengers in the event of a crash.

The preceding list provides a broad set of categories for different types of constraints but it is by no means exhaustive.

It should also be kept in mind that these constraints can be complex themselves and actually belong to more than one of these categories. For example, a car may have a limitation that all of the materials used must be recyclable, which could place it in both the environmental and implementation categories.

It should also be pointed out that some of these constraints lend themselves to different stages of the system life cycle. The system life cycle is an important concept that will be discussed in more detail later in this book.

Constraints are also often described as special types of needs as they are often represented as being related to specific needs rather than directly to the system itself. This will be discussed in more detail in *Chapter 6, Needs and Requirements,* which focuses specifically on needs.

Summary of system concepts

All of the concepts that have been introduced and discussed in this section may now be brought together to provide an overview of how they relate to the concept of a system:

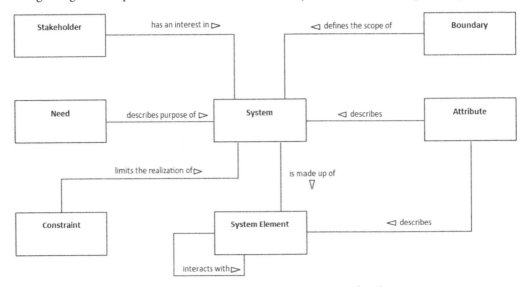

Figure 1.8 – Summary of the key concepts associated with a system

The diagram here shows a summary of the key concepts associated with systems that will be used throughout this book. It is important that these are all well understood as they will all be used from this point forward.

Defining systems engineering

There are many definitions of the term **systems engineering**, and there are various publications that discuss many of these and compare and contrast them (Holt and Perry 2019) (INCOSE 2018). For the purposes of this book, the main definition that will be used is taken from *ISO 15288* (ISO 2015), which, in turn, is used in the *INCOSE Systems Engineering Handbook* (INCOSE 108), which defines systems engineering as:

"The realization of successful systems"

This is shown pictorially in the following diagram:

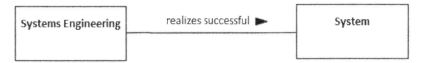

Figure 1.9 – Basic definition of systems engineering

The diagram in *Figure 1.9* shows the basic definition of systems engineering. This diagram may seem trivial but it will enable the general term to be related to all of the other concepts that are discussed consequently in this chapter.

This is a simple but effective definition of the term, but there are a few factors that must be kept in mind when reading this description:

- Systems engineering is a multidisciplinary approach that takes into account all areas of engineering, including mechanical, electrical, civil, software, and so on. Crucially, however, it should also be recognized that systems engineering is not just limited to engineering disciplines, but includes many other diverse areas, such as management, mathematics, physics, psychology, and just about any other area!

- Systems engineering is applied across the entire life cycle of a system and is not restricted to any single stage. This means that systems engineering is considered right from the point in time that the very first idea for the system is conceived until the system is ultimately retired. Even when working on a single stage, it is important that all stages of the life cycle are considered.

- Systems engineering does not remove the need for intelligence, as systems engineers must never blindly follow instructions, and requires a healthy dose of common sense in order to be effective.

With these considerations in mind, the initial definition may be expanded upon to be redefined as (Holt & Perry 2007):

Systems engineering is a multi-disciplinary, common-sense approach that enables the realization of successful systems

Now the definitions have been established, it is necessary to understand why systems engineering is needed in the first instance.

The need for systems engineering

The need for systems engineering is actually very simple. In real life, it is very easy for things to go wrong. Projects overrun, airplanes fall out of the sky, software and IT bring organizations to their knees, and whole societies are crippled by non-joined-up government and management, all of which are the result of system failures at one level or another.

Since it is so easy for things to go wrong, it is important to understand why. Fundamentally, there are three main causes for such system failures, which are as follows:

- **Complexity**, where complexity is not identified and, therefore, cannot be managed or controlled.

- **Communication**, where communication fails or is ambiguous.

- **Understanding**, where different points of view are not taken into account, and assumptions are made.

The problem is actually worse than this as these three main causes feed into one another, so unmanaged complexity will lead to communication failure and a lack of understanding; communication failure will lead to complexity and a lack of understanding; and a lack of understanding will lead to increased complexity and communication problems (Holt 2001).

These three causes are often referred to as the three evils of systems engineering and each will be discussed in more detail in the following sections.

Complexity

Complexity exists in every system and may be thought of as being one of two types, as shown in the following diagram:

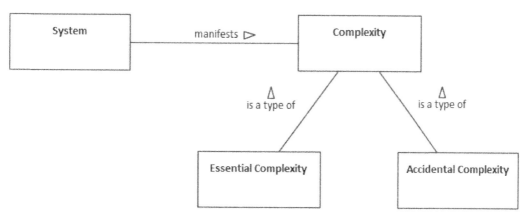

Figure 1.10 – Types of complexity

The diagram in *Figure 1.10* shows that systems manifest complexity. There are two main types of complexity:

- **Essential complexity** is the natural complexity that is inherent in the system. The term "essential" is used here as it refers to complexity that manifests in the essence of the system. It is not possible to lower the essential complexity of a system, but it is possible to manage and control this complexity providing, of course, it has been identified in the first instance.

- **Accidental complexity** is not natural and is introduced by inefficiencies in the peoples, processes, and tools that are employed to implement systems engineering, which will be discussed later in this chapter. Accidental complexity can certainly be lowered and this forms a natural part of systems engineering.

Complexity manifests itself in the relationships between things, whether these are between the system elements that make up the system or between systems themselves. There are many subtleties to complexity that will be discussed in more detail in the following sections.

An example...

In order to illustrate and, therefore, understand how complexity has changed and evolved over the last few decades, a simple example of a system will be introduced that will be used throughout this book to explain the various concepts and techniques that will be used as part of the overall approach to systems engineering.

For this example, the system that will be considered is a motor car, so now consider two such cars: one that was developed and built 50 years ago, around 1970, and one that was developed and built in the modern age, around 2020.

Consider the need for the system. The purpose of any car is to transport a number of people from point A to point B. The user interface of the car is, basically, a steering wheel, gear stick, and three pedals (accelerator, brake, and clutch pedals).

This basic need, or purpose, of a car has not really changed over the last 50 years, but the point of discussion here is that the complexity of the car has changed in four different ways, which will be discussed in turn in the following sections.

The complexity of the system elements

In order to illustrate how the complexity of the system elements has changed over the last 50 years, each of the cars will be discussed separately and then compared and contrasted.

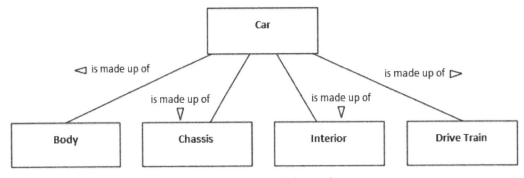

Figure 1.11 – Basic breakdown of a car

The diagram in *Figure 1.11* shows a simple example system of a car. There are four system elements at the next level down that make up the car, which are as follows:

- The body, which includes lower-level system elements such as wings, doors, mirrors, and so on.

- The chassis, which includes lower-level system elements, such as brakes, wheels, suspension, and so on.

- The interior, which includes lower-level system elements such as seats, dashboard, controls, and so on.

- The drive train, which includes lower-level system elements such as the motor and the gearing.

The system elements that make up the 50-year-old car are entirely mechanical and electrical in nature. On top of this, almost all of the system elements will be mechanical; only very few of them will be electrical.

Electrical system elements will be limited to the lights, indicators, fan, wipers, and starter motor, and that is really the extent of the electrical system elements. The mechanical elements, however, will make up all of the other system elements that relate to the body, chassis, drive train, and interior. The vast majority of the system elements, therefore, are mechanical with only a handful of them being electrical. This means that almost all of the interfaces between the system elements will be mechanical in nature, with only a few being electrical or electro-mechanical.

In order to build this car, it is largely a matter of integrating self-contained system elements that have well-defined interfaces. Also, any electrical connections will require quite simple point-to-point wiring.

Now consider the modern car. There are two new major types of system elements that now exist that did not exist at all on the 50-year-old car, which are electronic and software-based system elements. The vast majority of system elements on a modern car will fall into one of these two categories. Electronic system elements will include the following:

- Controllers (such as light controllers, indicator controllers, and so on)

- Sensors (such as temperature, pressure, rotation, and so on)

- Actuators (such as levers, small gears, motors, and so on)

- Display elements (such as dashboard lights, audio alerts, and so on)

All modern cars contain a vast amount of software and, in every case, this software will be split across multiple nodes across the whole vehicle. On top of the software itself, the software must be connected to its associated electronic component, which will, in turn, lead to the need for communication buses, such as **Controller Area Networks (CANs)**, which will themselves use communication protocols.

In order to build the modern car, it is no longer a matter of simply integrating system elements because the interfaces between the elements are now far more complex and will involve subtle changes in voltage and current levels, data transfer, communication protocols, and complex wiring.

The complexity of the system elements that make up the car has, therefore, greatly increased between the two vehicles. Indeed, not only has it increased in terms of the number of system elements but also in the nature of these system elements.

The complexity of constraints

It has already been stated that the basic need for a car has not really changed at a high level in the last 50 years. The basic need is to transport people from point A to point B. In the past, the emphasis of most cars was to make them go as quickly as possible with little regard for anything else. One of the major things that has changed over the last 50 years is not necessarily the basic needs, but the constraints that are now imposed on those needs.

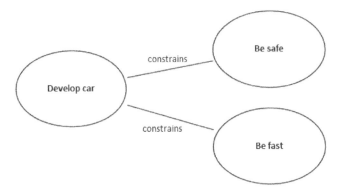

Figure 1.12 – Simple constraints

The diagram in *Figure 1.12* shows a simple need that is named **Develop car** and there are two main constraints associated with this, which are **Be safe** and **Be fast**. This diagram here represents, at a very high level, the basic needs and constraints associated with the 50-year-old car.

The number of constraints associated with the older car is very small compared to that of the modern car, which is shown in the following diagram:

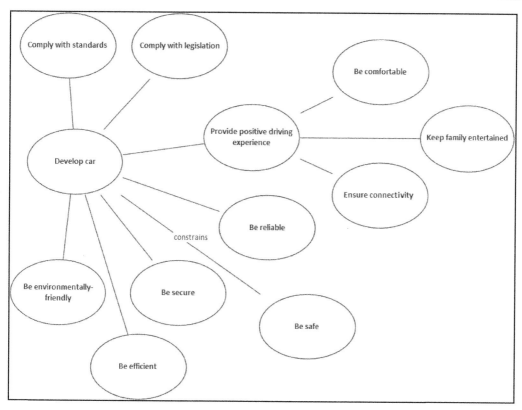

Figure 1.13 – Complex constraints

The diagram in *Figure 1.13* shows the constraints associated with the modern car. The first thing to notice when comparing the two sets of constraints is that the number of constraints themselves has increased dramatically. There are new sets of constraints that simply did not exist in the older car, for example, **Be secure** is now an issue that was not really a main consideration previously. Likewise, there is a whole set of new constraints associated with **Provide positive driving experience**. This increase in the number of constraints will lead to an increased number of relationships between the basic needs and constraints, which will naturally lead to an increase in the complexity of the needs and constraints.

It is not just the increase in the number of constraints that leads to an increase in complexity, but also the complexity of individual constraints has increased. There are a number of constraints now that are related to best-practice models, such as **Comply with standards** and **Comply with legislation**. This is interesting from a complexity point of view as these constraints will also relate directly to other constraints. Consider **Be safe**, which was previously seen as a standalone constraint. In the modern vehicle, this constraint will also have both of the compliance constraints associated with it. Since there are far more standards and legislation in place now that apply to cars that did not exist 50 years ago, the complexity of individual constraints has increased along with the increase of dependencies between constraints.

The complexity of a system of systems

Another area where the car has increased in complexity over the last 50 years occurs when a higher-level system of systems is considered. A system of systems is not just a collection of interacting systems, it is a collection of interacting systems that exhibits some behavior that is not exhibited by any of its constituent systems. Therefore, it can be argued that a fleet of vehicles is not a system of systems, as it is simply a collection of systems that does little more than make the overall system slightly more complex. A true higher-level system of systems may be the transport network that a car forms part of. The overall transport system of systems exhibits a number of behaviors, such as ensuring an efficient journey from end to end, keeping traffic moving when accidents occur, and providing seamless links with smart cites and other transport systems, such as rail.

A modern car is now truly part of a system of systems as the vehicle itself interacts with other systems, such as smart cities, smart roads, the cloud, satellites, and so on, that did not occur with an older vehicle. The modern car is also taking over some of the skills that were previously the sole domain of the driver, such as parking, maintaining constant speeds, identifying potential dangers, and so on.

The complexity of the car system has therefore increased due to the fact that the car is now truly part of a wider system of systems.

Complexity shift

The final aspect of increased complexity that will be discussed does not necessarily manifest as an increase in the same type of complexity but, rather, represents a shift in complexity due to increases in other aspects of complexity.

Consider again the older car and its motor. The motor in the 50-year-old car is an internal combustion engine that mainly comprises mechanical system elements with a handful of electrical system elements. The internal combustion engine may be considered to have quite a high level of mechanical complexity that is naturally exhibited.

Now consider a modern electric car. The motor on the modern electric car is an electric motor that has a single moving part, that of the motor shaft. The mechanical complexity of the modern car is practically non-existent when compared with the older car. The complexity of the modern car lives mainly in the software that monitors the rest of the car and controls the electric motor. There is no software whatsoever in the older car.

The older car, therefore, has high mechanical complexity and zero software complexity. The modern car has very low mechanical complexity and very high software complexity.

The complexity in the modern car has therefore shifted in nature – in this case, away from mechanical complexity and towards software complexity.

Bringing it all together

It can be seen that the complexity of a typical system has increased dramatically over the last few decades. In the example we have used, the car increases in complexity for four different reasons, which have been discussed.

This increase in complexity does not apply just to automotive systems but to any and all types of systems. In reality, these four types of increased complexity will actually have interdependencies, which in turn will also increase the overall complexity. For example, the increase in complexity of the system elements will also lead to a complexity shift and, potentially, an increase in the system of systems complexity, which in turn, will lead to an increase in the number of constraints.

Identifying complexity

The key to managing complexity is identifying where the complexity lives in a system. This is a topic that will be followed up throughout the book, particularly when artifacts and models are discussed.

The next section discusses the problems associated with communication, which, alongside complexity and understanding, is one of the three evils of systems engineering.

Communication

Communication is key to successful systems engineering. It has already been discussed that systems engineering naturally brings together people from multiple and disparate backgrounds, which will lead to an increase in potential communication problems. Poorly-specified information, language, and protocols lead to ambiguity, which will lead to poor or inefficient communication.

Communication can exist at many levels, such as the following:

- **Between people**: The obvious form of communication is between people. People interacting with other people is key to any successful project and is a matter that is more complex than it at first appears, as will be discussed in this section.

- **Between and within organizations**: A successful business relies on different organizations, or organizational units, within the same company being able to communicate effectively. The media for these communications may be through documents, agreements, contracts, and so on but the same communication problems will occur.

- **Between and within systems and system elements**: It is essential that the systems that are relied upon for our business and projects can also communicate effectively. This will include IT systems, other technical systems, and service-based systems, to name but a few.

When thinking about communication, another way to think about it is that communication must be effective and efficient between all stakeholders, whether they are represented by people, organizations, or things (such as systems). When considering communication in the world of systems engineering, it is inter-stakeholder communication that is being addressed.

These communication problems are further compounded by the fact that communication can also exist between these different types, such as between people and systems, people and organizations, and so on.

Defining common languages

One of the main solutions that is vaunted for improving communication is to get all parties to "speak a common language." This is an obvious solution and an important one, but speaking a common language is actually more complex than it may at first appear.

When considering a common language, there are actually two types of language that must be defined, as shown in the following diagram:

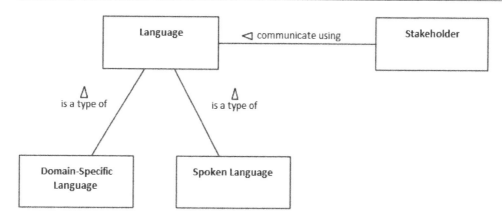

Figure 1.14 – Aspects of the common language

The diagram in *Figure 1.14* shows that stakeholders communicate using a **Language**, so it is essential that this **Language** is as clear and unambiguous as possible. This **Language**, however, has two aspects: **Spoken Language** and **Domain-Specific Language**.

The first aspect that will be considered is that of the **Spoken Language**, which provides a basic mechanism for communication. An example of **Spoken Language** is the fact that this book is written in the English language. In order to understand the information in this book, it is essential that the reader can speak English. Clearly, there are many more spoken languages than the English language, but the decision that has been made for this book (or system) was to select English as the chosen **Spoken Language**. This is clearly an obvious decision that needs to be made but, just because everyone reading this book speaks English does not mean that there will be no ambiguity nor misunderstandings. This is because the second aspect of **Language** that needs to be considered is **Domain-Specific Language**.

Domain-Specific Language defines the specific concepts and terminology that will be used for a given application or domain. For example, consider the word "function." The word "function" is a common English language word but a word that will actually take on different meanings depending on which stakeholder is reading it.

It is essential that the **Domain-Specific Language** is defined as it forms the cornerstone for successful systems engineering. This chapter actually defines the **Domain-Specific Language** for systems engineering that is used throughout this book. Each diagram in this chapter contributes towards defining the full set of concepts and the associated terminology that is used for systems engineering in this book.

Languages for systems engineering

When it comes to languages that can be used for systems engineering, both the **Spoken Language** and the **Domain-Specific Language** must be defined:

- In terms of the **Spoken Language**, there are several standard languages that can be adopted that are used throughout the industry across the world, such as the Unified Modeling Language, Systems Modeling Language, and Business Process Modeling Notation, among others. For the purposes of this book, the **Spoken Language** that has been selected is the **Systems Modeling Language (SysML)**, which will be discussed in more detail in *Chapter 2, Model-Based Systems Engineering*.

- In terms of the **Domain-Specific Language**, this will be different for every organization. A generic **Domain-Specific Language** for systems engineering is defined in this chapter and used throughout this book and may be used as a basis for readers to tailor into a language that fits their specific business.

Both types of language must be defined for successful systems engineering.

The next section discusses the problems associated with understanding, which, alongside complexity and communication, is one of the three evils of systems engineering.

Understanding

It is essential that all stakeholders share an understanding of the system, however, different stakeholders will perceive the system in different ways due to their different backgrounds and knowledge, which creates a potentially large problem. This problem may be addressed by considering the concept of "context." In order to understand the concept of context, consider a set of generic stakeholders, as shown in the following diagram:

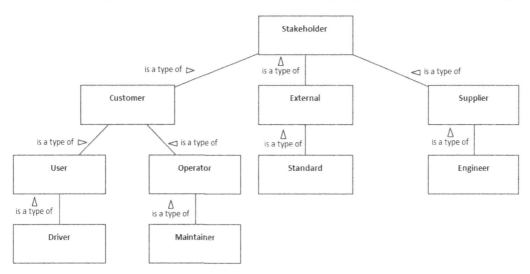

Figure 1.15 – Generic set of stakeholders

The diagram in *Figure 1.15* shows a generic set of stakeholders associated with the car system.

There are three broad categories of stakeholder, which are as follows:

- **Customer**, which represents the set of roles that will ultimately benefit from the system that is being developed. The diagram here shows that **Customer** has two types, which are **User**, such as the **Driver** of the vehicle, and **Operator**, such as the **Maintainer** of the vehicle.

- **External**, which represents the set of roles that have an interest in the system that will limit or restrict the system in some way. The diagram here shows that there is a single type of **External** stakeholder, which is **Standard**.

- **Supplier**, which represents the set of roles that are interested in developing and delivering the systems, such as **Engineer**.

The identification of stakeholders is an essential part of systems engineering, as it is this complete set of stakeholders whose expectations need to be understood and managed, rather than just the end user of the system.

When considering the complete set of stakeholders, it should be kept in mind that different stakeholders may look at the same system and perceive different needs or, as in almost all systems, they may look at the same need and interpret it in a different way depending on their point of view. When something is interpreted in a different way from a different point of view, this is referred to as a "context."

The concept of context is one of the single most important aspects of representing a system that must be understood for successful systems engineering, yet is one that is often overlooked or ignored altogether.

In order to illustrate this crucial concept of context, imagine that there is a statement of need associated with a system, which is *the system must be safe*. At first glance, this may seem like a straightforward statement with little or no room for ambiguity, but the actual meaning of this statement will be different for each of the different stakeholders. For example, from the point of view of the **Driver**, this statement may be interpreted as the car must have seatbelts, airbags, driver-assist technology, and so on. From the point of view of the **Maintainer**, this statement may mean that the drive train must be developed in such a way that the battery can be turned off to ensure that no parts of the car are live when maintaining the vehicle. From the point of view of the **Standard** stakeholder there may be several safety aspects, such as meeting specific requirements for crash impact. Finally, from the point of view of the **Engineer**, the system may have to satisfy a number of scenarios relating to the safety case for the vehicle.

The point here is that there are multiple interpretations for the same set of needs. In order to manage the expectations of all stakeholders, it is important that all of these different points of view, or contexts, can be understood.

Now that the three evils of systems engineering have been discussed, it is time to consider the implementation of systems engineering

The implementation of systems engineering

In order to implement systems engineering successfully, there are three aspects of implementation that must be considered, which are shown in the following diagram:

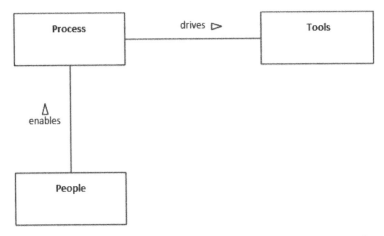

Figure 1.16 – The classic systems engineering mantra – people, process, and tools

The diagram in *Figure 1.16* shows three main concepts: **People**, **Process**, and **Tools**. These are referred to as the **Systems Engineering Mantra** (Holt & Perry 2019).

These three concepts are very important but it is the relationships between them that provide a true understanding of what information is being conveyed. It is important that these **People** enable the overall **Process** as the competencies associated with the **People** are worth nothing if they do not enable the overall approach. Also, the overall approach must drive the choice of **Tools**, rather than the **Tools** affecting the **Process**.

These concepts are expanded upon in the following diagram:

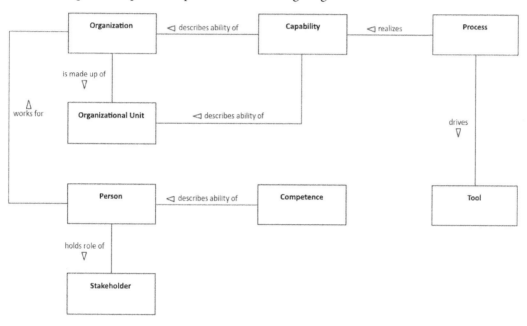

Figure 1.17 – Expanded concepts of People, Process, and Tools

The diagram in *Figure 1.17* shows the expanded concepts that were first introduced in *Figure 1.16*. By considering each of the main concepts in turn, it is possible to enhance the original descriptions:

- **People**: It is the competencies of the people that are of interest, rather than the presence of the people themselves. It is essential that people have the appropriate set of knowledge and skills and the attitude that is required to do the task at hand effectively and efficiently. It is also important not to confuse the concept of **People** with that of stakeholders. As was discussed previously, **People** may hold any number of stakeholder roles and it is a set of competencies associated with these roles that may be thought of as the ability of the individual.

- **Process**: It is the overall approach that is being followed, rather than just a set of individual processes. The term **Process** here may be thought of as the overall ability of the organization or organizational unit to carry out a specific task.

- **Tools**: The set of software, resources, or, in fact, anything that is intended to allow **People** to carry out their **Process** in a more effective or efficient manner. Such **Tools** may include software design and modeling tools, management tools, pen and paper, standards, notation, and so on.

Overall, it is important that there is a balance between **People**, **Process**, and **Tools** to enable successful systems engineering.

Summary

This chapter has introduced the main concepts and terminology associated with systems engineering, which may be thought of as the domain-specific language that will be used throughout this book. This domain-specific language is captured in all of the diagrams in this chapter. It is important to understand this domain-specific language, so these diagrams must be well understood and the following points considered:

- Each diagram is made up of a series of boxes with words in them that are joined together by lines.

- The main concepts for systems engineering are captured in the boxes and the lines between the boxes.

- The terminology for systems engineering is what is written inside the boxes and on the lines.

The relevance of these diagrams will be discussed further in the next chapter, in which models and modeling are introduced.

Questions

After reading the chapter, you should be able to answer the following questions:

1. Which definition of systems engineering works best for you?

2. How do spoken language and domain-specific language match the concepts and terminology used in your organization?

3. Redefine terms in each of the diagrams in this chapter to suit your own organization.

4. Identify any areas of ambiguity with these concepts in your organization.

5. Identify one key system that you work with and some of its characteristics.

References

- (Wilkinson 2011) Wilkinson L.A. (2011) Systems Theory. In: Goldstein S., Naglieri J.A. (eds) Encyclopedia of Child Behavior and Development. Springer, Boston, MA

- (Bertalanffy 1968) von Bertalanffy, L. 1968. General system theory: Foundations, development, applications. Revised ed. New York, NY: Braziller.

- (Holt 2001) Holt J., UML for Systems Engineering. 1st edition. Stevenage, UK: IEE; 2001

- (Holt and Perry 2019) Holt J., Perry S. SysML for Systems Engineering – a model-based approach, Third edition. Stevenage, UK: IET; 2008

- (Checkland 1999) Checkland, P. B. 1999. Systems Thinking, Systems Practice. Chichester, UK: John Wiley & Sons

- (ISO 2015) ISO/IEC. ISO/IEC 15288:2015 Systems and Software Engineering – System Life Cycle Processes. 1st edn. International Organisation for Standardisation; 2015

- (Holt & Perry 2008) Holt J., Perry S. SysML for Systems Engineering. Stevenage, UK: IET; 2008

- (INCOSE 2016) INCOSE. Systems Engineering Handbook – A Guide for System Life Cycle Processes and Activities. Version 4. INCOSE; 2016

2
Model-Based Systems Engineering

In this chapter, the main approach to systems engineering will be introduced and discussed and its key properties described. This approach is known as **model-based systems engineering**, or **MBSE**, which is the common abbreviation. The information contained in this chapter concerning MBSE is essential learning for any modern-day systems engineer. A good MBSE approach will provide a set of effective tools and techniques that will enable the realization of successful systems while managing the complexity of today's connected systems, and allowing all relevant aspects of the system to be understood in as simple a manner as possible. This will also enable all information concerning the system to be communicated to the appropriate stakeholders.

This chapter covers the following topics:

- **An introduction to MBSE**: Here, the key concepts associated with MBSE will be introduced and discussed, and collected together using "MBSE in a slide."

- **The evolution of MBSE**: Here, the transition from a document-based approach to a model-based approach to systems engineering will be discussed.

- **Modeling with MBSE**: In this section, the fundamentals of modeling for MBSE will be described.

- **The spoken language – the Systems Modeling Language (SysML)**: Here, the chosen notation, the Systems Modeling Language, or SysML, is described and an example given.

- **The domain-specific language – the ontology**: At this point, the ontology that forms the cornerstone of any MBSE endeavor will be introduced in detail.

This chapter will provide the basis for all of the techniques that are used throughout the rest of this book.

An introduction to MBSE

Before the main concepts of MBSE are discussed, it is important to understand a few key philosophical points.

Firstly, MBSE is not a subdivision, nor a subset, of systems engineering; MBSE is a complete approach to systems engineering and, therefore, is used for all aspects of systems engineering. One way to look at MBSE is that it is systems engineering that is achieved through a rigorous approach, and this is illustrated in the following diagram:

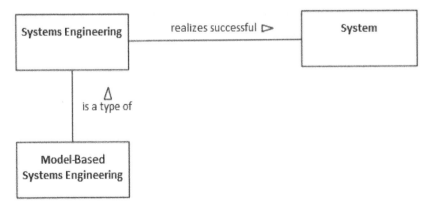

Figure 2.1 – MBSE is a type of systems engineering

The diagram in *Figure 2.1* shows that MBSE is actually a type of systems engineering, rather than being a subset or component part of systems engineering. This is essential to understand and you must be very clear about this matter.

The **International Council on Systems Engineering** (**INCOSE**) defines a worldwide vision of the future of systems engineering on a periodic basis. In the INCOSE Vision 2015 (INCOSE 2014), INCOSE society predicts that by the year 2025, all systems engineering will be model-based.

The question arises, therefore, of what exactly is meant by MBSE and how it is different from traditional systems engineering. The next few sections will discuss these questions in some detail.

Abstracting the system

When considering systems engineering, it is important to never lose sight of the goal of systems engineering, which is to **develop a successful system**. This seems like an obvious statement, but it is essential that every activity that is carried out as part of systems engineering contributes to this goal.

When considering MBSE, compared to traditional systems engineering, the main thing that must be understood is where the knowledge, information, and data concerning the system resides. In the case of traditional systems engineering, all of the knowledge concerning a system resides in the set of documents that describes the system. In the case of MBSE, all of the knowledge concerning the system resides in the **model** that abstracts the system:

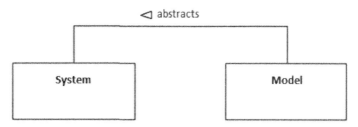

Figure 2.2 – The concept of the model

The diagram in *Figure 2.2* shows the most fundamental concept of MBSE, which is that the model abstracts the system. An abstraction may be thought of as a representation or simplification of the system. The model must be a simplification of the system; otherwise, it would *be* the system. As the model is a simplification of the system, it then follows, by its very nature, that the information contained in the model is incomplete. This sometimes leads to the fatuous argument that all models are wrong. The aim of a model, in MBSE, is to *provide an abstraction of the system in order to realize that system successfully*. The aim of the model in MBSE is not to contain as much information as possible, nor to attempt to capture *all* of the information concerning a system. The aim is to capture *enough* relevant information to realize the system successfully.

It is important to always remember this as it is very easy to generate more and more information as part of the model that is of no use to anyone. It is essential that all information contained in the model is useful.

The information that is contained in the model is grouped into specific collections that are known as **views**, as shown in the next diagram:

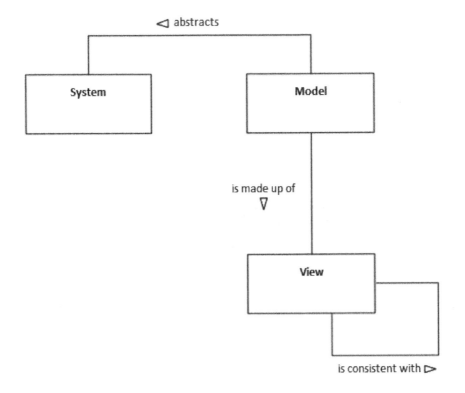

Figure 2.3 – The model is made up of views

The diagram in *Figure 2.3* shows that the model is made up of a number of **views**. Each of these views represents a collection of information; however, it is essential that this is relevant information that adds value to the overall systems engineering endeavor – otherwise, it is a waste of time. Therefore, in order to ascertain whether a collection of information is a view and, therefore, a valid part of the overall model, there is a number of questions that must be answered:

- **Which stakeholders would want to look at the view?** In order to answer this question, it is essential that each view is related to a set of stakeholders that are interested in the system. The concept of stakeholders was discussed in *Chapter 1, Introduction to Systems Engineering,* and it was stated that identifying the correct set of stakeholders is an essential part of systems engineering. Whenever any information is requested concerning the system, it is the stakeholders who make these requests.

- **Why would these stakeholders want to look at the view?** It is essential to understand why each relevant stakeholder wants to look at the view. Every view that is created as part of the model must add value to the systems engineering endeavor. In order to do that, at least one stakeholder must gain some sort of benefit from looking at the view.

- **What information must be contained in the view?** It is important to know what information, out of the complete model, must be made available for the relevant stakeholders to look at.

If it is not possible to answer these three questions for each of the views, then the result is quite simple – it is not a valid view and, therefore, must not be considered as part of the systems engineering endeavor. It is very easy to generate information in the form of views that is of no use to anybody. By asking these questions each time a view is considered, it means that the validity of each view can be guaranteed.

There is also a fourth question that should be considered once the first three questions have been answered successfully:

- **What language is the stakeholder expecting to use when looking at the view?** It is imperative when communicating with various stakeholders that the communication is carried out in a language that the stakeholder is fluent in. This applies to both the spoken language and the domain-specific language, each of which will be discussed later in this chapter. The importance of communication was discussed in *Chapter 1, Introduction to Systems Engineering*, and this is one of the areas where effective communication comes into play. Stakeholders may speak different languages and, when considering MBSE, this translates into the fact that different stakeholders may want to see a single view visualized in different ways.

It is essential that these questions are asked for every view; otherwise, there will be information contained in the model that adds no value, which is one of the biggest risks associated with MBSE.

The other big risk associated with the views that comprise the model is associated with the fact that the views must be consistent with each other. An essential and defining part of any model is consistency. If there is a set of views where each view is consistent with all other views, then it is a model. If there is a set of views where each view is not consistent with all other views, then it is data.

Once the model has been established (all views add value and are consistent), then it is used as the main repository for all information that relates to the system. This means that whenever any stakeholder wants to know anything concerning the system, then it is the model that is interrogated to ascertain the answer.

The model is sometimes referred to as a **single source of truth**. This is an important definition and consists of two main points:

- The model is the only representation of the system – it is the *single source*.
- All information in the model is viewed as being the truth as far as can be determined, hence the single source of truth.

This definition can be misleading as it does not imply that the model is contained in a single location. The idea is that conceptually, the model is a single entity even though, in reality, it may be split across several locations, databases, or tools.

The model may be imagined to be a large, complex collection of information and each view is analogous to opening up a small window into that model. It is necessary to open up enough of these windows to provide confidence to all of the stakeholders that the model is understood well enough to realize a successful system or, to put it another way, to carry out systems engineering.

One final aspect of views that needs to be understood is that a view may be visualized in many different ways or, to put it another way, may be communicated in any number of different languages. This is the same concept as different stakeholders speaking different languages and will be the focus of the next section.

Visualizing the model

The way that each view is visualized is crucial to the successful communication and understanding of the system among its stakeholders. In terms of MBSE, the various languages that each stakeholder may speak are referred to as **notations**, as shown in the following diagram:

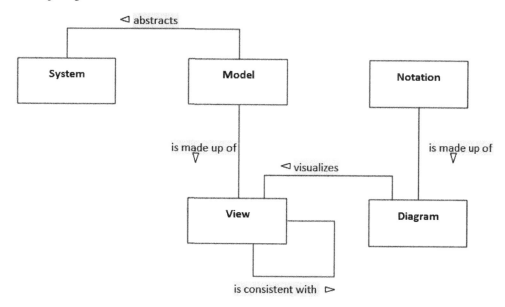

Figure 2.4 – Notations, diagrams, and visualization

The diagram in *Figure 2.4* introduces the concepts of **notations** and **diagrams** to the original definition of systems and models.

The notation represents some sort of language that is used to communicate with a number of stakeholders. This notation represents the spoken language that was introduced in *Chapter 1, Introduction to Systems Programming*, or, to put it another way, it represents a basic communication mechanism that can be used to communicate with a set of stakeholders.

The notation comprises a set of diagrams that provide the actual communication mechanism that is used by the notation. The term **diagram** is used in its most general sense here and the concept of a diagram may not even be graphical, as the notation may be realized by almost any language, as follows:

- The notation may be a visual, or graphical, language that uses graphics as its communication mechanism. Examples of this include the **Unified Modeling Language (UML)** (UML 2017), **SysML** (SysML 2017), the **Business Process Modeling Notation (BPMN)** (BPMN 2011), Flowcharts (ISO 1985), and so on.

- The notation may be mathematically based, using equations or some sort of formal method as its communication mechanism. Examples of this include languages based on first-order predicate calculus and set theory, such as the **Vienna Development Method (VDM)** (VDM 1998), Z (Z 1998), the **Object Constraint Language (OCL** 2014), and so on.

- The notation may be based on a natural language that uses structured or unstructured text as its basic communication mechanism.

The notation and its diagrams are used to visualize the views that comprise the model. If the model is imagined to be a large, complex collection of information and each view is analogous to opening up a small window into that model, then the diagrams may be thought of as applying different filters or lenses to each window. In the same way that it is possible to apply a number of different optical filters to change the appearance of whatever is on the other side of a window, it is possible to visualize each view in any number of different ways.

As an example of this, consider a view that contains text-based descriptions of a number of need statements, which will be referred to as a need description view. It needs to be established whether or not this is a valid view, and the following points address this:

- The stakeholders that are interested in the need description view are the requirements engineer and the requirements manager.

- The need description view is required so that the stakeholders can both gain a high-level appreciation for the number of needs as well as get a brief idea of what each need entails.

- The need description view contains a set of needs, each of which has a number of properties identified with it, such as its name, identifier, description, and priority.

The three basic questions have now been answered, so the view can be confirmed as a valid view. The next question to ask is *which language do the stakeholders speak?* and this will dictate how they are spoken to. In terms of the modeling, this will mean that different notations may be used, as follows:

- The need description view may be visualized using structured text, with each need being a paragraph and the properties being bullet points displayed under each paragraph.

- The need description view may be visualized using UML notation, specifically a diagram known as the **class diagram**, where each need is represented as a UML **class** and each property is represented by a UML attribute. Class diagrams in UML are very similar to block definition diagrams in SysML and, indeed, are the basis for block definition diagrams.

- The need description view may be visualized using SysML using a requirement diagram, where each need is represented by a SysML requirement block and each of its properties is represented by a SysML property.

This list represents just three possible options for visualizing the same view, making the point that any view may be visualized in any number of different ways.

For the purposes of this book, a single notation will be selected and used for all of the examples throughout. The notation that will be adopted is **SysML**, which will be discussed in a lot more detail later in this chapter. For the purposes of this book, therefore, the spoken language selected will be SysML.

Defining the approach

When developing a model by creating a number of views, it is obviously important that all of the views are created in the same way, and this is one of the areas where the approach comes into play, as shown in the following diagram:

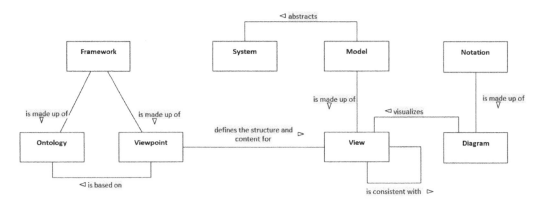

Figure 2.5 – Introducing the approach for MBSE

The diagram in *Figure 2.5* introduces part of the overall approach that is required for MBSE in the form of the **framework** and its associated **viewpoints** and **ontology**.

Consider a situation where it is desirable to ensure that all documents of a similar type have the same structure and contents. When dealing with documents, the answer to this is quite straightforward in that a template would be defined for the document to ensure that all future documents are consistent and have the same look and feel. When considering MBSE and the creation of views, the answer is the same in that a template of sorts is considered. The template for the views is referred to as a viewpoint, which, when defined properly, will ensure that all of the views that are created and that are based on the same viewpoint will be consistent.

This is achieved by answering three basic view questions and storing the answers as part of the viewpoint. Therefore, each viewpoint contains the answers to the following questions:

- Which stakeholders are interested in looking at the view?
- Why are they interested in looking at the view – or, to put it another way, what value will they realize?
- What information is contained in the view?

Each viewpoint, therefore, contains the answers to these three questions, which ensures that the structure and content of all views that are based on the viewpoint are consistent.

In order to ensure that all of these viewpoints are consistent with all of the other viewpoints, it is necessary to have a common set of concepts and associated terminology that form the basis of the content for the views. This is referred to as the ontology and is actually the domain-specific language that was introduced and discussed in *Chapter 1, Introduction to Systems Engineering*.

The ontology is arguably the single most important part of MBSE as all of the other elements that make up MBSE are ultimately traceable back to the ontology. The ontology will be discussed in a lot more detail later in this chapter.

When the ontology and the viewpoints are put together, they form what is known as a *framework*. A framework is created as a template, or blueprint, for a complete model. One of the common terms that you may have encountered is that of the architecture framework, which provides the template for system architecture.

There is a very close relationship between modeling and architecture but it is beyond the scope of this book to enter into a lengthy discussion and dialog concerning this relationship. It is sufficient for us to think about the two in this way: **all architectures are models, but not all models are architectures**.

The second part of the overall approach that must be considered is that of the process set, as shown in the following diagram:

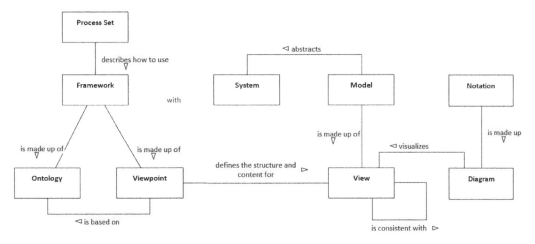

Figure 2.6 – Introducing the process set for MBSE

The diagram in *Figure 2.6* introduces the concept of the **process set** to the overall approach to MBSE. The process set represents the collective set of individual processes that are used by the framework in a number of ways:

- The process set is used to show how to develop the framework, its ontology, and its associated viewpoints.

- The process set is used to show how to develop the views that comprise the model, based on the definition of the viewpoints in the framework.

It is the combination of the framework and the process set that provides the overall approach to MBSE. There are some key points to bear in mind when considering these two parts of the approach:

- The framework focuses only on defining the structure, content, and consistency of the information that is produced and that is used to develop the model in terms of its views. The framework, therefore, may be thought of as defining the "what" of the approach: what information must be produced to develop the model?

- The process set focuses on the steps involved with both developing and using the framework. The process set, therefore, may be thought of as the "how" of the approach: how is the framework developed and used?

This conceptual separation between the framework (*what*) and process set (*how*) means that it is possible to have a number of different process sets that use the same framework. This is important as different projects may follow different processes, depending on the nature of the project, but the underlying framework will be the same. So, for example, there may be a research demonstrator project that has a timescale of only a few weeks that follows a set of high-level, technically light processes to develop its model. In the same organization, there may be another project that is business-critical and that may take a number of years to complete. The processes that are followed as part of this project will be far more detailed and rigorous and take far more time. However, the point here is that each project, despite following different process sets, may actually share the same framework. This means that the model produced by each project will use the same framework and, therefore, the views from each project may be compared and contrasted on a like-for-like basis.

At this point, it is a good idea to take a short interlude and reconsider what has been discussed so far in this chapter…

Grouping the MBSE concepts

The information discussed so far is crucial to understanding MBSE, so it is worthwhile to take a brief pause to revisit the information collated so far and to add another level of information.

To this end, the diagram that has evolved so far in this chapter has been grouped into three main areas, as shown in the following diagram, which is known in the systems engineering community as **MBSE in a slide** (Holt & Perry 2019):

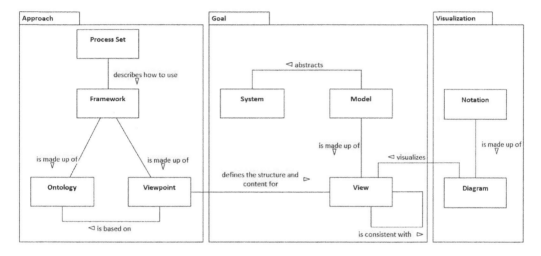

Figure 2.7 – "MBSE in a slide" – adding the groups

The diagram in *Figure 2.7* is used widely in the systems engineering community to disseminate the key concepts associated with MBSE.

The three groups that have been added here are as follows:

- **Approach**: Groups together the framework that comprises the ontology and viewpoints and the process set. Remember, the framework focuses on what information must be produced for the model, whereas the process set focuses on how that information must be produced and used.

- **Goal**: Groups together the system and the model and its associated views. Remember that the goal of any systems engineering endeavor is to develop the system. The goal of MBSE is also to develop the system, but this is achieved by developing the model and its associated views. Remember that each view is like opening a window to look at a small, focused part of the model.

- **Visualization**: Groups together the notation and its associated diagrams. The notation is the set of spoken languages that are being used as a basic communication mechanism for the systems engineering. Remember that each diagram is like opening a small window into the model and looking at it through a lens or filter.

All of the concepts that have been discussed so far may now be expanded upon by considering the **implementation** and **compliance** associated with MBSE.

Implementing the notation

The next step in looking at essential elements for MBSE is to look at how the visualizations of the views may be implemented in a pragmatic manner as part of an MBSE project. At this point, therefore, it is pertinent to introduce the idea of tools, by expanding MBSE in a slide, as shown in the following diagram:

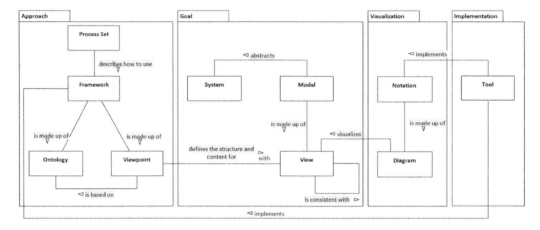

Figure 2.8 – Expanding "MBSE in a slide" to include implementation

Tools are an important part of MBSE and will allow the full range of benefits of MBSE to be realized.

There are two relationships that come out of the tools on the diagram: *the Tool implements the Notation* and *the Tool implements the Framework*. Let's take a look at these:

- **The Tool implements the Notation**: This is important as whichever notation is adopted must be adopted correctly according to the syntax and semantics of the underlying language. When considering tools, it should be kept in mind that different tools will offer different levels of support for the notation. For example, if a tool for a graphical notation such as SysML is being considered, then it is possible to use any tool with a basic drawing capability to create the diagrams, such as an Office tool. There is more to using SysML, however, than simply drawing the correct shapes and lines on a page as the language itself has an underlying syntax and semantics that must be followed. When using a good MBSE modeling tool, the knowledge of the syntax and semantics will be built into the tool and, therefore, the tool can enforce the correct notation by running syntactical and semantic checks on the model. When producing a text-based document that is written in English, any good word processor will allow the author to run spelling and grammatical checks on the text. Imagine the syntax and semantics checks on a modeling tool to be analogous with the spelling and grammar checks in an Office-based tool. Remember that the notation is the spoken language, so the tool will help to ensure that this spoken language is implemented correctly. By choosing an appropriate modeling tool, this means that the tool will speak the spoken language straight out of the box.

- **The Tool implements the Framework**: This is important as the framework is a large part of the overall approach and it means that the tool will therefore implement a large part of the approach. The approach itself may be implemented by embedding the ontology into the tool and by defining the set of viewpoints (by answering the key questions for each view) into the tool. The approach contains the ontology and as the ontology is the domain-specific language, this means that the tool can be tailored to speak the domain-specific language for the system. The tool will not be able to do this straight out of the box and this framework must be programmed into it. All good tools have the ability to create **profiles** that allow the tools to be tailored to implement, among other things, a specific framework.

Tools are an essential part of MBSE and it is important to choose one that satisfies the modeling needs of the project.

Showing compliance

The final enhancement to the MBSE in a slide diagram is to add in the concept of **compliance**. When this has been added, the diagram is complete and is referred to in the MBSE community as **MBSE in a slide and a bit**, as shown in the following diagram:

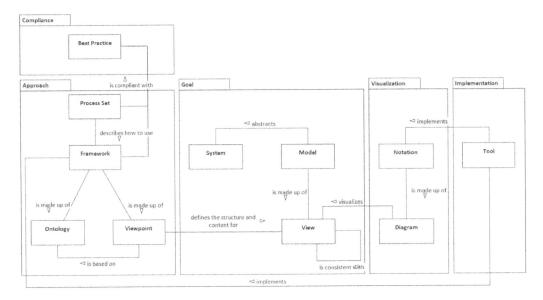

Figure 2.9 – Completed diagram – "MBSE in a slide and a bit"

The final piece of information that has been added is that of **Compliance**, which contains **Best Practice**, as it is important in systems engineering that every activity performed is carried out in a rigorous, robust, and repeatable manner. This is achieved by demonstrating that the MBSE approach complies with various best practice sources. These sources may be the following:

- **Process-based standards**, which may exist at different levels, such as international standards, industry standards, in-house standards, and so on. Typically, standards that relate to how to carry out an approach are based on processes; therefore, the process set must be shown to be compliant with the best practices. There are many process-based standards that exist and the most widely used standard for systems engineering is ISO 1588 – Software and systems engineering life cycles and processes (ISO 2015).

- **Framework-based standards**, which may exist at different levels, such as international standards, industry standards, and in-house standards. Typically, standards that are based on the information that must be produced as part of an approach are based on the framework, therefore this framework must be shown to be compliant with the best practices. There are many framework-based standards that exist. At the international level, the most widely used standard is ISO 42010 – Systems and software engineering — Architecture description (ISO 2011). There are also many industry standards, such as MODAF (MODAF 2010), DoDAF (DoDAF 2007), and NAF (NAF 2007), as well as now the UAF (UAF 2017) for the defense industry. Zachman (Zachman 2008) is also used extensively in the IT industry, among others.

- **Application-based standards**: Some applications of systems engineering have their own specific standards that may be used in any number of different industries. Examples of such standards include best practice sources for areas such as safety, security, usability, maintainability, and so on.

This set of best practice sources is not intended to be exhaustive but provides an indication of the types of standards and related sources that may be considered.

Using MBSE

The concepts shown in *Figure 2.7* and *Figure 2.9* must be understood in order to properly understand and, therefore, be able to implement systems engineering using MBSE.

These diagrams are also important for a number of other practical reasons when it comes to deploying MBSE into an organization.

These diagrams may be used as an indication of the current MBSE capability within an organization or organizational unit. Every organization must start its MBSE deployment somewhere and this diagram provides an overview of the five main areas, shown as the groups that must be considered as part of this deployment.

It must be stressed that the diagram is not read from left to right, and it is certainly not the case that the MBSE activities are also put into place in the same way. The diagram should be used in the first instance as a checklist to ascertain what capability exists for each group.

Once the capability for each group has been determined, it is then possible to perform a gap analysis and decide which groups need to be implemented, and then to prioritize each group.

In order to illustrate this, consider these two common examples:

- An organization has decided that it wants to implement MBSE and, as a first step, has decided to adopt the SysML notation and, as part of this adoption, has purchased a number of tools. There is nothing wrong with this as a first step *per se*, but the mistake that many organizations make is to think that MBSE can be successfully implemented simply by buying tools. It is clear from the diagram that there is no approach in place and, therefore, compliance cannot be demonstrated. Also, it will not be possible to tailor the tool to adopt the approach, as there is no approach in place. In this situation, it may be appropriate to look at getting the approach in place and then the compliance in order to deploy MBSE.

- An organization has decided that it wants to implement MBSE and so has identified an architecture framework that is used by a similar company, and has also identified that ISO 15288 is the standard that they would like to follow. Again, there is nothing wrong with this as a first step. The organization may think that it has a good approach in place, but it has confused the approach (architecture framework) with the compliance (standard). A process set must be developed that complies with the standard and suits the way that the organization works. Also, what is to say that the architecture framework that has been chosen is actually suitable for the nature of the business?

Problems such as the ones illustrated here are not necessarily easy to address and one way to get an additional insight into them is to consider the maturity of MBSE in the business by looking at its evolution. This will be discussed in the next section.

The evolution of MBSE

One key factor that must be considered when implementing MBSE into an organization is the maturity of the MBSE activities, which may be addressed by looking at the **evolution of MBSE**.

The evolution of MBSE may be thought of as ranging from a document-based approach to systems engineering, all the way to a full model-based approach to systems engineering. This is not a simple transition, however, and there are five conceptual stages that must be considered, as shown in the following diagram (Holt & Perry 2020):

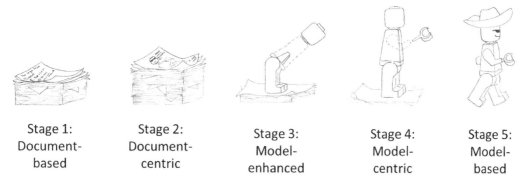

Figure 2.10 – The evolution of MBSE (Holt & Perry 2020)

The diagram in *Figure 2.10* shows the evolution of MBSE by identifying five key stages that help to understand how MBSE can be implemented and deployed into an organization. Each stage will be described by discussing the following criteria:

- **Outcomes**: In *Chapter 1, Introduction to System Engineering*, implementation of MBSE was covered very briefly by discussing how the people, process, and tools need to be effectively managed and balanced. Each stage, therefore, considers the people, process, and tools outcomes that will typically be in place for each of the stages.

- **Knowledge ownership**: The ownership of the knowledge and where the knowledge resides will change as the evolution progresses through the five stages and it is important to understand exactly how this happens.

- **Pre-conditional activities**: In order to be in any one of the stages, there are a number of activities that must have been performed before the stage can be entered.

Each stage will now be discussed according to these criteria.

Stage 1 – document-based systems engineering

Stage 1 of the evolution of MBSE is referred to as **document-based systems engineering**. For stage 1 in the diagram in *Figure 2.10*, a large pile of documents is depicted. This implies that there are lots of documents associated with this stage of the evolution. While this is true, it must also be kept in mind that the knowledge associated with the system is spread throughout these documents, rather than being contained in a single location.

At this stage, the people, process, and tools outcomes may be considered as follows:

- **People**: The people involved in this stage are assumed to have basic competence in systems engineering. The reality is that any organization that is delivering systems must have a systems engineering capability, even if it is a tacit capability that is not formally captured or documented. When people are in this situation, it may be that they claim to want to put a basic systems engineering capability in place before considering MBSE. This is a huge mistake. Remember that MBSE *is* systems engineering, so there is no point in doing both – just aim straight for MBSE.

- **Process**: The process that is in place may or may not be documented, but there will be a process in place. In either case, the main artifacts, that is, the inputs and outputs of the process, will be documents. These documents will be predominantly text-based and also include tables, graphs, lists, and so on.

- **Tools**: The tools involved in stage 1 will usually be Office-based tools, such as word processors, presentation applications, and spreadsheets.

In stage 1, all of the knowledge, information, and data concerning the system will be contained solely in the document set that is created as a result of executing the process. There is no model whatsoever in place, so everything is both contained and owned by the documentation.

The basic pre-condition for stage 1 is that there must be some sort of basic need for MBSE that has been identified within the organization.

Stage 2 – document-centric systems engineering

Stage 2 of the evolution of MBSE is referred to as **document-centric systems engineering**. For stage 2 in the diagram in *Figure 2.10*, a large pile of documents is again depicted, but this time with two main changes. Firstly, the pile of documents has increased slightly. Secondly, rather than being mainly text-based, there is some evidence of people starting to use notations as part of the documents. The knowledge associated with the system is still entirely contained in the documents as there is still no presence of a model.

In this stage, the people, process, and tools outcomes may be considered as follows:

- **People**: The people involved in this stage are assumed to have a basic competence in systems engineering, the same as in stage 1. This time, however, there will be evidence of people applying notations at an informal level. The reality of this is that what is being produced is a set of pictures rather than true views that will make up a model, but this is typical at this stage, as the people will be experimenting with different notations in an ad hoc manner.

- **Process**: In this stage, the artifacts associated with the process are still documents but, in line with the previous point, there will be the beginning of notations being used to support the text descriptions.
- **Tools**: In this stage, the tools will be the same as in stage 1 but the difference being that actual drawing packages may have been used to create the diagrams that form part of the documentation.

In stage 2, all of the knowledge, information, and dates concerning the systems are still solely contained in the document set. This is important as the diagrams that have been produced are not truly part of a model and cannot, therefore, own any of the knowledge associated with the system. Also notice that at this stage, the pile of documents has actually become slightly taller, which represents the increase in information. At this stage, like stage 1, all of the data, information, and knowledge associated with the system is contained in the documents. As the data, information, and knowledge are contained in the document and this is the only place where it resides, the documents may be thought of as owning all of this information.

The basic pre-conditions for stage 2 are the following:

- The goals for MBSE must be formally captured. This will include what the scope of MBSE implementation will be and which stakeholders exist. For each of the stakeholders, a set of benefits must be identified. This is crucial as otherwise it cannot be demonstrated whether the MBSE initiative has been successful or not. If the goals or needs for the initiative have not been identified and defined, then it is impossible to validate these needs.
- A basic assessment of the current MBSE in the organization must be ascertained. This will include identifying the current MBSE capability of the organization, which can be realized by looking at the MBSE in a slide that was introduced in the previous section in *Figure 2.7* and *Figure 2.9*. The second part of the assessment is that the current maturity of the MBSE capability must also be ascertained. This can be realized by looking at the evolution of MBSE in *Figure 2.10*.

During this stage, it may also be that some MBSE may be used to carry out the previous points without people actually realizing it. When this happens, it is often referred to as **MBSE by stealth**, where MBSE is actually being used in order to implement MBSE without people realizing that this is going on.

Stage 3 – model-enhanced systems engineering

Stage 3 of the evolution of MBSE is referred to as **model-enhanced systems engineering**. This is interesting as it is the first stage where the term **model** is introduced. The diagram in *Figure 2.10* shows the model starting to emerge from the pile of documents, which implies that the knowledge is now split between the model and the documents set.

In this stage, the people, process, and tools outcomes may be considered as follows:

- **People**: The people involved in this stage have now investigated notations in more detail and have received some sort of formal notational training so that they exhibit notational competence. Also, the people will have an awareness level of the competence of MBSE concepts or, to put it another way, they are familiar with the MBSE in a slide concepts that were introduced and described in *Figure 2.7* and *Figure 2.9*.

- **Process**: In this stage, the true model comes into existence and emerges from the documents. The model contains and owns some of the knowledge associated with the system. The knowledge is now split between the model and documents, rather than being solely owned by the documents. Also, the pile of documents starts to reduce in size. In this stage, MBSE will start to be applied in a serious manner, usually by implementing the emerging MBSE approach on a pilot project with a limited scope. By doing this, it is possible to demonstrate the benefits of MBSE, based on the goals identified previously, before rolling out across the rest of the organization.

- **Tools**: In stage 3, there is typically more than one tool that is being used as part of the modeling. It is always advisable to carry out a full tool evaluation where possible and, in such cases, there will be a set of candidate tools that have been previously identified for potential use in the organization.

In stage 3, all of the knowledge, information, and data associated with the system are split between the now-emerging model and the documentation set. This is important as it really represents the first time that MBSE is being applied properly in any project.

The basic preconditions for stage 3 are the following:

- People will have had some formal notation training to enable them to start modeling in an effective way, rather than in the ad hoc way that it has been applied previously.

- A formal tool evaluation should have been considered in order to narrow down the set of candidate tools to a single preferred tool.

In many cases, stage 3 may be an initial goal for MBSE in the short term in order to demonstrate the benefits of applying such an approach. Indeed, for some organizations, achieving stage 3 may actually be the final goal, but it is more usual for stage 3 to be a short-term goal.

Stage 4 – model-centric systems engineering

Stage 4 of the evolution of MBSE is referred to as **model-centric systems engineering**. At this stage, the model is almost complete, as shown in the diagram in *Figure 2.10*, and owns most of the knowledge associated with the system.

At this stage, the people, process, and tools outcomes may be considered as follows:

- **People**: The people involved at this stage now exhibit competence in MBSE and also in the use of the candidate tool. The people now have a very strong understanding of MBSE and are using it to great effect. The tool is being used in an efficient manner and is being driven by the MBSE approach that is in place.

- **Process**: In this stage, the approach is almost fully MBSE-based. The initial framework is now in place, including the ontology, and as a set of viewpoints that are being used as a basis for the modeling. Consistency is also enforced through the use of the framework, and the views in the model are created according to an initial process set. In this stage, the pilot project that was introduced in the previous stage is measured and assessed in order to demonstrate how effective the MBSE approach has been. The pilot project must be measured and assessed according to the goals that were established prior to stage 2.

- **Tools**: In stage 4, the preferred tool has been selected and is now being used on real projects.

In stage 4, almost all of the knowledge, information, and data associated with the system is contained and owned by the model with only small pockets still residing in the document set. As a consequence of this, the pile of documents is now significantly reduced.

The basic pre-conditions for stage 4 are as follows:

- Formal MBSE training has now taken place so that all relevant team members now have the right set of skills to implement the MBSE approach.

- The initial process set has been defined and is being applied to generate the views that make up the model.

- The initial framework, including the ontology and the viewpoints, have now been developed and are being applied to real projects.

- The preferred tool(s) has now been selected from the set of candidate tools. In large organizations, it is not unusual for several to have been selected.

- The people have been trained formally in the use of preferred tools.

Stage 4 sees MBSE being applied at an advanced level with many of the benefits that were anticipated now being realized.

Stage 5 – MBSE

The final stage of MBSE evolution, stage 5, is the ultimate goal for any MBSE endeavor. Stage 5 sees all of the knowledge associated with the system being contained and owned in the model, which has now fully emerged and exists as an entity in its own right. This stage is, of course, **MBSE**.

In this stage, the people, process, and tools outcomes may be considered as follows:

- **People**: The people involved in this stage now have mastery over MBSE and its application in the organization. The people strive to continuously maintain and even improve their competence so that the approach can be enabled as efficiently and effectively as possible.

- **Process**: The approach is now entirely model-based. The framework and process set are now mature and are being applied on multiple projects as part of a company rollout. Advanced application of MBSE is now being implemented, including the implementation of advanced applications, such as pattern identification, definition, and application; process and competence modeling; variant modeling; and so on.

- **Tools**: The tools that are being used are now tailored to allow the approach to be enforced automatically. This will include applying automatic domain-specific language consistency checks based on the ontology, automatic document generation, and other advanced tool functionality using profiles. In this stage, various different types of tools will also interoperate in a seamless fashion so, for example, management tools will interact with MBSE modeling tools, which will interact with mathematical modeling tools, and so on.

In stage 5, all of the knowledge, information, and data associated with the system are contained and owned by the model. The diagram in *Figure 5.10* shows that the model is now fully formed and exists in its own right. Although no documents are shown here, there will always be some documents that exist.

The point here is that the documents do not own any of the knowledge and, in fact, should be perceived as just another set of views that make up the model, albeit text-based views.

The basic pre-conditions for stage 5 are as follows:

- Advanced applications are being applied, including competence and process modeling, variant modeling, project-related applications, and so on.

- The MBSE approach that is in place is being continually measured, assessed, and improved by applying competency assessment, process maturity assessment, and model maturity assessment.

- The tool has been tailored by creating profiles that enable various types of automation to be possible.

Stage 5 is the ultimate goal, but it is essential that the whole MBSE approach is always continuously assessed and improved.

Cross-cutting concerns

As can be seen in the evolution of MBSE, the model has its origins in stage 2, starts to emerge in stage 3, is almost complete in stage 4, and is whole in stage 5. From the point of making the decision to implement MBSE (which is stage 1), it is important that several key mechanisms are put into place in order to ensure that the model can be properly managed and controlled throughout the whole evolution. These mechanisms are referred to as **cross-cutting concerns** and include the following:

- **Configuration management**: The model is a living entity and its evolution must be controlled by applying effective configuration management.

- **Change control**: It needs to be clear how changes are managed and what the process is for requesting and making changes to the model. Also, the permission must clearly define which stakeholders are allowed to view, edit, or create different parts of the model.

- **Consistency**: The model must be valid and therefore consistency must be ensured throughout the life of the system.

- **Traceability**: It is essential that all parts of the model, whether directly or indirectly, are traceable to all other parts of the model. This is important for impact analysis, change control, and so on.

- **Maintenance**: The model must be able to be edited, checked, and appended according to the change control processes, but the model must also be available to the relevant stakeholders using the tool.

Most of these cross-cutting concerns will be covered to a certain extent by existing engineering processes within a business.

Modeling with MBSE

This section introduces the key concepts of modeling as well as the spoken language that will be used throughout the rest of this book – the Systems Modeling Language, or SysML, as it is commonly known.

It is important to understand exactly what is meant by modeling and also why modeling is needed in the first place.

It is also very important to understand exactly what SysML is and what it is not, as there are many misconceptions associated with SysML and much confusion about how it fits in with the whole of MBSE. Indeed, one of the most common misconceptions is that SysML is actually the same as MBSE!

Before the main discussion begins, it should be pointed out that there are many different types of modeling, as discussed previously in this book. For the purposes of the discussion in this chapter and for the remainder of the book, when the term **modeling** is used, it is referring to visual modeling, which means that diagrams are being used as a basis for the spoken language.

At the heart of MBSE lies the act of modeling, so it is crucial that some key concepts concerning MBSE are both well-defined and well-understood, and it is also necessary to understand the need for modeling in the first instance

The need for modeling

The fundamental reasons as to why modeling is needed come back to the same fundamental reasons of why it is necessary to carry out systems engineering: the three evils of systems engineering, as discussed in *Chapter 1, Introduction to System Engineering*. These three evils will be revisited now but with an emphasis on how and why modeling can help to address them.

The first evil of systems engineering is identified as being the complexity that is manifested by a system, whether it is essential (inherent in the system) or accidental (caused by the people, process, and tools associated with the approach). Modeling can help with complexity as the visual nature of the views that are created provides an instant visual assessment of both the complexity and, importantly, where the complexity lives within the model. Identifying the complexity is key to managing and controlling it. For essential complexity, once the complexity has been identified, then the dependency on the parts of the system where the complexity manifests itself the most can be limited and, therefore, controlled. For accidental complexity, once the complexity has been identified, it can be rationalized and minimized to keep the level of complexity as low as possible.

The second evil of systems engineering is a lack of understanding at various points in the life cycle. Modeling can help here as there are two very simple rules that can be applied when modeling any sort of information. Rule 1 is that if the model is easy to generate, then it means that the source information is well-specified and, therefore, well-understood. In such situations, the model seems to naturally fall out of the source information and the modeling activity is very quick and straightforward. Rule 2 is the complement of Rule 1. If the model is very difficult to generate with lots of ambiguity, uncertainty, and missing information, then the source information is poorly understood and poorly specified. In such situations, the model is very difficult to abstract from the source information and the whole modeling activity is time-consuming and effort-intensive.

The third evil of systems engineering is identified as being poor communication between various stakeholders. Modeling helps in two ways here. It was discussed in *Chapter 1, Introduction to System Engineering*, how efficient and effective communication requires a common language, which actually requires both a spoken language and a domain-specific language. Modeling helps to realize both of these; the choice of notation is the spoken language and the definition of the ontology is the domain-specific language. Each of these is explored in more detail in the next two major sections.

So, modeling helps to address the three evils of systems engineering, which also explains why MBSE is such a powerful approach to realizing systems engineering itself.

Defining the model

The model was defined earlier in this chapter as being an abstraction of the system. Think of an abstraction as being a representation of the system, in this case using graphics or diagrams as the medium. As the model is an abstraction of the system, it is, by necessity, a simplification of the system, which means that it cannot contain every single possible piece of information associated with the system. The model must be a simplification of the system and, therefore, there will be information associated with the system that is not contained in the model. This does not mean that the model is wrong or incomplete, providing that all of the *relevant* and *necessary* information is contained in the model.

There is an inherent danger in this, as it means that it is important to be able to ascertain whether there is any missing relevant information or not. There is no way that this can be guaranteed 100% but by applying a good, solid MBSE approach in the form of a process set and framework, the risk of omitting such information is vastly reduced.

As well as being an abstraction of the system, the model was defined as comprising a number of views, each of which has a target audience, a need, and a defined set of information contained therein. The definition of each viewpoint is key in order to have confidence that no relevant information is missing.

The next part of the definition of the model was that each view must be consistent with every other view. This is essential. If the views are modeled and they are not consistent, there is no model, just a collection of pictures. If the views are modeled and they are consistent with each other, then there is a model. Consistency is king when it comes to modeling and this cannot be stressed enough.

The use of a good notation, such as SysML, is important as it will provide mechanisms within the notation that will demonstrate whether the diagrams that are used to visualize the views are consistent or not.

Two aspects of the model

When creating a model, it is important to understand there are always two **aspects** to the model: the **structure** and the **behavior**. Let's look at these in more detail:

- **Structure**: The structure of the model defines the *what* of the model – what the main elements in the model are, what the relationships between these elements are, and what each of the elements does. The structure will also allow hierarchies of the system both in terms of taxonomy (types of system elements) and the breakdown of conceptual levels (compositions of system elements). The relationships between the system elements are just as important as the system elements themselves, which is the key tenet of systems thinking.

- **Behavior**: The behavior of the model defines the *how* of the model. Here, we look at what order things happen in, under what conditions they happen, and what the timing constraints are. While structure allows the model to be broken down into hierarchies, the behavior tends to apply to specific levels of the hierarchy. Also, the relationships are considered dynamically, rather than statically.

Every model will have both structure and behavior associated with it, which, in real terms, means that there will be structural views and behavioral views that make up the model. As all of the views in the model must be consistent in order for it to be considered a model, this means that the structural and behavioral aspects of the model must be consistent with each other.

The notation that is used in this book is SysML, which describes nine different diagrams that can be used to visualize the structural and behavioral aspects of the model.

When and where to model

There is often a lot of debate about at which point in the life cycle (where) and under what circumstances (when) modeling should be applied. The answers to these two points are quite simple.

Modeling should be applied at any stage in the life cycle *where* the following apply:

- There is unidentified, unmanaged, or uncontrolled complexity in the system (evil number one).

- There is a need to understand any aspect of the system (evil number 2).

- There is a need to communicate effectively and efficiently with any of the stakeholders (evil number 3).

In terms of under what conditions, or *when*, modeling should be applied, it should *only* be applied **when value is being added by carrying out the modeling**.

This last point is quite abstract but crucial. Every activity that is performed as part of MBSE must add value and contribute toward realizing the system successfully. If this is not the case, then it should not be done! Sometimes it is necessary to go a step too far with the modeling and to arrive at the conclusion that, as there is no longer any value being added, the modeling should be stopped. The use of an effective framework will address this because the reasons why each view is needed will have already been decided and, providing that people adhere to the framework, no views will ever be created where there is no defined need or benefit.

The spoken language – the Systems Modeling Language (SysML)

SysML is a general-purpose visual modeling language. SysML is itself based on another general-purpose visual modeling language, known as **UML**. UML is a language that has its roots firmly in the software engineering world and was created for very pragmatic reasons. Prior to 1997, when the first version of UML was released, there was a whole plethora of modeling notations and methodologies that were being used for software engineering. In fact, there were over 150 different recognized approaches available.

Bearing in mind that one of the aims of a modeling notation is to provide a basic mechanism for communication, there were simply way too many available, which made the choice of notation both bewildering and difficult. In the mid-1990s, therefore, the software industry collectively decided that there were too many languages and that there should be a single, standardized, common language that everybody could use. It was important that the language would not be proprietary and, therefore, it was decided that the **Object Management Group** (**OMG**), which is an international standards body that owns, manages, and configures standards relating to object technology, would own the new language. In 1997, UML was formally released to the software engineering world.

As UML was a general-purpose modeling language, it actually had a far wider scope than just software and, indeed, it was used extensively in the systems engineering community (Holt 2001). UML was adopted so widely that in 2004 it was decided by INCOSE that there should be a variation of UML that could be applied specifically to the systems engineering world, hence SysML was born.

> **Important note**
> SysML is still owned, managed, and configured by OMG and the standard itself can be downloaded from the OMG website.

SysML is technically a **profile** of UML. You should think of the relationship between these two languages as UML being the parent language and SysML as a dialect of that language.

This section will begin by discussing exactly what the SysML is and what it is not. This is important as there are many myths concerning the nature of SysML. Nine SysML diagrams will then be introduced at a high level and more specific examples of structural and behavioral models will be provided.

What SysML is (and what it is not)

Many of the previously available modeling notations were actually methodologies in that they had an in-built process that was used alongside the notation that dictated which diagrams to use and at which point in the development.

SysML is purely a notation and has no inherent process. This is a very important point that needs to be very clear and well-understood. Looking back to MBSE in a slide in *Figure 5.7* and *Figure 5.8*, SysML sits on the right-hand side of the **Visualization** group. SysML is just one, albeit an essential, part of an overall MBSE solution; it is *not* MBSE.

The SysML diagrams

SysML may be thought of as a toolbox that contains nine different diagrams that collectively allow both the structural and behavioral aspects of the model to be visualized.

The structural diagrams are as follows:

* The **block definition diagram (bdd)**, which is by far the most widely used of all the SysML diagrams. Every model will contain views that are visualized using bdds, and it is important to have a good grasp of the basics of this diagram.
* The **internal block diagram (ibd)**, which is actually a variation on the bdd, and is used to show the structure inside specific blocks and configurations.

- The **requirement (rd)** diagram, which is a block diagram with a few specialized elements of notation that can be used to specify text-based requirements, or needs, and a set of predefined properties for each. Rds are used primarily for **requirements management**, as opposed to **requirements engineering**.

- The **parametric (par) diagram**, which allows properties of blocks (contained in block diagrams and internal block diagrams) to be reasoned about by applying constraints, such as equations and heuristics. The par forms the bridge between the visual world of MBSE modeling and the formal, mathematical world of **Model-Based Engineering (MBE)** modeling.

- The **package diagram (pd)**, which allows groups of elements on other diagrams to be collected together and partitioned. It is one of the lesser-used of the SysML diagrams, but packages can also appear on other diagrams, which is a more typical use.

One of the key points to observe here is that all the structural diagrams are closely related. In fact, they are all either a variation of, or very closely linked to, the bdd. When beginning with SysML, it is a good idea to simply default to using bdds for the structural aspect of the model and to bring in the other diagrams as and when they are required.

The behavioral diagrams are as follows:

- The **use case (uc)** diagram allows high-level behavior, such as context, to be visualized. It is particularly useful for needs modeling, such as requirements engineering. Uc diagrams are one of the more widely used SysML diagrams, but are also undoubtedly the most badly used of all the SysML diagrams!

- The **sequence diagram (sd)** allows scenarios to be modeled and focuses on the interactions *between* model elements, such as blocks. Sds typically used at high levels of the model and are a key tool for any systems model.

- The **state machine diagram (smd)** focuses on the behavior *inside* individual blocks and their instances. State machines are typically used at a low level of detail and may be driven by states or events and are widely used throughout systems engineering.

- The **activity diagram (ad)** allows very detailed behavior inside specific operations to be modeled. Ads are often used for the implementation modeling and reverse engineering of legacy systems. Activity diagrams are based on classic **flow charts** and, hence, many people will feel comfortable using them as they have seen something similar before.

The behavioral diagrams are typically applied at different levels of abstraction, whereas the structural diagrams allow multiple levels of abstraction to be shown on the same diagram.

There is obviously a very close relationship between diagrams of the *same type* (structure and behavior), but also between diagrams of *different types* (structure and behavior). It is these relationships that form the basis of the notation and of the consistency checks that can be applied to any SysML model to demonstrate that it is compliant with the underlying SysML notation.

It should be remembered that this book is not a book that is focused on SysML but rather, one that uses SysML as its preferred notation. With this in mind, the full syntax of SysML will not be covered in great detail but the basics of SysML will be introduced as and when they are used throughout the book.

The next section will introduce some of the key SysML diagrams by considering the existing example system of a car, but this time using SysML, rather than a generic "squares and lines" notation that has been used this far in the book.

Example structural modeling

It was mentioned in the last section that the go-to diagram for structural modeling in SysML is the bdd, which is an abbreviation of the term **block definition diagram**. In this section, the basics of bdds will be introduced and discussed. It should be remembered that these are only the basics and this is not intended to be an exhaustive description of bdd elements.

Identifying basic blocks and relationships

A bdd comprises two main elements, which are as follows:

- **The block**: This represents a concept of something that forms part of the system. A block is represented graphically by a rectangle with the word <<block>> in it. The <<block>> word is used to reference that it is a stereotype of a UML element called a **class**. Stereotypes are an advanced modeling concept that will be discussed later in the book. For now, it is enough to understand that the term <<block>> is used simply to identify a block.

- **The relationship**: This relates one or more blocks in the system to one another. There are various types of relationships that will be discussed as this section progresses.

In order to illustrate these two elements, consider the following diagram:

Figure 2.11 – Bdd – simple block and association

The diagram in *Figure 2.11* shows two blocks – **Driver** and **Car** – which are somehow related. The blocks are shown as rectangles with the term `<<block>>` and the relationship, known as an **association**, is shown by simply drawing a line between the two blocks.

Any SysML diagram should be able to be read out loud and it should make sense. If this diagram was read out loud, it would read as "there are two blocks – **Driver** and **Car** – and there is a relationship between them." This does read as a good sentence but does not convey too much information about the car or driver and about the relations between them. This diagram can be easily enhanced by adding some more information about the relationship, as shown:

Figure 2.12 – Bdd – named association

The diagram in *Figure 2.12* includes some adornment on the relationship, as the association has now been given a name and a direction. The name is **drives** and the *direction* shows that the association is to be read from left to right, which is indicated by the small triangle that is shown above the association line. This diagram now reads *Driver drives Car*, which is far more precise than what was shown in *Figure 2.11*.

Each block represents the concept of something, so both **Driver** and **Car** represent the concepts of **Driver** and **Car** rather than any specific, real-life examples of them. Such specific, real-life examples of a block are referred to as *instances*. So, for example, **Car** is a concept, whereas *Jon's car* is a specific, real-life example of a car and is, therefore, an instance.

When naming associations, the words written on the line are typically verb constructs that, when read out loud, will form a natural sentence. Here, *Driver drives Car* is a perfectly correct English sentence that will make sense to most people when they hear it.

The direction indicator shows which direction to read the association name in and is very important for the overall meaning of the diagram. It is also possible to show a two-way, or bidirectional, association by simply omitting the small rectangle. Caution must be exercised here, however, as if the direction is accidentally omitted, it has meaning in SysML!

This diagram may be enhanced further by showing numbers between the two blocks:

Figure 2.13 – Bdd – multiplicity

The diagram in *Figure 2.13* shows how numbers may be added to each end of the association, which is known in SysML as **multiplicity**. This diagram may be read as *one Driver drives one Car*. This sentence is correct, but there is a subtlety to the numbering that can easily be mistaken. The numbers on each end of the association do not refer to absolute numbers but actually refer to the ratio of instances of each block at each end of the association. This diagram does not imply that there is only one driver and only one car, which it may look like at first glance. What this actually states is that for *each* real-life example of **Driver**, there will be one real-life example of **Car**. The word "each" is important here as it conveys this meaning far less ambiguously than using the term "one." This diagram should be read, therefore, as *each Driver drives one Car*.

Each end of the association has its multiplicity shown and there are a number of standard options that can be used:

- **1** indicates one instance, as shown in this example.

- **1...*** indicates one to many instances.

- **0...1** indicates zero to one instance.

- **0...*** indicates zero to many instances.

- **1...10** indicates a range of between 1 and 10 instances.

- **2,4,6,8** indicates one of a set number of instances.

As an example of this, consider the following diagram:

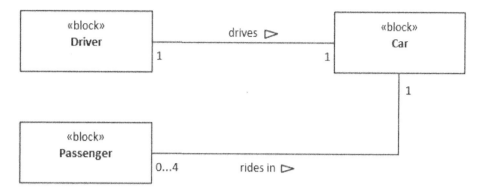

Figure 2.14 – Bdd – adding more blocks and multiplicities

The diagram shown in *Figure 2.14* has added a new block called **Passenger** that has an association with **Car**. This section of the diagram is read as *between zero and four passengers ride in each car*. Note how the multiplicity this time is shown as **0…4**, which shows that there may not even be any passengers, that passengers are optional, whereas the driver is not optional and must always be present.

It should also be noted that when writing the names of the blocks and the words that make up the association, the singular should always be used. Therefore, the block is *Passenger* and never *Passengers* and the verb constructs assume the singular, so the verb is *rides in* rather than *ride in*. Always show the blocks and verbs in their singular form and imply the plurality using multiplicity.

Associations typically show the relationships between multiple blocks, but it is also possible to show a self-association, that is, a relationship from one block back to itself, with the same multiplicity rules applying.

There is also a variation of an association that shows a relationship from a block to an association, rather than to another block, as shown in the following diagram:

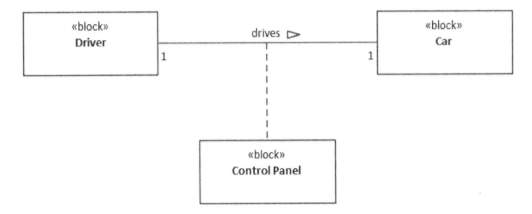

Figure 2.15 – Bdd – the association block

The diagram in *Figure 2.15* shows an **association block** that is named **Control Panel**. An association block relates a block to an association, rather than to another block. It is a good way to provide more detailed information about a relationship or interaction between blocks. The expression to use when reading an association block out loud is the word *via*. The diagrams here, therefore, reads as "Each Driver drives a Car via a Control Panel."

Describing a block in more detail

Each block may also be described in more detail, by identifying and defining its features – mainly, its **properties** that describe what the block looks like and its **operations** that describe what the block does.

When describing any block, there is the option to add more detail by identifying a number of properties that describe specific features of a block, as shown in the following diagram:

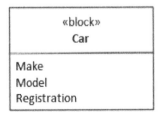

Figure 2.16 – Describing blocks – identifying properties

The diagram in *Figure 2.16* shows the **Car** block but this time a number of properties have been added that describe specific features of the block. Properties are shown by adding an additional **compartment** underneath the name of the block. A number of properties may then be added inside that compartment. Each property should describe a single feature of the block and should be a singular noun. In the example here, there are three properties that have been identified, which are as follows:

- **Make**, which refers to the manufacturer of the car

- **Model**, which refers to the specific variation or configuration of the car that is available to buy

- **Registration**, which refers to the unique registration number that is allocated to the actual car

It is important that each of these properties can take on a number of different values and these values are defined when the block is initiated. To illustrate this, consider the **Car** block, which has its three generic properties that will apply to all instances of **Car**. When a real-life example of **Car** is considered, let's use the instance of *Jon's Car*, then the properties will have their actual values defined, so the **Make** property may be set to the value **Mazda**, the **Model** property may be set to the value **Bongo**, and so on.

When properties have been identified, it is also important that they are defined in more detail, to avoid any unnecessary ambiguity, as shown in the following diagram:

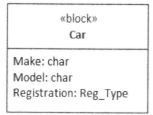
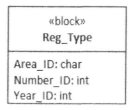

Figure 2.17 – Describing blocks – defining properties

The diagram in *Figure 2.17* shows the same **Car** block with its three properties but, this time, more information has been added to define the nature or **type** of values that each property may take. In SysML, everything is "typed," which means that everything must have a definition of the types of values that it may take on. These types may be simple or more complex.

Simple types are similar to standard variable types from the software engineering world, such as the following:

- `int`: Integer numbers
- `char`: Character
- `real`: Real number
- `bool`: Boolean, true or false

The list continues, but these are well-established types that are generally known and well-understood.

Each type is indicated by having a colon after the property name and then showing the type name immediately after it. It is also possible to show ranges of values and default values for each property, and these shall be described where appropriate as the book progresses.

It is also possible to define more-complex types, in which case it is possible to create another block, identify and define its properties, and then to use that as a type. An example of this is shown in the diagram with the block **Reg_Type**. The **Registration** property is not a simple type but is a construct of a number of alpha-numeric characters in a specific order with a specific meaning. In the UK, the standard registration number comprises three main elements, which are as follows:

- **Area_ID**: A set of two letters that indicates from where the car originated
- **Year_ID**: A set of two single-digit numbers that indicates which year, and which half of the year, the car was manufactured
- **Number_ID**: A set of three letters that provides the final part of the unique identifier for the car

This block may now be used as the type for the property of **Registration** on the **Car** block.

When defining the set of properties, SysML states that they should appear in alphabetical, rather than logical, order as, strictly speaking, no order should be inferred from the set of properties.

The properties of a block describe what a block looks like, and it is also possible to show what a block does by describing its **operations**, as shown in the following diagram:

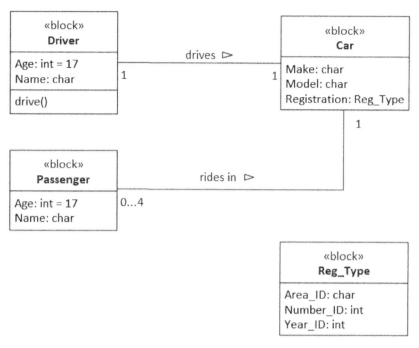

Figure 2.18 – Describing blocks – identifying operations

The diagram in *Figure 2.18* shows a more-complete diagram with more properties shown for the blocks that have been identified so far. Note that the two blocks **Driver** and **Passenger** each have a default value for **Age** indicated by showing it after the equals (=) sign after the type definition.

In addition to the properties, the **Driver** block has an additional compartment shown that has an operation identified as **drive** in it. Operations allow elements of behavior to be identified and defined that are associated with a specific block. It should be noted that operations show *what* the behaviors are, rather than *how* they behave – that is they're done using behavioral diagrams in SysML.

Each operation should be a verb to reflect its behavioral nature. These operations have parentheses after them, which allow **return values** and various **parameters** to be defined. Again, these will be dealt with when the need arises throughout the book.

Describing relationships in more detail

In the same way that blocks may be described in more detail, there are also several special types of relationships that allow more details to be added to the diagrams.

The basic type of relationship is the association, which has been discussed already and shows a simple relationship between one or more blocks. A variation on this, the association block, was also described, which allows a *via* relationship to be added.

Another standard type of relationship, which is actually a special type of association in SysML, is known as **composition** and is used to show structural hierarchies, as shown in the following diagram:

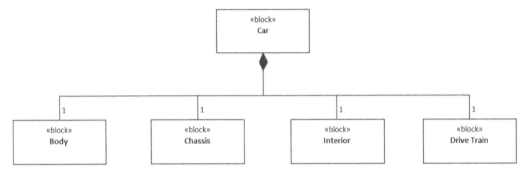

Figure 2.19 – Describing relationships – composition

The diagram shown in *Figure 2.19* shows the concept of composition, which is shown graphically as a filled-in diamond shape at one end of the association. When this symbol is seen, the words **is composed of** or **comprises** should be used when reading the diagram. The composition is read from the diamond end and the usual rules of multiplicity apply.

This diagram, therefore, reads as *Car is composed of one Body, one Chassis, one Interior, and one Drive Train.*

The diagram actually has four separate compositions on it, one for each lower-level block, but these are usually shown as overlapping, as is the case here, for reasons of clarity and readability.

Composition allows a block to be decomposed into lower-level blocks so that structural hierarchies may be shown. The diagram here only has a single level of decomposition, but there is no reason why multiple levels cannot be shown on the same diagram, and, indeed, this is quite common.

There is also a variation on a composition that is known as an **aggregation**. An aggregation also shows an *is made up of*-type relationship, but the main difference is that of ownership. Consider the following diagram:

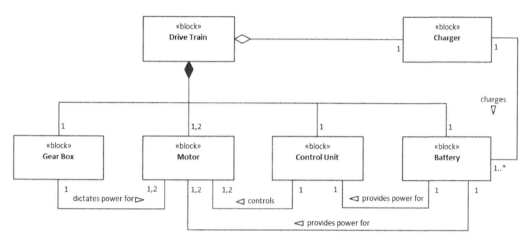

Figure 2.20 – Describing relationships – aggregation

The diagram in *Figure 2.20* shows a more complete and, as is often the case, more complex view that focuses on the breakdown of the **Drive Train** block. This increase in complexity is partly due to the fact that there are simply more blocks on this diagram, but also because this diagram is also showing the associations that exist between the various blocks, as well as the compositions. There is also an example of aggregation, which is represented by an empty diamond, as opposed to the filled-in diamond of the composition relationship. In order to illustrate the difference between the composition and aggregation relationships, consider the following:

- **The Drive Train is made up of a Gear Box, a Motor or two, a Control Unit, and a Battery**. This is expressed using a composition and it means that the four blocks that are part of the Drive Train via the composition are owned by that block. That is to say, the Drive Train owns the Gear Box, Motor, Control Unity, and Battery.

- **The Drive Train is made up of a Charger**. This is expressed using an aggregation and it means that the Charger is part of the Drive Train, but that it is not owned by the Drive Train.

This is a subtle difference, but an important one. The diagram actually shows that the Drive Train is made up of five blocks, four of which it owns, and one of which it does not. This means that the Charger is required to make sure the Drive Train is complete, but that it is owned by some other system element. The Drive Train needs the Charger; otherwise, it will not work, as there is nothing to charge the Battery.

However, this Charger may be part of any other systems element that happens to own a Charger. The difference between composition and aggregation is, therefore, one of ownership.

Both composition and aggregation are actually special types of association, but there is another very widely used type of relationship that is not a type of association and stands on its own. This is the *type of* relationship, referred to as either **specialization** or **generalization**. This is demonstrated as follows:

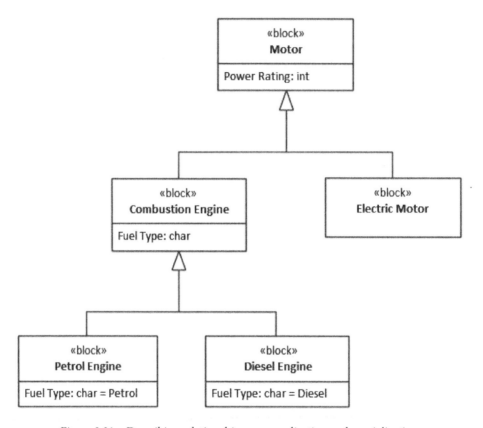

Figure 2.21 – Describing relationships – generalization and specialization

The diagram in *Figure 2.21* shows the *type of* relationship that allows generalization and specialization to be modeled and it is shown graphically as an empty triangle. This is a very powerful concept as it allows **classification hierarchies**, or **taxonomies**, to be modeled. The diagram shows that **there are two types of Motor, which are Combustion Engine and Electric Motor. Also, Combustion Engine has two types, which are Petrol Engine and Diesel Engine**.

The fact that there are two different terms for this *type of* relationship can lead to confusion, but the reality is actually straightforward as the difference between generalization and specialization is simply one of the reading direction of the relationship. This relationship can, therefore, be read in the following two ways:

- **Combustion Engine and Electric Motor are both types of Motor**. When reading up the relationship (toward the triangle), the blocks are becoming more abstract or more general. This is referred to as generalization.

- **Motor has the Combustion Engine and Electric Motor types**. When reading down the relationship (away from the triangle), the blocks are becoming less abstract or more specific. This is referred to as specialization.

The difference, therefore, is simply one of reading direction, which is purely a personal preference for the person reading the diagram. When two specializations of a block are present, there must be something that distinguishes them from each other, or that makes them "special." This is usually the set of properties, operations, or relationships that are specific to each specialized block.

When showing generalization and specialization, there is a very important concept known as **inheritance** that applies to any properties, operations, or relationships that relate to the blocks in the taxonomy. The Motor block has a property named Power Rating defined. As both Combustion Engine and Electric Motor are both types of Motor, then it is reasonable to assume that they will also have the same property, as they are specializations. This is known as inheritance, which states that any specializations associated with a block will inherit all of the properties and operations associated with its generalized block.

To put this another way, both Combustion Engine and Electric Motor will inherit the Power Rating property from the Motor block as they are types of Motor. Furthermore, as Combustion Engine has two types, Petrol Engine and Diesel Engine, these will also inherit the Power Rating property as the concept of inheritance applies to all levels of specialization.

Note that the Combustion Engine block has its own property, which is Fuel Type, which will be inherited by its specialization. It is not inherited by its generalized block, Motor, as inheritance *only* applies to specializations and *not* generalizations.

Inherited properties and operations are usually not shown on the blocks, therefore the Electric Motor block actually has the Power Rating property despite it not being shown on the block. The exception to this is when inherited properties are constrained in some way, such as with the Petrol Engine and Diesel Engine blocks, whose inherited properties are as follows:

- The Petrol Engine block shows its inherited property as the property value is always set to **Petrol** and it can never be changed.

- The Diesel Engine block shows its inherited property as the property value is always set to **Diesel** and it can never be changed.

When a property has a value that can never be changed, it is referred to as an **invariant** in SysML, and invariants are often the distinguishing feature between two specialized blocks.

Example behavioral modeling

The other aspect of modeling that must be considered as part of any model is the **behavior**. So far, the structural aspect of the model has been discussed, but the model cannot be complete without modeling the behavior.

As was seen with modeling structure with bdds, it is possible for several levels of abstraction to be shown on the same diagram, by using composition, aggregation, and generalization/specialization. It helps to think about this as a structure being able to show multiple levels of abstraction *vertically*.

Behavior, however, does not work like and this, and behavior views apply across single levels of abstraction. It helps to think about this as behavior being able to show a single level of abstraction *horizontally*.

Typically, these horizontal levels may be applied like so:

- **At the highest, contextual level**: This will focus on interactions between the system and its stakeholders, or enabling systems, and will allow interaction *across* the system boundary to be modeled. Typical SysML diagrams that will be used at this level include use case diagrams and sequence diagrams.

- **At the high level, between system elements**: This will focus on interactions *between* system elements, such as blocks on a bdd. Typical diagrams that are used at this level are sequence diagrams.

- **At the medium level, within a system element**: This will focus on interactions *within* a single system element, such as a block on a bdd. Typical diagrams that are used at this level are smds.

- **At the low level, within system element behaviors**: This will focus on interaction *within* a single system element behavior, such as an operation on a block in a bdd. Typical diagrams that are used at this level are activity diagrams.

It should be stressed that these are the typical diagrams that are used at each level and that the levels indicated here are themselves generic.

The common thread among all of these points is the word *interaction*, as behavioral modeling is concerned with *how interactions occur* at various levels of abstraction.

In order to illustrate modeling behavior, two of these levels will be considered in the first instance: modeling interactions *within* a system element and *between* system elements.

Modeling interactions within a system element

The first level of abstraction that will be considered is the medium level, where we will be looking at interactions within a system element.

In SysML, any block in a block diagram may have its behavior defined using an smd. For this example, consider again the following diagram:

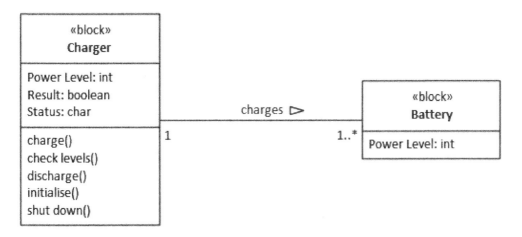

Figure 2.22 – Focus on Charger and Battery

The diagram in *Figure 2.22* shows a bdd that is a subset of the diagram shown in *Figure 2.20*, but this time it is specifically using the **Battery** and **Charger** blocks. Notice how each block has a number of features (properties and operations) defined. It is quite usual to show a high-level view with no features and then to focus on a subset in a separate view showing these features.

Each of these blocks may now have its behavior defined using an smd, so consider the behavior of **Battery**, as shown in the following diagram:

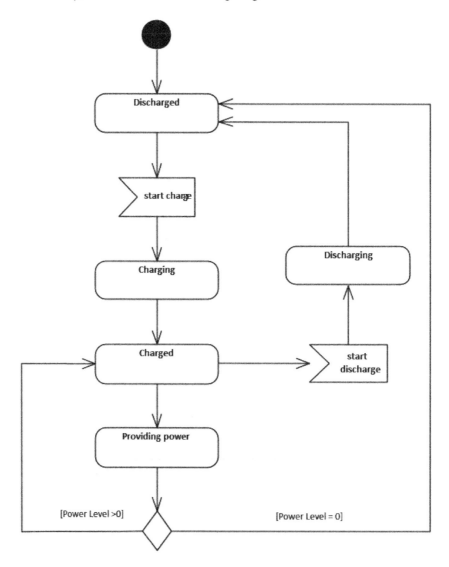

Figure 2.23 – Modeling behavior within a system element – smd for the Battery block

The diagram in *Figure 2.23* shows the behavior within a system element, in this case, the behavior of the Battery block, using an smd. A state machine is created for each system element that has behavior at the conceptual level. In SysML terms, this means that an smd will be defined for a specific block. This state machine, like the block, is conceptual. When the block is instantiated, its state machine is executed.

This means that if a block is instantiated multiple times, then the same state machine will be copied and executed multiple times. Therefore, it is entirely possible and usual for multiple copies of the same state machine to be executed simultaneously. Remember, define a state machine once for the block, then execute for each instance.

The basic model elements of a state machine are as follows:

- The **state**, which describes the situation of a block at a specific moment during its execution.

- The **transition**, which shows the legal paths to leave one state and execute another.

- The **event** and **condition**, which show what criteria must be met in order to cross a transition.

There are three types of state shown in *Figure 2.23*, which are as follows:

- **Start state**, which is shown graphically by the filled-in circle and represents the creation of an instance, or the birth, of a block.

- **End state**, which is shown graphically by the bull's-eye symbol, and represents the destruction, or the end of life, of a block.

- **State**, which is shown graphically by a box with rounded corners and represents a specific moment in time when the block is satisfying a particular condition, is performing an action, or is waiting for something else to occur.

There are a number of transitions on this diagram that are shown graphically by directed lines (lines with arrows on them) that show the possible execution paths between the various states.

There are also two types of event that are shown in the diagram, which are as follows:

- **Send event**, which represents sending some sort of **message** outside the boundary of the state machine. This is represented graphically by the five-sided shape showing a convex point.

- **Receive event**, which represents receiving some sort of message from outside the boundary of the state machine. This is represented graphically by the five-sided shape showing a concave point.

There are also two conditions that are shown on the diagram, each of which is shown in **square brackets** ([]) and represents a logical decision that is represented graphically by the diamond symbol. When making a decision and checking the values of a property, that property must exist on the block that owns the smd.

This is the first (of many) examples of consistency between the two different types of diagrams. One of the key points to check when considering more than one diagram is the consistency between different diagrams. Remember that the difference between pictures and a model is consistency. In this diagram, it can be seen that the property that is being checked as part of the decision check is also present on the parent block. In the following example, several more examples of consistency will be identified and discussed:

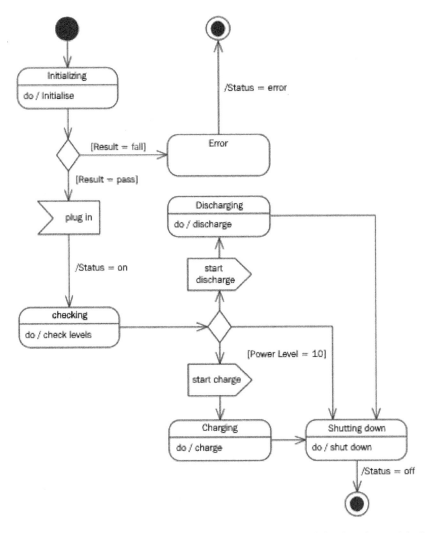

Figure 2.24 – Modeling behavior within a system element – smd for the Charger block

The diagram in *Figure 2.24* shows an smd for the Charger block. In this diagram, there is more detail and more consistency with the Charger parent block.

This diagram shows some explicit executable behavior, which in SysML may be defined at two levels of granularity:

- **Action**: This represents atomic behavior. This means that once started, the execution of the action cannot be interrupted. As a result of this, actions are often (but not always) short in terms of the time that they take to execute. In fact, many people consider actions to be instantaneous and take zero time, despite this being impossible. Actions are shown graphically by the / symbol followed by the action. In the diagram shown here, the actions are used to show how the value of the Status property is set at different points in the state machine. Actions may exist on transitions or inside states.

- **Activity**: This represents non-atomic behavior, which means that once started, it may be interrupted. As a result of this, activities are often perceived as taking time. Activities are shown graphically by the **do** keyword, which is immediately followed by / and that then references an operation from the parent block. Activities are shown inside blocks and may not be shown on transitions.

The use of actions and activities allows behavior to be added to the state machine as well as allows consistency to be enforced with the parent block.

Another aspect of consistency that may also be enforced is the send and receive events that are sent and received across the boundary of the various state machines. Consider the **start charge** and **start discharge** send events; they must go somewhere to be received.

Now consider again the smd for Battery that is shown in *Figure 2.23*. It can be seen that these same messages are also seen, but this time as receive events. Remember that send and receive events show the broadcast and receipt of messages, which must be consistent.

Modeling behavior between elements

This leads neatly on to looking at behavior modeling at a higher level of abstraction by modeling behavior between systems elements using sequence diagrams, as shown in the following diagram:

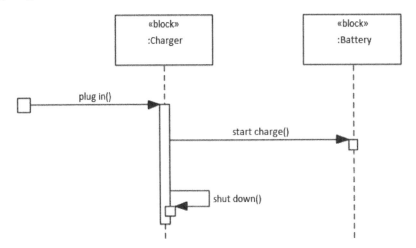

Figure 2.25 – Modeling behavior between system elements – sequence diagram showing a basic charging scenario

The diagram in *Figure 2.25* shows an example of modeling behavior between system elements using a sequence diagram. Sequence diagrams are the most widely used of all the behavior diagrams and they have a multitude of uses that will be explored throughout the book. In the first instance, sequence diagrams will be used to help us to understand how messages are passed between system elements in a single, simple **scenario**. A scenario shows a specific sequence of occurrences that result in a specific outcome and that allow "what ifs" to be explored. Unlike the smd, it is not possible to show all possible execution paths on a single diagram, which is why there will usually be several scenarios (using sequence diagrams) for different combinations of interacting blocks.

The basic modeling elements that comprise a sequence diagram are as follows:

- **Life lines**: These represent a number of instances to be shown. These are shown graphically as boxes with a block name preceded by a colon. This box has a dotted line underneath it that represents the passage of logical time, or the sequence of interactions that enter or leave the life line. As life lines represent collections of instances, they must relate directly back to blocks.

- **Interactions**: These show the communications between different life lines and allow the flow of messages to be visualized. Interactions are instances of associations from block diagrams and show messages that can be seen in other behavioral diagrams, such as the smd.

- **Gates**: These show an entry point to the sequence diagram without necessarily showing where it comes from. These are represented graphically by small boxes.

The sequence diagram in *Figure 2.25* shows several examples of consistency:

- The **:Battery** and **:Charger** life lines are consistent with the **Battery** and **Charger** blocks from the bdd.

- The **plug in** and **start charge** interactions are consistent with the **charges** association from the bdd.

- The **shut down** self-interaction is consistent with the **shut down** operation on the bdd.

- The **start charge** and **start discharge** interactions are consistent with the **start charge** and **start discharge** events on the smd.

The sequence diagram here shows a single normal scenario, where Charger is plugged in and the Battery charges successfully. Of course, there are a number of other normal scenarios that may be explored, such as discharging. One of the powerful uses of scenario modeling is to show abnormal, or atypical, scenarios, such as where things go wrong. The combination of normal and abnormal scenarios is often referred to as **sunny day** and **rainy day** scenario modeling. This will be explored in more detail when needs modeling is considered.

The domain-specific language – the ontology

The previous section provided a detailed discussion about the spoken language and, in particular, the use of SysML as this language. This section looks at the other half of having a common language – the domain-specific language or, to use the modeling term, the ontology.

The importance of the ontology will be discussed and then example ontology views will be presented that will be used throughout this book.

Understanding the ontology – the cornerstone of MBSE

The ontology is the single most important construct within MBSE as it provides the basis for the model. The ontology is used for almost every aspect of MBSE, including the following:

- **The domain-specific language**: The main concepts and their associated terminology must be defined for successful systems engineering, as discussed in *Chapter 1, Introduction to Systems Engineering*. The ontology is the visualization of the domain-specific language.

- **The basis for structure and content of viewpoints**: The model comprises a number of views and the consistency and rigor of the views are ensured through the use of templates or viewpoints that define the structure and content of each view. The viewpoint uses subsets of the ontology to identify and define what exactly is permitted to be visualized in each view.

- **The basis for consistency of the model**: The model must be consistent, otherwise it is a random collection of pictures, rather than a consistent set of views. This consistency must be enforced in terms of the spoken language, which is achieved through the use of SysML, and the domain-specific language, which is achieved through the use of the ontology. The relationships between all of the ontological elements provide all of the consistency paths needed to assure that the model is correct.

- **The basis for traceability**: It is essential that any artifact that is produced as part of the systems engineering approach can be followed backward (known as **traceability**) or forward (known as **impact**) in the model. This ensures that if any changes are made at any point in the project to any part of the model, then it can be easily and quickly established which other parts of the model may be affected.

The ontology, therefore, is an essential part of MBSE and one that it is important to get right. The next section will introduce the ontology that will be used and built upon throughout the book.

Visualizing the ontology

The domain-specific language was introduced in *Chapter 1, Introduction to Systems Engineering*, and a number of simple diagrams were used to show how the concepts related to one another.

Using the SysML that has been introduced so far in this chapter, it is now possible to define the ontology using the SysML notation to make it more precise and meaningful than the informal diagrams that were used in *Chapter 1, Introduction to Systems Engineering*, and at the beginning of this chapter.

The ontology that will be presented here will now be built upon and used for the rest of the book. This will be referred to as the **MBSE ontology** and is based on the best-practice MBSE ontology that is used extensively in the MBSE community (Holt & Perry 2014).

For reasons of clarity and readability, the MBSE ontology will be broken down into four diagrams. Here is the first one:

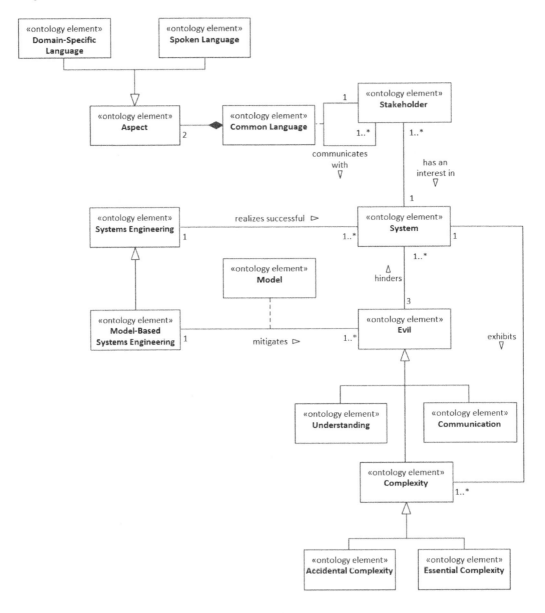

Figure 2.26 – The MBSE ontology – systems engineering

The diagram in *Figure 2.26* shows the MBSE ontology with a focus on systems engineering.

This diagram may be read as follows.

Systems engineering realizes successful systems. There are three evils that hinder systems engineering, which are **Understanding**, **Communication**, and **Complexity**. MBSE is a type of systems engineering that mitigates these evils via the model.

Each system exhibits complexity, of which there are two types: **Essential Complexity** and **Accidental Complexity**.

A number of stakeholders have an interest in the system and they communicate with each other via a common language. The common language has two aspects, which are the spoken language and the domain-specific language.

The next diagram follows on directly from this one and expands upon systems engineering by considering its implementation:

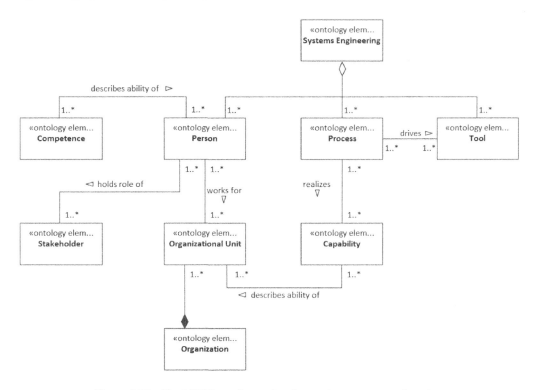

Figure 2.27 – The MBSE ontology – implementing systems engineering

The diagram in *Figure 2.27* shows the MBSE ontology with a focus on implementing systems engineering.

This diagram may be read as follows.

Systems engineering is made up of **people**, **processes**, and **tools**. The processes drive the tools and also realize a number of capabilities. The capabilities describe the ability of an **organizational unit** that comprises an **organization**.

A number of people work for a number of organizational units and people hold the roles of any number of stakeholders. Competence describes the ability of people.

The next diagram starts to consider the nature of a system:

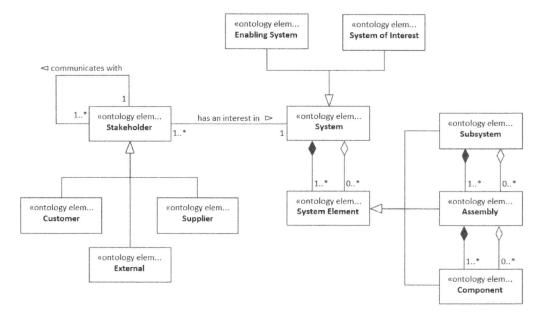

Figure 2.28 – The MBSE ontology – system structure

The diagram in *Figure 2.28* shows the MBSE ontology with a focus on the system structure.

This diagram may be read as follows.

A system has two types – **Enabling System** and **System of Interest** – each of which comprises a number of system elements that it owns, and may also be made up of a number of system elements that it does not own.

There are three types of system element:

- **Subsystem**, which comprises a number of assemblies that it owns, and may also be made up of a number of assemblies that it does not own

- **Assembly**, which comprises a number of components that it owns, and may also be made up of a number of components that it does not own

- **Components**, which is the lowest level of the system element

Stakeholders have an interest in the system and there are three types of stakeholders: customer, supplier, and external. Stakeholders also communicate with each other.

The next diagram also considers systems by expanding on other concepts associated with the system:

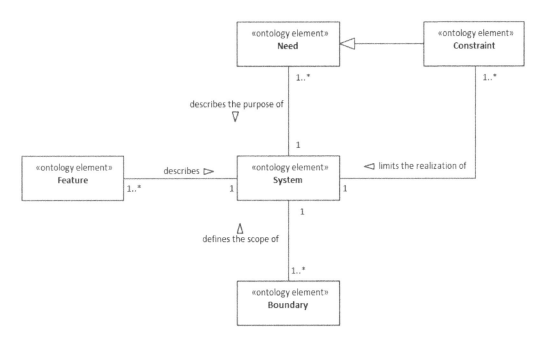

Figure 2.29 – The MBSE ontology – other system concepts

The diagram in *Figure 2.29* shows the MBSE ontology with a focus on other system concepts that were introduced previously in *Chapter 1, Introduction to Systems Engineering*.

This diagram may be read as follows.

Features describe each system and a number of boundaries define the scope of the system.

Needs describe the purpose of the system and constraints, which are a special type of need, limit the realization of the system.

Note how the descriptions for each of the diagrams that make up the ontology were created by simply reading the diagram out loud as a set of English sentences. This is how all good models should be read.

Summary

This chapter has introduced the concept of model-based systems engineers. It should always be remembered that MBSE is not a sub-branch of systems engineering, but it *is* systems engineering that is performed in a consistent and rigorous fashion.

In MBSE, all the knowledge information and data concerning the system is contained in a single source of truth that is the model, which is an abstraction of the system. Whenever any stakeholder needs to know anything concerning the system, the model is interrogated.

Now that the subject of MBSE has been introduced, the next chapter of the book focuses on a specific application of MBSE, that of systems and their associated interfaces, and how the concepts introduced in this chapter can be applied in more detail.

Self-assessment tasks

1. Revisit the MBSE in a slide diagrams in *Figure 2.7* and *Figure 2.9* and redraw them using SysML block diagrams. Focus on the relationship types and multiplicities.

2. Based on the new block diagrams, write out a description for each of the blocks, using consistent terminology used in the diagrams.

3. Consider the system structure concepts that were described in *Figure 2.28* and redraw it to represent your own organization.

References

- (INCOSE 2014) INCOSE. *International Council on Systems Engineering, A world in Motion, Systems Engineering Vision 2025*. INCOSE, 2014.

- (UML 2017) *The Unified Modeling Language (UML)*, version 2.5.1, Object Management Group, 2017

- (SysML 2017)*The Systems Modeling Language (SysML)*, version 1.5, Object Management Group, 2017

- (BPMN 2011) *Business Process Modeling Notation*, version 2.0, Object Management Group, 2011

- (ISO 1985) *Information processing – Documentation symbols and conventions for data, program and system flowcharts, program network charts and system resources charts.* International Organization for Standardization. ISO 5807:1985

- (VDM 1998) Alagar V.S. & Periyasamy K. (1998) *Vienna Development Method. In: Specification of Software Systems.* Graduate Texts in Computer Science. Springer, New York, NY

- (Z 1998) Spivey, J. M. (1998) *The Z Notation: A Reference Manual*, Second Edition. Prentice Hall International (UK) Ltd

- (OCL 2014) *Object Constraint Language (OCL)*, version 2.4, Object Management Group, 2014

- (Holt & Perry 2019) Holt, J.D. & Perry, S.A. (2019) *Don't Panic! The absolute beginners' guide to model-based systems engineering.* INCOSE UK Publishing, Ilminster, UK

- (ISO 2015) *ISO/IEC/IEEE 15288:2015(en) Systems and software engineering — System life cycle processes.* ISO Publishing 2015

- (ISO 2015) *ISO/IEC/IEEE 42010:2011(en) Systems and software engineering — Architecture description.* ISO Publishing 2011

- (MODAF 2010) *The Ministry of Defence Architectural Framework. Ministry of Defence Architectural Framework. 2010.* Available from `https://webarchive.nationalarchives.gov.uk/20121018181614/http://www.mod.uk/DefenceInternet/AboutDefence/WhatWeDo/InformationManagement/MODAF/` (Accessed February 2012)

- (DoDAf 2007) *DoDAF Architectural Framework* (US DoD), Version 1.5; 2007

- (NAF 2007) NATO Architectural Framework Version 4. Available from `https://www.nato.int/cps/en/natohq/topics_157575.htm`

- (UAF 2017) *Unified Architecture Framework Profile (UAFP)*, Version 1.0, Object Management Group, 2017

- (Zachman 2008) Zachman J. (2008) *Concise Definition of the Zachman Framework.* Zachman International;

- (Holt & Perry 2020) Holt, J.D. & Perry, S.A. (2020) *Implementing MBSE – the Trinity Approach.* INCOSE UK Publishing, Ilminster, UK

- (Holt 2001) Holt, J.D. (2001) *UML for Systems engineering – watching the wheels.* IET Publishing, Stevenage, UK

- (Holt & Perry 2014) Holt, J.D. and Perry, S.A. (2014) *SysML for Systems engineering – a model-based approach.* Second edition. IET Publishing, Stevenage, UK

Section 2: Systems Engineering Concepts

This section provides a concise definition of all the concepts and their associated terminology. This terminology must be understood in order for it to be effective in implementing Systems Engineering.

This section has the following chapters:

- *Chapter 3, Systems and Interfaces*
- *Chapter 4, Life Cycles*
- *Chapter 5*, Systems Engineering *Processes*

3
Systems and Interfaces

This chapter will focus on the two key concepts of **systems** and **interfaces**. In particular, the importance of different levels of abstraction of systems will be considered and the need to constrain the number of hierarchical levels. Once these systems and their levels have been discussed, the way that these different levels interact will be explored by introducing the crucial concepts of interfaces.

In particular, this chapter will cover the following topics:

- **Defining systems**: Here, we will introduce and discuss the key concepts that will be used throughout the chapter.

- **Describing interfaces**: This will show how to identify and define interfaces of different types and at different levels.

- **Defining the framework**: Here, all the views that are used in the chapter will be captured at a high level in the MBSE framework that is being developed in this book.

  Understanding systems and interfaces is one of the most important aspects of developing any system, as they form the backbone of the system model. The fundamental building blocks of any system are the system elements that make up the hierarchy and the interfaces between these various system elements.

Remember, the entire approach to MBSE is based on having a consistent and coherent ontology in place. Therefore, before the different levels of abstraction can be discussed in detail, it is important to understand how all of the views that comprise the model can be demonstrated to be consistent with the underlying MBSE ontology.

Defining systems

A key aspect of systems engineering that needs to be established as quickly as possible is that of the system itself. The first step in this chapter, therefore, will be to define the MBSE ontology with the concepts and terminology that relate to systems and interfaces. This will include identifying the key terminology, but also defining exactly what is meant by the following terms:

- **System hierarchy**: How many levels of hierarchy will be permitted to exist? Many people will think of the concept of a subsystem, but rarely think of any additional levels of abstraction that may exist below the subsystem. Therefore, the question needs to be addressed as to how many other levels exist below each subsystem.

- **Interactions between system elements**: What interactions will be permitted between similar system elements, for example, systems to systems, and subsystems to subsystems?

- **Interaction between levels**: What interactions will be permitted between levels of hierarchy, for example, between systems and the subsystem?

The cornerstone of successful MBSE is having a good **ontology** in place. The ontology provides the **domain-specific language**, as described in *Chapter 2, Model-Based Systems Engineering*, but also provides the basis for consistency of all the views that comprise the model, which will be discussed in this section.

A key part of defining the system and its system elements is, therefore, defining the MBSE ontology. The ontology will be developed in a step-by-step fashion and it will be demonstrated how this is then used to help to create **views**. In this case, these views will be related to the system and its interfaces.

Demonstrating consistency between the ontology and system hierarchy

When modeling a system, it is important that the model represents the **system of interest** as accurately as possible or, to put this another way, as accurately as is necessary to develop the system successfully.

All systems have a natural **hierarchy** and it is, therefore, an essential part of the modeling endeavor to capture this hierarchy and to ensure that all elements in the model adhere to the captured hierarchy. This is achieved by capturing the hierarchy of the system as part of the ontology. This was touched on briefly in *Chapter 2, Model-Based Systems Engineering*, when the concept of ontology was introduced. In this section, this will be looked at in more detail and the importance of what is captured in the ontology will be discussed, along with variations in the hierarchy.

The discussion will begin by considering the simplest of hierarchies, as shown in the following diagram:

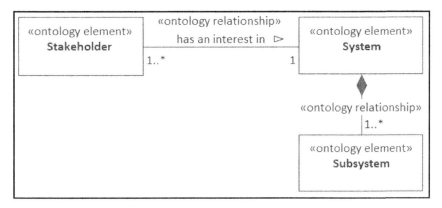

Figure 3.1 – A simple system hierarchy with a single level

The diagram in *Figure 3.1* shows a very simple **system hierarchy** with only one lower level of abstraction, that of the subsystem, using a SysML block definition diagram. The stakeholders that have an interest in the system sit at the same level of abstraction as the system. This may be inferred by the fact that the relationship between stakeholder and system is visualized using an association that makes both model elements exist *at the same level*. The relationship between system and subsystem, however, uses a composition that means that the subsystem sits *at a lower level* of abstraction than that of the system.

This is a good visual clue that can be easy to identify when looking at block diagrams. By locating the compositions (and aggregations, which will be discussed shortly), it is possible to quickly identify the various levels of abstraction that exist in the diagram and to easily identify the highest level. This is important as it provides a good starting point for reading the diagram. In this diagram, therefore, the natural place to start to read it is at the highest level of abstraction, which means that the diagram will be read as:

"One or more stakeholders have an interest in the system, and each system comprises a number of subsystems."

Each of the SysML modeling elements that exist on this diagram form part of the overall MBSE ontology that will be built upon throughout the book. Each of the blocks on the diagram represents an element in the ontology and this is shown visually by using the `<<ontology element>>` stereotype. Each of the relationships on the diagram, in this case an association and a composition, represent a relationship on the ontology and this is shown visually by using the `<<ontology relationship>>` stereotype. The entire ontology is made up of a set of **ontology elements** and **ontology relationships** and all the remaining ontology views that are shown in this book will follow this.

From this point forward, the `<<ontology element>>` stereotype will be shown, however, for reasons of clarity and for keeping the diagrams as clean and legible as possible. The `<<ontology relationship>>` stereotype will be omitted, but may be read as if it is present.

The preceding diagram uses a single composition between system and subsystem, which means that the concept of a system owns *all* of the subsystems that comprise it. This is where it is possible to introduce a slight variation to the ontology by adding in a new relationship, in this case an aggregation, as was discussed in *Chapter 2, Model-Based Systems Engineering*:

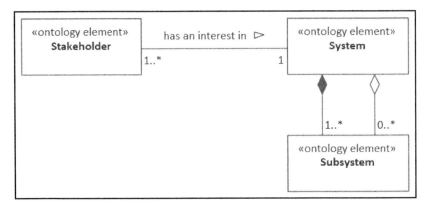

Figure 3.2 – A simple hierarchy showing one level with both composition and aggregation

The diagram in *Figure 3.2* shows the same basic hierarchy that was shown in *Figure 3.1*, using a SysML block definition diagram. This time, a new relationship has been introduced, which is the aggregation between system and subsystem.

This new addition is subtle but potentially very important for the entire structure of the system. This diagram may now be read as follows:

"One or more stakeholders have an interest in the system, and each system comprises a number of owned subsystems. The system may also be made up of optional subsystems that are not owned by the system."

This now means that the system itself is still made up of subsystems, but that these subsystems may be owned by the system of interest or may be owned by other systems. This allows for much more flexibility in terms of the systems that may be realized in the model. In order to illustrate this point, a number of views will be considered:

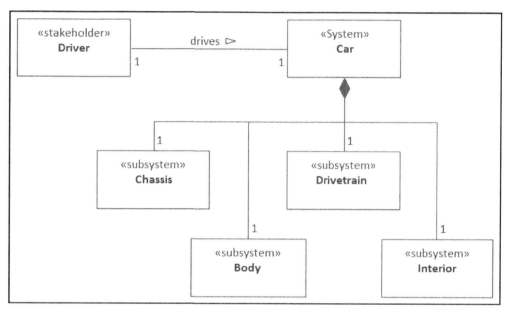

Figure 3.3 – Simple structural breakdown view showing consistency with the ontology

The diagram in *Figure 3.3* shows an example view that is based on, and is therefore consistent with, the ontology shown in *Figure 3.1*, using a SysML block definition diagram. If the diagram is consistent with the ontology, then it is a valid view. If, however, the diagram is not consistent with the ontology, then it is a picture. Remember, in MBSE, it is crucial that views are created as part of the model and not pictures. It is a simple matter to demonstrate that the diagram is consistent with the ontology by ensuring that every element on the diagram is an instance of one of more of the ontology elements or ontology relationships, as shown in the following list:

- **Driver** in the diagram is an instance of *stakeholder* from the ontology.

- **drives** in the diagram is an instance *of has an interest in* from the ontology.

- **Car** in the diagram is an instance of *system* from the ontology.

- **Chassis**, **Body**, **Drivetrain**, and **Interior** are all instances of *subsystem* from the ontology.

- All of the compositions between **Car** and **Chassis**, **Body**, **Drivetrain**, and **Interior** are instances of the composition between **system** and **subsystem** from the ontology.

As each element on the diagram is an instance of an ontology element or ontology relationship, it is a valid view and, just as importantly, is guaranteed to be consistent with any other views that use the same ontology, in this case, the one shown in *Figure 3.1*.

The diagram here shows its consistency by using the stereotypes stakeholder, system, and subsystem that are derived from the ontology. The same holds true for the relationships but, again, these are omitted from the diagram for reasons of clarity.

This is a good example of using stereotypes to enforce the ontology and it forms one of the key features of a profile that may be created using modeling tools.

The diagram in *Figure 3.3* is therefore consistent with the ontology in *Figure 3.1*, but it is also consistent with the ontology in *Figure 3.2*. This is because the diagram is consistent with a subset of the ontology and, therefore, is still consistent. The same is not true for the following diagram:

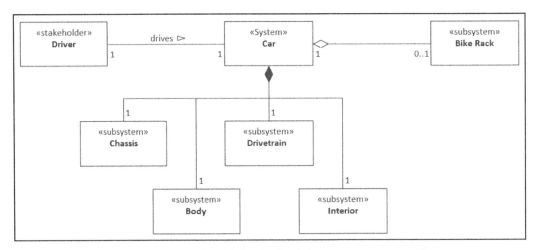

Figure 3.4 – Example structural breakdown view showing compositions and aggregation

The diagram in *Figure 3.4* shows the same basic system that was shown in *Figure 3.3*, but it has been enhanced by the addition of the bike rack, using a SysML block definition diagram. Notice that the 0..1 multiplicity implies that the bike rack is optional.

It is now possible to perform the same consistency check that was applied previously to demonstrate whether the diagram is consistent with the ontology as shown in *Figure 3.2*:

- **Driver** in the diagram is an instance of *stakeholder* from the ontology.
- **drives** in the diagram is an instance of *has an interest in* from the ontology.
- **Car** in the diagram is an instance of *system* from the ontology.

- **Chassis**, **Body**, **Drivetrain**, and **Interior** are all instances of *subsystem* from the ontology.

- All of the compositions between **Car** and **Chassis**, **Body**, **Drivetrain**, and **Interior** are instances of the composition between **system** and **subsystem** from the ontology.

- **Bike Rack** in the diagram is an instance of *subsystem* from the ontology.

- The aggregation between **Car** and **Bike Rack** is an instance of the aggregation between **system** and **subsystem**.

This demonstrates that the diagram is consistent with the ontology in *Figure 3.2*, but it cannot be consistent with the original ontology in *Figure 3.1* as the aggregation between the system and subsystem only exists in *Figure 3.2* and does not exist in *Figure 3.1*.

This is one of the most important points to understand in MBSE. All views must be consistent with the underlying ontology, otherwise they are not views and, therefore, are not part of the model.

The use of a set of stereotypes based on the ontology allows a simple way to quickly demonstrate consistency with ontology. From this point forward, all views shown in this book will use a set of stereotypes that originate from the MBSE ontology that will be evolved throughout the rest of this book.

The question that may arise at this point is which of these two ontologies is correct? The answer to this is that they are *both* potentially correct, but it will depend on exactly what information is to be included in the model. The ontology in *Figure 3.1* does not contain as much information as that in *Figure 3.2* and cannot, therefore, show as much information in the views. This does not mean that it is incorrect, however! It is important that, when defining the ontology, the implications of each ontology element and ontology relationship are fully considered before including them in the ontology. Remember, the aim is *not to model as much information as possible*, but *to model as much information as is necessary* in order to deliver a successful system.

Defining the system hierarchy

The system hierarchy may now be expanded to include a number of lower levels of abstraction, as shown in the following diagram:

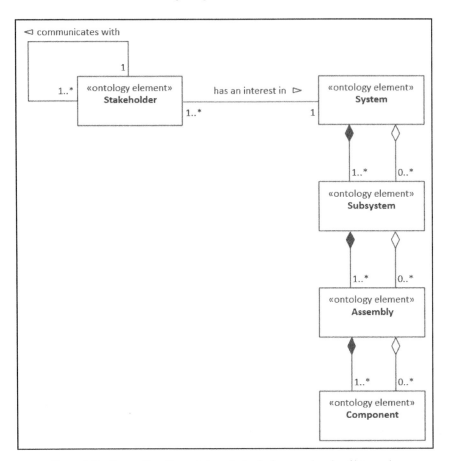

Figure 3.5 – Expanding the ontology to include more levels of hierarchy

The diagram in *Figure 3.5* shows an expanded ontology that defines several new levels of hierarchy, using a SysML block definition diagram. Each level is represented by stating a higher level and a lower level:

- Each *system comprises a number of owned subsystems* (shown by SysML composition) and may be made up of an optional number of non-owned subsystems (shown by SysML aggregation).

- Each *subsystem comprises a number of owned assemblies* (shown by SysML composition) and may be made up of an optional number of non-owned assemblies (shown by SysML aggregation).

- Each *assembly comprises a number of owned components* (shown by SysML composition) and may be made up of an optional number of non-owned components (shown by SysML aggregation).

This results in a set of four levels of system hierarchy that may be permitted to exist in the views.

The relationships between each of the levels is shown by both compositions and aggregations, as was discussed in the previous section. This allows for the flexibility of each level having both owned and non-owned lower-level elements. This will allow greater flexibility, but remember that the goal is not flexibility; the goal is to represent what is necessary in the hierarchy. Each of these relationships must be considered carefully before inclusion in, or exclusion from, the ontology.

The presence of these relationships shows the legal relationships that may be visualized in the views. Any relationships that are not present are, therefore, illegal in the views. For example, it is clear that it is legal for a system to comprise at least one subsystem, as it is in the ontology. The following relationships, however, are not legal:

- A system comprises a number of assemblies.

- A system comprises a number of components.

- A component comprises a number of subsystems.

This list shows just a few of the relationships that are illegal as their corresponding relationship does not exist on the ontology.

The ontology therefore shows the legal ontology elements and ontology relationships that may be visualized on views and prohibits the visualization of anything that is not on the ontology.

The diagram in *Figure 3.4* shows an example of legal visualizations of the ontology. Therefore, it is a valid view that forms part of the overall model.

Now that the basic system hierarchy has been discussed and is understood, it is time to consider the **interaction relationships** that exist between the elements at the same levels of the hierarchy.

Defining interaction relationships

The basic hierarchy has now been established, but it is also important to understand the legal interaction relationships between the individual levels of the hierarchy.

These interaction relationships can be seen on the following expanded ontology:

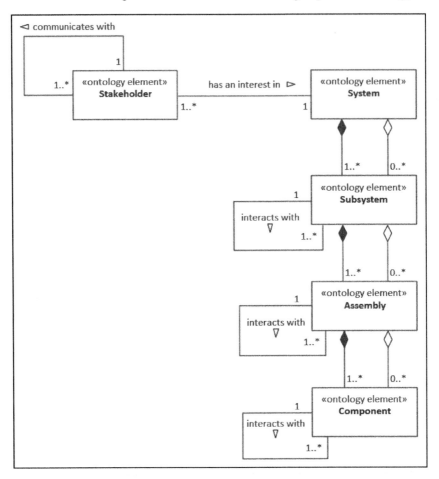

Figure 3.6 – Expanded ontology showing the interaction relationship between hierarchy levels

The diagram in *Figure 3.6* shows how the elements at individual hierarchy levels can interact with the same element at each level, using a SysML block definition diagram. In fact, there are five different types of interaction that can be identified from this diagram, which are as follows:

- **Stakeholder** to **Stakeholder**
- **Stakeholder** to **System**
- **Subsystem** to **Subsystem**
- **Assembly** to **Assembly**
- **Component** to **Component**

The associations on the diagrams, in this case of this ontology, identify points where the different elements that make up the view interact with one another. This not only clarifies where the points of potential interaction are, but also where interactions may not take place. This is very important as each line that appears on the ontology is weighted with meaning. This ontology, for example, currently does not allow for any of the following interactions:

- **System** to **System**
- **System** to **Subsystem**
- **Subsystem** to **Assembly**
- **Assembly** to **Component**

This is not intended to be an exhaustive list, but serves to illustrate the discussion. Consider the fact that there are no interactions allowed, according to this ontology, between systems and other systems. The immediate question that arises is, is this correct? In this case, the interaction between a system and another system is represented by the relationship between stakeholder and system, as other systems are considered to be stakeholders. This may be fine, but for a different organization, this may not be correct, in which case an additional relationship should be added, such as each system interacting with one or more other systems.

It is important to get away from the notion that there can only be one correct definition, as different organizations (and, indeed, different groups within the same organization) may look at the same concepts differently. The crucial thing to get right is to ensure that the ontology accurately reflects the domain-specific language of the organization of interest, rather than trying to create an ontology that satisfies the needs of all organizations. Note that these interactions are occurring horizontally between model elements that sit at the same level of abstraction in the system hierarchy.

The next set of illegal interactions to be discussed are those that exist between different levels of the system hierarchy: system to subsystem, subsystem to assembly, and assembly to component. In the case of the ontology shown here, there is no interaction permitted between adjacent levels or, for that matter, between any of the levels. This is an important aspect of the ontology to get right. It may be tempting to allow interaction vertically, between levels, as well as horizontally across the same levels. There is nothing wrong with this *per se* but, from the point of view of managing the complexity of the model, it is almost always advisable to constrain the number of interactions and not to allow every possible interaction for the sake of it.

In *Chapter 1, Introduction to Systems Engineering*, it was discussed that *complexity manifests itself on the interactions between model elements.* The ontology allows precisely this complexity to be managed and controlled, as it identifies and defines all the legal interactions and, by controlling the number and nature of these interactions on the ontology, it is a strong positive step toward managing complexity in the system as a whole.

Describing interfaces

Whenever such interactions have been defined, then there is also the potential to identify **interfaces** between these model elements. Controlling interfaces is a crucial part of systems engineering as it allows the control of interactions between different model elements. MBSE allows interfaces to be identified, defined, and managed using an established set of modeling views. This section will describe a set of views that allow any interface to be modeled.

Identifying interfaces

For the sake of this discussion, the relationship between the three lowest levels of the system hierarchy will be focused on, as shown in the following diagram:

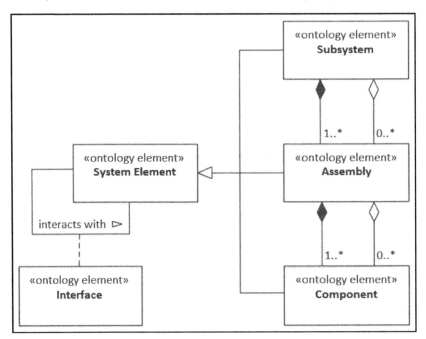

Figure 3.7 – Identifying generic interfaces between system elements

The diagram in *Figure 3.7* shows the concept of interfaces that exist between system elements, using a SysML block definition diagram. From a modeling point of view, note how a generalization relationship has been introduced to group the subsystem, assembly, and component together into a new, generic model element that is named **system element**. This diagram may be read as follows (ignoring for now the compositions and aggregations that were discussed previously):

There are three types of system element, which are subsystem, assembly, and component. Each system element interacts with one or more other system elements via an interface.

Note that the fact that there is an *interacts with* relationship between system element blocks means that this relationship is inherited down to its specialized blocks. This certainly makes the diagram more elegant than the alternative, which is shown here:

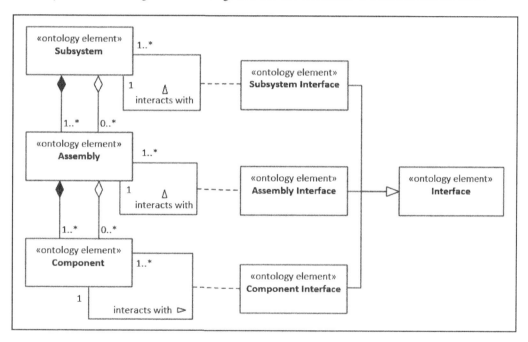

Figure 3.8 – Identifying explicit interface types

The diagram in *Figure 3.8* shows an alternative way to define interfaces, using a SysML block definition diagram, this time by defining explicit interfaces between specific levels of the system hierarchy. This diagram therefore reads as follows:

> *"Each subsystem interacts with one or more other subsystems via a subsystem interface. Each assembly interacts with one or more other assemblies via an assembly interface. Each component interacts with one or more other components via a component interface. Collectively, subsystem interface, assembly interface, and component interface are all types of interface."*

The ontology in *Figure 3.8* is clearly more complex than the one in *Figure 3.7* and, as can be seen by the text descriptions for each, the ontology that uses the system element generalization is, at first glance, certainly simpler and more elegant.

It is important, however, to look beyond the initial complexity and consider the precision of each of these ontologies. The simpler, more elegant ontology in *Figure 3.7* pays the price for its enhanced readability as it actually allows for more complex views, compared to the ontology in *Figure 3.8*.

The previous section discussed the fact that allowing more interaction between model elements can actually lead to an increase in the complexity of the model. This is the case in point here. By defining the new generalization of system elements and then defining a self-interaction of interacts with it, this does lower the number of types of interface defined and, therefore, the association blocks that are needed.

However, the ontology in *Figure 3.7* states that any system element may interact with any other system element. This actually means that a subsystem (a system element) may interact with an assembly (also a system element), which would be an interaction vertically between levels. Indeed, it is also possible that a component (being a system element) may interact with a subsystem (also a system element), which would be an interaction that actually jumps between more than one level.

Again, both of these are correct, but it is important to understand the implications of choosing to use different modeling constructs. Again, the aim is not to make the ontology as simple as possible, but to make it as simple as necessary in order to realize the system successfully.

Defining interfaces

The ontology has been used to explicitly identify where interfaces may exist in the overall model. Identifying interfaces is important, but it is also important to define exactly what is meant by an interface and what views may be used to represent the interface. This is achieved by expanding the ontology, specifically by expanding the interface ontology element, as shown in the following diagram:

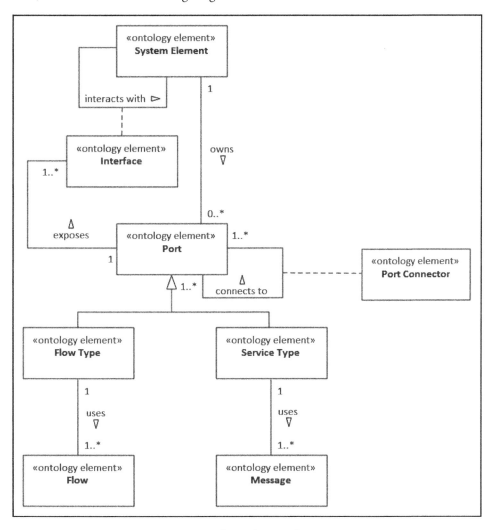

Figure 3.9 – Defining the interface concept

The diagram in *Figure 3.9* shows how the concept of the interface may be described further by defining other ontology elements and relating them to an interface, using a SysML block definition diagram.

The diagram here follows on from the ontology in *Figure 3.7*, but can also be easily related to the ontology in *Figure 3.8*. The definition of the interface itself is the same for both, the difference being that where there is only a single owns relationship between the system element and port, this would be expanded into three separate relationships between the port and each of subsystem, assembly, and component.

Reading the diagram, therefore, the following can be seen:

> *"Each system element interacts with one or more other system elements via an interface. Each system element may own zero or more ports and each port exposes one or more interfaces."*

Each system element may own zero or more ports, meaning that ports are optional, and it is possible to have a system element (whether it is a subsystem, assembly, or component) that does not own any ports. This allows for flexibility in the model. Each port may be thought of as a connection point between two elements. In real life, these may be almost anything where two elements join, and may be as diverse as electrical sockets, ports on a computer, doors between rooms, eyes and ears on a person, fingers, holes in a wall, and so on. It is important to not constrain the concept of a port to plugs and sockets on computers, which is often what people first think of when the term *port* is used. Real-life ports are incredibly varied and diverse in the world of systems engineering.

Each port exposes one or more interface which refers to what may be passed between ports, whether this be services or the flow of material. These will be elaborated upon shortly.

Continuing reading the diagram, it can be seen that one or more ports connect to one or more other ports via port connectors. There are two types of port – the flow type, which uses flows, and the service type, which uses messages.

Let's now turn our attention to the beginning of this sentence: One or more ports connect to one or more other ports via port connectors emphasizes that ports are the connection points between system elements. The medium that is used to make that connection is referred to as the port connector. As ports may take on many different forms in real life, the same holds true for port connections, examples of which include pipes, wires, air, corridors, and lenses.

There are two types of port – the flow type, which uses flows, and the service type, which uses messages, and all ports may be classified as one of these two types.

Service type ports use messages. A service may be thought of as a level of function that is made available to system elements and that may be realized by a number of processes (this will be discussed in more detail in *Chapter 5, Systems Engineering Processes,* which discusses modeling processes). Services are quite limited as to what they represent, and examples include software-type services (which is often what most people will be thinking of when referring to services) and also human-type services. A service is a behavioral construct (as opposed to a structural one) that is made available (rather than flowing) across an interface, and which allows the passing of messages across the interface.

Flow type ports use flows. A flow represents the passage of material that travels between one port and another. Flows can be many and varied and examples include power, force, fluids, gas, people moving, and data. A flow is a structural construct (as opposed to a behavioral one) that passes (rather than being made available) across an interface.

Modeling interfaces

This section considers how interfaces may be modeled using SysML. As with all modeling, there is always more than one way to model anything, so what is presented here will be based on best practice.

As with all models, it is necessary to consider both the structural and behavioral aspects of interfaces:

- When considering the structural modeling of interfaces, it is necessary to identify interfaces, define interfaces, ports, and their relevant flows and services, and also to define the connectivity of ports.

- When considering the behavioral modeling of interfaces, it is necessary to consider the sequence of services and their associated messages between ports, as well as any protocols that may exist.

Structural and behavior modeling is performed by creating a number of views, each of which will be visualized using a number of different SysML diagrams. Of course, it is possible to visualize the same views using any suitable notation but, for the purposes of this book, only the SysML notation will be considered.

Modeling the structural breakdown view

The first view that will be considered is one that allows ports and their associated interfaces to be identified for each of the system elements that own a port. It is possible, therefore, to consider any of the system elements that were described as part of the overall structure. For this example, consider the assemblies that make up the subsystem drivetrain, as described previously in *Chapter 2, Model-Based Systems Engineering*:

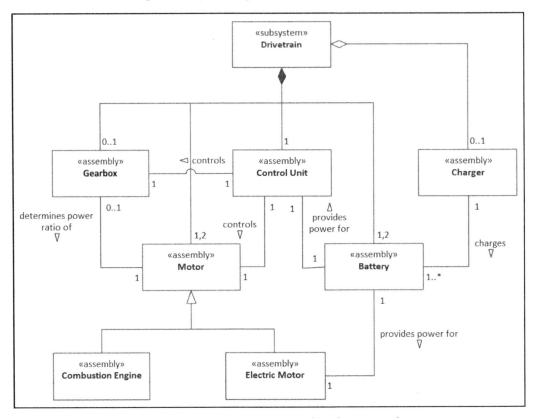

Figure 3.10 – Structural breakdown view of the drivetrain subsystem

The diagram in *Figure 3.10* shows a structural breakdown view of the drivetrain subsystem, using a SysML block definition diagram. Note the use of the term *view* here, as it is important to distinguish between the view and the visualization of the view by the SysML block diagram. Before continuing, consider the view, in this case, the structural breakdown view:

- It has a target audience of systems engineers, design engineers, and managers.

- The purpose of the view is to provide an overview of a single subsystem and to identify its constituent assemblies and the relationships between them.

- The content of the view is a single subsystem and one or more assemblies. Assemblies may be related to the chosen subsystem by either composition or aggregation. Assembly interaction relationships may also be shown along with types of assemblies.

In defining these points, it has now been established that it is a valid view.

The structural breakdown view is visualized using a SysML block definition diagram.

The structural breakdown view may be read as follows:

> *"The drivetrain comprises no gearbox, or just a single one, one or two motors, a single control unit, and one or two batteries, all of which it owns. It is also made up of no charger, or just a single one, that it does not own.*
>
> *The charger charges one or more batteries and each battery provides power for the control unit and electric motor. The control unit controls both the gearbox and the motor, of which there are two types: combustion engine and electric motor. No gearbox, or a single one, determines the power ratio of the motor."*

In showing the relationships between the different assemblies, the view also helps to identify potential interfaces between assemblies. In fact, every relationship between assemblies is a potential interface.

Modeling the interface identification view

The next diagram visualizes an interface identification view, which will allow interfaces to be identified and allocated to individual system elements:

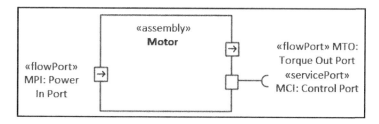

Figure 3.11 – Interface identification view: focusing on the motor assembly

The diagram in *Figure 3.11* shows an interface identification view that focuses, in this case, on a single assembly – the motor, using a SysML block definition diagram.

The SysML diagram used to visualize this view is a block definition diagram, but this time there is some advanced syntax introduced that will allow the modeling of interfaces. The next few paragraphs will, therefore, describe the SysML constructs and how they are used before they are applied fully to the example.

In SysML, connections between blocks may be shown by identifying a number of SysML ports. These are represented graphically by small rectangles that overlay the edge of the block. The diagram here therefore shows three ports, each represented by a small square that represents a connection point. It can be seen from the diagram that there are two different types of port shown here, which are as follows:

- **The standard port**, which is a simple rectangle (square on this diagram). This allows the identification of SysML interfaces, which facilitates the identification of a set of SysML services. The symbol for an interface is a line that emerges from the port with either a ball (not shown here, but shown on later diagrams) or a cup (as shown here), which represent either a provided interface (ball) or a required interface (cup). A provided interface represents a set of services realized by, or provided by, the block. A required interface represents a set of services that a block needs in order to operate.

- **The flow port**, which is shown as a rectangle (square on the diagram) with an arrow on it. A flow port allows flows to be represented and the arrow inside the rectangle shows the direction of the flow. The direction can be in (pointing toward the inside of the block), out (pointing toward the outside of the block), or it may be a two-way flow *inout* (a double-headed arrow).

This view, therefore, shows three ports. These are an **in**flow port named **MPI**, an **out**flow port named **MTO**, and a service port named **MCI**.

In SysML, ports are always typed, which is shown in the diagram as the name on the right-hand side of the colon that is next to the port name. In this example, therefore, we have the following:

- There is an *in*flow port named **MPI**, which is of the **Power In port** type.

- There is an *out*flow port named **MTO**, which is of the **Torque Out port** type.

- There is a standard port named **MCI**, which is of the **Control port** type.

Note that this view is only identifying where interfaces exist; it is not defining the nature, or type, of the interfaces, as that will be described in the next view.

The final point to make here concerns the use of stereotypes. As stated previously, the stereotypes (the words in the <<**chevrons**>>) refer to the ontology elements that are being realized in this view. This can lead to some confusion as the terminology used in the ontology (the domain-specific language) is very similar to the terminology used in SysML (the spoken language). The following list shows the mapping between the two:

- The interface identification view is visualized using a SysML block definition diagram.

- <<**assembly**>> from the ontology is visualized using a SysML block.

- <<**flow port**>> from the ontology is visualized using a SysML flow port (note that the two terms used are the same – one for the concept from the ontology, and one for the SysML construct).

- <<**service port**>> from the ontology is visualized using a SysML standard port.

This terminology can be quite confusing, but it is essential to be able to differentiate between ontological terms from the ontology and language-specific terms from the notation.

This view may now be expanded to include other assemblies, as shown here:

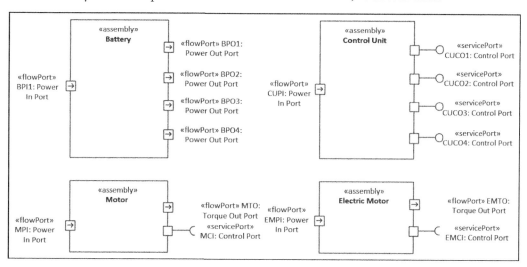

Figure 3.12 – Interface identification view showing multiple assemblies

The diagram in *Figure 3.12* shows an interface identification view, using a SysML block definition diagram, but, this time, multiple assemblies are shown. This is a very useful view as it can be seen as providing a library of standard elements that can be used when configuring systems – more on this in a later view.

Notice also that both provided (balls) and required (cups) interfaces are shown here as part of the definitions of different assemblies. These views can also be very technical and may not be as readable to a non-SysML expert as some of the other views due to the advanced SysML syntax that is being used. This is another reason why it is so important to consider which stakeholders will be looking at this view when deciding on its content.

Modeling the port definition view

Now that the interfaces have been identified via their ports, it is possible to describe each of these ports by creating a port definition view. A single port will be considered initially, as shown in the following diagram:

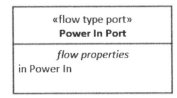

Figure 3.13 – Port definition view focusing on the Torque Output port

The diagram in *Figure 3.13* shows a port identification view that focuses on a single flow type port, in this case, the Power In port, visualized using the SysML block definition diagram. The flow type port is visualized in SysML using a block with a special compartment underneath that has the SysML label of flow properties. This compartment is used to identify the flows that pass across the port. In the case shown here, this is an incoming flow, indicated by the SysML keyword that is named *Power In*.

The port definition may also be enhanced by adding extra information in the form of properties, as described in *Chapter 2, Model-Based Systems Engineering*. An example of this is shown in the following diagram:

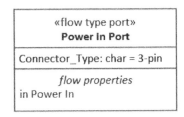

Figure 3.14 – Port definition view for the Power In port showing an additional property

The diagram in *Figure 3.14* is essentially the same as that in *Figure 3.13*, but it has been expanded to include further description of the flow type port using a SysML property, and visualized using a SysML block definition diagram. In this case, the property is named `Connector_type`. Note how this property has been typed to `char` and has a default value (an invariant constraint) set to `3-pin`.

In the preceding example, the property describes a physical feature of the port. In this case, it is stating the type of connector that is associated with the port. It could easily be expanded further to include other general features, such as size, position, manufacturer, material, and color, to name but a few.

The other type of port, the service type port, is also typed as a block, but uses different SysML syntax to describe it, as shown in the following diagram:

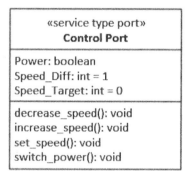

Figure 3.15 – Port definition view for Control Port

The diagram in *Figure 3.15* shows another port definition view, using a SysML block definition diagram. This time, it is describing a service type port rather than a flow type port. The SysML block has two compartments, which are as follows:

- **Properties**, shown here in the first compartment (the middle of the three boxes) and that are represented in the usual way in that they are typed and that can show default values. The properties on a service type port will often represent the data that is being used by the services, especially when software services are being modeled.

- **Services**, shown here in the second compartment (the lowest of the three boxes) and that are represented as SysML operations. These operations represent the services that are made available across an interface, whether they are perceived as being provided or required services.

It is also possible to define the flow types in a similar way by creating a flow type definition view, which will be discussed in the following section.

Modeling the flow type definition view

The flows that form part of the interfaces may also be defined in a similar way to the previous view. An example of the flow type definition view is shown in the following diagram:

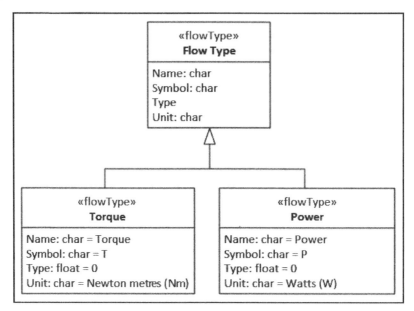

Figure 3.16 – Flow type definition view

The diagram in *Figure 3.16* shows a flow type definition view that is visualized using a SysML block diagram. The diagram shows a generic flow type that has four properties, which are as follows:

- **Name**, which is the full name of the flow type. This may seem like repetition as the name of the block is often the same as the value of this property name. This, however, is not always the case as the block name can often be an abbreviated form of the full name.

- **Symbol**, which shows the SI symbol (where there is one), or the short form, where there isn't.

- **Type**, which represents how the magnitude of the flow type is represented, be it an integer, short, long, float, and so on.

- **Unit**, which represents the official SI unit, where there is one.

This view also shows two specializations of flow type, which are torque and power. Notice how the values for each of the properties have been filled in using invariant constraints.

Modeling the interface connectivity view

All of the views that have been shown so far are generic in nature and may be used very effectively to form libraries that may be reused in different models. This is a very efficient way to use models as it means that the information only needs to be defined once and then never again. This is a very good time-saver and it automatically applies consistency to the model through reuse.

One of the main ways in which these libraries may be reused is to create different connectivity views that allow different configurations to be defined. There are two ways to show this in SysML, one using block definition diagrams, and one using a diagram known as the **internal block diagram**. The following diagram shows an example of where a block definition diagram is used:

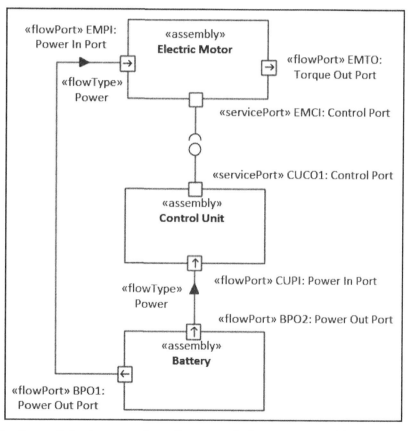

Figure 3.17 – Connectivity view: example configuration of a drivetrain using a block definition diagram

The diagram in *Figure 3.17* shows a connectivity view that shows an example configuration of a drivetrain using a SysML block definition diagram. Showing connectivity using a block diagram is typically done because there is only a single possible configuration of the system elements and only a single instance of each block.

The flow ports on the diagram are connected together using SysML **connectors** and then an **item flow**, which is typed as a flow type, is shown overlaying the connector line with a filled-in triangle. In the diagram here, the item flow is power.

The flow port definitions much be compatible, so the in- and out-flows must correspond on the diagrams. These ports need not necessarily be the same type, but the flows must be consistent. It is possible to have the same type definition for a port being used at both ends, even though the ins and outs on each port will be reciprocal. For example, in a situation where two ports have the same definition and a single flow, it will be an out-flow for one port and an in-flow for the other. This creates a potential problem, but this reciprocal relationship can be shown using the ~ symbol to show that one port is a **conjugated port**. A conjugated port is simply a port where the in-flows and out-flows have been reversed, while still using the same port definition. In such a situation, the ~ is shown next to the port on the diagram and the direction arrow in the port is reversed.

When connecting service ports together, the cup and ball symbols are used to show the provided and required interfaces and these must be of the same type. It should also be noted that a provided interface may only be connected to a required interface and it may not be connected to another provided interface. The cup and ball symbols provide a simple visual indicator of this.

The more usual diagram that is used to show connectivity is the internal block diagram, an example of which is shown here:

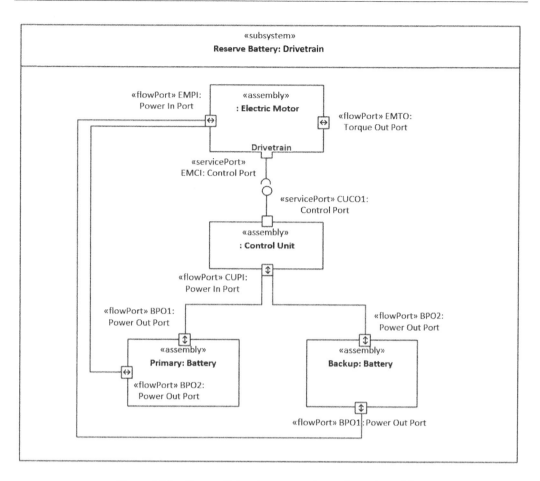

Figure 3.18 – Connectivity view: example configuration of the
drivetrain using an internal block diagram

The diagram in *Figure 3.18* indicates another way to show a possible configuration of the drivetrain, this time using a SysML internal block diagram.

The internal block diagram makes use of a very powerful concept in SysML, that of the **part**. In SysML, there are three levels of abstraction of concepts that may be modeled, and these are as follows:

- **The SysML block**. The block allows concepts to be visualized at the highest level. For example, blocks are typically used to show the overview of concepts of the car. The SysML syntax for a block is Car, where the block name is simply written inside the rectangle.

- **The SysML part**. This part allows collections of instances to be visualized to show configurations of system elements. For example, there are multiple configurations of a car that will be based on the generic concept of a car, and will provide the template for the instances of car. The SysML syntax for a part is Bongo:Car, where the part name is shown on the left-hand side of a colon, with the relevant block name shown on the right.

- **The SysML instance**. An instance allows a real-life example of a system element to be visualized. For example, an actual car that has been purchased is owned and may be driven around. The SysML syntax for an instance is JonsCar:Bongo:Car or JonsCar:Car. The colon is still used, but this time the whole name is underlined, indicating it is an instance, rather than a part. Either of these may be used, with the only difference being whether the part name is shown as well as the block name.

Internal block diagrams allow configurations to be specified using parts. The diagram here shows what looks like a large block that is named **Reserve Battery:Drivetrain**, but this is, according to the syntax, a part named **Reserve Battery** of the **drivetrain** block. Graphically, the part looks like a large block with several other parts contained within. The syntax here allows anything that is either a composition or an aggregation of a block to be shown inside its part without the need to show the composition or aggregation lines explicitly. Therefore, the diagram here shows that part of the **Powertrain** containing the following:

- **A single part of an electric motor**: This is an anonymous part, as it has nothing shown to the left of the colon. It is still a part, but the modeler has decided that no distinguishing name is required.

- **A single part of a control unit**: Again, this is an anonymous part with no name shown.

- **Two parts of the battery**: The two parts are shown with different explicit names, in this case, one is the primary and one is the backup.

The use of parts is very useful, therefore, as it allows multiple parts to be shown for a single block in the same configuration, as in the case of a battery.

Note how this view is still consistent with the structural breakdown view that was shown in *Figure 3.10* and, indeed, it is possible to show multiple connectivity views for a single structural breakdown view.

The internal block diagram, therefore, allows the internal connections and relationships of a block to be analyzed and specified by considering different configurations of its composite and aggregate parts.

It is possible to differentiate between compositions and aggregations in the internal block diagram as compositions are shown using solid lines for the boxes, whereas aggregations are shown using dashed lines for the boxes.

Modeling behavioral views for interfaces

It was previously stated that when modeling, it is necessary to model both the structural and behavioral aspects of the system, and interfaces are no different. Alongside the structural views that have been discussed so far, it is essential that behavioral views are also shown, otherwise they cannot be considered to be complete.

As interfaces show relationships between system elements, then the main diagram that is used to capture the behavior is the SysML sequence diagram, as this allows interactions between system elements to be modeled, as discussed in *Chapter 2, Model-Based Systems Engineering*.

The following sequence diagram shows a simple scenario for the drivetrain, based on the structural views:

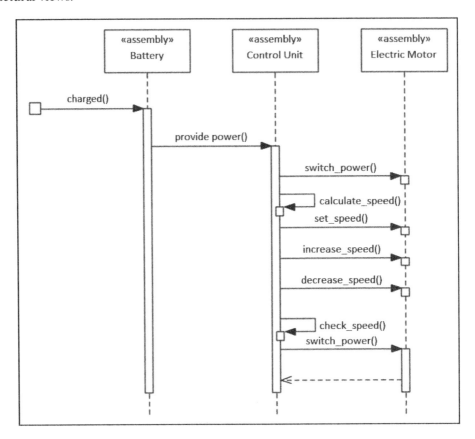

Figure 3.19 – Interface behavior view: example scenario for the drivetrain using a basic sequence diagram

The diagram in *Figure 3.19* shows an example scenario for the drivetrain using a simple SysML sequence diagram. As was discussed previously, any number of these behavior views may be created for the single structural breakdown view and its associated connectivity views. This may see quite a large increase in the number of views that are created as part of the overall model.

Note the consistency between the views:

- **Lifelines to blocks**: Each lifeline on the sequence diagram relates directly back to a block from the structural breakdown view.

- **Interactions with associations**: Each interaction between blocks relates back to an association between blocks from the structural breakdown view.

- **Interaction names to operations**: The names of the individual interactions relate back to the services on the port definition views that are visualized by operations on the block.

The application of the consistency ensures that the overall set of views for the interface definition provides a full and complete definition.

It is also possible to go into an extra level of detail using advanced notation on the sequence diagrams. It is possible to not only show the general interaction between lifelines (and, hence, blocks) but also to show the specific ports that are involved in these interactions. An example of this is shown in the following diagram:

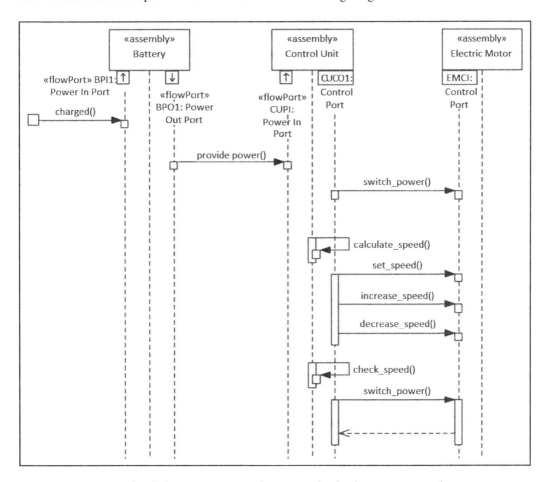

Figure 3.20 – Interface behavior view: example scenario for the drivetrain using a basic sequence diagram with advanced notations

The diagram in *Figure 3.20* shows the same scenario that was shown in *Figure 3.19*, still using a sequence diagram, but in this case some advanced syntax is being used.

Each lifeline now has its relevant ports shown underneath it, and the specific interactions between the ports are shown. Note how the self-interactions, for example, **check_speed**, are shown on the original lifeline as they represent internal interactions. These internal interactions will be shown as operations on the parent block, but will not be represented as service operations on the port definition, as these are internal operations, rather than operations being shown between blocks.

Again, this diagram is consistent with the structural breakdown view and its associated connectivity views, but it shows an extra level of detail.

Note how the more detailed a diagram becomes, then the more expert interpretation is required on behalf of the person reading the diagram. To put this another way, the more advanced syntax makes the diagram less readable to a non-SysML expert, and so caution must be applied when deciding which stakeholders will be shown any view that uses advanced SysML syntax.

Defining the framework

The views that have been created so far represent the center part of MBSE in a slide, which was discussed in detail in *Chapter 2, Model-Based Systems Engineering*. Each of the views have been visualized using SysML, which represents the right-hand side of MBSE in a slide. These views combine to form the overall model, but it is essential that these views are all consistent otherwise they are not views, but pictures! This is where the left-hand side of MBSE in a slide comes into play as it is important that the definition of all of the views is captured in the framework. The framework comprises the ontology and a set of viewpoints. Therefore, it is now time to make sure that these viewpoints are defined thoroughly and correctly, which is the aim of this section.

Defining the viewpoints in the framework

It was discussed in *Chapter 2, Model-Based Systems Engineering*, that it is necessary to ask a number of questions for each view to ensure that it is a valid view. There is also a set of questions that must be asked of the whole framework, as well as the views and the combination of these results in a set of questions that allow the whole framework to be defined:

- *Why is the framework required?* This question may be answered using a **framework context view**.

- *What are the overall concepts and terminology used for the framework?* This question may be answered using an **ontology definition view**.

- *What views are necessary as part of the framework?* This question may be answered using a **viewpoint relationship view**.

- *Why is each view needed?* This question may be answered using a **viewpoint context view**.

- *What is the structure and content of each view?* This question may be answered using a **viewpoint definition view**.

- *What rules should be applied?* This question may be answered using a **ruleset definition view**.

When these questions are answered, then it can be said that a framework has been defined. Each of these questions can be answered using a special set of views that is collectively known as the **Framework for Architecture Frameworks (FAF)** [Holt and Perry, 2019]. At this point, simply think about creating a specific view to answer each question, as described in the following sections.

Defining the framework context view

The framework context view specifies why the whole framework is needed in the first instance. It will identify the relevant stakeholders that have an interest in the framework and also identify what benefits each of the stakeholders hope to achieve from the framework.

There will be a single framework context viewpoint for each organization. This view will differ for each organization as different organizations will have a different set of needs in terms of the framework.

The framework context view will be visualized using a SysML use case diagram, and this will be described fully in *Chapter 6, Needs and Requirements*.

Defining the ontology definition view

The ontology definition view captures all the concepts and associated terminology associated with the framework in the form of an ontology. The good news is that this has already been done as the ontology for the system-related views was defined in *Figure 3.6*. The ontology elements shown on this view provide all of the stereotypes that have been used for the actual views that have been created so far in this chapter.

Defining the viewpoint relationship view

The viewpoint relationship view identifies which views are needed and, for each set of views, identifies a viewpoint that will contain its definition. These viewpoints may be collected together into a perspective, which is simply a collection of viewpoints with a common theme. In this chapter, the emphasis has been on defining a set of views relative to systems and interfaces. Therefore, it is appropriate to create the **systems perspective**. The basic set of views that has been discussed so far is shown in the following view:

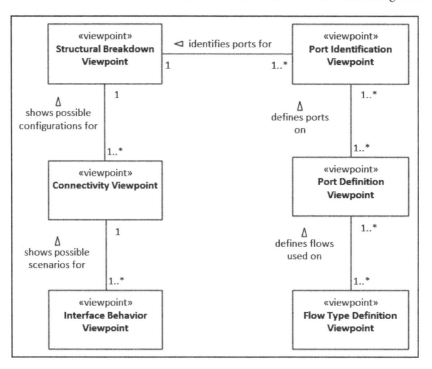

Figure 3.21 – Viewpoint relationship view for the system perspective

The diagram in *Figure 3.21* shows the viewpoint relationship view for the system perspective using a SysML block definition diagram. The concept of the viewpoint shown here is the one that was introduced in MBSE in a slide in *Chapter 2, Model-Based Systems Engineering*.

Each set of views has an associated viewpoint that contains the definition of the views. Alongside identifying these viewpoints, it is also important to identify the relationships between them, as these will come in useful later when it comes to defining rules associated with the framework.

It is also possible to use the SysML specialization relationship to show variations in terms of specific views, an example of which can be seen in the following diagram:

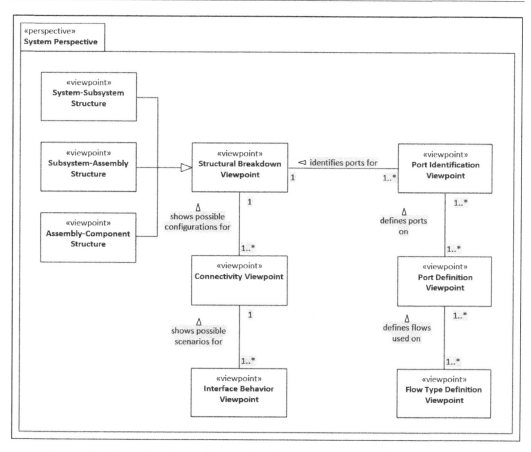

Figure 3.22 – Viewpoint relationship view for the system perspective showing greater detail

The diagram in *Figure 3.22* shows the viewpoint relationship view for the system perspective using a SysML block definition diagram. This time, however, the structural breakdown viewpoint has been expanded upon. Consider the ontology that was presented in *Figure 3.6*, which had four levels of abstraction: system, subsystem, assembly, and component. The same structural breakdown viewpoint may be applied at three levels, as follows:

- **System-Subsystem structure**, which focuses on a specific system and shows how it is broken down into various subsystems

- **Subsystem-Assembly structure**, which focuses on a specific subsystem and shows how it is broken down into various assemblies

- **Assembly-Component structure**, which focuses on a specific assembly and shows how it is broken down into various components

Each of these is actually a special type of structural breakdown viewpoint, which is shown in the diagram using a specialization relationship. It is by no means necessary to show this level of detail, but it is up to the modeler to decide whether or not adding the extra level of detail adds value to the model.

Defining the viewpoint context view

The viewpoint context view specifies why a particular viewpoint and, therefore, its set of views, is needed in the first instance. It will identify the relevant stakeholders that have an interest in the viewpoint and also identify what benefits each of the stakeholders hope to achieve from the framework.

There will be a viewpoint context view for each viewpoint. Each viewpoint context view will trace back to the framework context view as it must contribute to the overall expectations of the organization. The combined set of viewpoint context views will, therefore, satisfy the overall needs represented in the framework context view.

The viewpoint context view will be visualized using a SysML use case diagram, and this will be described fully in *Chapter 6, Needs and Requirements*.

Defining the viewpoint definition view

The viewpoint definition view defines the ontology elements that are included in the viewpoint. It shows the following:

- Which ontology elements are allowed in the viewpoint
- Which ontology elements are optional in the viewpoint
- Which ontology elements are not allowed in the viewpoint

An example of a viewpoint definition view for the structural breakdown viewpoint, specifically, the system-subsystem structure, is shown in the following diagram:

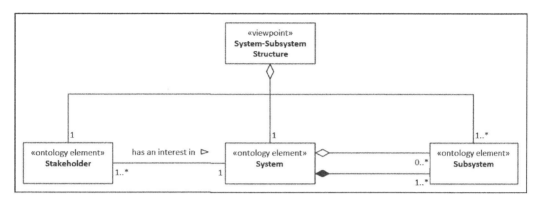

Figure 3.23 – Viewpoint definition view for the structural breakdown
view – System-Subsystem Structure

The diagram in *Figure 3.23* shows the viewpoint definition view for the structural breakdown viewpoint, using a SysML block definition diagram. This time, however, the diagram shows specifically the system-subsystem structure specialization of that viewpoint.

This view is a very important one as it defines the exact content of what is allowed in all the views that are described by the viewpoint. This viewpoint will always contain the following information:

- The **viewpoint** name, stereotyped by <<viewpoint>>, which is the focus of this view. The viewpoint that is identified here must come from the viewpoint relationship view that was shown in *Figure 3.22*.

- A number of ontology elements, stereotyped by <<ontology element>>. Each of these ontology elements must come from the ontology definition view shown in *Figure 3.6*.

This view may seem quite straightforward at first glance, as it contains a single viewpoint and then a subset of the ontology, but there are a number of subtleties associated with the ontology elements on this view.

The presence of each ontology element is clearly important as it identifies the ontology elements that are permitted to appear in this viewpoint. However, the multiplicities associated with each of the ontology elements and the ontology relationships.

Consider the following ontology elements:

- **Stakeholder** *must* appear on the diagram, as the multiplicity indicates 1. If stakeholder was an option, then the multiplicity would be 0...1 or 0...* or a variation thereof.

- **Stakeholder** has a multiplicity of 1, which means that there *must be one, and only one*, stakeholder shown on the viewpoint. If it was permitted for there to be more that a single stakeholder on this viewpoint, then the multiplicity would have to be set to 1..* or a variation thereof.

- **System** must appear on the diagram and, similar to the stakeholder, there must be *one and only one* system on the viewpoint.

- **Subsystem** *must* appear on the viewpoint, and there must be at least one subsystem.

Now consider the following ontology relationships:

- One or more stakeholders have an interest in the system. This means that there *must* be an association between stakeholder and system on the viewpoint.

- Each system is made up of one or more subsystems that it owns. This means that there *must* be at least one composition relationship between system and subsystem on the viewpoint. This is because of the 1…* multiplicity on subsystem that makes it mandatory.

- Each system is made up of zero or more subsystems that it does not own. This means that there *may or may not* be at least one aggregation relationship between system and subsystem. This is because of the 0…* multiplicity on the subsystem that makes it optional.

It is important to think very hard about every ontology element and ontology relationship that is present on the viewpoint definition view as this dictates the content of every view that is based on it.

Defining the ruleset definition view

The ruleset definition view identifies and defines a number of rules that may be applied to the model to ensure that it is consistent with the framework.

The rules are based primarily on the ontology definition view and the viewpoint relationships view. In each case, the rules are defined by identifying the key relationships and their associated multiplicities that exist:

- Between viewpoints on the viewpoint definition view
- Between ontology elements on the ontology definition view

Some examples of these rules are shown in the following diagram:

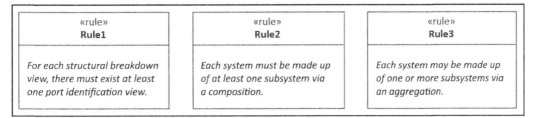

Figure 3.24 – Example ruleset definition view

The diagram in *Figure 3.24* shows an example of a ruleset definition view using a SysML block definition diagram. Each block on the diagram represents a rule that is derived from either the ontology definition view or the viewpoint relationship view.

These rules are defined as follows:

- For each structural breakdown view, there must exist at least one port identification view. This rule is derived directly from the viewpoint relationship view shown in *Figure 3.22*.

- Each system must be made up of at least one subsystem via a composition. This rule is derived directly from the ontology definition view shown in *Figure 3.6*.

- Each system may be made up of one or more subsystem via an aggregation. This rule is derived directly from the ontology definition view shown in *Figure 3.6*.

Of course, any number of other rules may be defined here, but not every relationship will lead to a rule, as this is at the discretion of the modeler.

Summary

In this chapter, the concept of a system and its interfaces was explored in more detail.

The different concepts associated with a system, such as the levels of abstraction and the interactions between these levels and the presence of stakeholders, were defined on the ontology. Where interaction between different elements occurs, it is possible to identify an interface.

interfaces were defined in terms of their different types, either service-based or flow-based, and several properties were defined for each, such as flows and services. It was then shown how to model these interfaces by describing a standard set of views that allow different aspects of any interface to be represented.

Finally, all of these views were captured as part of an overall framework definition using the Framework for Architecture framework. This framework itself comprises a number of views that are used to describe the model.

Understanding the fundamental structure of a system is an essential part of developing any successful system. If the system is not understood, then it can never be judged to be successful. Understanding the interactions between different system elements is an essential part of managing the complexity of the system and this is achieved through effective interface modeling. The skills that were therefore introduced in this chapter are essential for any systems engineering endeavor.

The success of the delivery of the final system will depend on the system satisfying its original needs, which will form the subject of the next chapter.

Self-assessment tasks

1. Create a structural breakdown view for part of a system in your organization based on the ontology described in this chapter. Choose a single system and identify its main subsystems.

2. Based on the answer to the previous question, consider the relationships between the levels of abstraction, in terms of composition and aggregation, as well as the relationships on each level of abstraction in terms of associations and where the interfaces exist.

3. Identify at least one interface that exists between the subsystems on your view and provide a description by creating an interface identification view, a port definition view, a flow definition view, a connectivity view, and an interface behavior view.

4. Define a configuration of your system, based on your previous answers.

5. Select any viewpoint from the viewpoint relationship view in *Figure 3.22* and create a viewpoint context view using text and a viewpoint definition view using a block diagram.

References

- [Holt and Perry 2019] Holt, JD, and Perry, SA. *SysML for Systems Engineering – A Model-Based Approach*. Third edition. IET Publishing, Stevenage, UK, 2019

4
Life Cycles

This chapter introduces the key concept of the life cycle and its relationship to systems engineering. Understanding and managing life cycles is crucial to the success of any systems engineering initiative.

The concept of a life cycle is relatively simple; however, there is a lot of hidden complexity associated with life cycles and, as a consequence, a lot of ambiguity and misunderstanding in this area. There are two main areas of misunderstanding – the types of life cycle and the interactions between life cycles, both of which will be discussed in this chapter.

In this chapter, we will study the following topics:

- **Defining the main concepts associated with life cycles**: The chapter begins by defining the main concepts associated with life cycles by expanding the MBSE ontology that has been developed so far in this book.

- **Discussing the different types of life cycles that may exist, along with examples**: The different types of life cycles that may exist will then be discussed, and examples will be provided. An in-depth example will be provided based on a systems engineering best-practice life cycle and its associated **stages**.

- **The execution of life cycles, with examples of how the chosen life cycle model influences project execution**: The execution of life cycles will be described and various examples of **life cycle models** will be discussed, along with the influence that they have on the overall project execution.

This chapter will give you a full understanding of the different types of life cycles that are relevant to MBSE and how to model them.

Defining life cycles

This section introduces the main concepts associated with life cycles. These concepts will be described using the modeling techniques that have been introduced so far in this book, specifically by expanding the existing MBSE ontology to include the life cycle concepts. As the MBSE ontology expands, the scope of the overall ontology will increase to include more concepts, but, very importantly, it will be consistent with everything else described so far in the book.

One of the key concepts associated with any life cycle is that of the stage, and this will form the start point of the discussion in the next section, which describes the key concepts associated with life cycles.

Defining life cycle concepts

There are several main concepts and associated terminology that need to be understood in order to perform systems engineering successfully. These main concepts are shown in the following diagram, which shows the first version of the ontology definition view for life cycle definition:

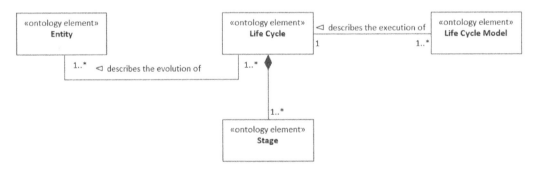

Figure 4.1 – An ontology definition view for life cycle concepts

Figure 4.1 shows the main **Life Cycle** concept. Any number of life cycles describe the evolution of one or more entities over time. There are many types of entities, and they will be explored later in this section, but for now, think of an entity as a system. Therefore, this part of the diagram may be read as follows:

One or more life cycles describe the evolution of one or more entities
(systems).

Each entity should be thought of as a living entity that will evolve over time. A system, therefore, may be thought of as something that evolves as it is developed and as it is deployed. The next important aspect of *Figure 4.1* to consider is that of **Stage**:

Each life cycle comprises one or more stages.

The basic constituent part of a life cycle is the **stage**. A stage represents a distinct period of time that describes a specific point in the evolution of an entity. We will study examples of the different types of stages later in this section.

The final part of *Figure 4.1* that will be considered is that of **Life Cycle Model**:

One or more life cycle models describe the execution of a life cycle.

A life cycle may be thought of as a *structural representation* of the evolution of an entity. It defines what stages are involved in the life cycle. A life cycle model, on the other hand, may be thought of as the *behavioral representation* of the evolution of an entity. Therefore, the *life cycle* shows *what*, while the *life cycle model* shows *how*. In relation to the stages that comprise the life cycle, the life cycle identifies what stages exist, whereas the life cycle model describes the order that these stages are executed in.

The stages that exist will depend on the nature of the entity that the life cycle is describing, and there are many types of entities that may be considered. Refer to the following diagram:

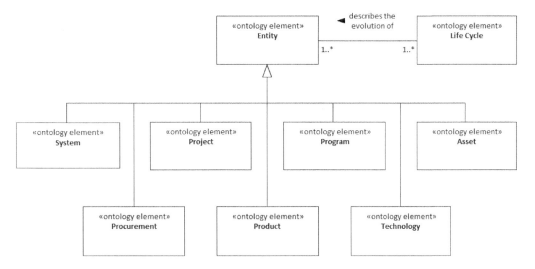

Figure 4.2 – An ontology definition view showing different types of entities

The preceding figure shows an ontology definition view that uses a SysML block definition diagram to show seven different types of entities, each of which will have a life cycle that describes its evolution. Examples of these life cycles and their associated stages will be discussed in the following sections.

Defining a life cycle for systems

The concept of a system is perhaps the main type of entity that is thought of in the world of systems engineering. It is also the one that will have its own life cycle, potentially interacting with other life cycles.

The term "system life cycle" is used frequently, but it is important to understand exactly what it means. The most widely used definition for a system life cycle is described in ISO 15288 and describes the development of a system. Indeed, sometimes the term "system development life cycle" may be used to describe a system. Refer to the following diagram now:

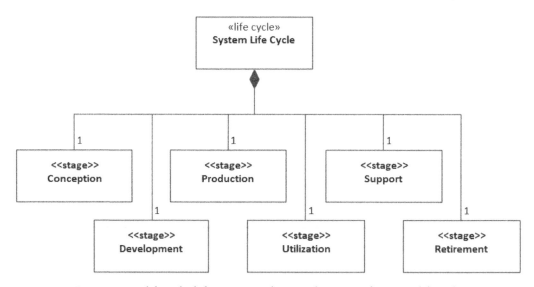

Figure 4.3 – A life cycle definition view showing the stages of a system life cycle

Figure 4.3 contains a life cycle definition view that shows the six stages that are identified for the system life cycle using a SysML block definition diagram:

- **Conception**: This stage is concerned with identifying and defining the needs of the system. This will also typically cover stakeholder analysis and the definition of verification and validation criteria for the needs.

- **Development**: This stage is concerned with identifying potential candidate solutions for the problem that are associated with the needs and finding the preferred solution. This stage may also involve developing a prototype prior to the production stage.

- **Production**: This stage takes the preferred solution and creates the actual system itself. This will also involve all of the various testing activities to ensure that the system is built right (verification) and that the right system is built (validation).

- **Utilization**: This stage describes what happens when the system is being used by the end users and the operator stakeholders. This stage will also include training the appropriate stakeholders to use the system effectively. This stage will take place in parallel with the support stage.

- **Support**: The support stage is concerned with providing all of the support services, such as reporting errors, maintenance, and so on, that will ensure that the system is being run effectively. This stage will take place in parallel with the utilization stage.

- **Retirement**: This stage describes how and when the system is to be decommissioned and disposed of in a safe and secure manner.

These stages may be executed in different sequences, depending on the nature of the system, which is described by the life cycle model.

These same six stages may also be used as the stages for the following:

- **Project life cycle**: The project life cycle describes the evolution of a specific project. It is possible for several project life cycles to be contained within a single system life cycle. Likewise, as a program comprises a number of projects, there is also a strong link between these two.

- **Program life cycle**: The program life cycle sits at a level of abstraction above the project life cycle, as a program comprises a number of projects. A program, therefore, relates to a number of projects or a portfolio of programs.

- **Product life cycle**: The product life cycle refers to the end result of a project or the thing that is sold to the end customer. There is a close relationship between a product and a system as it may be considered that all products are systems, but not all systems are products.

The use of the same set of stages for a number of different life cycles can lead to confusion, which is why it is so important to understand exactly the scope of the life cycle that is being considered.

Also, the natures of the entities that these life cycles describe are also very similar and easy to confuse with each other. So, programs and projects are very closely related, systems and products are closely related, projects and products are closely related, and so on.

It is essential, therefore, that when the term life cycle is being used, the exact nature of the life cycle is understood.

Defining a life cycle for procurement

The system life cycle describes the evolution of the development of a system. This system life cycle is often carried out within a higher-level life cycle, which is commonly known as a **procurement life cycle** or an **acquisition life cycle**.

These procurement life cycles are usually used by organizations that are not developing their own systems but issuing tenders for other organizations to bid on the development of their systems. A procurement life cycle will, therefore, often overarch one or more system life cycles. An example of a procurement life cycle is shown in the following figure.

In our previously considered car example, a car manufacturer may buy some of the subsystems, such as the motor, from other suppliers. A procurement life cycle allows this acquisition of motors to be captured and defined in the model. Refer to the following diagram:

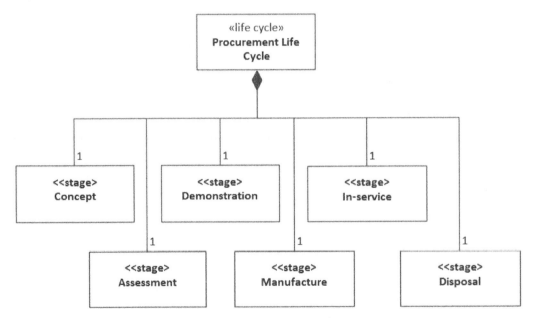

Figure 4.4 – A life cycle definition view showing the stages of a procurement life cycle

Figure 4.4 shows a life cycle definition view, using a SysML block definition diagram, that shows the six stages that are identified for the procurement life cycle:

- **Concept**: The **Concept** stage is concerned with understanding the needs of the system to be procured and issuing the tender that is used for the basis of bidding.

- **Assessment**: The **Assessment** stage is concerned with taking the bids that have been received against the tender and assessing them. On the basis of this assessment, one (or sometimes more) preferred bid will be chosen and taken forward to the next stage.

- **Demonstration**: The **Demonstration** stage is concerned with making sure that the preferred supplier is in a position to be able to manufacture the system by demonstrating their manufacturing capabilities.

- **Manufacture**: The **Manufacture** stage is concerned with undertaking production and ensuring the delivery of the final system.

- **In-service**: The **In-service** stage is concerned with providing all the support capability that is needed in order to ensure that the system performs correctly.

- **Disposal**: The **Disposal** stage is concerned with carrying out plans for efficient, effective, and safe disposal of the system.

The procurement life cycle is important as it will often sit at a higher level than the system life cycle but will have various interaction points.

Defining a life cycle for technology

The successful deployment of a system will depend on a number of technologies that are being used throughout the system life cycle. This is referred to as the **technology life cycle**. In cases where the system life cycle is very long, for example, if the system has long support and utilization stages, it is important to consider the life cycle of these technologies. For very long-term products, it may be necessary to ensure that the technology that was used as part of the solution remains available for the duration of the life cycle, even if the technology becomes obsolete. As an example of this, consider music media being played in a car.

In the 1980s, this would have been a cassette, in the 1990s, a compact disc, in the 2000s, a connected device (such as a phone or media player), and in the 2010s, this would tend toward direct streaming. It is important, therefore, to understand the stages that are involved in a technology life cycle, as shown in the following diagram.

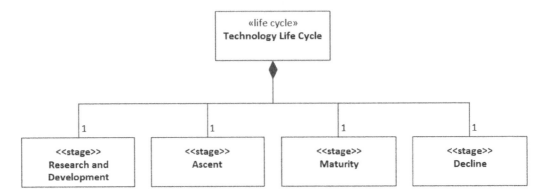

Figure 4.5 – A life cycle definition view showing the stages of a technology life cycle

Figure 4.5 shows a life cycle definition view, using a SysML block definition diagram, that shows the four stages identified for this life cycle:

- **Research and Development**: The **Research and Development** stage represents the point where investment is being made in new technology that has yet to establish a return. The risk of adopting such technology is high.

- **Ascent**: The **Ascent** stage represents the point where there is more widespread adoption of the technology. The risk associated with adopting such technology is lower than in the previous stage but still exists.

- **Maturity**: The **Maturity** stage represents a well-established technology where the risk associated with adoption is low.

- **Decline**: The **Decline** stage represents the point where the technology is no longer being used as widely as before and the end of its adoption can be foreseen. There is increased risk associated with adopting technology at this stage.

The technology life cycle is important as the system life cycle will depend on it, since it is dictated by the type of technology adopted as part of the system solution. This is particularly important where the system life cycle is long, for example, if it is measured in years, as technologies will become obsolete over time.

Defining a life cycle for assets

The final type of life cycle that will be considered is **Asset Life Cycle**. Again, the asset life cycle will be closely related to the system life cycle, as an example of an asset is a system. However, the scope of an asset is far wider, as an asset can be anything that has value to an organization and, therefore, may also be people, infrastructure, equipment, data, and so on.

It is important to understand the stages that are involved in the asset life cycle, which are shown in the following figure:

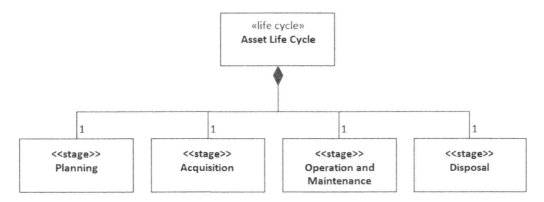

Figure 4.6 – A life cycle definition view showing stages for an asset life cycle

Figure 4.6 shows a life cycle definition view for an asset life cycle and is visualized using a block definition diagram. There are four stages that are identified for this life cycle:

- **Planning**: The **Planning** stage is concerned with establishing the asset needs, based on an evaluation of the existing assets and their potential to meet existing needs.

- **Acquisition**: The **Acquisition** stage includes the activities involved in procuring an asset.

- **Operation and Maintenance**: The **Operation and Maintenance** stage is concerned with providing all the support services that are required to ensure that an asset is installed, managed, and controlled in a way that ensures that it satisfies the original needs.

- **Disposal**: The **Disposal** stage is concerned with the safe and effective retirement of the asset from active service.

The asset life cycle is very closely related to the procurement life cycle and has some obvious overlaps. Indeed, the asset life cycle may be thought of as sitting at a higher level than the procurement life cycle, as one of the stages in the asset life cycle is the acquisition stage, which is concerned with the overall procurement of the asset.

Describing the Vee life cycle

One of the most common examples of a life cycle that is seen in the real world is the so-called **Vee model**. There is a very widespread misconception regarding the Vee model: contrary to popular belief, it does not describe a life cycle at all but actually shows relationships between processes that exist within a specific life cycle.

The Vee cycle, therefore, will be discussed in more detail in *Chapter 5, Systems Engineering Processes*, as that chapter is focused on processes.

There is a strong relationship between processes and life cycles and many people confuse stages and processes. In fact, processes are executed during each stage and in some cases, there is a one-to-one relationship between a stage and a process, which can lead to a blurring of the concepts.

This definition is shown clearly in the next section, where the life cycle ontology is expanded to include additional concepts.

Expanding the life cycle concepts

The life cycle ontology that was introduced in *Figure 4.1* may now be expanded to include several other key concepts, as shown in the following diagram:

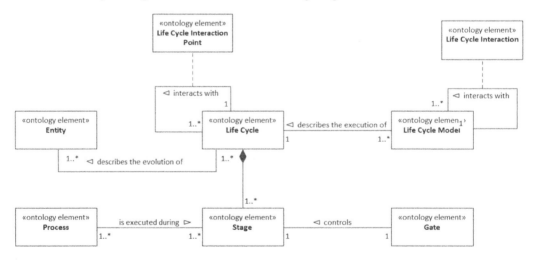

Figure 4.7 – Expanded ontology definition view for life cycle concepts

Figure 4.7 shows a life cycle definition view using a SysML block definition diagram that shows that the first new concept is that of **Gate**, which is associated with each life cycle **Stage**. A life cycle gate provides an assessment mechanism that controls the stage, which dictates the tests that must be applied at the end of each stage. It seems intuitive that once one stage comes to an end, another stage will begin its execution, but this is not always the case. This transition is controlled by the stage gate. A stage gate may result in one of several typical next steps:

- **Progress on to next stage**: If the stage has been completed successfully, then the next stage in the life cycle is executed.

- **Stay in current stage**: If the stage has not been completed successfully, then it may be necessary to stay in the current stage until all the success criteria for the stage have been met.

- **Go back to a previous stage**: If the stage has not been completed successfully and it is deemed that there are serious problems with the work carried out in the current stage, then it may be necessary to go back to a previous stage.

- **Cancel life cycle**: If the stage has failed catastrophically or something has happened to seriously disrupt the system development, then it may be necessary to cancel the whole life cycle. This is an extreme next step and not one that is usually desirable, but it is nevertheless one that must be taken into consideration.

In reality, a gate will be realized by an assessment process of some description, which will involve all relevant stakeholders and have a predefined set of success criteria associated with it. It is essential to consider life cycle gates in order to control and manage any life cycle successfully.

The next key concept is **Process**. *Chapter 5, Systems Engineering Processes* will be focused on processes and therefore will go into a lot of detail on the nature of and modeling of processes. For now, it is adequate to think of a process as a set of activities that is executed in order to result in a specific set of outcomes.

Any number of processes may be executed in any number of stages, which means the following:

- A single process may be executed in a single life cycle stage.

- Multiple processes may be executed in a single life cycle stage.

- The same single process may be executed in more than one life cycle stage.

- The same set of multiple processes may be executed in more than one life cycle stage.

It is crucial to be able to differentiate between a process and a stage. A stage represents a distinct period of time that describes different points in the evolution of an entity. A process represents a set of activities that is executed in order to achieve a set of outcomes. People often confuse the two concepts and think that the two are interchangeable, but this is simply not the case.

Another common misconception associated with processes and stages is that a single process is executed in each stage. Although this is possible, it is almost never the case in reality.

The ability to execute any number of processes in any number of stages makes the life cycle very flexible in terms of what can be achieved in each stage.

One key aspect of life cycles that has already been discussed briefly and is often overlooked is that there is more than one type of life cycle that exists at any point in time. This was explained by describing several different types of life cycles in the previous section. Another point that was touched upon was that some of these life cycles interact with each other. This leads directly on to the final two new concepts:

- **Life cycle interaction point**: This is a structural concept and identifies where two or more life cycles will interact, and it is applied to the life cycle and its stages.

- **Life cycle interaction**: This is a behavioral concept that describes the interaction of two or more life cycles. Life cycle interactions may be thought of as instances of life cycle interaction points.

Examples of both life cycle interaction points and life cycle interactions will be provided later in this chapter in the *Identifying interactions between life cycles* section

Now that the concepts have been described, it is time to look at some examples of the different types of life cycles in systems engineering.

Defining life cycle models

Life cycles are defined by identifying a set of stages that describe the evolution of an entity. A life cycle is a structural construct. A life cycle model, on the other hand, is a behavioral construct that describes the execution of a life cycle, specifically the order of execution of the stages.

In terms of visualizing the various life cycle models, as the emphasis is on the order of the execution of the stages that comprise the life cycle, a SysML sequence diagram will be used. This is good for the consistency of the overall model but can lead to diagrams that differ in appearance compared to some of the traditional visualizations of life cycle models. This is because most life cycle models are visualized using non-standard, ad hoc notations, which leads to a set of very different-looking and difficult-to-compare diagrams. This illustrates one of the benefits of using a standard notation, such as SysML, as all of the different life cycle models may be compared and contrasted easily as they are visualized in the same way.

There are several well-established life cycle models that may be used on different types of projects and will be described in the following sections.

Defining a linear life cycle model

In a **linear life cycle model**, the stages are executed in a simple linear sequence. The classic example that is often used to illustrate a linear life cycle model is the Waterfall model by Royce 1970. The Waterfall model is arguably the original life cycle model and, like many of them, it has its origins in the world of software engineering. An example of a linear life cycle model, based on the Waterfall model, is shown in the following figure:

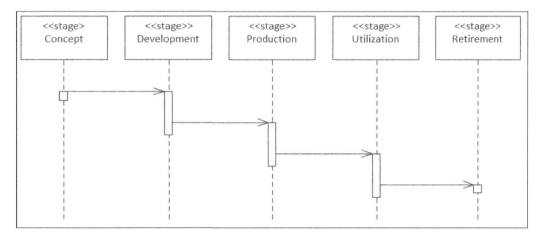

Figure 4.8 – A life cycle model view showing a simple linear life cycle model

Figure 4.8 shows an example of a life cycle model view visualized using a SysML sequence diagram. The execution of each stage from the life cycle is visualized using a lifeline and the interactions show the order of execution of the stages.

In a linear life cycle model, each stage is executed in a specific order and each stage is executed after the completion of the previous stage. There is typically no route to go back to a previous stage.

The linear life cycle model is used predominantly for projects where the original needs are well specified and not likely to change. Also, the product that is being developed and the technologies that are being used are typically well understood. In terms of the project, the resources are easily managed and readily available and the timeframe for such projects tends to be short.

There tends to be little variation, if any, in the processes that are executed in each stage and, indeed, it is very often the case that there is only a single process executed in each stage.

The linear life cycle model is still used extensively in industry, primarily for small, well-understood projects where the needs are robust. It has the advantage of being simple and easy to understand with a very clear process application and clearly defined gates for each stage.

This model is not suitable for large, complex projects and systems where the needs are prone to change. It does not work well for long-term projects as the products are delivered in a single release at the end of the project. Bearing in mind that systems engineering is typically applied to complex projects and systems, the linear life cycle model is not particularly well suited to it.

Defining an iterative life cycle model

The **iterative life cycle model** differs from the linear life cycle model in that instead of a single pass through the life cycle stages, there are several passes through the stages, which are known as **iterations**. Iterative life cycle models have been used successfully for decades and have seen a resurgence in the last two decades with the widespread use of Agile techniques, which employ an iterative life cycle model. Refer to the following figure:

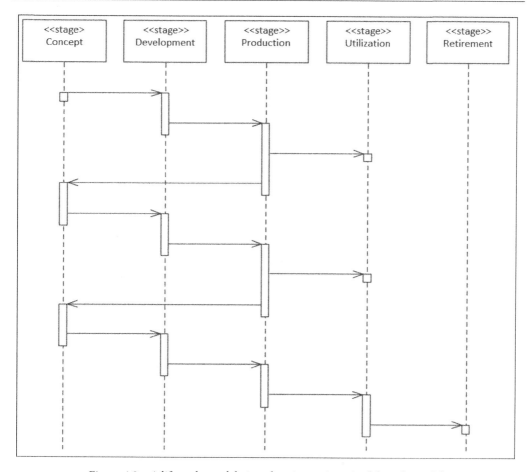

Figure 4.9 – A life cycle model view showing an iterative life cycle model

Figure 4.9 shows an example of an iterative life cycle model view that is visualized using a SysML sequence diagram. The execution of each stage from the life cycle is visualized using a lifeline and the interactions show the order of execution of the stages.

The basic approach of an iterative life cycle works on the assumption that if a linear life cycle model works well for short, well-defined projects and systems, then it is possible to break a large, complex system into a series of shorter, simpler projects. Each of these mini-life cycles is known as an **iteration**.

Each iteration represents a single pass through the stages, starting at the concept stage and progressing through until after the production stage and into utilization. The result of each iteration is a workable version of the final system that can be deployed in the target environment.

This has a number of advantages as each iterative release of the system is a more-complete and typically improved version compared to the previous one. This also means that if a specific release of the system does not work or is a disaster in some way, then it is relatively easy to go back to a previous release and restore some level of functionality.

Each iteration will also take a short period of time. In some cases, the first iteration may take longer than the subsequent iterations, in order to get the original working release completed. It is quite usual for these subsequent iterations to be very short indeed, and in many organizations that are employing an Agile approach, new versions of the system may be produced on a weekly or even daily basis.

The classic iterative approach is used heavily in the software world, rather than on large systems projects, due to the perceived ease of creating software releases. This also has the disadvantage that the emphasis is often on getting a release out on time rather than waiting for something that works.

There is often a misconception that MBSE cannot be applied to iterative approaches, but this is simply not the case. A model-based approach can be applied at any point in a life cycle where there is a need to control complexity, define understanding, and communicate with stakeholders.

One of the disadvantages of applying an iterative approach to systems projects is that the basic needs may be changed quite frequently by stakeholders, so it is important to have a good, robust needs process in place, which is often not the case.

Defining an incremental life cycle model

The **incremental life cycle model** is similar in some ways to the iterative life cycle model. In this, there is not just a single pass through the stages but multiple passes, so that the final system is deployed in a number of releases. Indeed, both iterative and incremental life cycle models are often known collectively as **evolutionary life cycle models**.

In this approach, the concept stage is executed as the first stage but will cover all the needs. The subsequent development and production of the system takes different subsets of the needs and produces a partial solution that does not comprise the whole system and can be deployed in the target environment:

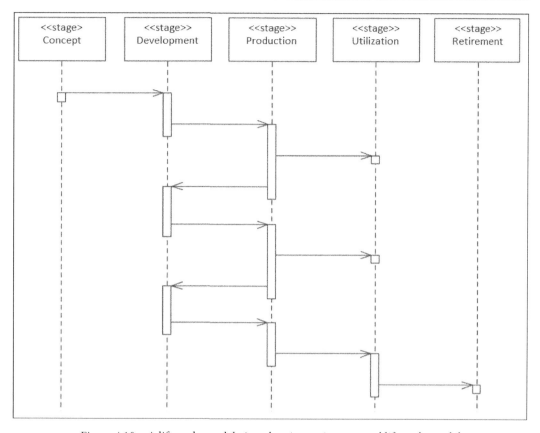

Figure 4.10 – A life cycle model view showing an incremental life cycle model

Figure 4.10 shows an example of a life cycle model view that shows a simple linear life cycle model, visualized using a SysML sequence diagram. The execution of each stage of the life cycle is visualized using a lifeline and the interactions show the order of execution of the stages.

The incremental life cycle model results in the system being deployed in an incremental fashion, rather than as a single release as in the case of the linear life cycle model. This is a clear advantage as the final system can be seen to be working and the system is deployed, albeit in a reduced form, compared to how it was relatively early in the project. The incremental life cycle model is, therefore, very good for very long projects where some functionality of the system is required before the end of the project.

There is a downside to this, as not all systems can be broken down into subsets of the overall system and, in such cases, this approach is not suitable.

This section has shown some of the different types of life cycles that relate to systems engineering. There is an added complexity that must be considered at this point, as these life cycles often co-exist and interact with each other. The following section discusses how these interactions between life cycles may be explored and defined using the model.

Interacting life cycles and life cycle models

The fact that there are various types of life cycles has already been discussed. Alongside this, the stages that comprise each life cycle may be executed in different sequences as life cycle models depending on the type of project or system. These life cycles and life cycle models rarely exist in isolation as they can interact with each other in different ways. Interactions, of course, lead to complexity, so it is important that these interactions can be modeled to be managed and that the interactions can be understood.

In order to understand these interactions, two new views will be introduced that allow interactions to be identified so their associated behavior can be understood—the **interaction identification view** and the **interaction behavior view**.

Let's see what each is.

Identifying interactions between life cycles

The interactions between life cycles are identified by considering the following:

- **A number of specific life cycles**: Each life cycle that will potentially interact is identified.

- **The stages in each life cycle**: For each of the identified life cycles, their associated stages are identified.

- **The interaction points between stages from different life cycles**: Rather than considering the interaction between stages for an individual life cycle, as has been the case so far, interactions between stages from different life cycles are identified, which are known as **life cycle interaction points**.

These life cycle interaction points existing between life cycles are then used for the basis of the modeling. Refer to the following figure:

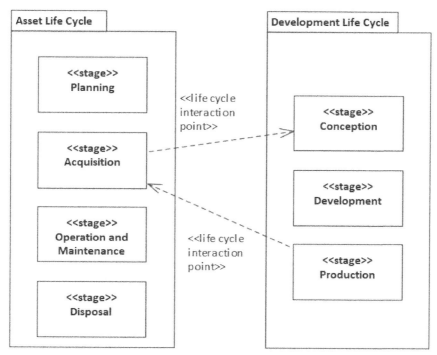

Figure 4.11 – Interaction identification view showing life cycle interaction points between life cycles

Figure 4.11 shows an interaction identification view that shows the life cycle interaction points that exist between different life cycles using a SysML block definition diagram.

The view here shows each life cycle using a SysML package with the name of the life cycle shown at the top of the package. Each package contains a set of blocks, each of which represents a single stage within the life cycle.

An interesting point to note here is that not all of the stages need to be shown in each package, only the ones that are relevant for the model. The example here represents the situation where one organization acquires a system from a second organization. The first organization uses an asset life cycle as they are interested in acquiring a system as an asset. The second organization is developing a system and is, therefore, using a development life cycle. In this example, however, the second organization is only developing the system and, therefore, is only implementing the first three stages of the life cycle—**Conception**, **Development**, and **Production**. The remaining stages of utilization, support, and retirement are not relevant and, therefore, are not included.

The potential life cycle interaction points between the stages of different life cycles are identified using SysML interactions, shown by the dotted line with the << **life cycle interaction points** >> stereotype being used. In this example, there are two life cycle interaction points that have been identified:

- **The life cycle interaction point between Acquisition (asset life cycle) and Conception (development life cycle)**: This life cycle interaction point shows that at some point during the acquisition stage, there will be an interaction, typically a transition, with the concept stage.

- **The life cycle interaction point between Production (development life cycle) and Acquisition (asset life cycle)**: This life cycle interaction point shows that there will be a return interaction from some point in the production stage back to the acquisition stage.

Note that the interaction identification view only shows the life cycle interaction points between the stages and does not show the exact point in the stage where the interaction occurs. This information can only be shown when the processes in each stage are considered, which will be discussed in *Chapter 5, Systems Engineering Processes*.

The interaction identification view is visualized using a SysML block definition diagram, which is, of course, a structural diagram. As is very often the case when modeling, once a structural view has been described, it is possible to describe a corresponding behavioral view. In this case, this is the interaction behavior view, which is discussed in the next section.

Defining the behavior of interactions

Now that the potential life cycle interaction points between stages in different life cycles have been identified, it is possible to model *how* these stages interact by considering an interaction behavior view. Observe the following figure:

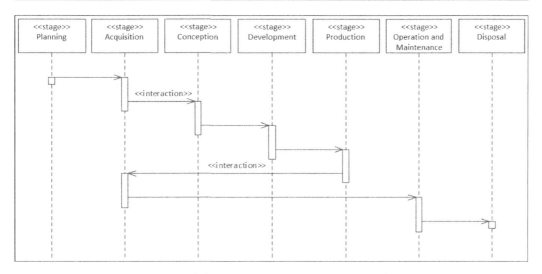

Figure 4.12 – An interaction behavior view showing the sequence of life cycle interactions

Figure 4.12 shows an interaction behavior view where the sequence of life cycle interactions is described using a SysML sequence diagram.

In this view, each stage is represented using a SysML lifeline in a similar way to the life cycle model view that was shown in *Figure 4.8*, *Figure 4.9*, and *Figure 4.10*. The life cycle model views only showed stages from a single life cycle, whereas the interaction behavior view shows its stages from different life cycles.

The interactions between stages are shown using SysML interactions (note that this is the SysML construct of interaction), whereas the interactions between stages from different life cycles are shown using the SysML interactions using <<interaction>>.

The interaction behavior view is really an expanded version of the life cycle model view but one that includes stages from different life cycles, rather than it being the usual situation of just a single life cycle.

This concludes the discussion of life cycles and how they may be modeled. The final section in this chapter defines the framework and its associated viewpoints that form the overall MBSE framework that is being developed throughout this book.

Defining the framework

The views that have been created so far represent the center part of the MBSE diagram that was discussed in detail in *Chapter 2, Model-Based Systems Engineering*. Each of the views has been visualized using SysML, representing the right-hand side of the MBSE diagram. These views come together to form the overall model, but it is essential that these views are all consistent, otherwise they are not views but pictures! This is where the left-hand side of the MBSE diagram comes into play, as it is important that the definition of all of the views is captured in the framework. The framework comprises the ontology and a set of viewpoints; therefore, it is now time to make sure that these viewpoints are defined thoroughly and correctly, which is the aim of this section.

Defining the viewpoints in the framework

It was discussed in *Chapter 2, Model-Based Systems Engineering*, that it is necessary to ask a number of questions of each view to ensure that it is a valid view. There is also a set of questions that must be asked of the whole framework, as well as of the views, to form a set of questions that will allow the whole framework to be defined. It is worthwhile, therefore, to have a reminder of what these questions are:

- Why is the framework required? This question may be answered using a **framework context view**.

- What are the overall concepts and terminology used for the framework? This question may be answered using an **ontology definition view**.

- What views are necessary as part of the framework? This question may be answered using a **viewpoint relationship view**.

- Why is each view needed? This question may be answered using a **viewpoint context view**.

- What is the structure and content of each view? This question may be answered using a **viewpoint definition view**.

- What rules should be applied? This question may be answered using a **ruleset definition view**.

When these questions are answered, it can be said that a framework has been defined. Each of these questions can be answered using a special set of views that are collectively known as the **Framework for Architectural Frameworks** (**FAF**), defined by Holt and Perry 2019. At this point, simply think about creating a specific view to answer each question, as described in the following sections.

Defining the framework context view

The framework context view specifies why the whole framework is needed in the first place. It will identify the relevant stakeholders that have an interest in the framework and also identify what benefits each of the stakeholders hopes to gain from the framework.

There will be a single framework context viewpoint for each organization. This view will differ for each organization as different organizations will have a different set of needs for the framework.

The framework context view will be visualized using a SysML use case diagram, and this will be described fully in *Chapter 6, Needs and Requirements*.

Defining the ontology definition view

The ontology definition view captures all the concepts and associated terminology associated with the framework in the form of an ontology. This has already been done, as the ontology for the life cycle-related views was defined in *Figure 4.1*, *Figure 4.2*, and *Figure 4.7*. The ontology elements shown in this view provide all of the stereotypes that have been used for the actual views that have been created so far in this chapter.

Ontology elements that are related will often be collected into a **perspective**, as was discussed in other chapters. In *Chapter 3, Systems and Interfaces*, a systems perspective was created that contained all the ontology elements that relate to systems and interfaces. In this chapter, a new perspective has been created that relates to life cycles.

Defining the viewpoint relationship view

The viewpoint relationship view identifies which views are needed and, for each set of views, identifies a viewpoint that will contain its definition. Remember that a viewpoint may be thought of as a type of template for a view. These viewpoints may be collected together into a perspective, which is simply a collection of viewpoints with a common theme. In this chapter, the emphasis has been on defining a set of views related to life cycles, so it is appropriate to create a **life cycle perspective**.

The basic set of views that has been discussed so far is shown in the following view:

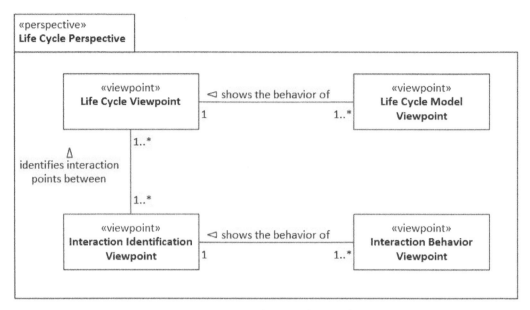

Figure 4.13 – A viewpoint relationship view for the life cycle perspective

Figure 4.13 shows a viewpoint relationship view for the life cycle perspective using a SysML package diagram. The perspective is shown as a SysML package that is stereotyped as <<**perspective**>> and simply collects together a number of viewpoints:

- **Life Cycle Viewpoint**, which defines the structure and content for the life cycle views, and identifies the stages for a specific life cycle. This is a structural view and was visualized using a SysML block definition diagram.

- The associated behavior for the life cycle viewpoint is shown in **Life Cycle Model Viewpoint**. Note that it is possible to have multiple instances of the life cycle model viewpoint (the life cycle model views) for each instance of the life cycle viewpoint (the life cycle view), as indicated by **1…***. This is because it is possible to have multiple different sequences of stages (life cycle models) for each structural set of stages (life cycle).

  The life cycle viewpoint and the life cycle model viewpoints focus on single life cycles, whereas the interaction identification viewpoint and the interaction behavior viewpoint focus on multiple life cycles and the relationships between them.

- **Interaction Identification Viewpoint** allows points where two or more different life cycles interact, by identifying life cycle interaction points. This is a structural view and was visualized using a SysML block definition diagram.

- The associated behavioral views associated with the interaction identification viewpoint come under **Interaction Behavior Viewpoint**. Whereas **Interaction Identification Point** identified where the different life cycles interact, **Interaction Behavior Viewpoint** shows how these interactions occur. As this is a behavioral view that focuses on interactions between elements, in this case, the life cycle stages, a SysML sequence diagram was used to visualize it.

Defining the viewpoint context view

The viewpoint context view specifies why a particular viewpoint and its set of views is needed in the first place. It will identify the relevant stakeholders that have an interest in the viewpoint and also identify what benefits each of the stakeholders hopes to gain from the framework.

There will be a viewpoint context view for each viewpoint. Each viewpoint context view will trace back to the framework context view as it must contribute to the overall expectations of the organization. The combined set of viewpoint context views will, therefore, satisfy the overall needs represented in the framework context view.

The viewpoint context view will be visualized using a SysML use case diagram, and this will be described fully in *Chapter 6, Needs and Requirements*.

Defining the viewpoint definition view

The viewpoint definition view defines the ontology elements that are included in the viewpoint. It shows the following:

- Which ontology elements are allowed in the viewpoint
- Which ontology elements are optional in the viewpoint
- Which ontology elements are not allowed in the viewpoint

The viewpoint definition view focuses on a single viewpoint and particular care and attention must be paid to not just the ontology elements that are selected but also the relationships that exist between these ontology elements. Obviously, the ontology elements and their relationship must be consistent with the original ontology, but it is possible to see some changes in the multiplicities between some of the elements, and this will be discussed in the next few sections.

An example of two viewpoint definition views will now be shown and a comparison between the two will be discussed to show some of the subtleties of the modeling that is used to visualize them. The first example is the life cycle viewpoint:

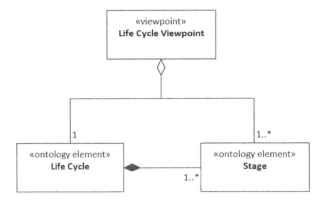

Figure 4.14 – A viewpoint definition view for the life cycle viewpoint

Figure 4.14 shows the viewpoint definition view for the life cycle viewpoint, using a SysML block definition diagram.

This view defines the exact content of what is allowed in all the views that are described by the viewpoint. This viewpoint will always contain the following information:

- *The viewpoint name*, stereotyped by <<**viewpoint**>>, which is the focus of this view. The viewpoint that is identified here must come from the viewpoint relationship view that was shown in *Figure 4.13*.

- *A number of ontology elements*, stereotyped by <<**ontology element**>>. Each of these ontology elements must come from the ontology definition view shown in *Figure 4.7*.

Notice how the SysML aggregation is used in the viewpoint description views, rather than the SysML composition between the viewpoint and the ontology elements. This is because the viewpoint *does not own* the ontology elements; it is just identifying which ontology elements are permitted to be contained in the viewpoint.

This view may seem quite straightforward at first glance, as it contains a single viewpoint and then a subset of the ontology, but there are a number of subtleties associated with the ontology elements on this view.

The presence of each ontology element is clearly important as it identifies the ontology elements that are permitted to appear in this viewpoint. However, the multiplicities associated with each of the ontology elements and the ontology relationships are also important.

Consider the following ontology elements.

- **Life Cycle** *must* appear on the view as the multiplicity is **1**. If the presence of the life cycle was optional, then the multiplicity would be **0...1, 0...***, or a variation thereof.

- **Stage** *must* appear on the view as the multiplicity of **1...***. If the presence of the life cycle was optional, then the multiplicity would be **0...1, 0...***, or a variation thereof.

Now consider the following ontology relationships:

- **Life Cycle Viewpoint is made up of one life cycle**: The multiplicity of **1** here is very important as it shows that the presence of the life cycle is mandatory in this view, as discussed previously. However, it also dictates that *one and only one* life cycle must be shown on the view. This means that it is *not possible to show more than one* life cycle in this view. Therefore, there will be one of these views for each life cycle that exists.

- **Each life cycle comprises one or more stages**: The means that not only must the stages be shown, but also the relationships between the stage and the life cycle, which is in this case visualized by the composition symbol.

It is important to think very hard about every ontology element and ontology relationship that is present in the viewpoint definition view as it is dictating the content of every view that is based on it.

For comparison purposes, consider the viewpoint definition view for the interaction identification viewpoint that is shown in the following diagram:

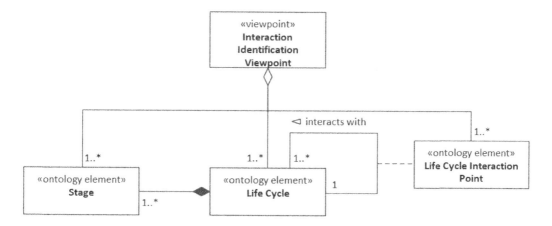

Figure 4.15 – A viewpoint definition view for the interaction identification viewpoint

Figure 4.15 is very similar to the one in *Figure 4.14*, with the most obvious difference being that there is an additional ontology element, that of **Life Cycle Interaction Point**. There are, however, some other subtle differences that make a big difference to the resulting views, which are listed as follows:

- The multiplicity of the aggregation to life cycle is **1…*** in *Figure 4.15*, whereas in *Figure 4.14* the multiplicity was only **1**. This small difference actually has a big impact on the view, as it means that the interaction identification views may contain multiple life cycles, whereas the life cycle views focus on one, and only one, life cycle.

- The association that shows each life cycle interacts with one or more other life cycles via the life cycle interaction point. Again, this is only possible due to the **1…*** multiplicity on the life cycle aggregation. If the multiplicity was only **1**, as in the life cycle view, it would not be possible to show any interactions as there would only be a single life cycle.

The point of discussing this is to illustrate just how important the multiplicities are when it comes to describing the viewpoint description views. Each multiplicity must be considered in turn as there are big implications with the resulting views for each number.

Defining the ruleset definition view

The ruleset definition view identifies and defines a number of rules that may be applied to the model to ensure that it is consistent with the framework.

The rules are based primarily on the ontology definition view and the viewpoint relationship view. In each case, the rules are defined by identifying the key relationships and their associated multiplicities that exist, which are in the following places:

- Between viewpoints in the viewpoint definition view
- Between ontology elements in the ontology definition view

Some examples of these rules are shown in the following figure:

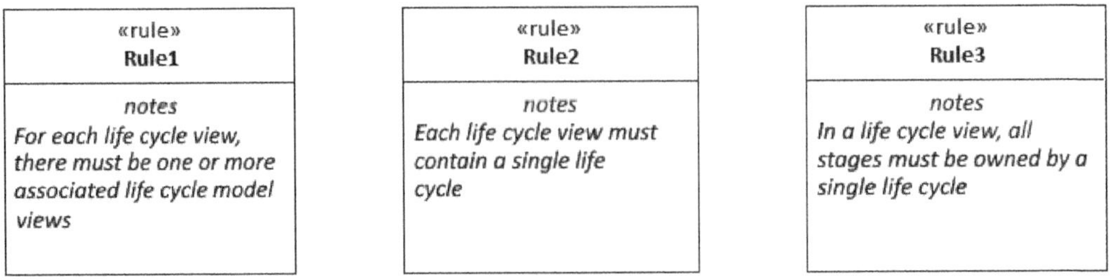

«rule» **Rule1**	«rule» **Rule2**	«rule» **Rule3**
notes *For each life cycle view, there must be one or more associated life cycle model views*	*notes* *Each life cycle view must contain a single life cycle*	*notes* *In a life cycle view, all stages must be owned by a single life cycle*

Figure 4.16 – Example ruleset definition view

Figure 4.16 shows an example of a ruleset definition view using a SysML block definition diagram. Each block on the diagram represents a rule that is derived from either the ontology definition view or the viewpoint relationship view.

These rules are defined as follows:

- **For each life cycle view, there must be one or more associated life cycle model views**: This rule is derived directly from the viewpoint relationship view shown in *Figure 4.13*. This rule helps to define how many views associated with each viewpoint may be created as part of the framework, which is indicated by the multiplicities.

- **Each life cycle view must contain a single life cycle**: This rule is derived directly from the ontology definition view shown in *Figure 4.7*. This rule enforces the subtlety that was discussed in the previous section regarding the number of life cycles that may be shown in the specific view.

- **In a life cycle view, all stages must be owned by a single life cycle**: This rule is derived directly from the ontology definition view shown in *Figure 4.7*. The rule also enforces the same subtlety that was discussed in the previous section regarding the multiplicities.

Notice how the rules are derived from the viewpoint relationship view, and therefore the viewpoints and the ontology definition view, and therefore the ontology elements. The actual rule descriptions themselves apply to the instances of the viewpoints (views) and instances of the ontology elements.

Of course, any number of other rules may be defined here, but not every relationship will lead to a rule, as this is at the discretion of the modeler.

Summary

In this chapter, the concept of the life cycle was explored in more detail.

Life cycles are an essential part of any systems engineering endeavor but one that is often oversimplified as they can exhibit a high level of complexity.

One of the most common incorrect assumptions that is made in the world of systems engineering is that there is only a single life cycle. There are, in fact, different life cycles that can be applied to many different aspects of systems engineering and it is therefore essential that these different life cycles are both identified and defined.

Following directly on from the point that there are multiple life cycles, these life cycles will interact with each other at different points. The concept of the life cycle interaction point was introduced, with each point showing where each life cycle interacts by identifying which stages are the start and end points for the interaction.

As with all views that comprise a model, there are structural views and behavioral views, which are closely related to each other.

Finally, all of these views were captured as part of an overall framework definition using the FAF; this framework itself comprises a number of views that are used to describe the model.

This chapter provided you with an overview of the different types of life cycles that relate to systems engineering and the ability to capture, analyze, and define any life cycles using the modeling techniques shown throughout the book.

The next chapter is closely related to life cycle modeling and introduces the idea of processes and how they relate to systems engineering.

Self-assessment tasks

1. Create a life cycle view for system development in your organization based on the ontology described in this chapter. Choose a single life cycle and identify its main stages.

2. Choose another aspect of systems engineering in your organization and define another, different life cycle. This may be based on the examples discussed in this chapter, such as acquisition, technology, or assets, or you may create one that was not discussed.

3. Create an interaction identification view to identify a set of life cycle interactions that exist between the two life cycles that were created in *question 1* and *question 2*. Identify which stages in each life cycle form the start and end points for the interactions.

4. Create at least one interaction behavior view that shows a possible scenario based on the interaction identification view that was created for *question 3*.

5. Select any viewpoint from the viewpoint relationship view in *Figure 4.13* and create a viewpoint context view using text and a viewpoint definition view using a block diagram.

References

- [Holt & Perry 2019] Holt, J.D. and Perry, S. A. *SysML for Systems Engineering – a model-based approach*. Third edition. IET Publishing, Stevenage, UK. 2019

- [Royce 1970] Royce, Winston. *Managing the Development of Large Software Systems*, Proceedings of IEEE WESCON, 26 (August): 1–9

5
Systems Engineering Processes

In this chapter, the focus will be on one of the fundamental aspects of systems engineering and, therefore, model-based systems engineering – the process.

Understanding processes is key to understanding systems engineering. Remember that systems engineering describes an *approach* to realizing successful systems. One of the main applications of process modeling is to understand approaches to doing things, therefore it is not surprising that processes lie at the heart of a good systems engineering approach. In fact, it is a framework alongside a set of processes that provide the overall **model-based systems engineering** (**MBSE**) approach that is described in this book. Think back to the MBSE diagram from *Chapter 2, Model-Based Systems Engineering*; the left-hand side of the diagram was focused on an approach that comprised the process set and the framework.

In the same way that modeling has been applied to the framework, modeling will also be applied to the process.

This chapter covers the following topics:

- First of all, some of the problems associated with processes will be discussed, along with the different types of processes and their desired properties.

- The subject of process modeling will be discussed by defining the concepts associated with processes in the now-usual way: by building up an ontology that will show the structure of a typical process and its related concepts. The different types of processes that may exist will then be discussed, which will provide an insight into some of the different ways that process modeling can be applied.

- The views that make up the process perspective that forms part of the larger framework will be introduced and some examples will be provided.

- Finally, some of the typical processes that are important for systems engineering will be used in an example based on ISO 15288. We shall discuss how processes are grouped into progress groups according to whether they are technical processes, management processes, organizational processes, or agreement processes.

Process modeling will also be used in all subsequent chapters of this book.

Understanding process fundamentals

This section introduces the fundamental aspects of processes that must be understood in order to define a good MBSE approach. This includes the following topics:

- Defining process properties, where the key features of processes will be discussed

- Defining process types, where different specializations of processes will be discussed

This section sets the scene for the rest of the chapter.

Defining process properties

The whole area of processes and process modeling is fundamental to MBSE and there are a number of desirable properties associated with processes that it is important to understand:

- **Processes must be repeatable**: It is essential that processes can be executed in a way that can be repeated by any stakeholders who choose to do so. This is important as consistency in execution is important. If processes can be executed in different ways, then the results of these processes cannot be compared.

- **Processes must be measurable**: According to the old adage, if something can't be measured, then it can't be controlled, and it is essential that processes can be controlled. Efficiency is a key part of any process and it is one of the reasons that is often cited that making processes more efficient will improve overall business performance. It is impossible to show how efficient something is if it cannot be measured.

- **Processes must be demonstrable**: Bearing in mind that processes form the heart of any approach, it is essential that this approach can be demonstrated to any relevant stakeholders in order to inspire confidence in the overall approach. Also, it is almost always desirable to show how processes comply with best practice sources, such as standards.

Alongside these desirable properties, there are a number of common problems that are associated with processes:

- **Processes can be complex**: Processes can be convoluted, particularly if the scope of the process is not well defined. It is quite common to find processes that are overly simplified (leading to hidden complexity) and processes that are over-specified (leading to too much complexity and detail). This is also one of the three evils of system engineering and, therefore, makes the subject of processes ideal for modeling and, indeed, forms the heart of any MBSE approach.

- **Processes can be difficult to understand**: Processes will often use language that is difficult to understand, whether it is spoken language, such as English, or, more usually, a domain-specific language, such as technical jargon. This problem can often be traced back to the fact that processes are often written by a different set of stakeholders than the ones that are involved in executing the process.

- **Processes can be unrealistic**: This follows on from the previous point because processes are often written by stakeholders that are not involved in the execution of the processes. Because of this discrepancy, the authors of the process will often not hold enough domain knowledge to make the process usable in the real world. What may seem like a good idea to outsiders is often impractical or wrong to stakeholders who are directly involved in the work.

- **Processes can be difficult to communicate to stakeholders**: The language used in some process definitions can be obscure or even incorrect. A lot of discussion of the importance of a common language has been had in this book, particularly on domain-specific language. It is essential that the correct terminology is used.

- **Processes can be irrelevant**: A lot of processes are actually irrelevant to the work activities that are being carried out, as their purpose has not been ascertained either properly or at all. Again, this is a common theme in MBSE as it is essential that the question *why* is asked for each process. This can be answered by ensuring that a process context is produced for each process.

- **Processes can go out of date**: Just because a process works when it is defined does not mean that it will still work at a later date. It is essential that the basic purpose of the process is revisited periodically in order to ensure that the process is still fit for purpose. Again, this can be addressed by reviewing the process context on a regular basis.

The next topic to consider is the different types of processes that may exist.

Defining process types

Processes exist at many levels and can take on different forms, such as very high-level processes (international standards), high-level processes (industry standards), medium-level processes (in-house processes and standards), low-level processes (in-house procedures), and very low-level processes (guidelines and work instructions).

The fundamentals of processes will now be discussed, before we move on to discuss process modeling.

Process concepts

This section will follow the same structure as *Chapter 4, Life Cycles*, by introducing and discussing process concepts and developing an ontology that will form part of the broader MBSE ontology.

The first few concepts that must be understood are shown in the following figure:

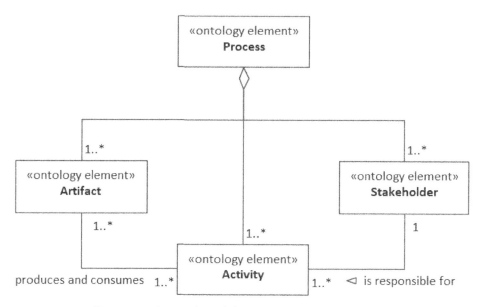

Figure 5.1 – An ontology definition view for process concepts

The diagram in *Figure 5.1* shows the initial ontology definition view for process concepts, visualized using a SysML block definition diagram.

The main concept in this view is the process, which describes an approach to doing something or achieving an aim of some description. As can be seen in the preceding figure, **Process** is made up of three main elements:

- **Activities**: An activity describes a behavioral step that must be performed in order to execute the process. A typical process will be made up of a number of these activities, each of which will have inputs, which are consumed, and outputs, which are produced by the activity. These inputs and outputs are referred to as artifacts.

- **Artifacts**: Each artifact represents a property of a process and may be realized by a document, a model or view, software, hardware, or electronics – in fact, anything that may be produced or consumed by an activity. Artifacts may be thought of as structural concepts, as they do not do anything, but they are produced by behavioral activities.

- **Stakeholders**: It was discussed in previous chapters that a stakeholder represents the role of a person, organization, or thing that has an interest in a system. When it comes to process modeling, then the system may be considered as a process, and therefore the stakeholders have an interest in the process. In fact, the stakeholders are responsible for the execution of the various activities.

Notice that a SysML aggregation is used in the diagram, rather than a composition, as the process does not own any of the artifacts, activities, or stakeholders, but merely groups them together.

These elements form the core of any good process but there are other concepts that sit alongside these, which are shown in the following diagram:

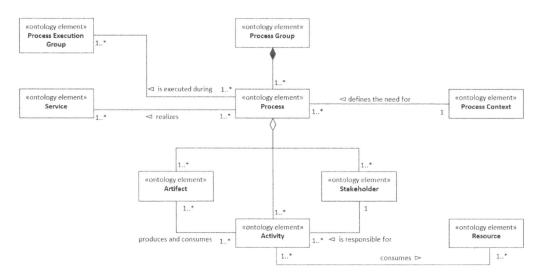

Figure 5.2 – An ontology definition view for expanded process concepts

Figure 5.2 shows an ontology definition view for expanded process concepts, visualized using a SysML block definition diagram.

The first new concept is the **process group**, which groups together a set of processes. Notice that the SysML composition symbol is used here, which implies that the processes that comprise the process group are actually owned by that process group. A process group provides a mechanism that allows processes that are related to the same topic to be grouped together. Most international standards provide a set of predefined process groups, an example of which can be seen in the following diagram:

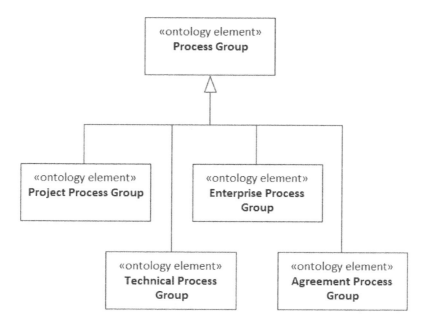

Figure 5.3 – An ontology definition view showing types of process group

The diagram in *Figure 5.3* shows a simple ontology definition view that shows the different types of process group, visualized by a SysML block definition diagram.

The diagram here shows that there are four types of process group:

- **Project process group**: The project process group collects together processes that are related to management in some way and that are applied on a project-by-project basis. Examples of such processes include planning, assessment, and control processes.

- **Technical process group**: The technical process group collects together processes that are typically associated with day-to-day systems engineering activities, such as stakeholder needs definition, architectural design, and implementation.

- **Enterprise process group**: The enterprise process group collects together processes that are applied across the entire business and includes processes such as enterprise management, investment management, and system life cycle management processes.

- **Agreement process group**: The agreement process group collects together processes that relate to whole customer/supplier relationships. This group covers processes such as acquisition and supply processes.

These process groups are used purely as a convenience to help people understand the set of processes at a higher level, rather than just having a flat set of processes. The names of the process groups shown here are based on those in ISO 15288. These process groups will be explored in more detail later in this chapter when modeling standards are discussed. It is important to have a good, high-level understanding of a typical set of processes as they form the heart of the systems engineering approach.

The next new process concept taken from *Figure 5.2* is that of the process context. In all aspects of systems engineering, it is essential to always ask *why* something is needed, and this can be captured using the concept of a context, in this case, the process context. It is essential that the purpose behind a set of processes and individual processes is well understood. If the basic need for something is not known, then it is impossible to demonstrate that this thing is fit for purpose. This makes sense, as the purpose would not be known! Indeed, the list of problems that was discussed in the previous section identifies the process context as the answer to addressing the problems. The whole topic of defining contexts for various purposes will be discussed in detail in *Chapter 6*, *Needs and Requirements*.

Each process is defined individually, but it is also important to define different ways that the processes can be executed in order to satisfy the process context. When processes are executed in a specific sequence, this is referred to as a **process execution group**. The process execution group is also used extensively in conjunction with life cycle modeling. In the previous chapter, life cycle stages were executed in a specific sequence in a life cycle model. Each of the stages may be broken down into more detail and the set of processes in each may be defined using the process execution group.

The process execution group may also be used in order to define a **service**. A service is a behavioral construct that offers a specific outcome according to a specific request. These services may be, for example, software-type services or human-type services. Services are realized by a set of processes.

The final concept in *Figure 5.2* is that of the **resource**. A resource is something that is required in order to execute one or more activity that forms part of a process. Examples of resources include people, money, time, building, rooms, equipment, and so on.

Now that the concepts have been introduced and discussed, it is time to apply them to process modeling.

Process modeling

This section builds on the previous discussion on process concepts and shows how they are applied to process modeling.

Defining the process context

It was mentioned in the previous section that understanding why a process, or a set of processes, is required is essential. The concept of a context has been mentioned on a number of occasions so far in this book. In this section, an example will be provided for the first time with a high-level explanation, as a detailed description of contexts will be provided in the next chapter.

The example of the car will be revisited for the process modeling views that will be presented, the first of which is shown in the following figure:

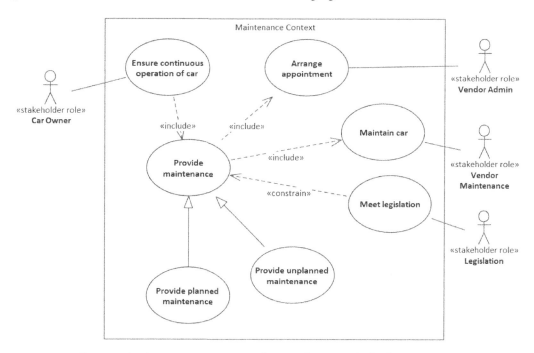

Figure 5.4 – A process context view showing the rationale for the process set

The preceding figure contains a process context view that shows the rationale for a set of processes, visualized using a SysML use case diagram. This is the first time that a use case diagram has been seen in this book and, therefore, a brief explanation of the basic notation is appropriate. A use case diagram comprises the following modeling elements:

- **Use case**: The main construct in a SysML use case diagram is, quite obviously, the use case, and each is visualized by an ellipse. A use case shows some sort of need of a system that is described from a specific point of view. Such points of view are known as **contexts** and, therefore, use case diagrams may be used to show different contexts associated with a system. A use case, therefore, shows the description of a need in a specific context.

- **Boundary**: A boundary in a use case diagram shows a conceptual border between what is considered inside the system – the use cases – and what lives outside the system – the actors. Each boundary represents a single context.

- **Actor**: A number of SysML actors can be seen in this diagram, each of which is visualized using a stick figure. An actor represents the role of something that lives outside the boundary of the context and that has an interest in some of the use cases inside the boundary. Actors are used to indicate stakeholders that have an interest in the system.

The subject area for this diagram concerns a set of processes that relates to the maintenance of a car. A context shows a set of needs that are represented from a specific point of view. The diagram in *Figure 5.4* may be read, therefore, in the following way:

- The main aim is to **Ensure the continuous operation of the car**.

- The **Car Owner** actor has an interest in **Ensure the continuous operation of the car**.

- There is a single use case that must be satisfied in order to achieve this, which is to **Provide maintenance**.

- There are two types of **Provide maintenance**: **Provide planned maintenance** and **Provide unplanned maintenance**.

- All types of **Provide maintenance** include the two use cases: **Arrange appointment**, which is of interest to the **Vendor Admin**; and **Maintain car**, which is of interest to the **Vendor maintenance** actor.

- The **Provide maintenance** use case is constrained by the use case **Meet legislation**, which is of interest to the **Legislation** actor.

The whole subject of contexts and their visualization using use case diagrams will be discussed in more detail in the next chapter.

Defining the process library

The next view that will be considered is the process content view. The process content view allows the set of processes that are being considered to be captured in a single view. This can be done in two ways: a process content view that focuses on a single process and a process content view that focuses on a set of processes.

An example of a process content view that focuses on a single process is shown in the following diagram:

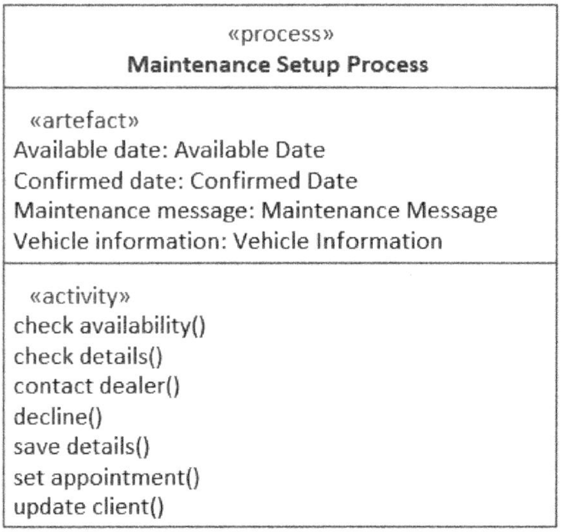

```
┌─────────────────────────────────────────────┐
│                «process»                      │
│         Maintenance Setup Process             │
├─────────────────────────────────────────────┤
│  «artefact»                                   │
│  Available date: Available Date               │
│  Confirmed date: Confirmed Date               │
│  Maintenance message: Maintenance Message     │
│  Vehicle information: Vehicle Information      │
├─────────────────────────────────────────────┤
│  «activity»                                   │
│  check availability()                         │
│  check details()                              │
│  contact dealer()                             │
│  decline()                                    │
│  save details()                               │
│  set appointment()                            │
│  update client()                              │
└─────────────────────────────────────────────┘
```

Figure 5.5 – A process content view showing a single process

The diagram in *Figure 5.5* shows a process content view that focuses on a single process, visualized by a SysML block definition diagram.

The process in question here is **Maintenance Setup Process**, visualized by a single SysML block. The use of the SysML block here allows a clever piece of modeling to be applied by the use of SysML properties and SysML operations.

It was discussed in the ontology in *Figure 5.2* that each process comprises the following:

- A number of **artifacts**: Each artifact represents something that is produced or consumed by an activity. Each of these may be represented rather neatly by using a SysML property.

- A number of **activities**: Each activity represents something that must be done in order to perform the process. Each activity may be represented rather neatly by a SysML operation.

This means that all the artifacts and activities associated with a single process may be shown in a single SysML block using properties and operations.

Each artifact represented by a SysML property may be typed, and these types are defined using blocks in the information view, which will be discussed presently.

It is very useful to be able to represent a single process in this way, but it is also useful to be able to see more than one process in a single view, as seen in the following diagram:

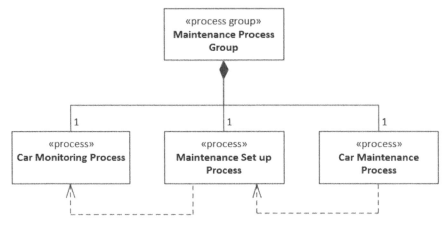

Figure 5.6 – A process content view showing multiple processes

Figure 5.6 shows a process content view that contains multiple processes and is visualized using a SysML block. This diagram, as opposed to the one in *Figure 5.5*, shows more than one process: **Car Monitoring Process**, **Maintenance Setup Process**, and **Car Maintenance Process**. Also notice that these processes do not show any of the artifacts or activities for the processes. This is actually completely optional and it is up to the modeler to decide whether or not they should be shown in this particular view. Bear in mind that the artifacts and activities will be present in the model even if they are not shown in this specific view. Remember that it is possible to filter the information that is shown in any view.

This view also shows a new type of SysML relationship that has not been seen before, which is the SysML **dependency**. A dependency is shown graphically by a dotted line with an arrow on the end indicate the direction of the dependency relationship. In order to illustrate the meaning of this, consider the following relationship: *Maintenance Setup Process depends on Car Monitoring Process*. This can mean the following:

- If **Car Monitoring Process** changes in some way, then it may have an impact on **Maintenance Setup Process**.

- The execution of **Maintenance Setup Process** is dependent on the previous execution of **Car Monitoring Process**.

The diagram in *Figure 5.6* showing multiple processes also shows the process group that owns these processes, and that is called the **maintenance process group**. The process group is really just a container for a number of like-themed processes and allows the processes to be managed more easily than if they just existed in a flat structure.

The process content view allows processes to be gathered together to form a library of processes. This is particularly useful at the beginning of a project when it is necessary to understand exactly what capabilities are required by a project and also what capabilities the organization possesses.

The processes on a process content view show the artifacts and activities from the ontology but do not show the stakeholders, which are discussed in the next section.

Defining the process stakeholders

The one concept that comprises each process that was not discussed in the previous section is that of the **stakeholder**. Stakeholders have already been introduced previously in this book as one of the essential concepts for understanding systems. Understanding stakeholders is essential to have a good systems engineering approach in place, and so it is not surprising that stakeholders crop up again when processes are considered.

This is also a very good example of being able to re-use specific views for different aspects of systems engineering, as can be seen in the following familiar-looking diagram:

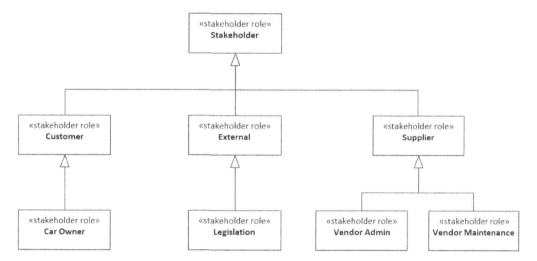

Figure 5.7 – A stakeholder view showing the maintenance process group stakeholders

The preceding figure shows a stakeholder view for the maintenance process group and is visualized by a SysML block definition diagram.

The stakeholder view shows a taxonomy, or classification hierarchy, of the different types of stakeholder that exist and uses a specialization relationship. The general pattern of this view has been seen before in this book and the top level of specializations shows that **there are three types of stakeholders: Customer, External, and Supplier.**

The next level of specializations shows the following:

- **There is one type of Customer stakeholder, which is the Car Owner**
- **There is one type of External stakeholder, which is the Legislation.**
- **There are two types of Supplier stakeholder, which are the Vendor Admin and the Vendor maintenance**.

Understanding stakeholders is crucial for process modeling and one of the key aspects of each process so that they are allowed to show is the responsibility of each stakeholder. Remember from *Figure 5.1* that **each stakeholder is responsible for one or more activities**, and this is something that will be explored in more detail when the process behavior view is described in a subsequent section.

Defining the process artifacts

The artifacts that are associated with each process allow the inputs and outputs of the activities and, therefore, the processes, to be represented in the model. The artifacts associated with each process are captured in an information view, an example of which is shown in the following figure:

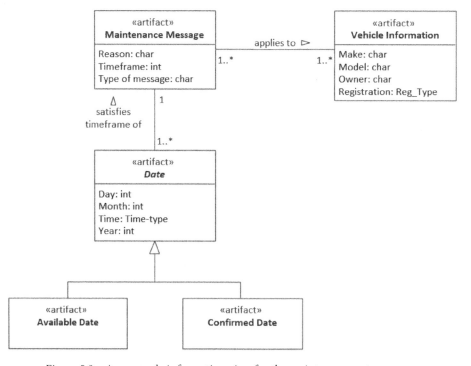

Figure 5.8 – An example information view for the maintenance setup process

The previous figure shows an example of an information view for the maintenance setup process visualized with a SysML block definition diagram.

Each artifact that was identified as being part of the process in *Figure 5.8* is represented by a SysML block on the diagram. Also, each process will have its own information view.

The main aim of this view is to show each artifact but, more importantly, the relationships between these artifacts. This is essential for traceability between the artifacts and can be used to identify audit trails.

Notice also that various properties have been shown for some of the artifacts, which allows more information about them to be captured.

The information view may also be used at a slightly higher level of abstraction in order to focus on the relationship between the processes, not just within a single process, but between multiple processes. An example of this can be seen in the following diagram:

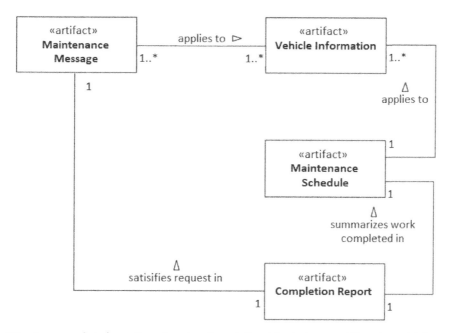

Figure 5.9 – An example information view showing relationships between artifacts in multiple processes

The diagram in *Figure 5.9* shows more example information, this time focusing on the relationships between artifacts from multiple processes, which is, again, visualized by a SysML block definition diagram.

The syntax of this view is the same as in *Figure 5.8*, where each artifact is visualized using a SysML block. This time, however, the properties of each artifact are not being shown, although this is optional and they may be shown if so desired.

The artifacts shown here, however, come from two different processes, rather than a single process. In this case, the artifacts are **Maintenance Schedule** and **Completion Report**. Note how the associations are now showing the relationships between artifacts in a single process but also the relationship between artifacts from two different processes.

This higher-level view is used predominately for identifying audit trails and also for identifying relationships and dependencies between processes that may be performed by stakeholders in different workgroups. When two or more processes are executed in different groups, it identifies a working interface between these two groups and helps to establish the information, in the form of the artifacts, that is passed between them.

Defining the process behavior

The views that have been considered so far have been mainly concerned with the structure of the processes. One of the views that is most associated with process modeling is the process behavior view, an example of which is shown in the following diagram:

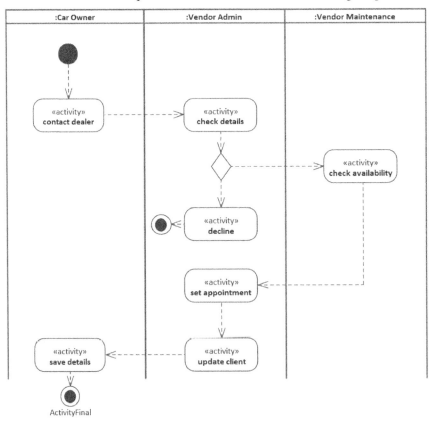

Figure 5.10 – An example of a process behavior view for the maintenance setup process

The diagram in *Figure 5.10* shows an example process behavior view for the maintenance setup process visualized using a SysML **activity diagram**.

The SysML activity diagram has not been considered in any detail so far in this book, so it is worth taking a little time to look at the syntax of the diagram.

The activity diagram allows behavior to be modeled, usually at a detailed level. In this case, the activity diagram will be used to model the detailed behavior of a block. Remember that the process content view in *Figure 5.5* visualized a process using the following SysML constructs:

- A SysML block to show a single process
- SysML properties to show the process artifacts
- SysML operations to show process activities

When modeling the behavior of a block using an activity diagram, the following syntax is used:

- The whole activity diagram represents the block.
- **Objects** show artifacts. Each object is represented graphically by a rectangle.
- **Actions** show activities. Each action is represented graphically by a rounded box.

Remember that behavior diagrams show the order of execution of things and, in this case, it is the order of execution of the actions that is shown.

The syntax of an activity diagram is similar to that of a state machine diagram, which has already been discussed – indeed, the activity diagram is actually a special type of state machine diagram. The start states (represented graphically by a solid circle) and the end state (represented graphically by the bull's-eye symbol) are the same as in a state machine diagram and show the creation and destruction of an instance of a block, respectively.

There is a new piece of syntax on this diagram that has not been seen before, which is known as a **swim lane** in SysML and is shown graphically by the large bottomless rectangles. A swim lane allows different groups of behavior to be collected together according to their responsibility. Each swim lane is titled with whatever holds the responsibility. In this example, each swim lane is titled by referring to a stakeholder from the process model. All of the behavior that is the responsibility of the stakeholder is contained in the swim lane. In this example, these behaviors are the activities from the process model.

This is a very convenient construct when applying process modeling as it has already been discussed that stakeholders are responsible for activities.

This view is particularly interesting when it comes to considering consistency between all of the views that have been discussed so far. This includes the following:

- The activities in this view are the same as the activities that were shown on the process content view in *Figure 5.5*. In this view, the activities are represented graphically by SysML actions, whereas in the process content view, they are represented graphically by SysML operations.

- The artifacts in this view are the same as the artifacts that are shown in both the process content view in *Figure 5.5* and the information view in *Figure 5.8*. In this view, the artifacts are visualized by SysML objects, whereas in the process content view, they are visualized using SysML properties, and in the information view, they are visualized using SysML blocks.

- The stakeholders in this view are the same as the stakeholders that are shown in both the stakeholder view in *Figure 5.7* and the process context view in *Figure 5.4*. In this view, the stakeholders are visualized using SysML swim lanes, whereas in the stakeholder view, they are visualized using SysML blocks, and in the process context view, they are visualized using SysML actors.

As can be seen, the process behavior view really emphasizes the consistency between several of the other views. It is worth noting here that a concept, or ontology element, in one view may be visualized using different modeling elements in different views. This is a good example of different visualizations being relevant for a single entity, as was discussed in *Chapter 2, Model-Based Systems Engineering*.

The process behavior view focuses on the behavior within a process, but it is also useful to be able to model the behavior between processes, which will be discussed in the next section.

Defining a sequence of processes

A process behavior view shows detailed behavior inside a process, but it is also important to be able to execute processes in a number of different sequences, which is shown using a process instance view, an example of which can be seen in the following diagram:

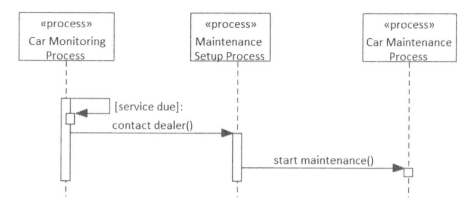

Figure 5.11 – An example process instance view showing the behavior between processes

The diagram in *Figure 5.11* shows an example of a process instance view that shows the behavior between processes, and it is visualized using a SysML sequence diagram.

In this view, each process is visualized using a SysML lifeline and the information and messages passed between these processes are shown using SysML interactions.

The process instance view is particularly useful for two main reasons:

- It shows that processes are consistent with one another in terms of the artifacts that are passed between processes. This is very important when it comes to ensuring that the complete set of processes is consistent.

- It allows the processes to be validated against the original rationale that was captured in the process context view.

The process instance view also provides several very strong consistency relationships with the other process modeling views:

- The processes in this view are the same as the processes in the process content view in *Figure 5.6*. Each process in this view is visualized using a SysML lifeline, whereas in the process content view, each process is visualized using a SysML block.

- The second consistency check is unusual in that the entire process instance view is consistent with a single need in the process context view in *Figure 5.4*. In this view, the entire view is visualized by the SysML sequence diagram, whereas in the process context view, the need is visualized using a SysML use case.

As can be seen, the consistency between all of the views is very strong and through enforcing this consistency, the confidence in the process model becomes very high.

The views that have been presented so far are known collectively, and quite unimaginatively, as the seven-views approach to process modeling. This approach is very flexible and very powerful and can be applied to a number of applications, including modeling standards, which will be discussed in the following section.

Modeling standards using process modeling

One of the key aspects of MBSE that was introduced in the MBSE diagram from *Chapter 2, Model-Based Systems Engineering*, is the idea of **compliance**. It is important that everything that we do in MBSE is demonstrable to the relevant stakeholders in terms of the quality of the work that is being carried out. An obvious way to achieve this is to show compliance with key standards, and an excellent way to do this, and also an excellent application of MBSE, is to apply process modeling to standards.

In this chapter, therefore, the following points will be considered:

- **Standards**: Why standards are so important and what the key systems engineering-related standards are
- **Modeling standards**: How the *seven-views* approach to process modeling may be applied to a specific standard
- **Types of process**: How to use this process model to identify the different processes that may be used as part of a wider MBSE application

This is just one of the many applications of process modeling and it will be revisited throughout the book. In the next few chapters, some specific processes for MBSE will be considered, and then they will be mapped back onto the best practice standard model that is developed in this section.

Identifying systems engineering standards

Standards play an important role in any MBSE endeavor as they provide an example of best practice that may be used as a basis for compliment. This is important as it is essential that any defined approach to MBSE may be demonstrated to comply with established best practice. Bearing in mind that the whole approach to MBSE that is advocated in this book has been defined using MBSE techniques, it makes sense that the compliance with best practice should also be carried out using MBSE techniques. This is an excellent application for process modeling, as the seven-views approach may be used to capture an understanding of any standard.

In the case of MBSE, the main standard that will be considered is **ISO 15288 – software and systems life cycle processes**. This is the most widely used systems engineering standard in the world and is mandated by many organizations that use systems engineering at any level.

The standard itself is not focused on modeling but on general systems engineering concepts. However, it has been stated on a number of occasions in this book that MBSE is just a way of achieving systems engineering, and, if this is indeed true, then there should be a clear mapping between best-practice systems engineering and MBSE concepts.

Modeling ISO 15288

When modeling any process-based standard, such as ISO 15288, it is possible to apply the seven-views approach to creating the associated standard model.

When modeling process standards, it should be borne in mind that standards are aimed at quite a high level of abstraction when it comes to their application. Standards, therefore, tend to dictate what should be done and produced rather than going into detail and dictating how things should be done and produced. Because of this, only a subset of the seven views will be used to model the standard.

ISO 15288 – The need context view

The need context view shows why a particular process or process set is needed and, therefore, when applied to a standard will show why a particular standard is needed. The need context view for ISO 15288 is shown in the following diagram:

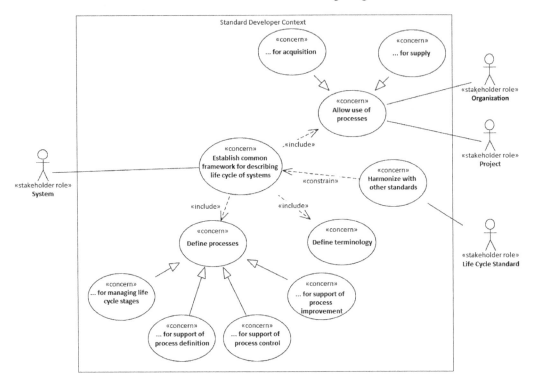

Figure 5.12 – The need context view for ISO 15288

The diagram in *Figure 5.12* shows the need context view for ISO 15288 visualized using a SysML use case diagram. The use cases on this diagram are shown to be of type <<**concern**>>, which are basically the needs for the standard. These may read as follows:

- The main aim of the standard is to **Establish common framework for describing life cycle of systems.** This summarizes everything that the standard is concerned with.

- One of the next use cases is to **Define processes**, which has an include relationship with the main use case, **Establish common framework for describing life cycle of systems**. The processes that need to be defined cover four areas, which are shown by the four specializations of this use case.

- **Define processes** is specialized by **…for managing life cycle stages**. This covers the life cycle definition and analysis such as was described in *Chapter 4, Life Cycles*.

- **Define processes** is specialized by **…for support of process definition**. This covers the definition of processes, and the seven-views approach described in this chapter can be used to achieve this.

- **Define processes** is specialized by **…for support of process control**. This covers managing and controlling the execution of processes, and the seven-views approach described in this chapter can be used to achieve this.

- **Define processes** is specialized by **…for support of process improvement**. This covers improving the processes and ensuring that they remain fit for purpose over a period of time. The seven-views approach described in this chapter can be used to achieve this.

- **Define terminology** that is an inclusion on the main use case **Establish common framework for describing life cycle of systems**. This relates to the fact that this standard defines a standard set of concepts and associated terminology for systems engineering. This has been covered extensively in this book by ontology modeling.

- **Allow use of processes** has an include relationship with the main use case, **Establish common framework for describing life cycle of systems**. This provides a mechanism for setting the scope of what areas of the process the standard covers and has two specializations.

- **Allow use of processes** is specialized by **…for acquisition**. This shows that the standard is concerned with acquisition-type processes; this may be modeled using the seven-views approach.

- **Allow use of processes** is specialized by **…for supply**. This shows that the standard is concerned with supply-type processes; this may be modeled using the seven-views approach.

- Finally, **Harmonize with other standards** covers compliance with other standards, which is covered in this very section and may be performed using the seven-views approach.

Notice how all of the use cases that are shown here and that represent the needs of ISO 15288 may be met by using the seven-views approach. This goes to show how powerful and flexible this approach is for many aspects of processes and process modeling.

One of these use cases, Define terminology, may be satisfied by creating an ontology, which is shown in the following section.

ISO 15288 – The process structure view

The process structure view defines the ontology for the standard and as such defines the main concepts and terminology associated with the standard. The ontology for ISO 15288 is shown in the following diagram:

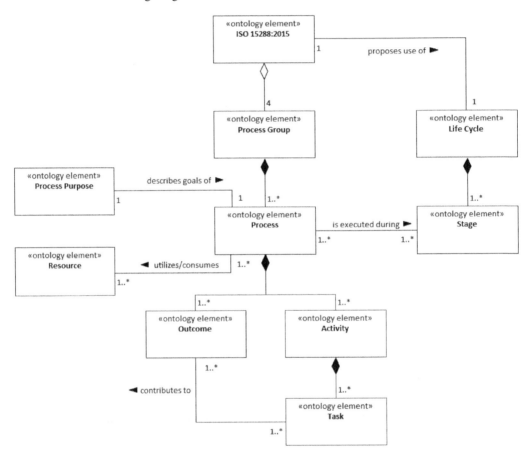

Figure 5.13 – A process structure view for ISO 15288

The diagram in *Figure 5.13* shows the process structure view for ISO 15288 visualized using a SysML block definition diagram.

It can be seen that **ISO 15288:2015 is made up of four process groups** and that **each process group comprises and owns a number of processes**.

Moreover, **ISO 15288:2015 also proposes the use of a life cycle.**

Refer to the following properties:

- **Focusing on the process**: Each process comprises a number of outcomes and a number of activities.

- **Focusing on the activity**: Each activity comprises a number of tasks, one or more of which contributes to one or more outcomes.

- **Returning back to process**: Each process has a single process purpose that describes the goals of the process, and one or more processes utilizes/consumes a number of resources.

- **Focusing on life cycle**: Each life cycle comprises one or more stages and one or more processes is executed during one or more stage.

It should be quite clear from this ontology that there are obvious similarities with the MBSE ontology that is used in this book. This is because ISO 15288 is one of the main best-practice references that is used throughout the book.

It is now possible to focus on the life cycle concept and to break this down into more detail, as shown in the following diagram:

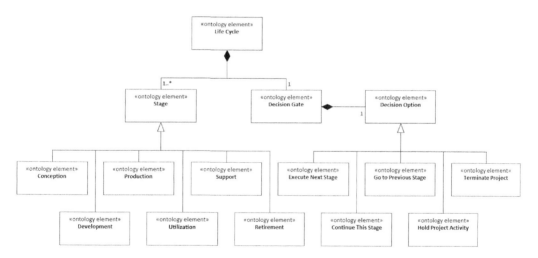

Figure 5.14 – A process structure view focusing on the life cycle concept

The diagram in *Figure 5.14* shows an additional process structure view, but this time with a focus on the life cycle concept, visualized using a SysML block definition diagram.

The diagram shows that **each life cycle comprises a number of stages and a number of decision gates**. Furthermore, **each stage is controlled by a single decision gate** as explained in the following points:

- **Focusing on the decision gates**: Each decision gate comprises a single decision option, of which there are five types: **Execute Next stage, Continue this stage, Go to Previous stage, Hold Project activity** and **Terminate Project**.

- **Focusing on the stages**: The different types of stage are **Conception, Development, Production, Utilization, Support**, and **Retirement**.

Again, notice the similarities between this ontology for ISO 15288 and the one that was introduced in *Chapter 4, Life Cycles* concerning life cycles.

ISO 15288 – the stakeholder view

The stakeholder view is concerned with identifying the stakeholders that have an interest in the system. In this case, the system is the standard itself, so the stakeholder view is concerned with identifying the stakeholders that have an interest in the standard, as shown in the following diagram:

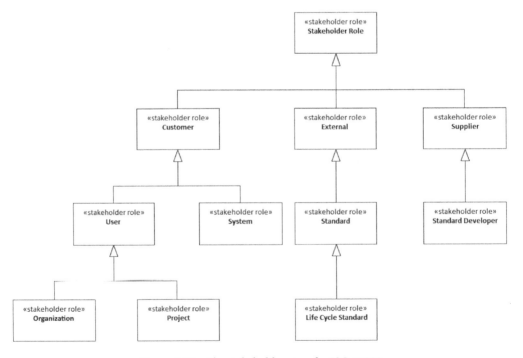

Figure 5.15 – The stakeholder view for ISO 15288

The diagram in *Figure 5.15* shows the stakeholder view for ISO 15288, which is visualized by a SysML block definition diagram.

Notice the same high-level structure for the three basic types of stakeholders that have been seen several times already in this book: the **Customer**, **External**, and **Supplier** stakeholders.

The **Customer** stakeholders are broken down into two sub-types:

- **User**, which is split into two further types: **Organization** and **Project**, both of which are identified as the main benefactors applying the standard

- **System**, which will benefit by having been systems engineered in a rigorous fashion by applying the standard

The **External** stakeholder has a single type, **Standard**, which itself has a single type, which is **Life Cycle Standard**. This refers to the fact that ISO 15288 relates to life cycles and the processes associated with those life cycles.

The **Supplier** stakeholder has a single type, which is **Standard Developer**, who is responsible for the creation, development, and maintenance of the standard.

ISO 15288 – the process content view

The process content view shows an overview of the processes that are available for inclusion in the life cycle and that may be thought of as a process library. In terms of ISO 15288, the process content view is by far the most populous of the views.

A high-level process content view that focuses on the process groups from the ontology is shown in the following diagram:

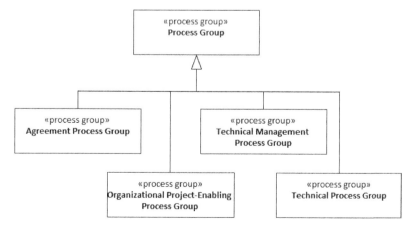

Figure 5.16 – A process content view for ISO 15288, focusing on process groups

The preceding figure shows a high-level process content view for ISO 15288 that focuses on the process groups and is visualized using a SysML block definition diagram.

The diagram shows that there are four types of **process group**:

- **Agreement Process Group**, which is concerned with all processes that relate to the customer and supplier relationships and covers areas such as acquisition and supply

- **Organizational Project-Enabling Process Group**, which is concerned with processes that apply across the entire organization and are relevant to everyone in the business

- **Technical Management Process Group**, which is concerned with processes that are applied on a project-by-project basis to manage the technical activities

- **Technical Process Group**, which is concerned with the sort of processes that are usually associated with systems engineering activities, such as needs modeling, design, verification and validation, and so on

Each of these process groups may be broken down to show individual processes, which will be discussed in the next four sections.

Process content view for the technical process group

This section shows the processes that comprise the technical process group, as shown in the following diagram:

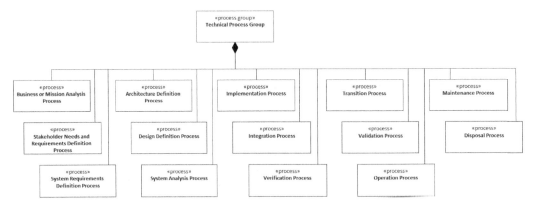

Figure 5.17 – A process content view for ISO 15288, focusing on the technical process group

The previous figure shows a process content view for ISO 15288 that focuses on the technical process group and is visualized using a SysML block definition diagram.

The diagram shows that there are 14 processes that make up this process group:

- **Business or Mission Analysis Process**, which is concerned with the definition of the business, mission problem, or opportunity; characterizing the solution space; and determining potential solutions for the system.

- **Stakeholder Needs and Requirements Definition Process**, which is concerned with the definition of the stakeholder needs and subsequent requirements for the system in the target environment.

- **System Requirements Definition Process**, which is concerned with the transformation of the stakeholder needs and requirements into a technical view of a solution.

- **Architecture Definition Process**, which is concerned with the generation of the system architecture options and the selection of one or more alternatives that satisfy the original needs.

- **Design Definition Process**, which is concerned with the provision of a system model to enable the implementation of a solution that is consistent with the views of the system architecture.

- **System Analysis Process**, which is concerned with the provision of a rigorous basis of the system model for technical understanding to aid decision-making across the life cycle.

- **Implementation Process**, which is concerned with the realization of a specified system element. This includes transforming the needs, architecture, and design models, including the interfaces, into a system element.

- **Integration Process**, which is concerned with the integration of a set of system elements into a realized system that satisfies the original needs.

- **Verification Process**, which is concerned with providing objective evidence that a system or system element fulfills its specified needs.

- **Transition Process**, which is concerned with the transition of a system to the operational environment.

- **Validation Process**, which is concerned with providing objective evidence that the system, when in use, fulfills its intended purpose in its intended operational environment.

- **Operation Process**, which is concerned with the use of the system in its target environment to deliver its services.

- **Maintenance Process**, which is concerned with sustaining the ability of the system to provide its intended purpose.

- **Disposal Process**, which is concerned with the disposal of a system element or system and ensuring that it is appropriately handled, replaced, or retired.

Each of these processes may be shown in more detail, also using a process content view, an example of which is shown in the following figure:

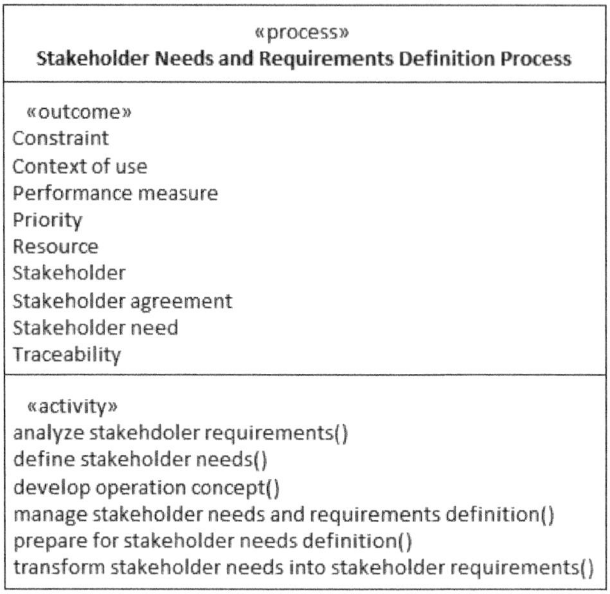

```
                    «process»
    Stakeholder Needs and Requirements Definition Process

     «outcome»
    Constraint
    Context of use
    Performance measure
    Priority
    Resource
    Stakeholder
    Stakeholder agreement
    Stakeholder need
    Traceability

     «activity»
    analyze stakehdoler requirements()
    define stakeholder needs()
    develop operation concept()
    manage stakeholder needs and requirements definition()
    prepare for stakeholder needs definition()
    transform stakeholder needs into stakeholder requirements()
```

Figure 5.18 – A process content view for ISO 15288, focusing on the Stakeholder Needs and Requirements Definition Process

The diagram in *Figure 5.18* shows the process content view for ISO 15288, focusing on the **Stakeholder Needs and Requirements Definition Process** and is visualized using a SysML block definition diagram. The individual parts of the diagram are visualized as follows:

- The process itself is visualized using a SysML block.
- Each artifact is visualized using a SysML property.
- Each activity is visualized using a SysML operation.

This process, and some of the other processes in the various process groups, will be discussed in more detail in subsequent chapters of this book.

Process content view for the agreement process group

This section shows the processes that comprise the agreement process group, as shown in the following diagram:

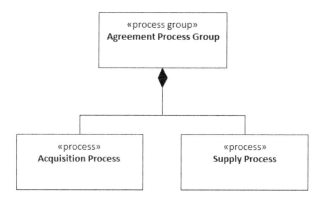

Figure 5.19 – A process content view for ISO 15288, focusing on the agreement process group

The diagram in *Figure 5.19* shows the process content view for the ISO 15288, this time focusing on the agreement process group, visualized using a SysML block definition diagram.

The processes that comprise the agreement process groups are as follows:

- **Acquisition Process**, which is concerned with obtaining a product or service in accordance with the customer's needs

- **Supply Process**, which is concerned with providing a customer with a product or service that meets the agreed needs

Notice that there are only two processes shown here, as opposed to 14 in the technical process group. This demonstrates how the emphasis in this standard is on the technical and engineering activities.

Process content view for the organizational project-enabling process group

This section shows the processes that comprise the organizational project-enabling process group, as shown in the following diagram:

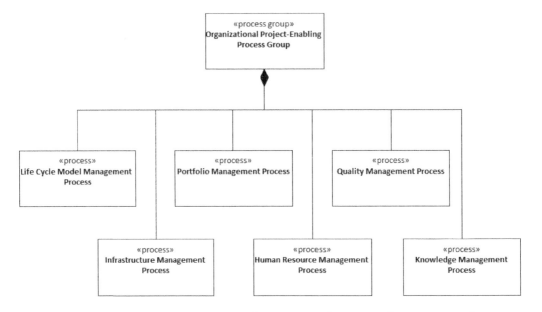

Figure 5.20 – A process content view for ISO 15288, focusing on the organizational project-enabling process group

The diagram in *Figure 5.20* shows the process content view with an emphasis on the organizational project-enabling process group, visualized using a SysML block definition diagram.

The processes that comprise the organizational project-enabling process group are as follows:

- **Life Cycle Model Management Process**, which is concerned with the definition, maintenance, and assurance of the availability of life cycle processes used by the organization

- **Infrastructure Management Process**, which is concerned with the provision of infrastructure and services to projects to support the organization and project throughout the life cycle

- **Portfolio Management Process**, which is concerned with the provision of suitable projects in order to meet the strategic objectives of the organization

- **Human Resource Management Process**, which is concerned with the provision of appropriate people with the appropriate competencies according to the organization's business needs

- **Quality Management Process**, which is concerned with ensuring that the quality process sets meet organizational and project quality objectives and achieve customer satisfaction

- **Knowledge Management Process**, which is concerned with creating the capability and assets needed to enable the organization to meet its commercial objectives

Again, note the number of processes here in comparison to the other two process groups that have been discussed so far.

Process content view for the technical management process group

This section shows the processes that comprise the technical management process group, as shown in the following diagram:

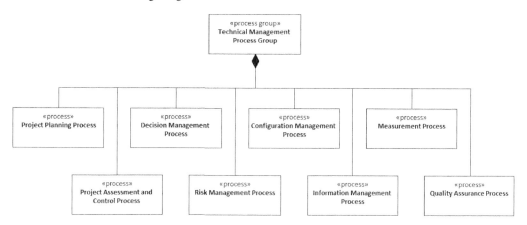

Figure 5.21 – A process content view for ISO 15288, focusing on the technical management process group

The diagram in *Figure 5.21* shows the process content view for ISO 15288 with an emphasis on the technical management process group, visualized using a SysML block definition diagram.

The processes that comprise the technical management process group are as follows:

- **Project Planning Process**, which is concerned with producing effective and workable plans

- **Project Assessment and Control Process**, which is concerned with assessing and ensuring that the management plans are consistent and feasible

- **Decision Management Process**, which is concerned with providing a structured analytical framework for decision-making at any point in the life cycle

- **Risk Management Process**, which is concerned with identifying and analyzing risks throughout the life cycle

- **Configuration Management Process**, which is concerned with managing and controlling system elements and their configurations over the life cycle

- **information Management Process**, which is concerned with the control, dissemination, and disposal of information to the relevant stakeholders over the life cycle

- **Measurement Process**, which is concerned with collecting, analyzing, and reporting data and information to support effective management and demonstrate the quality throughout the life cycle

- **Quality Assurance Process**, which is concerned with ensuring the effective application of the organization's processes

Again, notice the difference in the number of processes within each process group, which provides an indication of where the emphasis of this standard lies, which is mainly in the technical and technical management areas.

Demonstrating compliance with ISO 15288

One of the main applications of a model of a standard is to use it as basis for compliance.

If a process set is developed using the seven-views approach and then a number of standards are also modeled using the same approach, then the resulting models may be directly related together to demonstrate any areas of compliance and non-compliance. Indeed, this is an application that will be explored in subsequent chapters of this book, where specific techniques for MBSE will be discussed and their provenance demonstrated by mapping them back to the ISO 15288 process model.

Now that process modeling has been discussed, we will look at the framework that defines the views that we have described so far in this chapter.

Defining the framework

The views that have been created so far represent the center part of the MBSE diagram that we discussed in detail in *Chapter 2*, *Model-Based Systems Engineering*. Each of the views has been visualized using SysML, and they come together to represent the right-hand side of the MBSE diagram. These views combine together to form the overall model, but it is essential that these views are all consistent, otherwise they are not views but pictures! This is where the left-hand side of the MBSE diagram comes into play, as it is important that the definition of all of the views is captured in the framework. The framework comprises the ontology and a set of viewpoints; therefore, it is now time to make sure that these viewpoints are defined thoroughly and correctly, which is the aim of this section.

Defining the viewpoints in the framework

It was discussed in *Chapter 2*, *Model-Based Systems Engineering*, that it is necessary to ask a number of questions for each view to ensure that it is a valid view. There is also a set of questions that must be asked of the whole framework, as well as of the views. A combination of these, results in a set of questions allowing the whole framework to be defined. It is worthwhile, therefore, to have a reminder of what these questions are:

- Why is the framework required? This question may be answered using a **framework context view**.

- What are the overall concepts and terminology used for the framework? This question may be answered using an **ontology definition view**.

- What views are necessary as part of the framework? This question may be answered using a **viewpoint relationship view**.

- Why is each view needed? This question may be answered using a **viewpoint context view**.

- What is the structure and content of each view? This question may be answered using a **viewpoint definition view**.

- What rules should be applied? This question may be answered using a **ruleset definition view**.

When these questions are answered, it can be said that a framework has been defined. Each of these questions can be answered using a special set of views that is collectively known as the **framework for architecture frameworks (FAF)** [Holt and Perry 2019]. At this point, simply think about creating a specific view to answer each question, as described in the following sections.

Defining the framework context view

The framework context view specifies why the whole framework is needed in the first place and, in this case, will define the basic need for the seven-views approach to process modeling in the form of a process perspective, which is shown in the following diagram:

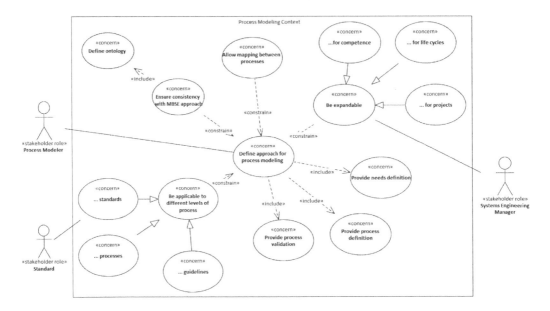

Figure 5.22 – A framework context view for the seven-views approach to process modeling

The diagram in *Figure 5.22* shows the framework context view for the seven-views approach to process modeling, visualized using a SysML use case diagram.

The main aim of the seven-views approach to process modeling is to **Define approach for process modeling**, an approach that includes the following three needs:

- **Provide needs definition**, which allows the basic purpose of the process set to be modeled to be defined

- **Provide process definitions**, which allows the processes in the process set to be defined

- **Provide process validation**, which demonstrates how the process set satisfies the original needs

The main aim is also constrained by the following:

- **Ensure consistency with MBSE approach**, which *includes Define ontology*. This makes sure that the overall approach is based on MBSE best practice.

- **Allow mapping between processes**, which allows compliance with other processes to be demonstrated.

- **Be expandable**, which has three specializations: **...for competence, ...for life cycles**, and **...for projects**. This makes sure that the approach is flexible and can be adapted for other process-related applications.

- **Be applicable to different levels of process**, which has three specializations: **... standards, ...processes**, and **...guidelines**. This makes sure that the approach is flexible enough to be applied at different levels of abstraction of process.

This is only a brief explanation, as use case diagrams will be covered in depth in the next chapter.

Defining the ontology definition view

The ontology definition view captures all the concepts and associated terminology associated with the framework in the form of an ontology. This has already been done as the ontology for the process-related views was defined in *Figure 5.1*, *Figure 5.2*, and *Figure 5.3*. The ontology elements shown in this view provide all of the stereotypes that have been used for the actual views that have been created so far in this chapter.

Ontology elements that are related will often be collected into a **perspective**, as was discussed in all previous chapters. In this chapter, a new perspective has been created that relates to processes.

Defining the viewpoint relationship view

The viewpoint relationship view identifies which views are needed and, for each set of views, identifies a viewpoint that will contain its definition. Remember that a viewpoint may be thought of as a type of template for a view. These viewpoints may be collected together into a perspective, which is simply a collection of viewpoints with a common theme.

In this chapter, the emphasis has been on defining a set of views relations to life cycles, so it is appropriate to create the **process perspective**. The basic set of views that has been discussed so far is shown in the following view:

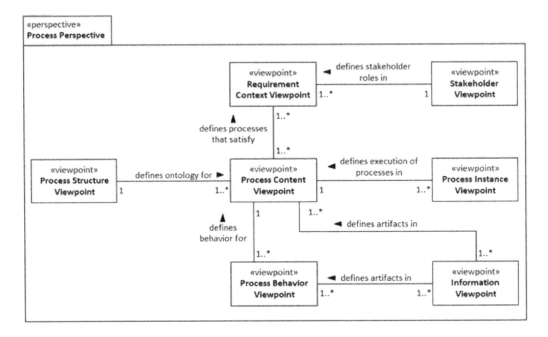

Figure 5.23 – A viewpoint relationship view for the process perspective

The diagram in *Figure 5.23* shows the viewpoint relationship view for the process perspective using a SysML block definition diagram.

The process perspective is shown using a SysML package, stereotyped as `<<perspective>>`, that simply collects together a number of viewpoints, as follows:

- **Process Structure Viewpoint**, which allows the ontology to be captured.

- **Process Content Viewpoint**, which defines a process library for the process set.

- **Requirement Context Viewpoint**, which defines the need for each process in the process set

- **Stakeholder Viewpoint**, which allows all relevant stakeholders to be identified

- **Process Behavior Viewpoint**, which specifies how a single process operates internally

- **Information Viewpoint**, which defines the artifacts associated with either a single process or the process set and their inter-relationships

- **Process Instance Viewpoint**, which allows sequences of processes to be executed in order to satisfy the original need

The number of viewpoints defined here gave rise to the original name for the approach: the seven-views approach to process modeling.

Defining the viewpoint context view

The viewpoint context view specifies why a particular viewpoint and, therefore, its set of views is needed in the first place. It will identify the relevant stakeholders that have an interest in the viewpoint and also identify what benefits each of the stakeholders hopes to gain from the framework.

There will be a viewpoint context view for each viewpoint. Each viewpoint context view will trace back to the framework context view as it must contribute to the overall expectations of the organization. The combined set of viewpoint context views will, therefore, satisfy the overall needs represented in the framework context view.

The viewpoint context view will be visualized using a SysML use case diagram, and this will be described fully in *Chapter 6, Needs and Requirements*.

Defining the viewpoint definition view

The viewpoint definition view defines the ontology elements that are included in the viewpoint, showing the following:

- Which ontology elements are allowed in the viewpoint

- Which ontology elements are optional in the viewpoint

- Which ontology elements are not allowed in the viewpoint

The viewpoint definition view focuses on a single viewpoint and particular care and attention must be paid to not just the ontology elements that are selected but also the relationships that exist between these ontology elements. An example of a viewpoint definition view is shown in the following diagram:

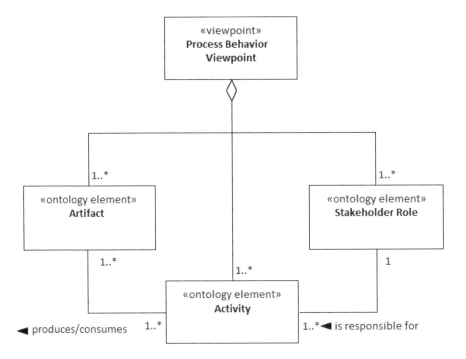

Figure 5.24 – A viewpoint definition view for the process behavior viewpoint

Figure 5.24 shows the viewpoint definition view for the process behavior viewpoint, using a SysML block definition diagram.

The process behavior viewpoint, therefore, contains the following ontology elements:

- One or more **artifacts**
- One or more **activities**
- One or more **stakeholders**

Alongside these ontology elements, the following ontology relationships are also included in the viewpoint:

- **One or more activities produces/consumes one or more artifact.**
- **Each stakeholder is responsible for one or more activities.**

Remember, not all ontology relationships from the ontology need be included, only the ones that manifest themselves in the views.

Defining the ruleset definition view

The ruleset definition view identifies and defines a number of rules that may be applied to the model to ensure that it is consistent with the framework.

The rules are based primarily on the ontology definition view and the viewpoint relationships view. In each case, the rules are defined by identifying the key relationships and their associated multiplicities that exist in the following places:

- Between viewpoints in the viewpoint definition view
- Between ontology elements in the ontology definition view

An example of a rule for the process perspective is shown in the following diagram:

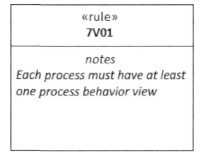

Figure 5.25 – Example ruleset definition view

Figure 5.25 shows an example of a ruleset definition view using a SysML block definition diagram. Each block on the diagram represents a rule that is derived from either the ontology definition view or the viewpoint relationship view.

The rule is as follows:

- **Each process must have at least one process behavior view**. This is based on the relationship between the **process content viewpoint** and the **process behavior viewpoint** from the viewpoint relationship view.

Of course, any number of other rules may be defined here, but not every relationship will lead to a rule, as this is at the discretion of the modeler.

Summary

This chapter has introduced the concepts of processes and why they are so important to MBSE. Processes are collected together into a process set to form the heart of any good MBSE approach, alongside the framework.

An approach to modeling processes was introduced that is known as the seven-views approach to process modeling and was used to show how a process may be defined.

The same approach was then also used to show how a standard may be modeled; this will be referred back to in subsequent chapters in this book.

Finally, the framework for the process perspective was defined.

The next chapter looks at the whole area of needs modeling. The process modeling that we have learned about in this chapter will also be used to define a needs-based process.

Self-assessment tasks

1. Consider the ontology for processes that was presented in *Figure 5.1* and map this onto the concepts and terminology in your organization.

2. Identify a single process in your organization and create a set of seven views to model this process.

3. Take the process model created in question 1 and map it onto the ISO 15288 process model that was created in this chapter. Use the process structure view to map between concepts and the process content view to map between processes.

References

- [Holt & Perry 2019] Holt, JD and Perry, SA. *SysML for Systems Engineering – a model-based approach*. Third edition. IET Publishing, Stevenage, UK. 2019

Section 3: Systems Engineering Techniques

In this section, you will learn some specific techniques that will allow you to realize the concepts discussed in *Section 2, Systems Engineering Concepts* of the book.

This section has the following chapters:

- *Chapter 6, Needs and Requirements*
- *Chapter 7, Modeling the Design*
- *Chapter 8, Verification and Validation*
- *Chapter 9, Methodologies*
- *Chapter 10, Systems Engineering Management*

6
Needs and Requirements

This chapter focuses on introducing one of the most important techniques associated with MBSE, that of modeling **needs** and **requirements**.

Understanding needs is crucial to the success of any system as they provide the definition of all aspects of the system, such as the intended use, performance, function, form, and intent of the system.

Without understanding the needs of a system, it is impossible to say whether the delivered system is fit for purpose. This is because the purpose of that system is not known, as it is the needs that *describe* its purpose. Therefore, it is crucial that all needs are well defined and also that they are well understood by all of the stakeholders of the system. This is important as different stakeholders may interpret these need statements in different ways, depending on their context. Indeed, the topic of context will be described in detail as it is one of the most important aspects that must be clearly specified before the needs can be truly understood and accepted.

This chapter covers the following:

- Introducing needs and requirements
- Visualizing needs using different SysML diagrams
- Defining the framework

Our discussion begins by considering the fundamental concepts associated with needs and requirements.

Introducing needs and requirements

This section introduces the key concept of needs and discusses how different types of needs exist, such as **requirements**, **capabilities**, and **goals**. We will discuss the importance of defining the exact meaning of the terminology and the MBSE ontology that has been developed throughout this book so far will also be expanded upon to introduce these new concepts. We will start by looking at what needs actually are…

Defining needs

One of the most important concepts associated with systems engineering is that of the **need**, as shown in the following diagram:

Figure 6.1 – Ontology definition view showing basic needs

The diagram in *Figure 6.1* shows an ontology definition view that introduces the concept of a need and its relationship to a system, which is visualized using a SysML block definition diagram.

The diagram shows that one or more needs describe the purpose of one or more systems. The concept of a need is important for several main reasons:

- It provides a statement of a desired feature of a system.

- It provides an agreed consensus between the customer and supplier stakeholder roles as to what is to be delivered as part of the system.

- It is the means by which a system may be accepted by the customer. To put this another way, a system may only be accepted by the customer once it has been demonstrated that all of the agreed needs have been satisfied.

Remember from *Chapter 1, Introduction to Systems Engineering*, that the main aim of systems engineering is to realize a successful system, and it is satisfying these needs that ensures that the system is successfully realized.

Also, the needs will be traced back through the development life cycle to ensure that the project is consistently and continuously satisfying its overall purpose.

There are three main areas of needs that will be discussed in the following sections: defining the different types of needs that exist, describing each need using use cases, and validating use cases and needs using scenarios.

Defining types of needs

The concept of a need is a generic one, and there are many different types of need that may be identified, depending on the type of system that is being developed and the domain in which the system will be deployed. Some examples of different types of need are shown in the following diagram:

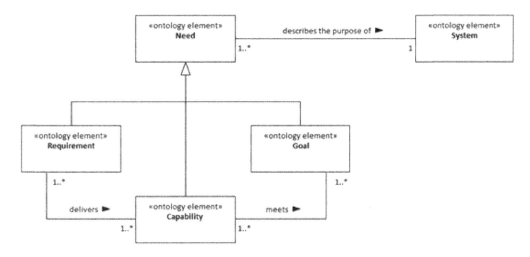

Figure 6.2 – Ontology definition view types of need

The diagram in *Figure 6.2* shows the basic concept of a need by showing three different types of need, visualized using a SysML block definition diagram.

It can be seen that there are three types of need, which are as follows:

- **Requirement**: Contributes to describing the purpose of the system and delivers one or more capabilities. A requirement describes a specific need of a system and may be applied at different levels of system elements, such as the system, subsystem, and so on (note that this is not shown in this diagram).

- **Capability**: Contributes to describing the purpose of the system that is delivered by one or more requirements and that meets one or more goals.

- **Goal**: Contributes to describing the purpose of the system that is met by one or more capabilities.

These types of needs are often referred to as functional needs as they describe a specific function of a system that has to be delivered. This term will not be used explicitly in this book; only the terminology that is specified in the ontology definition views.

Notice that at this point, the needs themselves are not being described individually as this will be done in two ways in the next section when need descriptions and use cases are discussed. Several examples of these different types of needs will be provided at that point.

It should be stressed that the three types of need that are shown here are examples and, as such, are provided for guidance only, and it is up to you to define the types of needs that suit your own ends.

There is also another type of need that must be considered at this point and that may be applied to all three needs, and that is shown in the following diagram:

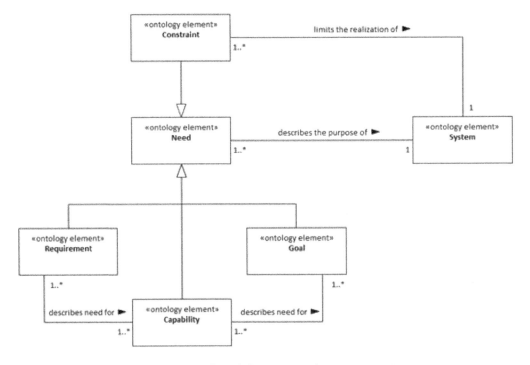

Figure 6.3 – Ontology definition view showing constraints

The diagram in *Figure 6.3* introduces the concept of the **constraint**, and is visualized using a SysML block definition diagram.

A constraint is a special type of need but it sits alongside the three types of needs that were introduced in *Figure 6.2*. This is a subtle yet important point from a modeling point of view. When two separate specializations are used, as seen here, they are actually considered different types of specialization altogether. Therefore, the following three situations are possible:

- A need may be both a type of requirement and a type of constraint.

- A need may be both a type of capability and a type of constraint.

- A need may be both a type of goal and a type of constraint.

This is a very powerful modeling mechanism that provides considerable flexibility when defining specialization in SysML.

One or more constraints limit the realization of a system in some way. Needs state a desired feature of a system whereas constraints, while still being needs, will limit the way that a need may be realized in the system.

Constraints are often referred to as non-functional requirements, but this term will not be used explicitly in this book; only the terminology that is specified in the ontology definition views.

Constraints can often be more difficult to satisfy than standard needs. Also, it is possible to develop a system that satisfies all of the original needs but, without also satisfying the constraints, it will be impossible to deploy the system.

There are many different types of constraints that may exist, such as the following:

- **Quality constraints**: Satisfying a particular standard; for example, all cars in Europe must satisfy the basic requirements of ISO 26262: Road Vehicles – functional safety, otherwise they are not permitted to be used on public roads.

- **Environmental constraints**: Limiting the emissions of a system; for example, a car may be limited to using an electric motor, rather than an internal combustion engine, due to the levels of emissions generated by a petrol or diesel engine.

- **Performance constraints**: Specifying efficiency measures associated with a system; for example, the power of a motor may need to be less than what is possible according to its parameters as there may be a constraint associated with ensuring a predefined distance that needs to be traveled between refueling or recharging.

- **Implementation constraints**: Using a specific material or prohibiting the use of a specific material in the construction of the system; for example, only certain types of solder may be used in the construction of the circuit boards in a car due to the lead content of some solders.

Of course, this is not intended to be an exhaustive list of constraints but should provide you with some indication of the sheer diversity of constraints that may limit the realization of the system in some way.

Constraints, as will be seen later in this chapter, must be related to other needs, or to put it another way, they must constrain an existing need.

Describing needs

Both needs and constraints (themselves a special type of need) are conceptual and must be described in some way. This will be achieved in two ways: by creating need descriptions and by defining use cases for the needs. The following diagram introduces the first of these two – the need description.

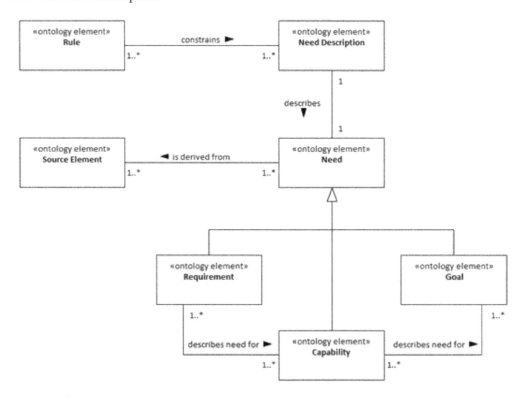

Figure 6.4 – Ontology definition view for need descriptions

The diagram in *Figure 6.4* expands to introduce several new concepts using a SysML block definition diagram. There are three new concepts in this diagram, which are as follows:

- **Need description**, which provides a set of text-based features that describe an individual need. These features are typically a list of attributes, such as name, description, identifier, and priority, among others, that must be defined for each need description.

- **Source element**, which provides a reference to the origin of the need. All needs must come from somewhere and the source element provides a set of legal sources for the needs.

- **Rule**, which provides guidance that may limit the way that a need description may be defined. Rules will constrain a need description so, for example, a rule may prohibit the use of some words, such as should, could, reasonable, and so on.

Need descriptions are an important part of describing a set of needs but there is a major pitfall that will often manifest itself when describing needs using only text-based need descriptions, which is the context of the need description. In many cases, it is difficult to explicitly see the context, or point of view, from which the need description has been written. This can lead to different stakeholders having different interpretations of a single need description, without these differences being apparent. This can be catastrophic for gaining a true understanding of the needs as a whole and, therefore, it is essential that needs are also described using use cases, which are shown in the following diagram.

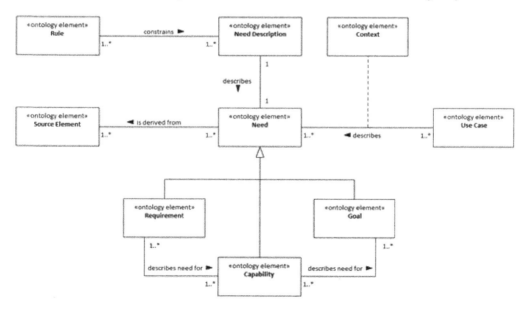

Figure 6.5 – Ontology definition view showing use cases

The diagram in *Figure 6.5* shows several new concepts that have been realized using a SysML block definition diagram. There are two new concepts in this diagram, which are as follows:

- **Use case**, which provides a context-based description of a need. This context may completely change the interpretation of a specific need depending on which context has been selected.

- **Context**, which describes the point of view from which the use case has been defined.

There is potential for confusion between a need description and a use case as both describe a need. The difference between the two, which is absolutely crucial to understand, is that use cases describe needs explicitly via a specific context, whereas need descriptions do not. Both are important for different reasons:

- Need descriptions will often provide a contract for a project to deliver a system.

- Need descriptions are used extensively for needs management, rather than engineering (understanding) the need.

- Use cases provide context and, therefore, a true understanding of the many different interpretations of a single need.

It is possible and usual, therefore, to have a single need description for a single need, and also for that single need to have multiple interpretations that are captured in the model by multiple use cases.

Validating needs and use cases

If it is accepted that a single need can have multiple interpretations in the form of multiple use cases, then the way that each need may be validated will also be open to multiple interpretations. These multiple validations are captured in the model using **scenarios**, which are introduced in the following diagram.

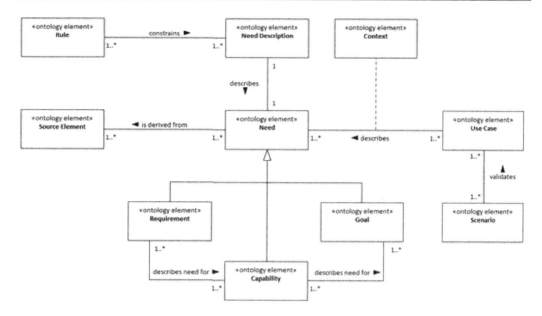

Figure 6.6 – Ontology definition view showing scenarios

The diagram in *Figure 6.6* shows that scenarios provide a mechanism for validating a need via its use cases. It is essential to demonstrate that each need can be satisfied in order for the system that is being developed to be successful. As each need may have multiple use cases, it is important that each of these may be demonstrated to have been satisfied. This is achieved by defining a number of scenarios that validate each use case.

A scenario may be realized in the following two different ways:

- **Operational scenarios**, which show a sequence of events or actions that results in a specific outcome. These operational scenarios are typically sequential in nature.

- **Performance scenarios**, which allow parameters of a system to be changed in order to demonstrate that it can satisfy specific outcomes. These performance scenarios are typically mathematical in nature.

The concepts that have been introduced to us in this section provide the ontology definition view for needs. We will discuss the realization of a number of views based on this needs ontology in detail in the next section, which discusses visualizing needs.

Visualizing needs using different SysML diagrams

The previous section defined the concepts associated with needs in the form of the needs ontology. This section looks at each of these in more detail and shows how needs may be realized using a number of different views, each of which will be visualized using the SysML notation.

Visualizing source elements

This section discusses the importance of defining source elements and introduces the source element view, which is used to visualize these source elements. There are five basic reasons why we need to identify these source elements, which are as follows:

- **To identify the origin of all the needs that are defined for a system**: This is something that is often overlooked or neglected altogether, but this is important for a number of reasons.

- **To demonstrate the provenance of all needs**: It is essential to be able to identify where each need originated. This must include an actual reference to the origin so that the source information may be identified and also checked in the event that the need is queried in some way.

- **To identify the source stakeholder**: If a need cannot be traced back to a stakeholder, then it is not a need! Stakeholders have been defined as having an interest in the system, therefore all needs must trace back to one or more stakeholders.

- **To prevent unspecified needs**: It is a common problem that some needs are actually introduced by workers on a project and have not been formally identified by a specific stakeholder. This can result in extra needs being introduced that are not required or needs that are detrimental to the system.

- **To identify what is a legal source element**: Depending on the nature of a system and how critical it is, it is important to identify what constitutes a legal source element and what does not.

The ontology element that must be considered, therefore, is that of the source element, but it is always advisable that the different types of source elements are specified explicitly by expanding the ontology definition view, as shown in the following diagram.

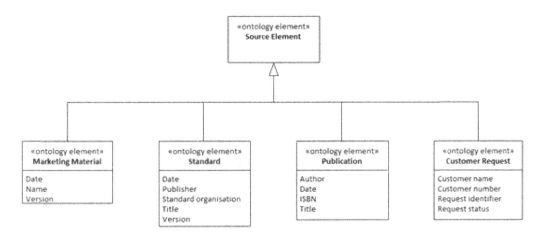

Figure 6.7 – Expanded ontology definition view showing types of source elements

The diagram in *Figure 6.7* shows the four new types of source elements introduced here that are indicated using the SysML specialization relationship and are as follows:

- **Marketing material**, which represents information that is used by the marketing stakeholders in order to provide an indication of the final product that is being developed. In the case of a car, this may be sales literature, for example, that provides features of a new car that may be desirable for potential customers and that may have to be introduced into a new car system that is under development.

- **Standard**, which represents some sort of best practice reference that is relevant to the car. This may be a safety standard, such as ISO 26262 or the ENCAP rating standard that is used as part of the promotion for new cars. Of course, these standards may cover any aspect of the system or the project that is being run to develop that system.

- **Publication**, which may be a book (such as this one!) or a scientific paper that may give rise to needs. For example, a book may be used as the industry-standard for best practice in a particular field, such as MBSE.

- **Customer request**, which may be a specific request from existing customers. For example, customers using an old version of a car may all have a similar complaint that may be resolved by introducing a new need to subsequent versions of the car.

Note that each of the new types of source element has a number of properties associated with it that allows reference to be made to the specific source element.

In the same way that legal source elements may be identified, it may also be desirable to identify source elements that will not be accepted as valid, as shown in the following diagram.

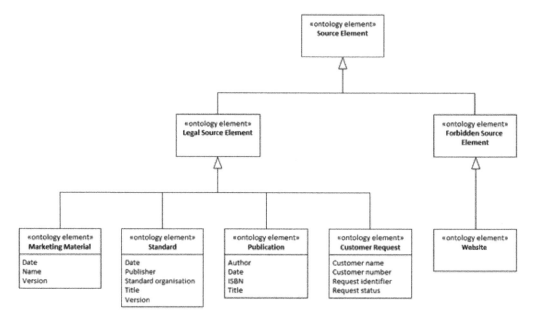

Figure 6.8 – Ontology definition view showing legal and forbidden source elements

The diagram in *Figure 6.8* shows another expanded ontology definition view that introduces a new level of specialization of source elements.

The diagram in *Figure 6.7* shows types of source elements, but *Figure 6.8* introduces a new level of classification by defining the following:

- **Legal source element**, which is the same collection of types of source elements that was seen previously. This time, however, they are explicitly identified as being legal and, therefore, may be permitted in the model.

- **Forbidden source element**, which provides a new collection of source elements (in this case, only one – **Website**) that is deemed to be illegal. Note that there are no additional properties on the forbidden source elements as they may not be added to the model and, therefore, do not require an explicit specification.

This provides a very neat way of stating exactly what is permitted and not permitted to be a source element. Also, in the case of legal source elements, the properties required to reference the source element precisely are identified.

This expanded ontology may then be used as a basis for a **Source Element View**, an example of which is shown in the following diagram.

Figure 6.9 – Example Source Element view

Each block in the diagram in *Figure 6.9* represents a single source element but uses stereotypes that are taken from the expanded ontology definition view from *Figure 6.6*, all of which are types of source elements. Notice how each of the source elements now has its property values filled in to specify exactly what the source element is.

The Source Element View is visualized here using a SysML block definition diagram but it could have very easily been visualized using text or a simple table. The use of the block definition diagram, however, has a number of advantages over using only text:

- **The view must be part of the model**: As discussed in *Chapter 2, Model-Based Systems Engineering*, it does not matter how each view is visualized provided that the view is truly part of the model and is consistent with all the other views (which is the very definition of a view!). By using SysML to visualize the view and with an underlying ontology, this is far simpler than using text.

- **The view provides a bridge to the actual source element**: Each source element on the view is a reference to the actual source element, for example, the block **Car Brochure** is not the actual brochure but is a reference to it. All SysML tools will allow a hypertext link to be inserted as part of the block description, which will allow a direct bridge between the model, in this case, the source element, and the actual document, such as the **Car Brochure**.

- **Traceability is assured**: Following on from the previous two points, full traceability across the model is now assured as everything in the model and the source element files that sit outside the model is now fully traceable.

The source element view is often overlooked but it is a very important view that must always be present in any needs model.

As with all the views in a particular framework, there is no inherent order for creating the views and, therefore, the source element view may be created at any point. In some cases, it may be the first view that is created if, for example, the start point of the needs modeling is a set of source documents. As another example, the start point of the needs modeling may be creating contexts, in which case the source element view would not be the first view to be created.

Visualizing need descriptions

When defining needs of any kind (requirements, capabilities, or goals, according to the ontology presented here), it is both natural and intuitive to want to describe each need in turn using text. This is both useful and important and forms a key part of any needs modeling exercise. In many cases, this will be the first view that is generated due to the historical tradition of defining needs using text as part of a needs management activity.

When defining an individual need, it is common to identify a number of properties that relate to each need and that, when taken together, form the description of that need. This is captured in the ontology by the **Need Description**.

There is no definitive set of properties that must be defined for each need and it is ultimately up to the modeler to decide which are appropriate, but a typical set is shown in the following diagram.

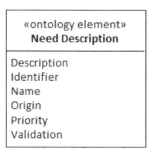

Figure 6.10 – Ontology definition view focusing on need description

The diagram in *Figure 6.10* shows a single ontology element shown on the view, which is the need description that was discussed previously in this chapter, shown in *Figure 6.1*. This time, however, a number of properties have been identified, which are as follows:

- **Description,** a text-based description that uses plain English to describe the need in detail.

- **Identifier**, which provides a unique reference for the need description that can be used later for traceability purposes.

- **Name**, which provides a high-level label that can be used as a simple description of the need.

- **Origin**, which refers directly to the stakeholder that was responsible for identifying the original need that relates to this need description.

- **Priority**, which provides an indication of how important the need is; typically, this may be set as mandatory, desirable, or optional.

- **Validation**, which refers directly to the number of scenarios that will be used to demonstrate that the need has been satisfied. Scenarios will be discussed later in this chapter.

Each need that has been identified will have a single need description associated with it and these may be modeled using a **SysML requirement diagram**. The SysML requirement diagram is a new diagram that has not been discussed in detail so far in this book. The requirement diagram is actually a variation of the SysML block definition diagram and comprises two basic elements:

- **Requirement**, which is a special type of block that is stereotyped as `<<requirement>>` in SysML and has two predefined properties associated with it: `id`, which provides a unique identifier, and `text`, which allows a text description to be defined

- **Relationships**, which allow requirement blocks to be related together

These SysML requirement diagrams, therefore, may be used to visualize a set of need descriptions in a need description view, an example of which is shown in the following diagram.

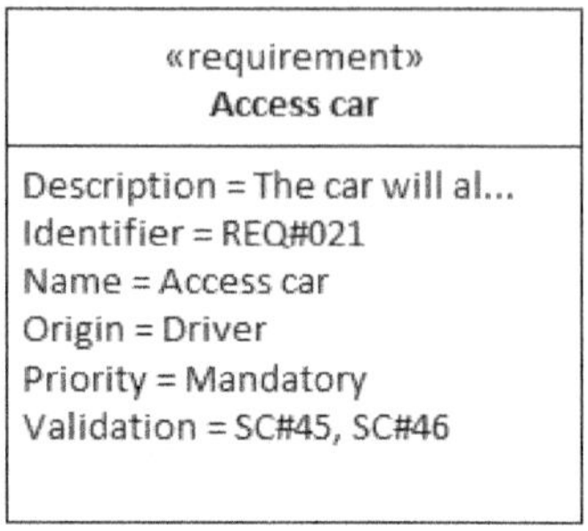

Figure 6.11 – Example need description view for a single need description

The diagram in *Figure 6.11* shows a need description view that focuses on a single need description and that is visualized using a SysML requirement diagram.

In this example, there is a single need description named **Access car** that is represented on the diagram using a SysML requirement block. Notice how the properties for the need description have been filled in with appropriate values.

This diagram also shows how the basic SysML language must be tailored, in some cases, to suit the specific needs of the project. In the SysML language, there are only two predefined properties on a requirement block, which is not nearly enough to fully describe a need description. However, this is not an oversight of SysML and is actually quite deliberate. By only specifying a small number of properties (in this case, just the ID and the text properties), it allows the modeler to define their own set of properties to suit their own ends. In this example, the properties that are used are the ones that were defined on the ontology and depicted in *Figure 6.9*.

The example here focuses on a single need description and, of course, in a real project, there would never be a need description view that contains only a single need description, as it would be more typical to show multiple need descriptions and the relationships between them. An example of this can be seen in the following diagram.

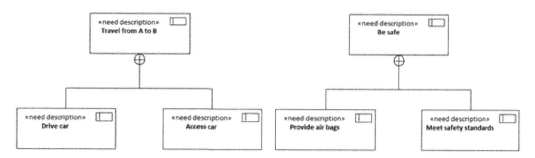

Figure 6.12 – Example need description view showing multiple need descriptions

The diagram in *Figure 6.12* shows another need description view that shows multiple need descriptions and that is visualized using a SysML requirement diagram.

In this example, there are two high-level need descriptions that are shown along with their associated lower-level need descriptions. This decomposition is shown in SysML by using a nesting symbol (the circle with the cross), which is just one of the many relationships that may be used on a SysML requirement diagram. The nesting construct allows need descriptions to be broken down into lower-level need descriptions.

Another useful relationship that may be used on requirement diagrams is that of the <<**trace**>> relationship. Refer to the following diagram:

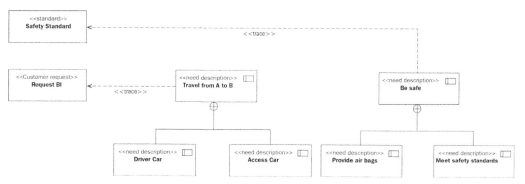

Figure 6.13 – Need description view showing traceability

The diagram in *Figure 6.13* shows another need description view showing traceability, which is visualized using a SysML requirement diagram.

In this example, the <<**trace**>> relationship has been used to show explicit traceability between need descriptions and source elements (in this case, the two specializations of source element: <<**standard**>> and <<**customer request**>>). The ability to show traceability is very powerful, but it is essential that whatever traceability path is being shown is consistent with the ontology. In this case, the <<**trace**>> relationship shows explicit traceability between the need description and the source elements. This is consistent with the ontology in *Figure 6.3*, which shows a traceability path from need description to need and then on to the source element. If this traceability path did not exist on the ontology, then the <<**trace**>> relationship on this view would be incorrect and would break the model! Everything on each one of the views, including both the elements and relationships, must be a direct instance of ontology elements and ontology relationships from the ontology.

There are several other types of relationships that may be used on a requirement diagram, which are as follows:

- **Copy**, which shows that a SysML requirement is an exact and direct copy of another. This is useful when disparate source elements may result in multiple copies of a single need description.

- **Derive**, where one SysML requirement has been created that did not exist previously, directly as a result of an existing SysML requirement.

- **Refine**, where one SysML requirement has been changed or modified based on an existing SysML requirement. This may be, for example, where the wording has been correct or, as will be seen in the next section, as a result of some use case modeling.

- **Satisfy**, where other aspects of the model may be related back to a SysML requirement to show either verification or validation.

Caution must be exercised when using SysML requirement diagrams as they are intended to be used for managing needs, rather than understanding those needs. Historically, the SysML requirement diagram was based on standard views from several commercial requirements management tools, hence the names of the standard relationships may be familiar to some readers.

There is a great potential danger in this as many people will produce text descriptions of needs (need description views) and then mistakenly believe that they have engineered those needs. This is simply not true, as this type of view and the associated SysML requirement diagram are intended for use in managing needs rather than engineering them. As a result of this, there can be little or no confidence in a set of needs that consists solely of need description views.

The need description view is an important view, but it is only a single view. In order to gain a complete, thorough, and rigorous understanding of the needs, it is essential to consider the complete set of views that is presented there. An essential aspect of the other views that must be considered is the concept of the context, which is often ignored or missed out altogether when only text-based descriptions are considered.

This crucial concept of context, and how it may be modeled, is described in the following section.

Visualizing the context definition

The next view that will be discussed is the **Context Definition View**. When modeling needs, identifying and defining contexts is essential to gain an understanding of the underlying needs.

Each context provides a point of view, from which each need is considered. Looking at needs from different contexts provides a very rich understanding of the different interpretations of each need, which is essential for engineering the needs correctly. These contexts may be based on a number of different sources and two will be considered in this chapter: **stakeholder contexts** and **system contexts**.

A number of different contexts may be identified based on different stakeholders that exist for the system. This is a very common source of contexts and one that is mandatory for any rigorous needs modeling exercise.

Each stakeholder that exists for the system may look at a single need and, potentially, each stakeholder may interpret that need in a different way. These different interpretations are known as **use cases** and these will be discussed in the next section. For now, the important thing is to have a good idea of what stakeholders exist. This is good news as identifying stakeholders is something that has already been discussed previously in this book, as stakeholder identification is an essential part of any systems engineering endeavor. Consider, therefore, the set of stakeholders that has been identified in the following diagram.

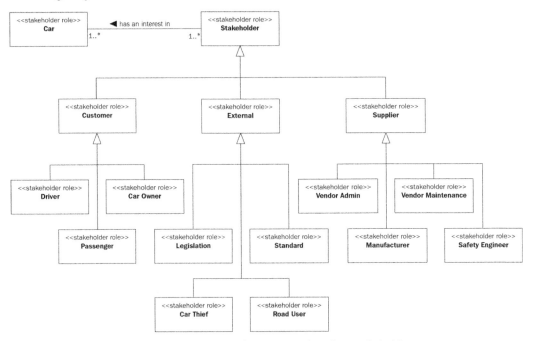

Figure 6.14 – Context Definition View based on stakeholders

The diagram in *Figure 6.14* shows a Context Definition View that is visualized using a SysML block definition diagram. This is very similar to some of the stakeholder views that have been seen previously in this book, but this view has a different name. This is because this view may not necessarily be based on stakeholders but may be based on the system structure, for example, in which the diagram would look different (this will be considered in the next diagram). Therefore, the term Context Definition View is used as this allows the view to focus on other sources for the context, not just stakeholders.

Note that the classification hierarchy of the stakeholders is the same as was seen previously but, this time, there have been more stakeholders added to the view. There are 11 different stakeholders in total shown on this view, which means that, potentially, there will be 11 different interpretations of each need as there are 11 different contexts. Initially, this can be quite intimidating as it can lead to a lot of work being carried out to provide a thorough understanding of the needs. This is true, but it is a very good example of how complex needs can be and makes the case for modeling. If the modeling was not carried out, then the different interpretations of each need may become hidden and would not be considered at this point. This hidden complexity almost always leads to problems later on in the life cycle when these different interpretations come to light.

Another source of contexts that should always form part of a thorough needs modeling exercise is that of the system structure. In order to illustrate this, consider the following diagram.

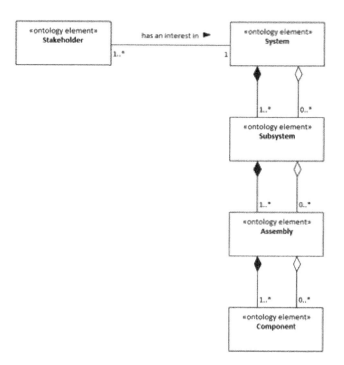

Figure 6.15 – Context Definition View based on system structure

The diagram in *Figure 6.15* shows how this view is the same type of view as the one in *Figure 6.14* but it looks very different as the emphasis in this view is on the system structure, rather than the stakeholders. Indeed, notice how **System** was present in *Figure 6.14* as a single block with the stakeholders being shown in detail, whereas **Stakeholder** is present in *Figure 6.15* and the system is shown in detail.

When considering contexts based on stakeholders, each type of stakeholder gives rise to its own context. When considering contexts based on system structure, then it is each level in the system hierarchy that gives rise to a context.

Now that these Context Definition Views have been defined, it is now possible to look at the contexts themselves and to consider use case modeling, which will be discussed in the next section.

Visualizing contexts

The previous section identified a number of contexts and this section will look at how each context can be modeled. This requires looking at use cases and for each need, a SysML use case diagram will be used to model these use cases. The SysML use case diagram has been seen already in this book, particularly when looking at contexts for framework and viewpoint definitions, but they were only considered at a very high level. In this section, use case diagrams will be discussed in detail and the various modeling constructs will be illustrated based on the existing car example.

The SysML use case diagram is one of the most widely used diagrams but it is very often misused or is not used correctly. The main reason for this is that use case diagrams are intended to be very simple, which leads to the misconception that they are easy to produce. The simplicity of a good use case diagram can, therefore, be deceptive as it can take a lot of effort and structured thinking to get them right.

The use case diagram has four main modeling constructs, which are as follows:

- **Use case**: Each SysML use case represents a conceptual use case from the ontology. (This leads to confusion as the two terms are the same! Note that when capitalized, use case refers to the ontology element, whereas when in lower case, use case refers to the SysML modeling element.) Each SysML use case is visualized by an ellipse in the use case diagram.

- **Actor**: Each SysML actor represents a stakeholder from the ontology. Each actor is visualized by a stick person in the use case diagram.

- **Boundary, which represents the actual context**: Each boundary is visualized using a large rectangle that encapsulates use cases and that has actors outside.

- **Relationships, which represent relationships between use cases and between a use case and actor**: These are represented by various lines, depending on the nature of the relationship. These will be discussed in more detail later in this section.

One of the ways that SysML use case diagrams are typically used is to capture source needs in the form of SysML use cases. This is often seen as a somewhat straightforward exercise and consists of taking source needs and redrawing each one in an ellipse so that it becomes a SysML use case, and then joining these up with SysML actors. The result of such an exercise will often look something like the following diagram.

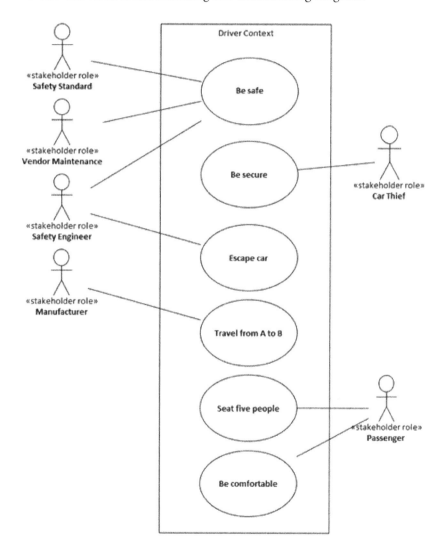

Figure 6.16 – Example of how not to create SysML use case diagrams

The diagram in *Figure 6.16* shows an example of how not to create a SysML use case diagram. The reasons why this diagram is unacceptable are discussed ahead.

The SysML use case diagram is one of the most widely used of all the SysML diagrams, but is almost certainly the most badly used of all the diagrams! This is mainly because of the confusion about what exactly a SysML use case represents.

In the diagram in *Figure 6.16*, a set of initial need descriptions has been taken and, essentially, this has been redrawn using a SysML use case diagram by creating a SysML use case for each need description. Indeed, consider the two use cases **Be safe** and **Travel from A to B** and then compare them to the need descriptions from *Figure 6.11*. It should be very clear that these are the same. The SysML use cases shown here, therefore, directly represent the need descriptions that were initially identified. This is fundamentally wrong as the SysML use cases should be representing use cases from the ontology, not need descriptions.

This can be quite confusing due to the same terms being used in SysML and in the modeling world, so consider the following points:

- Each need is described by a single need description. This is taken directly from the ontology definition view in *Figure 6.1*.
- Each need is described by one or more use cases, via a context. This is also taken directly from the ontology definition view in *Figure 6.1*.

The difference, therefore, between the ontology elements of need description and use case is that the use case is based on context, whereas the need description is not.

Now consider the SysML use case diagram and its associated SysML use cases:

- Each SysML use case must represent the ontology element of a use case (a description of a need in context).
- Each SysML use case must not represent the ontology element of need description directly, as there is no context defined.

The first major problem with the diagram in *Figure 6.16* is that the SysML use cases are representing need descriptions and not use cases.

The second major problem with the diagram in *Figure 6.16* is concerned with the fundamentals of systems engineering and systems thinking. The diagram here has no relationships between the SysML use cases and, therefore, there is no indication of the complexity of the view that is being shown. One of the key aspects of modeling is that modeling will identify areas of complexity due to the fact that relationships between key model elements are shown visually and are not ignored, which leads to hidden complexity.

There are several basic types of relationship between SysML use cases that may be used to identify relationships and dependencies between SysML use cases, as shown in the following diagram:

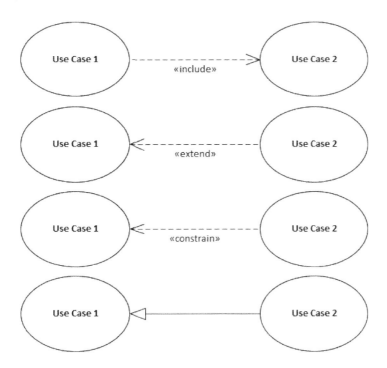

Figure 6.17 – Basic SysML use case diagram relationships

The diagram in *Figure 6.17* shows the basic SysML use case diagram relationship visualized using a SysML use case diagram.

There are four basic types of relationship that may be used between SysML use cases, which are as follows:

- The <<**include**>> relationship. This is read as **Use Case 1 includes Use Case 2**. This means that use case 1 will always contain use case 2 or, to put this another way, in order to satisfy use case 1, then use case 2 must also be satisfied. This may be thought of as a mandatory dependency between the two SysML use cases.

- The <<**extend**>> relationship. This is read as **Use Case 2 extends the functionality of Use Case 1**. This means that use case 1 will sometimes contain use case 2, depending on the circumstances and specific conditions. To put this another way, it may be read that in order to satisfy use case 1, it is sometimes necessary to satisfy use case 2. This may be thought of as an optional dependency between the two SysML use cases.

- The <<**constrain**>> relationship. This is read as **Use Case 2 constrains Use Case 1**. To put this another way, it means that use case 2 will limit the way that use case 1 can be realized.

- The **generalization/specialization** relationship. This is read as **Use Case 2 is a type of Use Case 1** or **Use Case 1 has a type of Use Case 2**. This works in exactly the same way as the generalization/specialization from the block definition diagram, including inheritance on the specialization.

These four basic types of relationships allow dependencies between the SysML use cases to be defined and provides a powerful mechanism for increasing the understanding of the underlying use cases.

There is one other type of relationship that is drawn between actors and SysML use cases and that identifies some sort of interest in a particular SysML use case by a specific actor.

In order to illustrate how these relationships work, consider the following diagram, which expands upon *Figure 6.15* by adding some new use cases but, more importantly, shows how the relationships may be used.

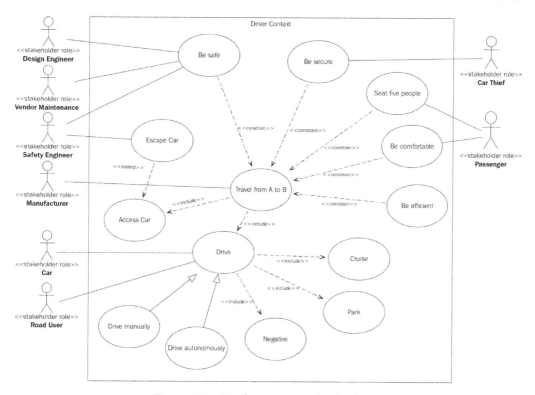

Figure 6.18 – Need context view for the driver

Figure 6.18 shows that there are many interesting facets to this diagram from a modeling point of view. Firstly, the need context view represents a single context. In this case, the context is based on the point of view of the **Driver** stakeholder. When describing a context based on stakeholders, the context must be based on one of the stakeholders that exist in the Context Definition View; in the case of this example, this is the diagram shown in *Figure 6.14*.

Potentially, each stakeholder from the Context Definition View may have its own context, which will result in there being a need context view for each one of the stakeholders.

The name of the context – in this case, **Driver** – is written inside the boundary box (the large rectangle) on the diagram. The fact that the use case diagram has a boundary shows that it is representing a context. It is possible to have use case diagrams that do not have boundaries and, therefore, do not represent a context. In such cases, these use case diagrams will be decompositions of higher-level use cases from another use case diagram. In this way, it is possible to need context use case diagrams but, ultimately, the highest level must be a context with its own boundary.

The boundary, therefore, indicates a context and, as a result of this, the associated stakeholder will not be shown on the diagram. For this example, there is no need to show the **Driver** stakeholder on the diagram, as the whole diagram itself is representing the driver's point of view or context.

The boundary shows the SysML use cases that are relevant to the context inside the boundary and the actors that have an interest in the context sit outside the boundary of the context. If a stakeholder has an interest in a context, it is represented by a SysML actor and then an association is drawn between the actor symbol (stick person) and the SysML use cases that it has an interest in. This is shown graphically by a straight, unadorned line and examples of this can be seen in *Figure 6.18*, such as between **Safety Standard** and **Be safe**, and **Vendor Maintenance** and **Be safe**, among others.

When reading a SysML use case diagram, it is useful to look for the highest-level SysML use case as a start point. In this case, it is the **Travel from A to B** use case. This is because it has its own inclusions, but is not included in any higher-level use cases. The use cases in this diagram, therefore, may be read in the following way:

- **Travel from A to B includes Drive and Access car**: The <<include>> relationship means that the two included use cases must always be satisfied in order for **Travel from A to B** to be satisfied.

- **Travel from A to B is constrained by Be safe, Be secure, Seat five people, Be comfortable, and Be efficient**: This means that the constraining use case will limit the way that **Travel from A to B** can be realized. For example, it would be possible to satisfy the **Travel from A to B** use case by producing a system where the passengers are balanced precariously on top of the car. Although this would satisfy **Travel from A to B**, it would not satisfy **Be safe** and therefore would limit how **Travel from A to B** could be realized.

- **Access car is extended by Escape car**: This means that **Escape car** is not always part of **Access car** but may be depending on certain conditions. In this case, the conditions may be related to an emergency occurring such as crashing the car. Extensions are often used for atypical conditions that, in an ideal world, will never have to be satisfied but, for safety (in this case), must still be considered.

- **There are two types of Drive, which are Drive manually and Drive autonomously**: Each of these types will include all three of the inclusions that sit below **Drive**. Any differences between the two specializations may be added to their specific use cases.

- **Drive includes Navigate, Park, and Cruise**: Again, these use standard <<include>> relationships as discussed previously in this list.

These relationships are very important and provide a more complete understanding of the use cases. In fact, changing one of the relationships can completely change the overall meaning of the diagram. Say, for example, the **Navigate** use case had an <<**extend**>> relationship, rather than an <<**include**>>. This would mean that navigation would not be needed all of the time, whereas with the original <<**include**>> it would always be needed.

Exploring different contexts

The defining feature of a use case, as opposed to a need description, is that use cases have context and, therefore, may take on different interpretations, depending on the viewpoint of the stakeholder. In this section, this will be explored in more detail and some examples of these different interpretations will be provided. In order to illustrate this, we will consider the use case **Be safe** and explore its meaning from several contexts. The SysML use case **Be safe** has been created from the need descriptions in *Figure 6.10* but, in order for it to become a true modeling use case (from the ontology), it may take on a different meaning according to its context.

The first context that will be considered is that of the **Driver** and is shown in the following diagram.

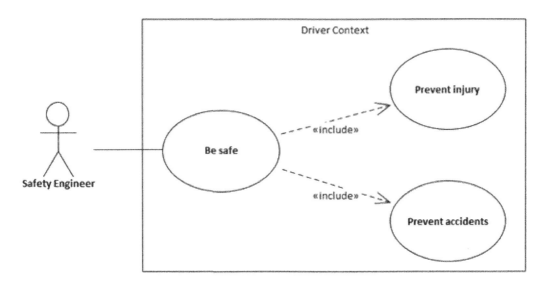

Figure 6.19 – Need Context View focusing on Be safe from the Driver context

The diagram in *Figure 6.19* shows the **Need Context View** from the **Driver** context that focuses on the **Be safe** use case, and that is visualized using a SysML use case diagram.

The exact meaning of the **Be safe** use case may be explored by adding on additional use cases and adding in the relevant relationship to **Be safe**.

From the **Driver** Context, it can be seen that **Be safe** has two inclusions, which are: **Prevent injury** and **Prevent accidents**.

Understanding the context is quite straightforward: just imagine that you are the driver in this example and ask the question what does **Be safe** mean to you? When this is answered, it provides a true use case, that is to say, a specific interpretation of the **Be safe** use case from the point of view of the driver.

Notice that the **Safety Engineer** stakeholder is represented here by a SysML actor that sits outside the boundary of the context. This will become important in the next discussion when the context of the **Safety Engineer** is considered.

Now consider the same use case but from a different context, as shown in the following diagram.

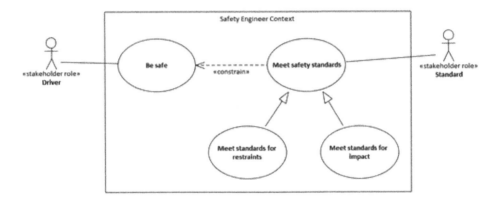

Figure 6.20 – Need Context View focusing on Be safe from the Safety Engineer context

The diagram in *Figure 6.20* shows that, in order to understand the use case of **Be safe** from the **Safety Engineer** context, you should carry out the same exercise – imagine that you are the safety engineer and ask the same question: what does **Be safe** mean to you? In this context, the answer is that **Be safe** is all about meeting safety standards, which is shown by the constraint **Meet safety standards**. In fact, this then goes one step further by specifying two different types of safety standards by introducing two new use cases: **Meet standards for restraints** and **Meet standards for impact**.

Notice here the presence of the **Driver** stakeholder, which is shown by a SysML actor outside the boundary of the system. This stakeholder must exist here as *Figure 6.17* showed the context for the **Driver** and the **Safety Engineer** stakeholder was shown as an actor. If, therefore, the **Driver** context has an interest from the **Safety Engineer** stakeholder, then the converse must also be true – the **Safety Engineer** context must have the **Driver** stakeholder as an actor outside the context boundary. Indeed, the association line between the **Safety Engineer** actor and the **Be safe** use case in *Figure 6.17* is the same line as between the **Driver** actor and the **Be safe** use case in *Figure 6.18*. This shows that the two use cases are connected in some way. In this example, these two use cases have the same name, but this needn't be the case. In fact, this is a powerful way to identify which use cases are related and, therefore, if they are complementary, the same, or in conflict with each other.

The following diagram shows the same SysML use case from another context that will allow its own interpretation to be understood.

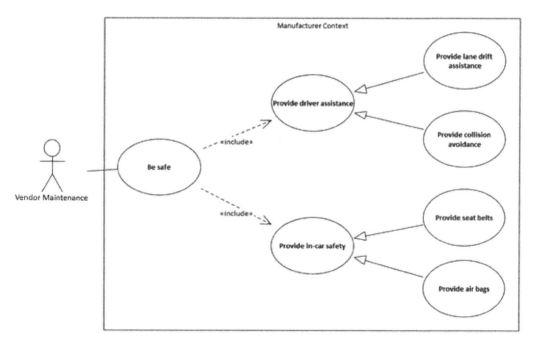

Figure 6.21 – Need Context View focusing on Be safe from the Manufacturer context

The diagram in *Figure 6.21* shows the **Need Context View** from the manufacturer context. The emphasis is on providing features for the car that relate to safety. Again, this is a very different interpretation of the **Be safe** use case.

Notice that there is a stakeholder on the diagram that is represented by the **Vendor Maintenance** actor. This will mean that there will be a context for the **Vendor Maintenance** stakeholder and that **Manufacturer** will appear on this as a stakeholder. Indeed, this can be seen in the following diagram.

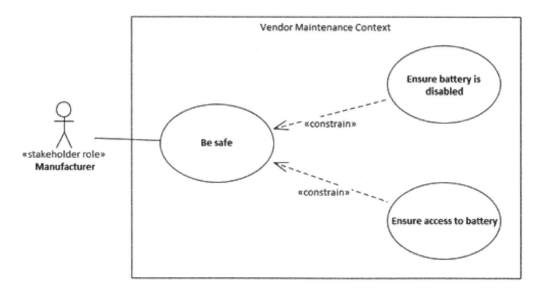

Figure 6.22 – Need Context View focusing on Be safe from the Vendor Maintenance context

The diagram in *Figure 6.22* shows that, in this context, the emphasis is on making sure that the car is safe when it is being maintained.

All four of these examples demonstrate that there can be many interpretations of a single need that are captured in the model using use cases. It is essential that multiple contexts are considered in order to gain a thorough understanding of the needs of the system.

Contexts based on stakeholders are an essential consideration as they provide a very good understanding of exactly what the different stakeholders' expectations of the system are. Even if the final goal is to understand the needs of the system, it is impossible to do this successfully without understanding what the stakeholders require of the system.

When considering the system, again, considering context is key to gaining a thorough understanding of what the system needs are. The system context may be based on the level of abstraction of the system, which provides different interpretations of the same need in the form of different use cases.

Consider the need description that is named **Be efficient** and now consider the four different levels of abstraction that were defined for the system in *Figure 6.13*. For each of these levels of abstraction, the following interpretations may apply:

- **System level**: This may be the car itself and **Be efficient** may refer to the car having to travel a minimum number of miles between refueling or recharging.

- **Subsystem level**: This may refer to the motor in the car and **Be efficient** may refer to delivering a certain power throughput for a given use of fuel.

- **Assembly level**: This may refer to an electronic motor control assembly, which may use different algorithms to achieve different efficiency modes.

- **Component level**: This may apply to a specific bolt, which may have to be made of an especially light material that will reduce the weight of the whole car, making it more efficient.

Again, different interpretations and, therefore, use cases, for different contexts, this time based on the levels of abstraction.

The concept of context is an essential one and it leads directly to the next topic, which is validation. If it is accepted that different interpretations of a single need exist (use cases), then the ways that it is demonstrated that these needs have been satisfied will all differ, depending on the use case. This whole topic of validation is addressed by considering scenarios, which will be discussed in the next section.

Visualizing scenarios

One of the most important aspects of a systems engineering project is to be able to demonstrate that the original needs of the system have been satisfied. Satisfying the original needs is referred to as **validation** and a system cannot be accepted into service unless it can be validated.

There is an important distinction that needs to be made clear at this point, as the term validation is often confused with the term verification. The definitions that are used in this book are as follows:

- **Verification** allows us to demonstrate that we have built the system right.

- **Validation** allows us to demonstrate that we have built the right system.

This is a subtle but important difference as it is essential that any system can be verified and validated.

Validation is concerned with demonstrating that the right system has been built or, to put it another way, that it satisfies the original needs. Therefore, it is important to have a thorough understanding of all the original needs.

The previous section introduced the concept of context and discussed how different contexts lead to different interpretations of the same need. Therefore, if the interpretation of needs may be different, then it becomes important that all of these different interpretations can be satisfied. As a result of this, the needs of the system are satisfied by demonstrating that their associated use case can be satisfied.

The mechanism that is used in modeling to perform validation is to create a number of scenarios for each use case.

A scenario may be realized in two different ways:

- **Operational scenarios,** which show a sequence of events or actions that results in a specific outcome. These operational scenarios are typically sequential in nature.

- **Performance scenarios,** which allow parameters of a system to be changed in order to demonstrate that it can satisfy specific outcomes. These performance scenarios are typically mathematical in nature.

SysML may be used to visualize both types of scenarios, as will be discussed in the next two sections.

All the SysML use cases in each context must be validated using either type of scenario, or both.

Visualizing operational scenarios

Operational scenarios are a very powerful and essential part of any needs modeling exercise. They allow different options to be explored by asking *what if* for each of the use cases. The following diagram shows an example of an operational scenario.

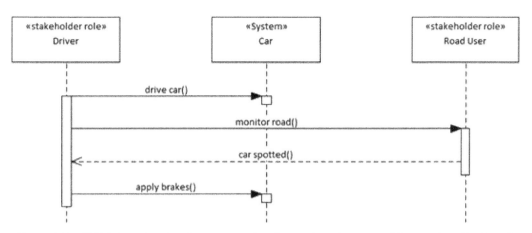

Figure 6.23 – Validation view showing an operational scenario – the successful manual application of brakes for the Drive manually use case

The diagram in *Figure 6.23* shows that a scenario is defined as an instance of a use case. Instances of blocks have already been discussed in *Chapter 2, Model-Based Systems Engineering*, and were used to represent a real-life example of a block. Instances of SysML use cases work in exactly the same way in that a number of real-life examples of how a use case may be realized are explored.

The first step is to identify a SysML use case that needs to be validated. In the example here, the SysML use case that has been selected is **Drive manually** from the **Driver** context that is shown in *Figure 6.18*. The next step is to identify any stakeholders that have an interest in the selected use case. In this example, it can be seen that both **Car** and **Road User** are related to the **Drive manually** use case and are inherited via its parent use case, **Drive**.

It is now possible to create a sequence diagram using the context stakeholder as a SysML lifeline and the two related stakeholders as other lifelines.

Next, it is necessary to think of an unintended outcome of the selected use case, give it a name, and then think of a sequence of events that leads up to this outcome being realized.

In this example, the scenario may be named the successful manual application of brakes. This name sums up the intended outcome nicely and succinctly.

Next, the events are drawn onto the diagram. The first event is an interaction between the **Driver** and the **Car**, which has been named **drive car**. Next, there is an interaction between the **Driver** and a **Road User**, which is called **monitor road**, and then there is a direct response to this, which is **car spotted**. The **Driver** then interacts with the car again with the **apply brakes** interaction.

When defining scenarios for use cases, the language that is used to name the interactions is deliberately written at a high, non-technical level. The language used should be one that the target stakeholder who will be looking at this diagram will understand. At this point, the main goal is to make the scenario easy to understand and communicate, so the language is written with this in mind.

The sequence diagram must be consistent with the SysML use case diagram, and the following SysML consistency checks must be applied:

- Each lifeline on the sequence diagram must be an actor or boundary on the use case diagram.

- Each interaction on the sequence diagram must be an instance of an association between an actor and use case on the use case diagram.

If the two diagrams are not consistent, then either the sequence diagram or the use case diagram needs to be changed to make them consistent. For example, if there was a lifeline on the sequence diagram that was not on the use case diagram, then it would either need to be added to the use case diagram or removed from the sequence diagram.

It is usual to show multiple scenarios for each use case and to explore how the model can react to different events for the same outcome to understand how the system must behave under typical conditions. These scenarios are often referred to as **sunny-day scenarios** as they represent everything going well. A very powerful aspect of this is to explore what happens when something goes wrong and to explore so-called **rainy-day scenarios**. An example of this is shown in the following diagram:

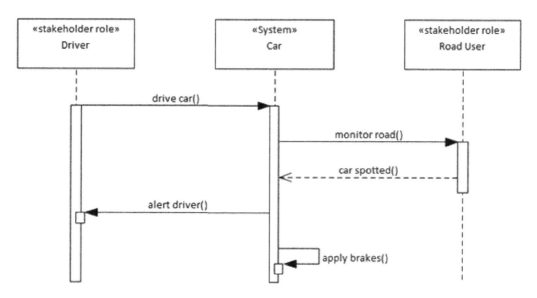

Figure 6.24 – Validation view showing an operational scenario – the automatic application of brakes for the Drive manually use case

The diagram in *Figure 6.24* shows a scenario for the same use case as the scenario in *Figure 6.22* but it looks quite different. In this example, the scenario considers what happens if the **Driver** is driving the **Car** and the **Car** itself spots another **Road User** and then applies the brakes itself. This scenario is titled the automatic application of brakes.

The scenario starts in the same way, with the **Driver** interacting with the **Car**, but this time, it is the **Car** that is monitoring the road for other **Road Users**. The brakes are still applied but, this time, the brakes are applied by the **Car**, rather than the **Driver**.

The number of scenarios generated for each use case can also be interesting and reveal something about the level of abstraction of each use case. Consider the following three rules of thumb:

- **Only one scenario for a single use case**: The use case is too detailed and should be abstracted up into a higher-level use case.

- **Between two and nine scenarios for a single use case**: A good number of scenarios demonstrating a clear understanding of the use case.

- **More than 10 scenarios for a single use case**: The use case is too high-level and should be broken down into lower-level use cases.

These three rules are actually quite powerful as they provide another level of checking for the use case diagram.

The second type of scenarios, performance scenarios, will be discussed in the next section.

Visualizing performance scenarios

Performance scenarios work in the same way as operational scenarios in that they allow different what-ifs to be explored. However, rather than being based on a sequence of events with a specific outcome, they consider how values of parameters may be varied in order to result in a specific outcome.

Performance scenarios are visualized using SysML parametric diagrams but, in order for a parametric diagram to be used, there must also be an associated block definition diagram that defines a number of parametric constraints. An example of this can be seen in the following diagram.

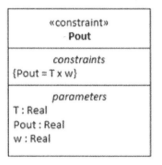 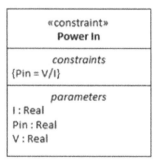 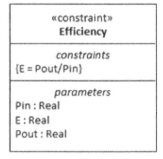

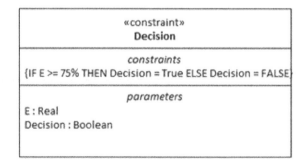

Figure 6.25 – Validation view showing constraint definition for the Be efficient use case

The diagram in *Figure 6.25* shows a validation view that shows constraint definitions for the **Be efficient** use case, and that is visualized using a SysML block definition diagram.

For this example, consider the use case **Be efficient** from the **Driver** context in *Figure 6.17*.

The diagram here shows four blocks that are stereotyped as **<<constraint>>**, which is a standard SysML construct. Each constraint block has three compartments:

- **Name**: The name of the constraint
- **Constraint definition**: The definition of the constraints using an equation, heuristic, rule, or any other notation
- **Parameter definition**: The definition of each of the parameters that is used in the constraint definition

In this example, there are four constraints that have been defined:

- Power out (**Pout**), defined by the product of torque and angular velocity
- Power in (**Pin**), defined by the product of voltage and current
- Efficiency (**E**), defined by the ration of **Pout/Pin**
- **Decision**, which is defined by a simple heuristic

These constraints may be predefined as part of a standard library or defined specifically for the system. In either case, it is possible to build up a library of constraints that may be used across multiple projects.

The constraints are used by instantiating them and then connecting them together to form a network using a SysML **parametric diagram**, an example of which can be seen in the following diagram.

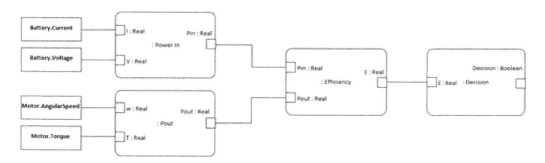

Figure 6.26 – Validation view showing parametric usage for the Be efficient use case

The diagram in *Figure 6.26* shows a validation view for the **Be efficient** use case that is visualized using a SysML parametric diagram.

In SysML, parametric diagrams comprise three main elements, which are as follows:

- Parametric, which is visualized with a box with rounded corners. Each parametric is an instantiation of one of the constraints that were defined in *Figure 6.24*. Note the use of the colon to separate the name of the parametric usage from its type (the constraint). Each parametric also has a number of parameters associated with it that are visualized by the small rectangles on the inside of the main box.

- Parameter blocks, which are visualized by the rectangles on the left-hand side of the diagram. These reference a block from somewhere in the model and then a specific property of the block that is the origin of the required parameter. The notation that is used to separate the block name from its property is a full stop (.) with the block name on the left and its property on the right.

- Connections, which are visualized by lines. The connections link together the parameters from the model with the specific parameters of the parametric constraint.

These parametric diagrams show the network of parametric constraints and their connections. In this way, it is possible to change some of the input parameters and to monitor the resulting output. For example, it would be possible to try different scenarios where the parametrics represent different batteries to see if the car would still satisfy the **Be efficient** use case.

The potential value of parametric diagrams is very large indeed; however, this value is often not realized due to the widely varying capabilities of different tools. The parametric diagrams form a natural bridge between the visual world of SysML and the mathematical world of, for example, simulation. It is often desirable, therefore, to be able to use such parametric diagrams in conjunction with mathematical tools in order to realize the full benefits of the model. This then becomes a major tool issue as the interoperability of the tools becomes of paramount concern.

For real projects, the use of operational scenarios and performance scenarios together is a very powerful mechanism that allows many different scenarios to be explored and, hence, the underlying use cases and needs to be satisfied. If it is possible to define these scenarios and then obtain agreement from the relevant stakeholders that they are correct, then they will form the heart of the validation and, hence, acceptance of the final system. This is a very good thing to have defined as soon as possible in any project, as all subsequent design work may be demonstrated to trace back and satisfy these scenarios, providing continuous validation through the project life cycle.

Life cycle and processes

The needs modeling that has been discussed in this chapter is carried out during a typical development life cycle. With this in mind, consider the following development life cycle model, which was introduced in *Chapter 4, Life Cycles*.

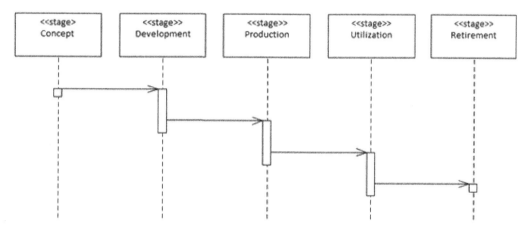

Figure 6.27 – Example development life cycle model

The diagram in *Figure 6.27* shows an example development life cycle that is visualized using a SysML sequence diagram. The stages in this life cycle model are those from ISO 15288 and the execution of the stages is a simple linear sequence.

The obvious place for the needs modeling to occur is during the first stage in the diagram, **Concept**. This is where the majority of the needs modeling will take place, but the needs will also be revisited throughout the entire life cycle as needs will change as time goes on and, very importantly, some of the contexts associated with the needs may change.

The approach to needs modeling must map onto best practice and this is an example of how the process modeling from *Chapter 4, Life Cycles*, may be used for compliance. Using the seven-views approach that was discussed in *Chapter 5, Systems Engineering Processes*, the following process content view may be used, which was abstracted from ISO 15288.

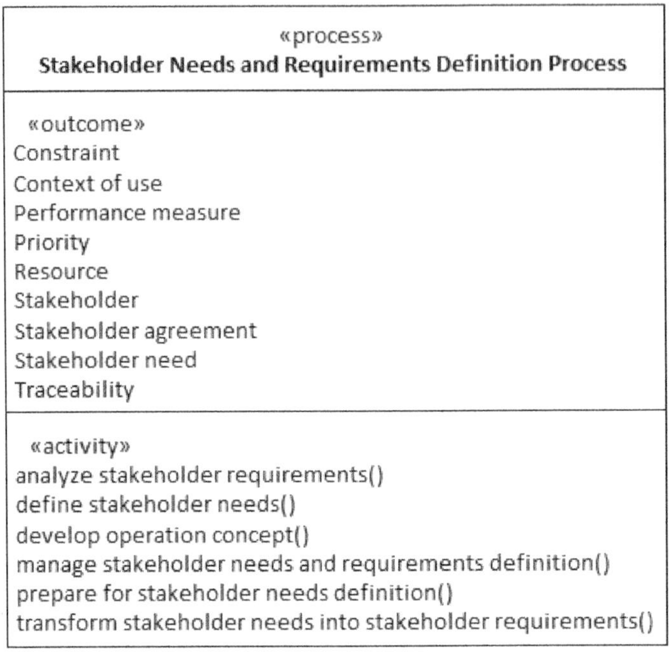

Figure 6.28 – Process context view for the Stakeholder Needs and Requirements Definition Process from ISO 15288

The diagram in *Figure 6.28* shows the process context view for the Stakeholder Needs and Requirements Definition Process from ISO 15288 and is visualized using a SysML block definition diagram.

The whole process is represented by the SysML block, whereas the outcomes are shown using SysML properties and the activities are shown using SysML operations. The process shown here represents the minimum recommended activities and resultant outcomes rather than a prescriptive approach. If it is possible to map the needs modeling techniques that have been discussed in this chapter to this best-practice process, then it provides both credibility and provenance to the modeling approach.

The activities that are required by ISO 15288 map onto the modeling as follows:

- **Prepare for stakeholder needs definition**: In modeling terms, this relates to identifying the source elements that will be used for the needs modeling and will result in the creation of the source element view.

- **Define stakeholder needs**: This relates to capturing the initial needs in the form of the need description view.

- **Analyze stakeholder requirements**: This relates to analyzing the contexts, which involves both identifying the relevant contexts and then defining each of the contexts. This will result in a number of context definition views being created and then their associated need context views being developed.

- **Develop operation concept**: This relates to developing the operational scenarios and performance scenarios that will allow the concept of operation to be explored. This will result in the creation of various validation views.

- **Transform stakeholder needs into stakeholder requirements**: This relates to applying the same modeling techniques at a different level of abstraction. For example, the ontology would have two types of needs defined: stakeholder needs and stakeholder requirements, which would be related to each other. Each of these two types of needs could have any or all of the need views defined for them.

- **Manage stakeholder needs and requirements definition**: This relates to the overall management and traceability of the needs model. Thanks to the ontology, traceability is inherent in the model and the framework view definitions provide all of the management, in terms of the rationale, content, and structure of each view along with the view traceability.

The outcomes that are required by ISO 15288 are mapped onto the model views as follows:

- **Constraint**: This maps onto any use cases that have a <<**constraint**>> relationship associated with them.

- **Context if use**: This maps onto the operational scenarios.

- **Performance measure**: This maps onto the performance scenarios.

- **Priority**: This is a property of a need on the need description view.

- **Resource**: Again, this will map onto a property of a need on the need description view.

- **Stakeholder**: This will map onto the stakeholders on the context definition views.

- **Stakeholder agreement**: The combined set of views will provide the stakeholder agreement.

- **Stakeholder need**: This maps onto the need description views.

- **Traceability**: This is captured in the framework by the ontology definition view and the viewpoint relationship view.

These modeling views may now be collected together and defined from the needs perspective, which will be discussed in the next section.

Defining the framework

The views that have been created so far represent the center part of the *MBSE in a slide* diagram, which was discussed in detail in *Chapter 2, Model-Based Systems Engineering*. Each of the views has been visualized using SysML, which represents the right-hand side of *MBSE in a slide*. These views combine together to form the overall model, but it is essential that these views are all consistent, otherwise they are not views, but pictures! This is where the left-hand side of *MBSE in a slide* comes into play as it is important that the definition of all of the views is captured in the framework. The framework comprises the ontology and a set of viewpoints; therefore, it is now time to make sure that these viewpoints are defined thoroughly and correctly, which is the aim of this section.

Defining the viewpoints in the framework

It was discussed in *Chapter 2, Model-Based Systems Engineering*, that it is necessary to ask a number of questions for each view to ensure that it is a valid view. There is also a set of questions that must be asked of the whole framework, as well as the views, and the combination of these results in a set of questions that allow the whole framework to be defined. It is worthwhile, therefore, to have a reminder of what these questions are:

- Why is the framework required? This question may be answered using a **Framework Context View**.

- What are the overall concepts and terminology used for the framework? This question may be answered using an **Ontology Definition View**.

- What views are necessary as part of the framework? This question may be answered using a **Viewpoint Relationship View**.

- Why is each view needed? This question may be answered using a **Viewpoint Context View**.

- What is the structure and content of each view? This question may be answered using a **Viewpoint Definition View**.

- What rules should be applied? This question may be answered using a **Ruleset Definition View**.

When these questions are answered, then it can be said that a framework has been defined. Each of these questions can be answered using a special set of views that is collectively known as the **Framework for Architecture Frameworks (FAF)** [Holt and Perry 2019]. At this point, simply think about creating a specific view to answer each question, as described in the following sections.

Defining the Framework Context View

The **Framework Context View** specifies why the whole framework is needed in the first instance. It will identify the relevant stakeholders that have an interest in the framework and also identify what benefits each of the stakeholders hopes to achieve from the framework:

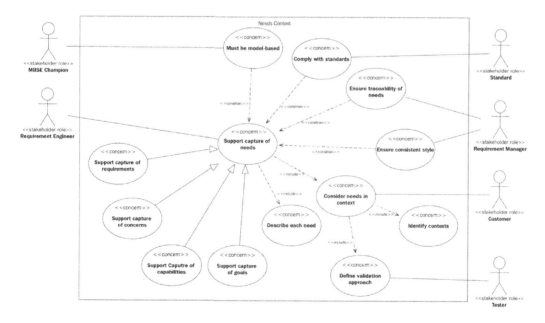

Figure 6.29 – Framework Context View for the needs framework

The diagram in *Figure 6.29* shows the **Framework Context View** for the needs framework, which is visualized using a SysML use case diagram.

Note the application of the use case diagram here to capture the context, the approach of which was described in this chapter. This is the SysML diagram that will be used from this point forward in this book to define any context.

This diagram is read as follows:

- The main use case is to **Support capture of needs**, which is done in four different ways: **Support capture of concerns**, **Support capture of requirements**, **Support capture of capabilities**, and **Support capture of goals**.

- The main use case includes the lower-level use cases to **Describe each need** and to **Consider needs in Context**, which itself includes both **Define validation approach** and **Identify contexts**.

- The main use case is also constrained in four ways: **Must be model-based**, **Comply with standards**, **Ensure traceability of needs**, and **Ensure consistent style**.

Notice that in this diagram, each of the SysML use cases is stereotyped as a **<<concern>>**. A concern is a need that relates specifically to a framework or one of its viewpoints.

Defining the Ontology Definition View

The Ontology Definition View captures all the concepts and associated terminology associated with the framework in the form of an ontology. This has already been done as the ontology for the life cycle-related views was defined in *Figure 6.5*. The ontology elements shown on this view provide all of the stereotypes that have been used for the actual views that have been created so far in this chapter.

Ontology elements that are related will often be collected into a **Perspective**, as was discussed in other chapters. In this chapter, a new **Perspective** has been created that relates to needs.

Defining the Viewpoint Relationship View

The Viewpoint Relationship View identifies which views are needs and, for each set of views, identifies a viewpoint that will contain its definition. Remember that a viewpoint may be thought of as a type of template for a view. These viewpoints may be collected together into a perspective, that is, simply a collection of viewpoints with a common theme. In this chapter, the emphasis has been on defining a set of views' relations to life cycles, therefore it is appropriate to create a **Need Perspective**. The basic set of views that has been discussed so far is shown in the following view:

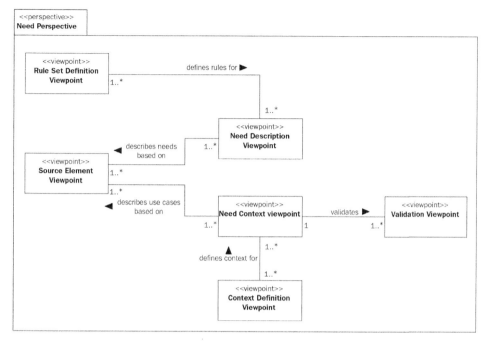

Figure 6.30 – Viewpoint Relationship View for the need perspective

The diagram in *Figure 6.30* shows the Viewpoint Relationship View for the need perspective using a SysML block definition diagram.

The need perspective is shown using a SysML package, stereotyped as **<<perspective>>**, which simply collects together a number of viewpoints. There are six viewpoints that are defined in the needs perspective:

- **Source Element Viewpoint**, which identifies all the sources for the needs that will form the model. Both the **Need Description Viewpoint** and the **Need Context Viewpoint** are based on the **Source Element Viewpoint**.

- **Rule Set Definition Viewpoint**, which defines the rules that will constrain the information contained in the **Need Description Viewpoint**.

- **Need Description Viewpoint**, which provides a text-based description of each individual need and is constrained by the **Rule Set Definition Viewpoint** and based on the **Source Element Viewpoint**.

- **Need Context Viewpoint**, which describes a set of use cases that are based on the information contained in the **Source Element Viewpoint**, and has its context defined by the **Context Definition Viewpoint**. The **Need Context Viewpoint** is also validated by the **Validation Viewpoint**.

- **Context Definition Viewpoint**, which defines the context for the various **Need Context Viewpoints**.

- **Validation Viewpoint**, which validates the use cases that are defined in the **Need Context Viewpoint**.

Each of the viewpoints that have been identified here may now be described by its own Viewpoint Context View and its Viewpoint Definition View.

Defining the Viewpoint Context View

The Viewpoint Context View specifies why a particular viewpoint and, therefore, its set of views, is needed in the first instance. It will identify the relevant stakeholders that have an interest in the viewpoint and also identify what benefits each of the stakeholders hopes to achieve from the framework.

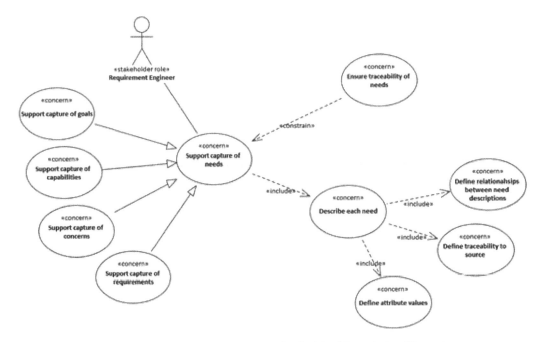

Figure 6.31 – Viewpoint Context View for the Need Description Viewpoint

The diagram in *Figure 6.31* shows the Viewpoint Context View for the Need Description View, visualized using a SysML use case diagram.

Notice that, at first glance, this diagram looks very similar to the one in *Figure 6.29* and this makes sense as each of the Viewpoint Context Views must be consistent with the higher-level framework Context View. Indeed, it is quite common for the higher-level use cases on the Viewpoint Context View to be taken directly from the Framework Context View, as is the case here.

The main differences are what is included in this view and what is omitted from this view:

- The diagram includes the use case **Describe each need**, which is then broken down into three lower-level use cases, which are: **Define attribute values**, **Define traceability to source**, and **Define relationships between need descriptions**.

- The diagram deliberately excludes the use case *Define need in context* from *Figure 6.29* as this is not one of the concerns for this viewpoint but, rather, will be included in the Viewpoint Context View for the Need Context Viewpoint.

Care must be taken here to include only the use cases that are relevant to the viewpoint under scrutiny, as this is the whole point of a context.

Now that the reason why the viewpoint must exist has been established, the Viewpoint Definition View may be considered.

Defining the Viewpoint Definition View

The Viewpoint Definition View defines the ontology elements that are included in the viewpoint and shows the following:

- Which ontology elements are allowed in the viewpoint

- Which ontology elements are optional in the viewpoint

- Which ontology elements are not allowed in the viewpoint

The Viewpoint Definition View focuses on a single viewpoint and particular care and attention must be paid to not just the ontology elements that are selected, but also to the relationships that exist between these ontology elements.

An example of a Viewpoint Definition View for the Need Description Viewpoint is shown in the following diagram.

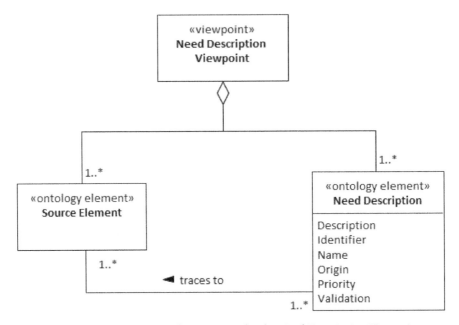

Figure 6.32 – Viewpoint Definition View for the Need Description Viewpoint

The diagram in *Figure 6.32* shows the **Viewpoint Definition View for the Need Description Viewpoint**, using a SysML block definition diagram.

This view defines the exact content of what is allowed in all the views that are described by the viewpoint. This viewpoint will always contain the following information:

- **The viewpoint name**, stereotyped by <<**viewpoint**>>, which is the focus of this view. The viewpoint that is identified here must come from the **Viewpoint Relationship View** that was shown in *Figure 6.30*.

- **A number of ontology elements**, stereotyped by <<**ontology element**>>. Each of these ontology elements must come from the **Ontology Definition View**, shown in *Figure 6.1*.

The two ontology elements that are legal on the views associated with this viewpoint are as follows:

- **Source Element**, which represents the origin of the needs

- **Need Description**, which, along with the properties that are shown here, will describe each need

The viewpoints and the ontology elements that are permitted in each viewpoint are constrained by a number of rules, which will be described in the **Ruleset Definition View** for the needs perspective.

Defining the Ruleset Definition View

The **Ruleset Definition View** identifies and defines a number of rules that may be applied to the model to ensure that it is consistent with the framework.

The rules are based primarily on the **Ontology Definition View and the Viewpoint Relationships View**. In each case, the rules are defined by identifying the key relationships and their associated multiplicities that exist:

- Between viewpoints on the **Viewpoint Definition View**

- Between ontology elements on the **Ontology Definition View**

Some examples of these rules are shown in the following diagram.

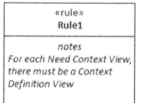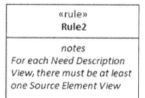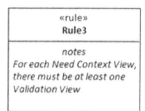

Figure 6.33 – Example Ruleset Definition View

The diagram in *Figure 6.33* shows an example of a **Ruleset Definition View** using a SysML block definition diagram. Each block on the diagram represents a rule that is derived from either the **Ontology Definition View or the Viewpoint Relationship View**.

These rules are defined as follows:

- **For each Need Context View, there must be a Context Definition View**: This rule is derived directly from the **Viewpoint Relationship View** shown in *Figure 6.29*. This rule helps to define how many views associated with each Viewpoint may be created as part of the framework, which is indicated by the multiplicities.

- **For each Need Description View, there must be at least one Source Element View**: This rule is derived directly from the **Viewpoint Relationship View** shown in *Figure 6.30*. This rule helps to establish that the traceability for all need descriptions is mandatory, indicated by the **1…*** multiplicity.

- **For each Need Context View, there must be at least one Validation View**: This rule is derived directly from the **Viewpoint Relationship View** shown in *Figure 6.30*. This rule establishes that validation for each use case that is in the **Need Context View** is mandatory. Otherwise, there is usually a pop-up like, *Error! Reference source not found.*

Notice how the rules are derived from the **Viewpoint Relationship View** and, therefore, the viewpoints and the **Ontology Definition View** and, therefore, the ontology elements. The actual rule descriptions themselves apply to the instances of the viewpoints (views) and instances of the ontology elements.

Of course, any number of other rules may be defined here, but not every relationship will lead to a rule, as this is at the discretion of the modeler.

Summary

In this chapter, the concept of needs has been explored and modeling associated with the different concepts covered has been discussed.

Initially, the importance of the concept of needs and the different types of needs, such as requirements and capabilities, was discussed. This led to understanding how to analyze needs in two ways: by describing each need using text-based properties and descriptions, and by gaining a true understanding of the underlying need by exploring the contexts of each need.

Context was introduced as one of the single most important aspects of needs modeling and, in order to establish this understanding, how important it is to understand the stakeholders that have an interest in the system. Each of these stakeholders has the potential to interpret each need in a different way to all other stakeholders, which is known as a modeling use case.

Each use case, and therefore its related need descriptions, must be validated, and two ways of validation were discussed: performance validation and operational validation, which were modeled using scenarios and captured in validation views.

The importance of best practice was also discussed and this was related to the views by considering a specific process from ISO 15288 and relating the modeling view directly to its activities and outcomes.

Finally, all of these views were captured as part of an overall framework definition using the FAF. This framework itself comprises a number of views that are used to describe the model.

This chapter has shown, therefore, how to take simple, text-based needs and fully explore and understand them using MBSE modeling techniques.

The next chapter moves forward from needs modeling and discusses design and how to model its different aspects.

Self-assessment tasks

1. The concept of a concern was introduced as a need that relates specifically to a framework or viewpoint definition. Revisit *Figure 6.6* and add on the concept of concern.

2. Consider a set of stakeholders that is specific to your organization and capture these in a **Context Definition View**.

3. Choose a single need that relates to any project that you are familiar with and describe it using text by creating a **Need Description View**.

4. Based on your answers to questions 1 and 2, take your need description and consider it from three or four different stakeholders' points of view. For each, create a **Need Context View**.

5. Choose any use case from the **Need Context Views** and define some validation views. Try out performance-based scenarios and operational scenarios. Now compare and contrast each scenario.

6. There is an inconsistency in *Figure 6.31* as an ontology relationship has been omitted from the diagram. Check each ontology element and its relationships and deduce which is missing.

References

- [Holt & Perry 2019]: Holt, JD and Perry, SA. *SysML for Systems Engineering – a model-based approach.* Third edition. IET Publishing, Stevenage, UK. 2019

- [Royce 1970]: Royce, Winston. *Managing the Development of Large Software Systems*, Proceedings of IEEE WESCON, 26 (August): 1–9

7
Modeling the Design

This chapter discusses how solutions may be defined by developing effective designs. Various levels of design abstraction are discussed, such as architectural designs and detailed designs. Also, different aspects of design, such as logical, functional, and physical designs, are introduced, and the relationships between them are defined. There is then a discussion on how designs fit into the systems life cycle and which processes are relevant and how to comply with them. This chapter is, therefore, structured as follows:

- We'll look at defining designs, where different types of design are considered and discussions concerning architectural design and detailed design will be had. These are both important yet different in many ways.

- The three different aspects of designs are introduced and examples are given of logical, functional, and physical system elements and how design views may be used to model each.

- The modeling techniques that may be used for these different types and aspects of design are then related to international best practice, by mapping the various views onto ISO 15288.

- The views that are discussed are then captured in the **Model-Based Systems Engineering (MBSE)** framework, specifically the design perspective that has been developed throughout this book.

Finally, there will be a number of self-assessment tasks for you to carry out to test your achievement of the learning objectives of this chapter.

Defining designs

When considering the development of any system, there are three concepts that may be considered in the early stages of the life cycle:

- **Understanding the need**: This involves identifying the needs of the system, such as the goals, capabilities, and requirements of the system. This was covered in *Chapter 6, Needs and Requirements*. This is typically carried out in the concept stage of the ISO 15288 life cycle.

- **Understanding the problem**: This involves analyzing the needs of the system in order to understand the problem or problem domain. In systems engineering, this is addressed by context modeling and scenario modeling, which were also discussed in *Chapter 6, Needs and Requirements*. This is typically carried out in the concept stage of the ISO 15288 life cycle.

- **Understanding the solution**: This is concerned with solving the problem that arises as a result of understanding the needs of the system. This is typically carried out in the development stage of the ISO 15288 life cycle.

Designs are to do with the third of these three points.

There are many ways to solve a problem and, therefore, there are many techniques that may be applied to designs. It is important to consider not just one but several solutions to a given problem. These different solutions can then be assessed and the most appropriate one can be selected. These different solutions are referred to as **candidate** solutions and they may be considered at any level of design.

In this chapter, we will be looking at some of the modeling techniques that may be applied when carrying out a design.

There are two main levels that a design may be applied at, which are **architectural design** and **detailed design**.

Architectural design

An architectural design, or high-level design, as it is sometimes referred to, is mainly concerned with considering the system as a single entity and how it breaks down into subsystems. These architectural design views are also often conceptual in nature. The following diagram shows the system structural view that was first introduced in *Chapter 2, Model-Based Systems Engineering*, and will form the basis for our discussion of architectural designs:

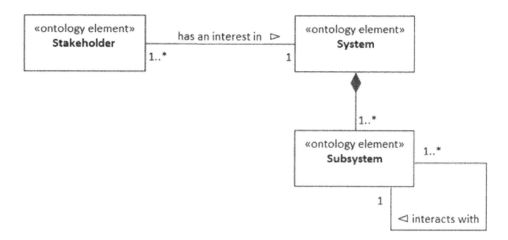

Figure 7.1 – An ontology definition view showing high-level system concepts

The diagram in *Figure 7.1* shows an ontology definition view that shows the high-level system concepts, visualized using a SysML block definition diagram.

An architectural design mainly comprises the following:

- One or more stakeholders interact with the system.
- Each system comprises a number of subsystems, some of which are owned and some of which are not owned.

An architectural design, therefore, is mainly focused on the system and the way that it interacts with entities at the same level of abstraction (stakeholders) and its composition (subsystems). An architectural design solves a problem by considering the system and the associated interfaces.

Any design aspects that are applied at lower levels than this are considered as part of the detailed design.

Detailed design

Whereas an architectural design is concerned with the system and its associated stakeholders and subsystems, a detailed design is concerned with the lower levels of abstraction, as shown in the following diagram:

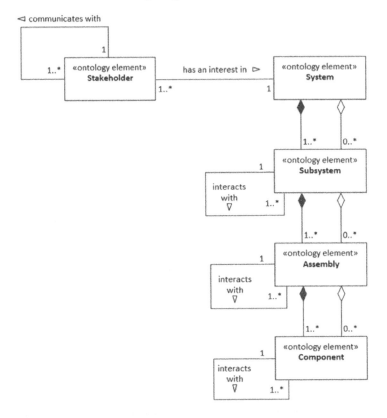

Figure 7.2 – Expanded ontology definition view showing more detailed system concepts

The preceding figure is an expanded ontology definition view that shows more detailed levels of system structure, visualized using a SysML block definition diagram.

A detailed design is concerned with taking each of the subsystems and breaking them down into their constituent parts, in this case, assemblies and their components.

In a detailed design, the focus is on understanding the subsystems, assemblies, and components and their interfaces.

In both design cases, we use the following views to represent the design:

- **System structure views**, where system elements and their relationships are considered

- **System configuration views**, where specific relationships between system elements for individual configurations are considered

- **system behavior views**, where the interactions between system elements are considered

- **Interface identification views**, where the location of the ports on various system elements are considered

- **Interface definition views**, where each individual port and interface is specified

- **Interface behavior views**, where the interactions between ports and interfaces are considered

All of these views were introduced in *Chapter 3, Systems and Interfaces*, and, on top of these, some new views will be introduced that are aimed at functional modeling:

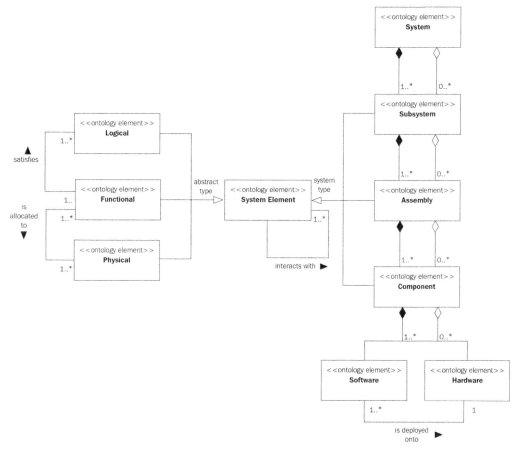

Figure 7.3 – Expanded ontology definition view showing abstract types of system elements

The diagram in *Figure 7.3* shows another ontology definition view that has been expanded to show abstract types of system elements, visualized using a SysML block definition diagram.

The diagram shows that there are three types of system element:

- **Logical system element**: Satisfied by a functional system element.
- **Functional system element**: Satisfies logical system elements. Allocated to one or more physical system elements.
- **Physical system element**: To which functional system elements are allocated.

There is an interesting SysML modeling construct in this diagram, as it can be seen that there are two specialization relationships that emerge from the system element. Usually, these would all be joined with a single generalization, but it is possible to show two completely different types of generalization that are related to the same model element. These two generalizations are differentiated by adding a qualifying term, in this case, **abstract type** and **system type**, which are known as **discriminators**. Therefore, the diagram tells us that there are two different generalizations:

- **Abstract type**, which shows three types of system element that are based on the type of abstraction of the system element
- **system type**, which shows the different types of system elements based on the system hierarchy

When these discriminators are used, it is possible for the parent block, in this case, the **system element**, to have two types associated with it, one from the **abstract type** and one from the **system type**. For example, it is possible for a system element to be both **logical** and a **subsystem**. This provides tremendous flexibility as it now means that it is possible for each of **subsystem**, **assembly**, and **component** to be one of **logical**, **functional**, and **physical**.

It should be stressed at this point that the definitions of these terms, defined using the ontology definition view, are entirely up to the modeler. This is important as it means that what is presented in *Figure 7.3* is only the definition of the concepts and terms that will be used in this book. The ontology must be defined to satisfy your own needs and must represent the way that you work in your organization.

In this chapter, we will be considering how to use these specifically to carry out three different types of modeling that may be applied at the architectural and detailed levels: **logical modeling**, **functional modeling**, and **physical modeling**.

Defining logical model elements

In a logical model, each of the model elements represents an abstract concept of something. Crucially, elements in a logical model are independent of any particular solution. As an example of this, consider the following diagram:

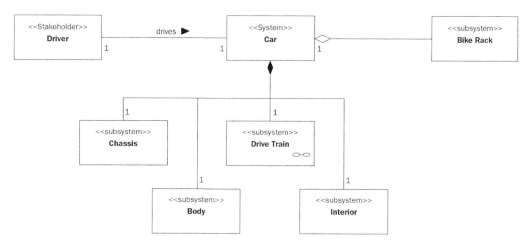

Figure 7.4 – Logical system structure view for the Car system

The diagram here shows the logical system structure view for the Car system, visualized using a SysML block definition diagram.

Each of the blocks in this diagram represents a logical element. Each logical element is a concept and is independent of any solution. Therefore, **Drive Train** is the concept of a drive train and does not refer to any specific implementation of a drive train. This is a very powerful modeling technique and logical models are very common in real-life projects. One of the reasons for this is that it is possible to have a common logical model that can be applied across all projects but realized in different ways in different projects.

The **Drive Train** logical system element may now be broken down into more detail, as shown in the following diagram:

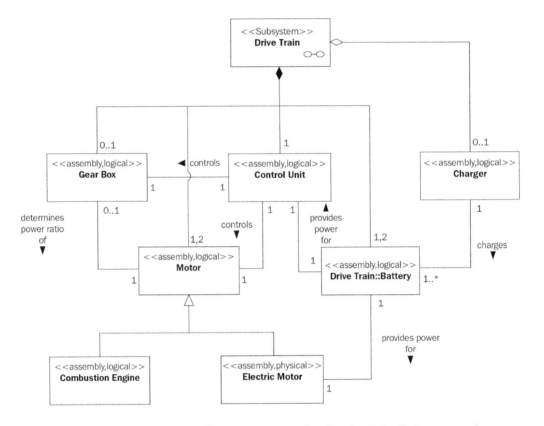

Figure 7.5 – Logical system structure view showing Drive Train

The diagram in *Figure 7.5* shows a logical system structure view that focuses on **Drive Train**, visualized using a SysML block definition diagram.

This diagram was discussed previously in *Chapter 3, Systems and Interfaces*, but it now takes on more meaning as we now know that it is a logical view and, therefore, that each of the blocks in the diagram represents a logical system element. This can be confusing as you may wonder how is it possible to know that each of the system elements on the diagram is logical, rather than functional or physical. This can be cleared up quite easily and neatly by using multiple stereotypes, as shown in the following diagram:

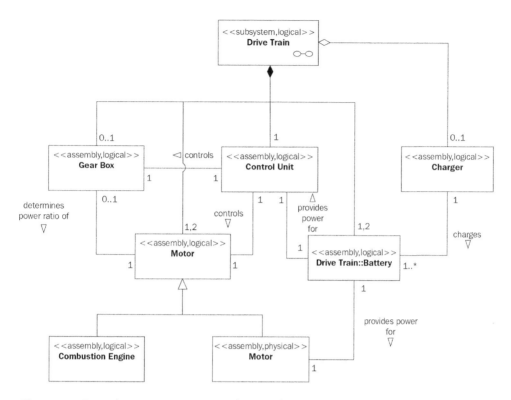

Figure 7.6 – Logical system structure view showing the Drive Train using multiple stereotypes

The diagram here shows the same logical system structure view that was shown in *Figure 7.5*, but this time it uses multiple stereotypes, and it is still visualized using a SysML block definition diagram.

Each of the system elements in this diagram now has two stereotypes, which is perfectly legal in SysML. The two stereotypes correspond to the two different sets of specializations that were defined in the ontology definition view in *Figure 7.3* and qualified using SysML discriminators. So, looking at these stereotypes, it is clear to see that **Drive Train** is both a subsystem (in terms of the type of the system element) and logical (in terms of its abstract type). Each of its lower-level system elements is both an assembly (in terms of the type of the system element) and logical (in terms of its abstract type). In this way, it is now totally clear exactly what each element in the diagram represents.

The use of these logical system elements means that the concept of a logical **Drive Train** will always have the same basic structure. However, as these are logical system elements, there is no implication of how each of these blocks will be realized in a real project. This is useful for defining something that is often known as a **reference model** or something that's part of a **reference architecture**. When defining a reference model, the logical views form a baseline from which all of the more solution-oriented views, such as the functional and physical views, may be derived. This allows a common set of logical elements to be defined that can then be specialized for specific solutions. This will be expanded upon the next two sections where both functional and physical system elements will be discussed.

Defining functional model elements

In this section, the concept of functional model elements will be discussed, and one of the main new concepts that will be introduced is that of the function. The term **function** is arguably one of the most contentious terms used in almost any industry, as it can take on so many different meanings in different domains. The following list is just a small sample of some of the possible different interpretations of the term **function**:

- A function may be a mathematical function that, based on a set of input parameters, performs one or more mathematical operations and then returns a result.
- A function may be a department in an organization; for example, there may be an engineering function, a management function, a human resources function, and so on.
- A function may be a job title; for example, a person may have a systems engineering function that defines their job in a business.
- A function may be a unit of activity that is performed by a system element; for instance, a brake pedal in a car may invoke a braking function.
- A function may be a software function, where a set of parameters are passed to a distinct module that performs some transformation, before returning a specific value.
- A function may be a party or social event.

This is by no means an exhaustive list of all the different interpretations of the term but is given here to show the diversity of different meanings that may be attributed to the word.

The term **function**, therefore, will be defined in the following diagram, but you must bear in mind that this is the definition that will be used throughout this book and that the definition may very well be different in your own organization:

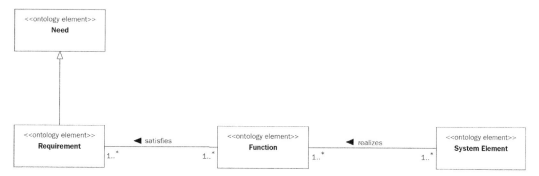

Figure 7.7 – An ontology definition view introducing the term function

The diagram here shows an ontology definition view that introduces the term **function** to the ontology that has been developed throughout this book, and it has been visualized using a SysML block definition diagram.

The term **function** is defined as follows:

- **One or more system elements realizes one or more functions**: A function represents some sort of task that is realized by the combined execution of one or more system elements. Remember that system elements may be subsystems, assemblies, or components; therefore, functions may exist at any or all of these levels.

- **One or more functions satisfies one or more requirements**: The execution of a single function, or a combination of functions, results in one or more of the requirements for the system being satisfied.

It should also be borne in mind that functions are, in a similar way to logical elements, independent of any specific solution. Defining specific solutions to a problem will be discussed when we consider physical system elements.

The addition of the new function ontology element also has wider implications for the broader ontology, as shown in the following diagram:

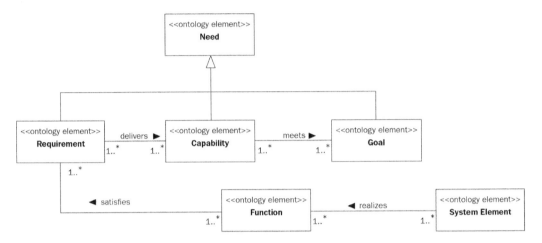

Figure 7.8 – Ontology definition view showing Function and expanding on Need

The diagram here shows an ontology definition view that shows the term **Function** again, but this time expanding on the types of **Need**, realized by a SysML block definition diagram.

The concept of **Need** has been expanded to include the two other types of need that were defined in *Chapter 6, Needs and Requirements*, those of **Capability** and **Goal**. This makes the concept of the function very important for the wider ontology as it provides a crucial link between the world of needs modeling and the solution, in terms of system-related views. The concept of a function, therefore, is an essential part of traceability across the model. For example, it is now possible to trace the relationship between a system element and any of the types of need by following the path between the ontology elements. For example, it is possible to trace the relationship between a system element and one of the original goals by following the following path:

1. **System element realizes function**

2. **Function satisfies requirement**

3. **Requirement delivers capability**

4. **Capability meets goal**

Traceability is a very important concept that applies across the whole of systems engineering and is a basic requirement of ISO 15288, which dictates that all needs must be traceable across the whole system life cycle.

This is another excellent use of the ontology as, when there is an ontology in place, the traceability of the whole system development is inherent in the model. When this is implemented using a modeling tool, then this traceability may be automated to make it effortless. Traceability is important for many reasons, including the following two:

- **Impact analysis**: Here, the traceability is applied in a forward manner, to see what impact a change in a need may have on the solution. For example, if one of the goals changes, then it is possible to then trace its related elements across the whole model up to, in this instance, the system elements.

- **Regression analysis**: Here, the traceability is applied in a backward manner, to see what effect a change on the solution may have on the needs. For example, if a system element changes, it is possible to trace back to any of the original needs (requirements, capabilities, and goals) it may be related to.

The function also has an important relationship to all of the different types of system element, as shown in the following diagram:

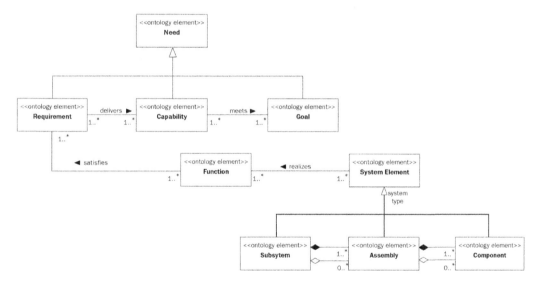

Figure 7.9 – Ontology definition view showing Function and expanding on System Element

The diagram here shows an ontology definition view that shows **Function**, but that has the concept of the system element expanded, visualized using a SysML block definition diagram.

The ontology now has the concept of the function relating directly to the concept of the system element. This provides an interesting insight, as system elements have three specializations: **subsystem**, **assembly**, and **component**. As the specialization relationship has been used, the concept of inheritance applies from the system element to its three types. This means that the relationship between the function and the system element is now inherited by the three specializations. From this, we may now infer that the function may be applied at any of the three levels of abstraction (indicated by the compositions and aggregations) that apply to the system element.

This may lead to some confusion, as when the term function is used, it will need to be made clear what level of the system element hierarchy it applies to. This may be achieved implicitly in the diagram or explicitly when the structure of the function is considered.

Defining the structural aspect of functions

It is always a good idea to be explicit wherever possible as relying on implicit concepts leads to people making assumptions about the model. There are two main ways that the relationship between functions and system elements may be represented in the model, the first of which is shown in the following diagram:

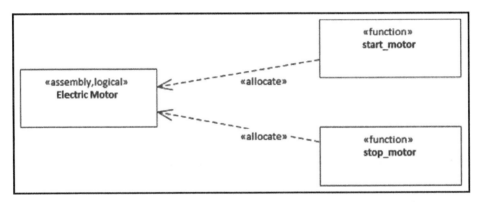

Figure 7.10 – A function allocation view showing explicit relationships using allocations

The diagram in *Figure 7.10* shows how to model explicit relationships between a function and a system element using allocations, visualized by a SysML block definition diagram.

The diagram shows several blocks, which are qualified using two stereotypes:

- <<**assembly**>> : This is a type of system element and represents the owning block to which the functions will be allocated. This is shown as the **Electric Motor** block, stereotyped as <<**assembly**>>.

- <<**function**>>: This represents the actual functions, which are represented as stereotyped SysML blocks and will be allocated to the owning <<**assembly**>> block. These are shown as the **start motor** and **stop motor** blocks, where the <<**function**>> stereotype has been applied.

The functions and assemblies are related using the SysML construct of an **allocation**. An allocation is shown in SysML by using a dependency relationship where the <<**allocate**>> stereotype has been applied.

This is a very good way to show the allocation of functions to system elements, in this case, assemblies, explicitly. However, this can become quite cumbersome when there are a large number of functions, as each function is represented as a block, which can lead to a large amount of space on the diagram being taken up with <<**function**>> blocks.

An alternate way to show the allocation of functions to system elements is shown in the following diagram:

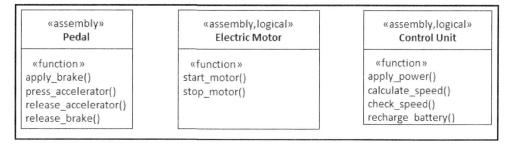

Figure 7.11 – A function allocation view showing explicit relationships using a function compartment

The diagram in *Figure 7.11* shows an alternative way to show the explicit allocation of functions to systems elements using a function compartment, realized using a SysML block definition diagram.

In this example, the same set of functions (**start motor** and **stop_motor**) are shown as allocated to the same system element (the assembly named **Electric Motor**). Rather than the function allocation being shown with a relationship to a stereotyped block, the functions are given their own compartment on the owning block, stereotyped as <<**function**>>.

Notice how much less space this approach takes up on the diagram. A second <<**assembly**>>, named **Pedal**, and a third named **Control Unit** have been included in the diagram, yet the diagram takes up less space than that in *Figure 7.10*.

As to which of these two representations is better, it is up to the discretion of the modeler to make that decision, as there are pros and cons to each:

- The use of the <<**allocate**>> dependency makes the allocation far more visually striking. Also, it is possible to show relationships between the functions, if necessary. For example, it may be desirable to show dependencies between various functions that may be used when defining the behavior of the functions.

- The use of the <<**function**>> compartment makes the diagram smaller and, it may be argued, more elegant. It is certainly possible to show far more allocations on a single diagram compared to the previous approach.

Now that the structural aspects of the functions have been defined, it is now possible to consider the behavioral aspects of functions.

Defining the behavioral aspect of functions

The standard way of modeling that has been promoted throughout this book has been to always consider the structural and behavioral aspects of the model. So far, we have considered the structural aspect of defining the exact meaning of a function and how to allocate functions to system elements at different levels of abstraction. The next step, therefore, is to look at how the functions interact with each other by considering the behavioral aspect of functions.

In order to do this, we will be using the SysML activity diagram that was first introduced in *Chapter 5, Systems Engineering Processes*. In order to illustrate this, consider the **Pedal** <<**assembly**>> from *Figure 7.11*, which has a number of functions; therefore, it is possible to construct the following diagram:

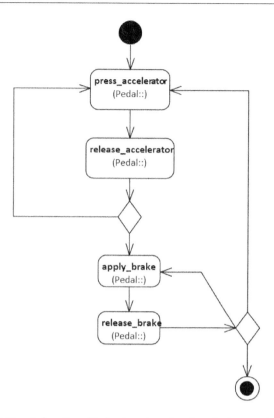

Figure 7.12 – A functional behavior view showing the interaction between functions for the Pedal system element

The diagram here is a functional behavior view that shows the interactions between functions for the **Pedal** system element, visualized using a SysML activity diagram.

The diagram shows the basic flow of execution of the various functions, as follows:

1. The first function is to **press accelerator**.

2. Immediately following this, the next step must always be to **release accelerator**.

3. Once the accelerator has been released, there are two possibilities: go back and **press accelerator** again or to move forward and **apply brake**.

4. Immediately following **apply brake**, the next function is always to **release brake**. Following this, there are three options: **press accelerator**, **apply brake**, or finish the diagram.

This functional behavioral view only applies to the single system element block of **Pedal**, which is perfectly valid from a modeling point of view. This view may be expanded to include the use of SysML swim lanes to show functional allocation across various system elements. This is illustrated in the expanded functional behavioral view that is shown in the following diagram:

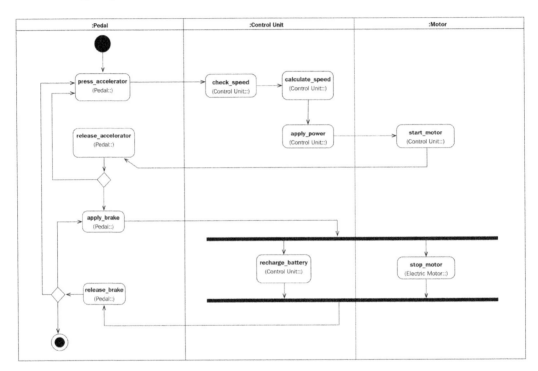

Figure 7.13 – A functional behavior view showing the interaction between functions across several system elements

The diagram here shows an expansion of the functional behavior view that shows the interactions between functions, but this time across several system elements, visualized using a SysML activity diagram.

In this view, SysML swim lanes have been used to represent the three system elements (<<**assembly**>>) that were shown in *Figure 7.11*. Each of the swim lanes shows the relevant system element, in this case, **Pedal**, **Electric Motor**, and **Control Unit**; but, very importantly, the functions for each of these are shown in their appropriate swim lanes. This allows the functional flow between different system elements to be shown in a single diagram, which is a very powerful mechanism indeed.

Note the differences between *Figure 7.12* and *Figure 7.13*, especially these:

- When considering a single system element, as in *Figure 7.12*, it is only possible to show the functional flow within that system element. Therefore, the flow goes directly from **press accelerator** to **release accelerator**.

- When considering the functional flow across multiple system elements as shown in *Figure 13*, it is easier to see the flow between functions from different system elements. Therefore, the flow from **press accelerator** now goes to **check speed**, which is a function that is allocated to the **Control Unit** system element.

The whole concept of functional modeling should still be independent of any particular solution, and this is what will be discussed in the next section, where we will be discussing physical modeling.

Defining physical elements

In a physical model, each of the model elements is a concrete representation of a real-life artifact. Whereas both logical elements and functional elements were firmly in the conceptual world, physical elements are rooted in the real world. When we looked at logical and functional elements, we were considering a conceptual solution to a problem that could be realized in a number of ways depending on the specific technologies and techniques that could be applied. When we are considering physical elements, we are looking at real solutions to a problem using specific technologies and specific techniques.

Modeling the system structure of physical elements

In order to illustrate this, we shall consider the breakdown of the **Electric Motor** system element. So far, we have considered the electric motor as a logical system element, but it is also possible to think of it as a physical system element. This is shown in the following diagram:

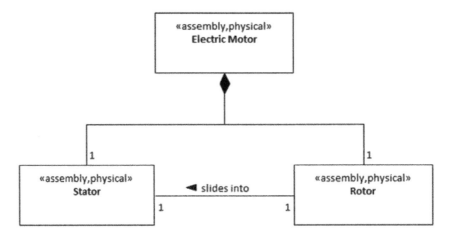

Figure 7.14 – A physical structure view showing the breakdown of Electric Motor

The diagram here is a physical structure view that shows the breakdown of the **Electric Motor** system element, visualized using a SysML block definition diagram.

There are several interesting points to consider regarding this diagram:

- Firstly, notice again the use of multiple stereotypes to allow the two different types of system element that were defined using SysML differentiators.

- The second point is that the **Electric Motor** block is now stereotyped as <<**assembly**>> and <<**physical**>>. This differs from when we saw it in *Figure 7.10*, when the stereotypes applied were <<**assembly**>> and <<**logical**>>. This is perfectly acceptable from a modeling point of view but it is essential that both occurrences of **Electric Motor** in the model must be separate model elements. This can potentially lead to some confusion as there will now be two model elements with the same name but that have different stereotypes applied.

- The next point is that there is a situation here where there is a block that is stereotyped as <<assembly>> and is made up of two other blocks that are also stereotyped as <<assembly>>. This actually does not comply with the original ontology, as it would require a composition or an aggregation (or both) from **assembly** back to itself. This is a good example of how the ontology will evolve over time to reflect the application of the modeling of the system.

This diagram can be read as follows:

- **Electric Motor** comprises a single **Stator** and a single **Rotor**.

- **Rotor** slides into **Stator**.

- All three blocks represent physical system elements that are assemblies.

Each of the blocks is a physical assembly, so this is an actual solution representing a real-life electric motor. The stereotypes help to convey the fact that this is a physical model rather than a logical model. The fact that this is a solution, rather than being logical, means that when the stator and rotor are broken down into more detail, we will also be dealing with physical system elements, as shown in the following diagram:

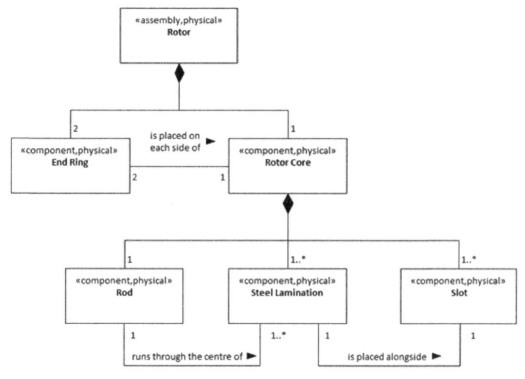

Figure 7.15 – A physical structure view of the Rotor assembly

The diagram here shows a physical structure view for the **Rotor** assembly, visualized using a SysML block definition diagram.

This system structure view is focused on decomposing a single assembly (the rotor) into its constituent components. Also, each of these components is also a physical system element. This is indicated, again, through the use of two stereotypes on each block to show exactly what the block is representing.

This diagram may be read as follows:

- **Rotor** comprises two **End Ring** blocks and a single **Rotor Core**.

- The two **Rotor Ring** blocks are placed on each side of **Rotor Core**.

- **Rotor Core** comprises a single rod, one or more **Steel Lamination** blocks, and one or more **Slot** blocks.

- **Rod** runs through the center of one or more **Steel Lamination** blocks.

- Each **Steel Lamination** is placed alongside a **Slot** block.

Notice how the system structure view is imprecise about exact numbers of some of the composite blocks, using **1…*** rather than a specific number. Also, the relationships do not explicitly represent interfaces between blocks, but they will be consistent with the interfaces. Both the interfaces and the specific numbers of instances of blocks will be considered when configuration views are created in the next section.

The following diagram shows a breakdown of the other major assembly, the **Stator**:

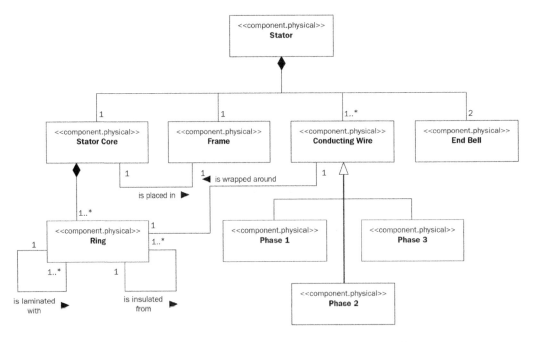

Figure 7.16 – A physical structure view of the Stator assembly

The diagram here shows the physical structure view for the **Stator** assembly and is visualized using a SysML block definition diagram.

Again, this diagram uses multiple stereotypes to show that all system elements are physical and that there is a single assembly and multiple components associated with it.

This diagram may be read as follows:

- **Stator** comprises a single **Stator Core**, a single **Frame**, one or more **Conducting Wire** blocks, and two **End Bell** blocks.

- **Stator Core** is placed in **Frame** and comprises one or more **Ring** blocks.

- Each **Ring** is laminated with one or more other **Ring** blocks and is also insulated from one or more other **Ring** blocks.

- **Conducting Wire** is wrapped around **Ring**.

- There are three types of **Conducting Wire**, which are **Phase 1**, **Phase 2**, and **Phase 3**.

This view is quite straightforward and simple to read, as all views should be; however, there is something here that deserves a second look. When considering any view, it is important to look for anomalies that may lead to potential questions about the view itself. In this case, consider **End Bell** and notice that, apart from the composition, it has no relationship with any other element on the diagram. This is unusual on any diagram and should always be questioned. In many cases, a block with no relationships to other blocks will indicate that there is a relationship missing. In this case, there should be a link between **End Bell** and the **Ring** piece on the diagram.

It is important to always be on the lookout for such modeling anomalies and to always question them. It is the responsibility of the modeler to answer such questions, and this should be viewed as constructive feedback rather than criticism. Remember that the goal is to end up with a model that is correct and that the model will evolve as the project progresses, so querying any diagram is a good way to ensure that the content is correct.

Modeling the configuration of physical elements

Now that the generic structure of the system has been modeled, it is possible to model the specific configurations of the solution. The idea of modeling configurations was introduced in *Chapter 3, Systems and Interfaces*, but this now starts to make more sense when we consider physical modeling, as each configuration will show a specific solution for the system.

The following diagram shows an example of this:

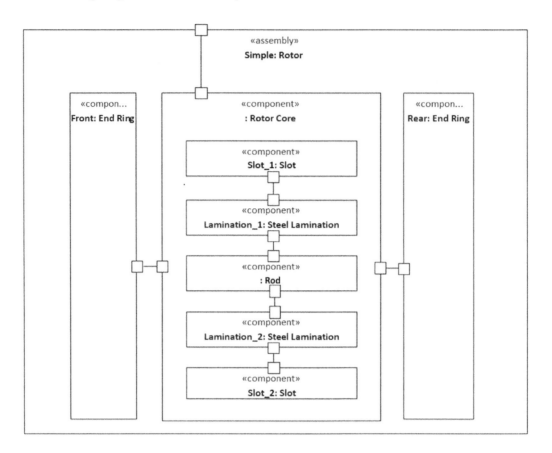

Figure 7.17 – A physical configuration view for a simple rotor with two laminations

The diagram here shows a physical system configuration view for a specific configuration of a simple rotor, visualized using a SysML block definition diagram.

Notice how this diagram is consistent with the physical structure view that was shown in *Figure 7.15* for the rotor assembly.

In this example, the configuration is for a simple rotor, which has been indicated by the assembly part name, which is defined as **Simple:Rotor**. It has just two laminations, which can be seen in the diagram. This is a useful mechanism as it allows multiple different configurations to be defined. These different configurations may form different candidate solutions. In this case, the candidate solution may just be represented by a different configuration, or, of course, it may be a completely different structure using different system elements. In order to illustrate this, consider the following configuration:

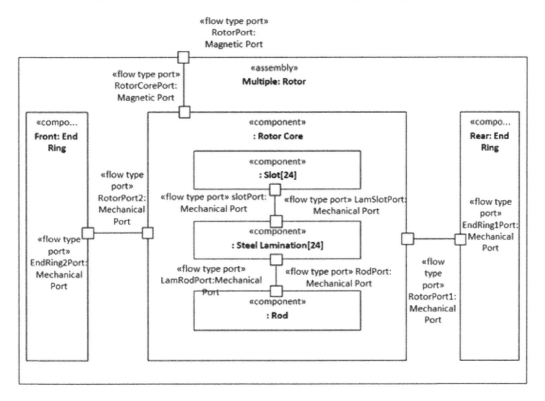

Figure 7.18 – A physical configuration view for a more-complex rotor with multiple laminations

The diagram here shows another possible physical configuration view, this time showing a more complex configuration of a rotor with multiple laminations, visualized using a SysML block definition diagram.

Notice how this diagram is also consistent with the physical structure view that was shown in *Figure 7.15*. This is important as it demonstrates how it is possible to have the same physical structure view but have multiple configurations using physical configuration views associated with it that, in this case, show multiple candidate solutions.

There are also some interesting modeling observations that can be made about this more complex configuration:

- Multiplicity on the <<**component**>> parts. Notice how there is a multiplicity of **[24]** associated with the **:Slot**, **:Steel Lamination**, and **:Rod** components. This is a useful mechanism that allows us to show that there are actually multiple parts, without having to show each one explicitly. This may be considered as a way to show a short-hand version of repeated elements, where shown all of them on a single view would make the view far too complex and, therefore, unreadable.

- More detail on the port definitions. In this view, the port definition has its types and names shown. This adds more detail to the view but does make the diagram busier and potentially less readable.

Both of these points are important as they demonstrate how the skill and judgment of the modeler are important. When considering visualizing any view, it is important to think about which stakeholder will be reading the diagram. For example, if it was an engineer reading the view, then it may be more appropriate to show more detail, as in *Figure 7.18*, whereas if it was a simple-minded manager looking at the view, it may be better to show a simple view, as in *Figure 7.17*. It comes down to the discretion of the modeler, but either way, it is important to make an informed decision.

Defining system behavior

The focus so far has been very much on structural views but, as has been one of the themes in this book, it is important to consider both structure and behavior. Wherever we have views that show system elements and their structure, particularly when there are specific configurations, it is vital to show some possible behaviors associated with these different configurations. An example of this can be seen in the following diagram:

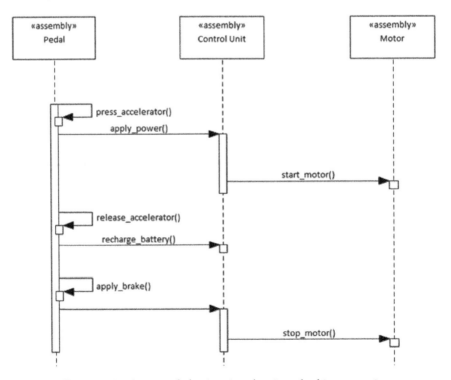

Figure 7.19 – A system behavior view showing a braking scenario

The diagram here shows a system behavior view for a braking scenario that is visualized using a SysML sequence diagram.

System behavior views, such as the one shown here, are very flexible and powerful as they can be applied to almost any structure view. For example, the example here relates to the logical assemblies that were described in *Figure 7.10* and *Figure 7.11*, so the behavior relates to logical assemblies. However, the same type of view, the system behavior view, could just as easily be applied to physical configuration views, such as those in *Figure 7.17* and *Figure 7.16*. This demonstrates how flexible this view can be and is also a good example of consistency between different views.

The views that have been discussed so far have used good modeling practice, and it is now time to consider how this modeling relates to international best practice, by looking at ISO 15288 again and, specifically, the processes that relate to design activities.

Complying with best-practice processes

The techniques for applying model-based techniques to architectural designs and detailed designs that have been introduced and discussed so far in this chapter may be used to comply with international best practice, in this case, ISO 15288 – software and systems engineering life cycle processes.

The two processes that are of interest are both taken from the technical process group and are the **architecture definition process** and the **design definition process**. Each of these will be discussed in the following two sections.

Complying with the ISO 15288 architecture definition process

The ISO 15288 process that is relevant for architectural design is the architecture definition process. This has been captured and modeled using the approach described in *Chapter 5, Systems Engineering Processes*. Refer to the following diagram:

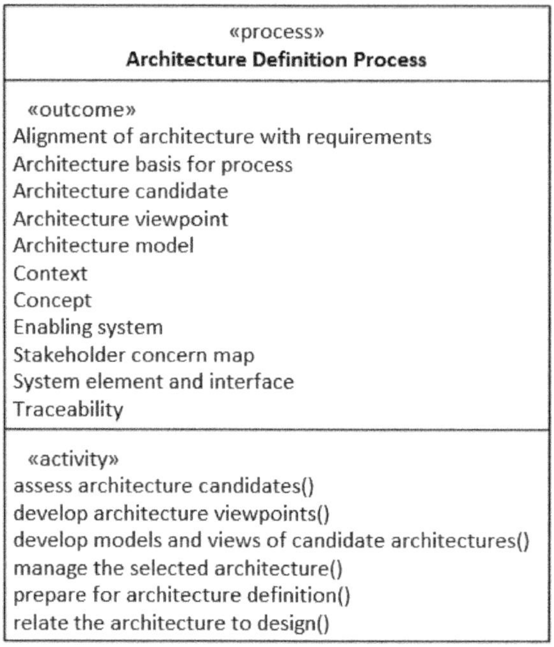

```
+-----------------------------------------------------+
|                   «process»                         |
|            Architecture Definition Process          |
+-----------------------------------------------------+
|  «outcome»                                          |
|  Alignment of architecture with requirements        |
|  Architecture basis for process                     |
|  Architecture candidate                             |
|  Architecture viewpoint                             |
|  Architecture model                                 |
|  Context                                            |
|  Concept                                            |
|  Enabling system                                    |
|  Stakeholder concern map                            |
|  System element and interface                       |
|  Traceability                                       |
+-----------------------------------------------------+
|  «activity»                                         |
|  assess architecture candidates()                   |
|  develop architecture viewpoints()                  |
|  develop models and views of candidate architectures() |
|  manage the selected architecture()                 |
|  prepare for architecture definition()              |
|  relate the architecture to design()                |
+-----------------------------------------------------+
```

Figure 7.20 – A process content view for the ISO 15288 process architecture definition process

The diagram here shows the process content view for the ISO 15288 **architecture definition process**, shown using a SysML block definition diagram.

The diagram uses standard SysML to represent the process perspective ontology concepts as follows:

- The block name shows the process name.

- The middle compartment shows the outcomes associated with the process, represented as stereotyped SysML properties.

- The bottom compartment shows the activities associated with the processes, represented as SysML operations.

The outcomes associated with the ISO process map onto the views that have been discussed so far as follows:

- **Alignment of architecture with requirements**: This is to do with establishing traceability from the architectural design view back to the needs. As there is an ontology in place, this traceability is inherent in the model.

- **Architecture basis for the process**: This is to do with establishing processes for the architectural design that can be integrated with all of the other processes across the life cycle. Again, this is already covered in the model by defining specific processes using the seven-views approach and mapping them back to best practice. This was discussed in detail in *Chapter 5, Systems Engineering Processes.*

- **Architecture candidate**: There will be multiple solutions for the system that are expressed as different sets of architecture views. These candidate architecture views are then assessed and narrowed down to find the preferred solution.

- **Architecture model**: This is a collection of views that have been deemed necessary to form the architecture. This will include, for example, all of the views that have been discussed in this chapter, the systems- and interface-related views that were discussed in *Chapter 3, Systems and Interfaces*, the life cycle views developed in *Chapter 4, Life Cycles*, the processes that were developed in *Chapter 5, Systems Engineering Processes*, and also the needs models that were discussed in *Chapter 6, Needs and Requirements*. Indeed, the architecture model may contain any of the views that are discussed throughout this book.

- **Architecture viewpoint**: These viewpoints are defined as part of the overall framework along with the ontology. These frameworks have been developed throughout this book and form a complete MBSE framework.

- **Concepts**: These concepts are defined as part of the ontology that forms part of the overall MBSE framework that is being developed throughout this book.

- **Context**: The context of the architecture defines the reason why the framework is needed. This has been defined for each of the perspectives that have been developed throughout the book and is described using the approach to needs modeling from *Chapter 6, Needs and Requirements.*

- **Enabling systems**: The enabling systems are covered in the ontology that was developed in *Chapter 3, Systems and Interfaces*, and exist outside the boundary of the system of interest. These may also be considered as a special type of stakeholder.

- **Stakeholder concern map**: This maps the views in the architecture back to the original context for the architecture, which comprises a number of stakeholder concerns.

- **System elements and interface**: Again, this has been covered by the design views in both this chapter and *Chapter 3, Systems and Interfaces*.

- **Traceability**: This is a subject that is key to systems engineering but one that is addressed implicitly when applying an MBSE approach, as all the traceability is established in the framework through both the ontology and the viewpoint definitions.

The activities that are identified in the process are mapped onto the modeling activities as follows:

- **Assess architecture candidates**: This activity is concerned with taking the various candidate architectures and their associated views and assessing them for compliance with the underlying needs, including the constraints. As a result of this, the preferred solution is selected in the form of the candidate architecture.

- **Develop architecture viewpoints**: This activity is concerned with ensuring that the framework for the architecture is sufficiently defined.

- **Develop models and views of candidate architectures**: This activity is focused on populating the architecture views based on the architecture framework. This is where the model itself and its associated views are created.

- **Manage the selected architecture**: This activity is focused on ensuring that processes are in place that will allow the architecture to evolve and grow as the project develops. These processes will cover areas such as governance of the architecture, developing an architecture strategy, and ensuring that it is met.

- **Prepare for architecture definition**: This activity ensures that the original context for the architecture and how will be evaluated are defined. This will also include having enough of an understanding of the relevant stakeholders (including the enabling system) that the architecture can be developed, as well as identifying any specific tools and notations that are to be used.

- **Relate the architecture to the design**: Again, this activity relates to the traceability of the architecture, this time to the design. Once again, all the traceability paths are defined as an inherent part of the framework.

Notice how all of the modeling that has been described in this book is now coming together to form part of the overall architecture. It is interesting at this point to revisit MBSE framework:

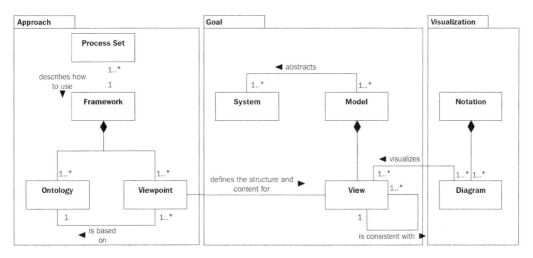

Figure 7.21 – MBSE revisited

The diagram here shows the MBSE framework that was originally introduced in *Chapter 2, Model-Based Systems Engineering*. The original diagram was shown using no specific notation but, at this point in the book, it is pertinent to show it realized using a SysML block definition diagram.

All of the information in ISO 15288 that relates to the architecture definition process can easily be mapped onto MBSE. Indeed, if the word **Model** in the diagram was replaced with the word **Architecture**, it would be a perfect visualization of what needs to be done as a part of the process.

This also serves to show how closely related architecture and MBSE are. It is worth remembering that all architectures are models, whereas not every model is an architecture. Modeling, therefore, is an essential part of any architecture definition.

In the same way that modeling is essential to architectural design activities, the same is true for detailed designs.

Complying with the ISO 15288 design definition process

The ISO 15288 process that is relevant for detailed designs is the design definition process. This has been captured and modeled using the approach described in *Chapter 5, Systems Engineering Processes*. The process content view for this process is shown in the following diagram:

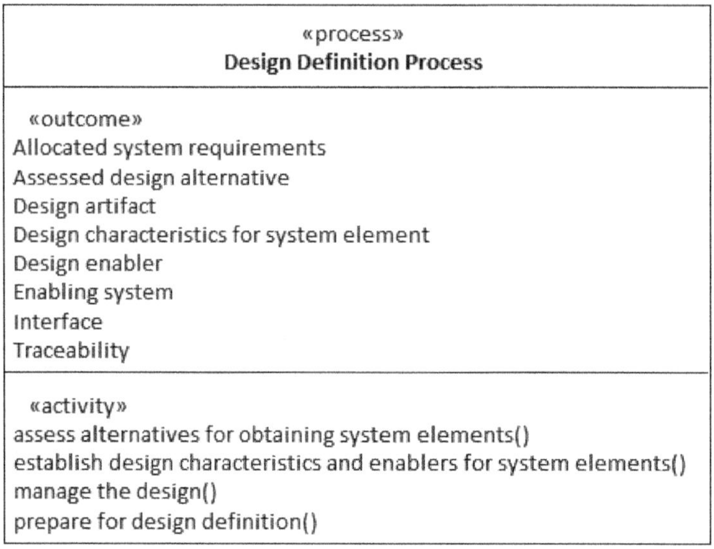

```
┌─────────────────────────────────────────────────────────────┐
│                          «process»                           │
│                   Design Definition Process                  │
├─────────────────────────────────────────────────────────────┤
│   «outcome»                                                   │
│   Allocated system requirements                               │
│   Assessed design alternative                                 │
│   Design artifact                                             │
│   Design characteristics for system element                   │
│   Design enabler                                              │
│   Enabling system                                             │
│   Interface                                                   │
│   Traceability                                                │
├─────────────────────────────────────────────────────────────┤
│   «activity»                                                  │
│   assess alternatives for obtaining system elements()         │
│   establish design characteristics and enablers for system elements() │
│   manage the design()                                         │
│   prepare for design definition()                             │
└─────────────────────────────────────────────────────────────┘
```

Figure 7.22 – A process content view for the ISO 15288 design definition process

The diagram here shows the process content view for the ISO 15288 process design definition process, shown using a SysML block definition diagram.

The outcomes associated with the ISO process map onto the views that have been discussed so far as follows:

- **Allocated system requirements**: All of the system elements must be allocated to the original needs. This is a traceability exercise and one that is, once more, straightforward, as traceability between all system elements and the different types of needs is established and inherent in the framework.

- **Assessed design alternatives**: In the same way that there were several potential candidate architectures that had to be assessed, there may also be multiple candidate designs for specific system elements. Again, these are assessed and the preferred design is selected.

- **Design artifact**: This is a generic term that applies to any of the views that relate to any aspect of the detailed design. These views have been discussed both in this chapter and in *Chapter 3, Systems and Interfaces*.

- **Design characteristics for system elements**: Each system element may have a number of design-related characteristics associated with it. These may be, for example, performance-related characteristics, quality characteristics, environmental characteristics, and so on. The terms that are used to describe these different types of characteristics may look familiar and there is a good reason for this. These characteristics may be derived directly from the constraints that were identified when modeling the needs. Bearing in mind that all the detailed design views may be traced back to the needs, it is relatively straightforward to see which constraints apply to which system elements using the traceability relationships that are inherent in the framework. These were discussed in detail in *Chapter 6, Needs and Requirements*.

- **Design enablers**: These design enablers may include selecting specific methodologies, techniques, notations, or tools that are required or recommended for specific design-related activities.

- **Enabling systems**: This is very much the same as in the previous section. The enabling systems that interact with specific system elements must be identified and modeled to such a degree that the system elements themselves may be designed.

- **Interfaces**: The interfaces between the system elements and the external interfaces to enabling systems must be identified and defined, and their connections must be specified. Interfaces were discussed in detail in *Chapter 3, Systems and Interfaces*.

- **Traceability**: Yet again, traceability is inherent in the framework and, therefore, is already well established.

The activities associated with the ISO process map onto the views that have been discussed so far as follows:

- **Assess alternatives for obtaining system elements**: This activity relates to the assessment of various candidate solution, this time for the system elements.

- **Establish design characteristics and enablers for system elements**: This covers the identification of the various constraints that must be applied to the system elements.

- **Manage the design**: This covers the processes that must be in place in order for the detailed design views to be managed, configured, and governed during the project life cycle.

- **Prepare for design definition**: This activity ensures that the original context for the detailed design and how it will be evaluated are defined. This will also include having enough of an understanding of the relevant stakeholders (including the enabling systems) that the detailed design views can be developed, as well as identifying any specific tools and notations that are to be used.

The whole approach that has been introduced and discussed in this chapter has been shown to comply with current international best practice in the form of ISO 15288. The views that have been shown must be defined as part of the overall framework, and the next section builds on the existing framework views by adding some of the architectural design and detailed design views to the framework.

Defining the framework

The views that have been created so far represent the center part of the MBSE diagram that was discussed in detail in *Chapter 2, Model-Based Systems Engineering*, and that was also revisited in the previous section. Each of the views has been visualized using SysML, representing the right-hand side of the MBSE diagram. These views come together to form the overall model, but it is essential that these views are all consistent, otherwise they are not views but pictures! This is where the left-hand side of the MBSE diagram comes into play, as it is important that the definition of all of the views is captured in the framework. The framework comprises the ontology and a set of viewpoints; therefore, it is now time to make sure that these viewpoints are defined thoroughly and correctly, which is the aim of this section.

Defining the viewpoints in the framework

It was discussed in *Chapter 2, Model-Based Systems Engineering*, that it is necessary to ask a number of questions of each view to ensure that it is a valid view. There is also a set of questions that must be asked of the whole framework, as well as the views and the combination of these results, to allow the whole framework to be defined. It is worthwhile, therefore, to have a reminder of what these questions are:

- Why is the framework required? This question may be answered using a **framework context view**.

- What are the overall concepts and terminology used for the framework? This question may be answered using an **ontology definition view**.

- What views are necessary as part of the framework? This question may be answered using a **viewpoint relationship view**.

- Why is each view needed? This question may be answered using a **viewpoint context view**.

- What is the structure and content of each view? This question may be answered using a **viewpoint definition view**.

- What rules should be applied? This question may be answered using a **ruleset definition view**.

When these questions are answered, then it can be said that a framework has been defined. Each of these questions can be answered using a special set of views that is collectively known as the **framework for architecture frameworks (FAF)** [Holt and Perry 2019]. At this point, simply think about creating a specific view to answer each question, as described in the following sections.

Defining the framework context view

The framework context view specifies why the whole framework is needed in the first place. It will identify the relevant stakeholders that have an interest in the framework and also identify what benefits each of the stakeholders hopes to gain from the framework:

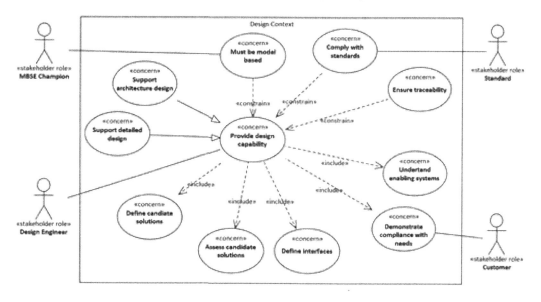

Figure 7.23 – Framework context view for the design framework

The diagram here shows the framework context view for the design framework, visualized using a SysML use case diagram.

Note the application of the use case diagram here to capture the context, an approach that was described in *Chapter 6, Needs and Requirements*.

This diagram may be read as follows:

- The main aim of the design framework is to **Provide design capability**. This is a generic term that is used to capture, in a single statement, the overall intent of the entire context. It is useful to be able to identify which of the use cases in any given context diagram is the main one. This can be achieved by looking out for use cases that have multiple <<**include**>> relationships coming out of them and multiple <<**constrain**>> relationships going into them. This will typically identify a high-level use case and it is the suggested starting point for reading any context view.

- There are two main types of design, which are shown by the two specialization relationships from the main use case: **Support architectural design** and **Support detailed design**. This is a powerful construct to use here as it means that anything that is attached to the parent use case, in this case, **Provide design capability**, will also be inherited down to the specializations, for both of the child use cases.

- The overall design capability **Must be model based**. This is a common use case that will appear on all of our systems engineering context views; as MBSE is the approach advocated by this book, it is not surprising to see it repeated here.

- Another common theme throughout this book is to **Comply with standards** so, again, it appears as a use case here. This will enforce best practice for everything that we do in systems engineering and allow our overall approach to be demonstrable to any interested stakeholders.

- One of the common activities that is mentioned in almost every systems engineering standard relates to **Ensure traceability**. This is vital to demonstrate compliance with the original needs as well as allowing engineering to carry out impact analyses when changes have been made to the model.

- There are four <<**include**>> relationships on the main use case, the first of which is **Define candidate solutions**. An important aspect of any robust design is to consider multiple solutions that explore different ways to solve the same problem.

- Following on from the previous point, it is also necessary to be able to compare and contrast the solution in order to **Assess candidate solutions**. This will provide a mechanism for ensuring that the assessment is fair and covers all of the criteria explored during the needs modeling.

- A key part of any design at any level is to **Define interfaces**, so this becomes an important part of both architectural designs and detailed designs.

  It is impossible to define a good solution without considering what goes on outside the boundary of the system of interest, and this is achieved by being able to **Understand enabling systems**. This allows the wider context of the system to be understood and a design to be developed that integrates with any enabling systems.

- Finally, it is essential at any point in the life cycle to be able to **Demonstrate compliance with needs**. This forms the heart of delivering any successful system and is the main goal of systems engineering.

Notice that in this diagram, each of the SysML use cases is stereotyped as a concern. A concern is a need that relates specifically to a framework or one of its viewpoints.

Defining the ontology definition view

The ontology definition view captures all the concepts and terminology associated with the framework in the form of an ontology. This has already been done, as the ontology for the design-related views was defined in *Figure 7.2*. The ontology elements shown on this view provide all of the stereotypes that have been used for the actual views that have been created so far in this chapter.

Ontology elements that are related will often be collected into a **perspective**, as was discussed in other chapters. In this chapter, a new perspective has been created that relates to design.

Defining the viewpoint relationship view

The viewpoint relationship view identifies which views are needed and, for each set of views, identifies a viewpoint that will contain its definition. Remember that a viewpoint may be thought of as a type of template for a view. These viewpoints may be collected together into a perspective, which is simply a collection of viewpoints with a common theme.

In this chapter, the emphasis has been on defining a set of views related to design, so it is appropriate to create the **design perspective**. The basic set of views that has been discussed so far is shown in the following view:

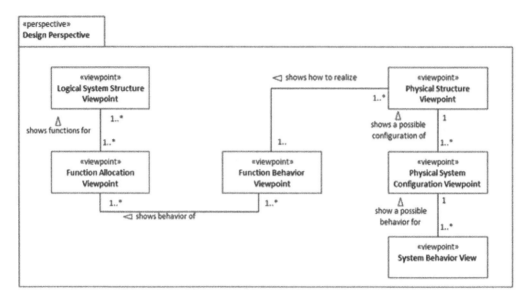

Figure 7.24 – A viewpoint relationship view for the design perspective

The diagram here shows the viewpoint relationship view for the design perspective using a SysML block definition diagram.

The need perspective is shown using a SysML package, stereotyped as <<**perspective**>>, that simply collects together a number of viewpoints. There are six viewpoints that have been defined in this chapter that make up the design perspective. There are actually more possible views for this perspective, which will be discussed after these basic viewpoint descriptions:

- **Logical system structure viewpoint**: Identifies the high-level logical system elements and the basic relationships between them

- **Function allocation viewpoint**: Identifies the key functions and allocates them with various system elements at different levels of abstraction

- **Function behavior viewpoint**: Allows specific functions to be broken down and their behaviors described

- **Physical structure viewpoint**: Shows how the various functions may be realized using physical system elements

- **Physical system configuration viewpoint**: Shows a number of different configurations for specific physical system elements

- **System behavior viewpoint**: Shows a number of possible behaviors for each of the configurations

This set of viewpoints is focused on the design of the system. Of course, this is just an example, and there may be many more viewpoints that are described and relate to design. For example, all the interface-related viewpoints that were described in *Chapter 3, Systems and Interfaces*, will also be included in this perspective.

It should also be pointed out that at this point, people may start to refer to the design perspective as the architecture of the systems. Although the architecture will certainly include all the design viewpoints, the architecture has a far-wider scope. For example, any of the viewpoints and their perspectives, such as the life cycle perspective (*Chapter 4, Life Cycles*), process perspective (*Chapter 5, Systems Engineering Processes*), and needs perspective (*Chapter 6, Needs and Requirements*), will also be included in the wider architecture framework.

Each of the viewpoints that has been identified here may now be described using its own viewpoint context view and its viewpoint definition view.

Defining the viewpoint context view

The viewpoint context view specifies why a particular viewpoint and, therefore, its set of views, is needed in the first place. It will identify the relevant stakeholders that have an interest in the viewpoint and also identify what benefits each of the stakeholders hopes to gain from the framework, as shown in the following diagram:

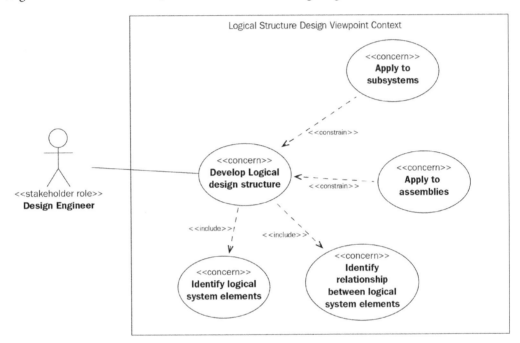

Figure 7.25 – A viewpoint context view for the logical system structure viewpoint

The diagram here shows the viewpoint context view for the logical system structure viewpoint, visualized using a SysML use case diagram.

This diagram may be read as follows:

- The main aim of the logical system structure viewpoint is to **Develop logical design structure**. Note that this has been identified as the highest-level use case due to the fact that it has two <<**include**>> dependencies coming out of it and two <<**constrain**>> dependencies that go into it.

- **Identify logical system elements** is important as it sets the scope for which types of system elements this viewpoint is focusing on. In this case, it is explicitly the logical system elements, and we may infer from this that it does not apply to the functional system elements nor the physical system elements. When modeling, it is important to see what is in the scope of a viewpoint but also what is not included in the scope.

- **Identify relationships between logical system elements** is again important as it explicitly states relationship and does not specify actual interfaces. This tells us that only generic relationships will be shown and not specific interfaces or their connections.

- **Apply to subsystems** and **Apply to assemblies**. These two use cases allow us to see that the logical system elements are only applied at two levels of abstraction: the subsystem level and the assembly level. Again, we can infer from this that these logical system elements do not apply to the system or the component system elements.

Now that the reason why the viewpoint must exist has been established, the viewpoint definition view may be considered.

Defining the viewpoint definition view

The viewpoint definition view defines the ontology elements that are included in the viewpoint. It shows the following:

- Which ontology elements are *allowed* in the viewpoint

- Which ontology elements are *optional* in the viewpoint

- Which ontology elements are *not allowed* in the viewpoint

The viewpoint definition view focuses on a single viewpoint and particular care and attention must be paid to not just the ontology elements that are selected, but also the relationships that exist between these ontology elements.

An example of a viewpoint definition view for the need description viewpoint is shown in the following diagram:

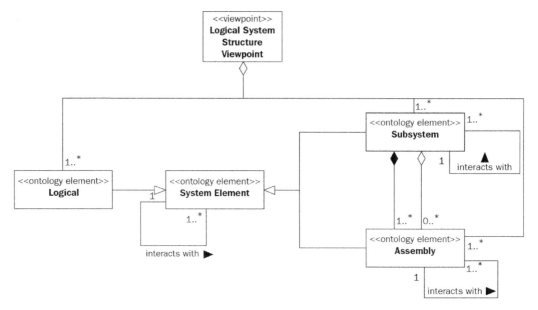

Figure 7.26 – A viewpoint definition view for the logical system structure viewpoint

The diagram here shows the viewpoint definition view for the logical system structure viewpoint, using a SysML block definition diagram.

This view defines the exact content of what is allowed in all the views that are described by the viewpoint. This viewpoint will always contain the following information:

- **The viewpoint name**, stereotyped by <<**viewpoint**>>, which is the focus of this view. The viewpoint that is identified here must come from the viewpoint relationship view that was shown in *Figure 7.24*.

- **A number of ontology elements**, stereotyped by <<**ontology element**>>. Each of these ontology elements must come from the ontology definition view shown in *Figure 7.3*.

The ontology elements that are allowed on the views associated with this viewpoint are as follows:

- **Logical**, which refers to the logical system elements. This is important as the other two types of functional and physical are not shown here, which limits the scope of this viewpoint.

- **Aubsystem** and **assembly**. These are also important as they exclude both the system and components from the scope.

These subtleties regarding the scope are important as it goes to show just how important explicitly defining the viewpoint definition view can be. Another subtlety is that the **system element** is not included in this viewpoint as there is no aggregation relationship to the viewpoint name. This is because the **system element** has no direct instances; it is abstract and therefore is not explicitly included in the viewpoint.

The viewpoints and ontology elements that are permitted in each viewpoint are constrained by a number of rules, which will be described in the ruleset definition view for the needs perspective.

Defining the ruleset definition view

The ruleset definition view identifies and defines a number of rules that may be applied to the model to ensure that it is consistent with the framework.

The rules are based primarily on the ontology definition view and the viewpoint relationships view. In each case, the rules are defined by identifying the key relationships and their associated multiplicities that exist in the following places:

- Between viewpoints in the viewpoint definition view
- Between ontology elements in the ontology definition view

Some examples of these rules are shown in the following diagram:

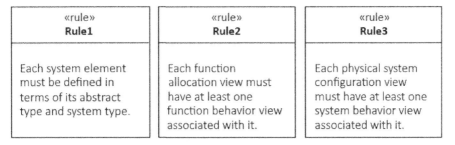

Figure 7.27 – Example ruleset definition view

The diagram here shows an example of a ruleset definition view using a SysML block definition diagram. Each block on the diagram represents a rule that is derived from either the ontology definition view or the viewpoint relationship view.

These rules are defined as follows:

- **Rule1: Each system element must be defined in terms of its abstract type and system type**: This rule is taken from the ontology definition view that was shown in *Figure 7.3*, showing that each system element has two different specializations associated with it, defined by the SysML discriminator.

- **Rule2: Each function allocation view must have at least one function behavior view associated with it**: This rule is taken from the viewpoint relationship view that was shown in *Figure 7.24*.

- **Rule3: Each physical system configuration view must have at least one system behavior view associated with it**: This rule is also taken from the viewpoint relationship view that was shown in *Figure 7.24*.

Notice how the rules are derived from the viewpoint relationship view, and, therefore, the viewpoints and the ontology definition view, and, therefore the ontology elements. The actual rule descriptions themselves apply to the instances of the viewpoints (views) and instances of the ontology elements.

Of course, any number of other rules may be defined here, but not every relationship will lead to a rule, as this is at the discretion of the modeler.

Summary

In this chapter, the fundamental issue of design has been discussed. Design involves providing the solution to a specific problem that is specified by given needs. Design may be applied at two broad levels, which are generally referred to as the architectural design level and the detailed design level. It was discussed that architectural design is generally more abstract and applies at a high level, such as the system and subsystem level. Detailed design, on the other hand, focuses more on detailed aspects of the overall solution and focuses on the structure of subsystems, assemblies, and components.

It was also discussed that the system elements that we saw previously in *Chapter 3, Systems and Interfaces*, actually may take on different types. In the example ontology in this chapter, these types were logical, functional, and physical. It was seen that functional system elements satisfy logical system elements, whereas physical system elements realize functional system elements.

The importance of best practice was also discussed, and this was related to views by considering a specific process from ISO 15288 and relating the modeling view directly to its activities and outcomes.

Finally, all of these views were captured as part of an overall framework definition using the framework for architecture frameworks. This framework itself comprises a number of views that are used to describe the model.

In the next chapter, we will be looking at verification and validation modeling techniques that will be used to test the design views shown in this chapter.

Self-assessment tasks

1. Revisit the ontology definition view in *Figure 7.3* and consider how this applies to your organization. Change, where necessary, the different types of system element to reflect your organizational needs.

2. Think about the term "function" and what it means to you in your organization. Update the ontology to reflect your specific interpretation of this term. Relate it to both the design-related terms that have been used in this chapter and the needs-related terms that were used in *Chapter 6, Needs and Requirements*.

3. Compare and contrast the two different ways to visualize the allocation of functions in *Figure 7.11* and *Figure 7.12*. Which do you prefer, and why?

4. There is an inconsistency between what is shown in *Figure 7.14* and the ontology shown in *Figure 7.3*. Identify this inconsistency and correct it on the ontology.

5. Add to the viewpoint relationship view in *Figure 7.24* to include any other perspectives that you feel may be important to create a viewpoint relationship view for an architecture.

6. Define the viewpoint context view and the viewpoint definition view for at least one other viewpoint that was shown in *Figure 7.24*.

References

*   [Holt & Perry 2019] Holt, JD and Perry, SA. *SysML for Systems Engineering – a model-based approach*. Third edition. IET Publishing, Stevenage, UK. 2019.

8
Verification and Validation

The modeling that has been introduced so far in this book has been concerned with the creation of a number of views that are related to specifying and defining the system and that contribute to delivering the successful system. Remember that the main aim of systems engineering is to deliver successful systems.

Alongside these modeling activities, it is also important to be able to test that what we have produced is correct, and this is done in two main ways, which are as follows:

- **Verification**: This helps us to demonstrate that the system works. This was summed up, very famously, by Boehm by asking the question *have we built the system right?*"

- **Validation**: This helps us to demonstrate that the system actually does what it is supposed to – that it is fit for purpose. This was again summed up neatly by Boehm by asking the question *have we built the right system?*

It is essential that the system can be both verified and validated, and it must be remembered that achieving one of these by no way means that we have necessarily achieved the other.

This chapter is structured as follows:

- Defining testing concepts: In order to understand verification and validation, it is necessary to understand the concepts associated with testing. This will be done by the now-familiar approach of building up the MBSE ontology to cover testing concepts.

- Modeling verification and validation: In this section, we discuss why modeling the testing context is important, along with modeling the testing setup and the execution of the actual testing activities.

- Using existing views for testing: This is a crucial part of MBSE, as the more that we can reuse existing views from the model, the more value we will add with our MBSE activities.

- Complying with best practice: Again, we shall map everything that we discuss in this chapter to the processes contained in ISO 15288.

- Defining the framework: This is where we define some of the views that were introduced in this chapter.

Finally, we will wrap up with some conclusions and a set of self-assessment exercises.

Defining testing concepts

Before considering the main testing concepts, it is necessary to take a step back and to consider what can be tested in any given system. In modeling terms, the contents of the model are defined by the views and, in turn, these views have their structure and content defined by a set of viewpoints that comprise part of the framework. This was covered in detail in *Chapter 2, Model-Based Systems Engineering*. The viewpoints themselves are based on the ontology, which, it has been demonstrated throughout this book, is the cornerstone to achieving successful MBSE and, hence, systems engineering. The ontology, we can therefore infer, forms the heart of the views (and, therefore, the model) as each element that appears on a view is actually an instance of an ontology element.

If we now ask the question "which elements that make up the model can be tested?", then the answer is that any element in the model may be tested to some degree or other.

We can now infer that testing may be applied to any ontology element. This is shown in the following diagram:

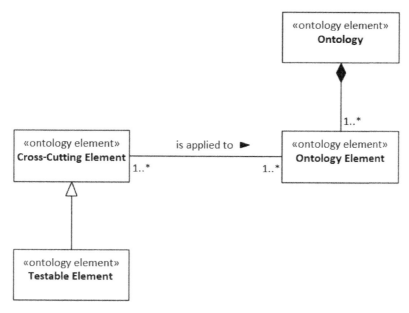

Figure 8.1 – Meta-model showing cross-cutting element

The diagram here shows a meta-model that focuses on the cross-cutting element and that is visualized using a SysML block definition diagram.

This diagram introduces a new generic modeling concept, which is that of the **metamodel**. A metamodel, in its simplest terms, may be defined as a **model of a model**. In fact, we have seen a number of metamodels in every chapter of this book as an ontology is actually a special type of metamodel, as it is a model of a model that allows us to identify concepts and terminology for a specific system. Indeed, every ontology is a metamodel, but not every metamodel is an ontology.

The use of the metamodel in this diagram allows us to relate a new concept to every type of ontology element that comprises the ontology. An ontology element that may be applied to any number of other ontology elements is referred to as a **cross-cutting element** as it may be applied across the entire gamut of model elements.

The diagram in *Figure 8.1* may be read as follows:

- An **Ontology** comprises one (or more) **Ontology Element**.
- One or more **Cross-Cutting Element** is applied to one or more **Ontology Element**.
- There is a single type of **Cross-Cutting Element**, which is the **Testable Element**.
- Therefore, using the law of inheritance, one or more **Testable Element** is applied to one or more **Ontology Element**.

This is a very powerful mechanism as we have now defined a new ontology element that can be applied to potentially any other ontology element. If this was done using just the MBSE ontology, then it would be necessary to draw an association between the cross-cutting element and every single ontology element that comprises the ontology, which would render the ontology unreadable!

It is now possible to take the concept of the testable element and to expand upon it to identify and define a number of other testing-related concepts, as shown in the following diagram:

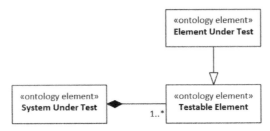

Figure 8.2 – Ontology definition view showing system under test

The diagram here shows an ontology definition view that focuses on the concept of a system under test, and that is visualized using a SysML block definition diagram.

This diagram may be read as follows:

- Each **System Under Test** comprises one or more **Testable Element**.

- There is a special type of **Testable Element**, which is an **Element Under Test**.

The concept of a system under test may be thought of as just a special type of system (not shown in the diagram) that is specifically being tested. In the same way, there is a special type of testable element, which is specifically the element under test. This special type of testable element is needed as not all testable elements will be tested in every single test case, therefore it is a useful mechanism that allows us to differentiate between the two.

This ontology may now be expanded, as shown in the following diagram:

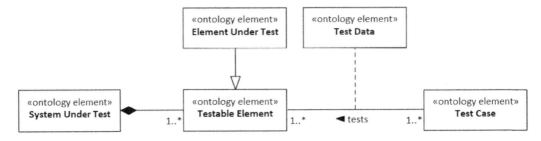

Figure 8.3 – Expanded ontology definition view showing the concept of a **Test Case**

The diagram here shows an expanded ontology definition view that has included the new concept of a **Test Case**, and that has been visualized using a SysML block definition diagram.

The concept of the test case represents an individual test that will be applied to a specific set of testable elements. It can also be seen that the **Test Case** tests the **Testable Element** using **Test Data**. This is important as there is usually a specific dataset that must be used for each test case in order to make sure that the appropriate aspects of the testable element are tested and that the test case may be repeated using the same input criteria.

Each test case is executed on the testable elements according to a specific structure, which is shown in the following diagram:

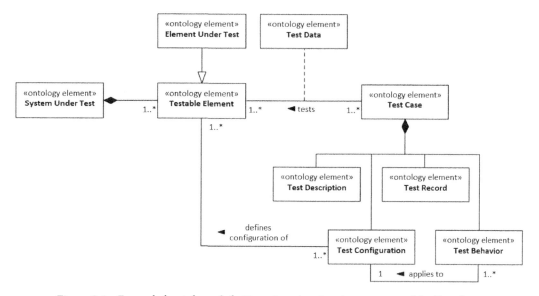

Figure 8.4 – Expanded ontology definition view showing the structure of the Test Case

The diagram here shows an ontology definition view that has been expanded to show the structure of a **Test Case**, and that is visualized using a SysML block definition diagram.

It can be seen that a **Test Case** comprises four elements, which are as follows:

- **Test Description**: This provides a simple text-based description of the **Test Case**, such as the name of the **Test Case**, a unique identified version number, and so on. This would be used largely as a management enabler.

- **Test Configuration**: This provides details on how the testable elements must be configured in order for the **Test Case** to be executed. This is important as the **Test Case** may require a specific set of connections, for example, between the testable elements.

- **Test Behavior**: This provides a series of sequential steps that must be followed in order to carry out the **Test Case** successfully. This **Test Behavior** will also be applicable to a specific **Test Configuration** in order for it to be valid.

- **Test Record**: This provides a mechanism for capturing the results of each **Test Case**.

These test cases are grouped together, as shown in the following diagram:

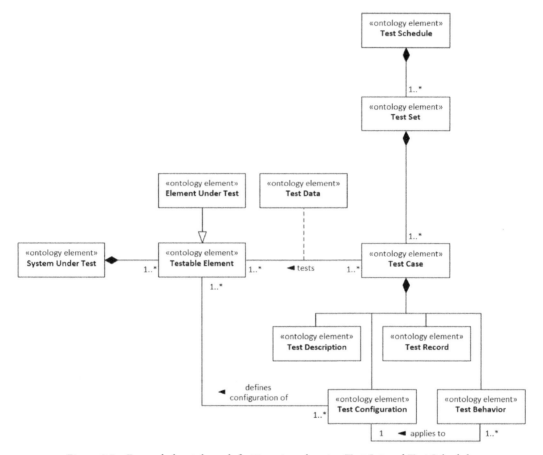

Figure 8.5 – Expanded ontology definition view showing Test Set and Test Schedule

The diagram here shows an expanded ontology definition view that focuses on the concepts of **Test Set** and **Test Schedule**, and that is visualized using a SysML block definition diagram.

Test cases are collected together into two higher-level groupings which are as follows:

- **Test Set**, which collects test cases into a set that has a specific purpose.

- **Test Schedule**, which collects together all of the test sets and, therefore, all of the test cases into a single entity. The **Test Schedule** describes a complete set of test cases.

These groupings are a good way to introduce levels into testing, which allows effective management. However, there is still something crucial that is missing from this ontology and that is the concept of a **Testing Context**, which is shown in the following diagram:

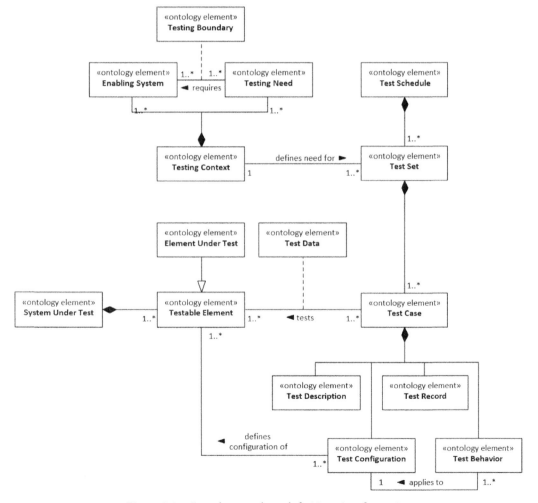

Figure 8.6 – Complete ontology definition view for testing

The diagram here shows the complete ontology definition view for testing that introduces the **Testing Context**, and that is visualized using a SysML block definition diagram.

One of the themes that run through this book is to always ask why something is being done, and this has been captured in the model using various types of context, as described in *Chapter 6, Needs and Requirements*. The concept of testing is no different and it is essential to understand the rationale behind why the testing is being carried out in the first instance. Of course, the obvious answer to this question is to make sure that the system works as it should, but we have already discussed that there are two broad reasons to test anything, which are verification and validation. There are also many other types of testing that exist, for example, testing may be applied at different levels of abstraction of the system. These are as follows:

- **Unit testing**: This is applied at the lowest level of abstraction of the system and, referring to the examples that we have used throughout this book, would apply to the component level of our system.

- **Integration testing**: This brings together the unit tests and aggregates them into higher levels. In the examples that have been used throughout this book, integration testing would apply to the assembly and subsystem levels of the system.

- **System testing**: This brings together the integration tests and aggregates them at the highest level. In our examples, this would apply to the system as a whole.

All these types of testing may be thought of as verification techniques as they are testing that the system works against various specifications and design artifacts, which would be the model views. However, it is also important that we apply testing for validation purposes, such as the following:

- **Acceptance testing**, where it is demonstrated to the appropriate customer stakeholder that the system actually satisfies its original needs.

- **Alpha testing**, where the system is released internally to the supplier stakeholders so that it can be operated in a near real-world environment to test whether it meets the original needs.

- **Beta testing**, where the system is released to a typically limited set of customers so that they can put the system through its paces in a real-world environment and test to see whether it satisfies the original needs.

There are also other types of testing that apply to the non-functional aspects of the system, such as performance testing, load testing, recovery testing, soak testing, and so on. All of these types of non-functional testing must relate back to the constraints that were originally applied to the needs of the system and then carried through the analysis and design of the system.

The types of testing that are identified here are really just a small sample of the different types of testing that may be applied to a system and there are literally hundreds to choose from. Due to this plethora of different testing techniques, each of which has its own set of purposes, it is essential that the reason behind the testing is captured in the model, which is achieved by creating the testing context. When defining the testing context, there are several concepts that need to be captured. These are as follows:

- **Testing need**: This captures why the testing is being applied.

- **Enabling system**: This refers to any other system that is required in order for the testing to be carried out.

- **Testing boundary**: This identifies the scope of the testing and identifies exactly what is included in the test set.

Now that the concepts associated with testing and verification and validation have been discussed, it is appropriate to consider how these concepts may be realized using modeling techniques.

Modeling verification and validation

It should be clear by now that verification and validation are important to delivering a successful system and, therefore, are essential parts of MBSE. In this section, we shall consider how modeling techniques may be applied to visualize the different aspects of testing and verification and validation.

One of the major advantages of modeling compared to a model-based approach comes into play now, as it is possible to reuse many of the views that have been generated so far as part of systems development for testing purposes. The more views that can be reused, then the more value that is added to the overall project as a direct result of modeling.

There are also other benefits to reusing existing views. One such advantage is that by using the same views that were used to develop the system, it is guaranteed that all of the information that is being used for the testing activities will be consistent, as it is using the same model. Remember that all the way back in *Chapter 2, Model-Based Systems Engineering*, the model was referred to as the **single source of truth**, and this is an excellent example of this.

Modeling the testing context

It has been discussed that understanding why the testing is required is important and that this may be captured by creating a testing context. The testing context is created in the same way as all the other contexts in this book, by using the techniques discussed in *Chapter 6, Needs and Requirements*. An example of a testing context for the example car system is shown in the following diagram:

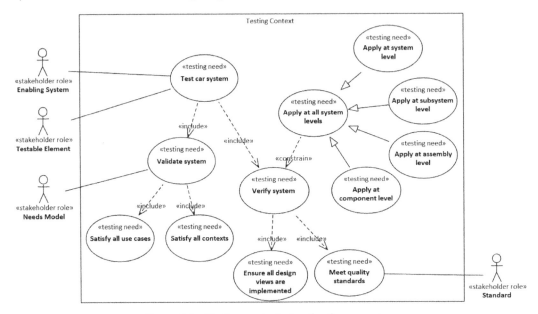

Figure 8.7 – Testing context view for the car system

The diagram here shows the testing context for the car system, and that is visualized using a SysML use case diagram.

The use cases in this diagram represent the testing needs and are stereotyped as <<**testing need**>>. These testing needs are as follows:

- **Test car system**: This is the highest-level <<**testing need**>> and applies to the testable elements that are being tested and also the enabling systems that are required for the testing to be carried out successfully.

- **Validate system**: This means that there is a need to demonstrate that the system satisfies all of its original needs and, because of this, there is a link to the need model.

- **Satisfy all use cases**: This is part of the validation but explicitly refers to the use cases that exist in the system model.

- **Satisfy all contexts**: This, again, is a part of the validation but refers to the contexts that contain the use cases in the system model.

- **Verify system**: This means that there is a need to demonstrate that the car system works and has been developed according to its various specifications and designs, which will, of course, refer to the model views that have been created as part of the system development.

- **Ensure all design views are implemented**: This forces the checking of the system against the model. This is important as it also provides a coverage check that ensures that the model in its entirety, or specified parts of the model, are implemented.

- **Meet quality standards**: This is a quality check against a set of identified standards, and that applies to the standard stakeholder.

- **Apply at all system levels**: This is a high-level constraint that means that all of the verification use cases must be applied at the four levels specified in the diagram, which are: **Apply at system level**, **Apply at subsystem level**, **Apply at assembly level**, and **Apply at component level**.

The diagram in *Figure 8.7* is modeled at a high level and the use cases are still quite generic. Of course, any of these use cases may be broken down into their own diagram and specific techniques may be identified.

This goes to highlight another interesting point associated with the reuse of model views, as this testing context view may be applied as a start point of almost any type of system. At the moment, the diagram refers specifically to the car system but, if this was changed to refer to a generic system, then this diagram would be applicable to almost every system.

The reuse of these generic views not only saves much time and effort but is also useful as an initial start point that may be viewed as a sophisticated checklist. For example, using this view as a generic start point will remind the testers that there is a minimum set of needs for the testing, represented by the use cases in the testing context.

The testing activities that will satisfy these use cases must be structured in some way, and this is discussed in the next section, which considers modeling the testing setup.

Modeling the testing setup

The structure of the **Test Schedule**, **Test Set**, and **Test Case** was shown in the diagram in *Figure 8.6* and this can be visualized very neatly using a single view, as shown in the following diagram:

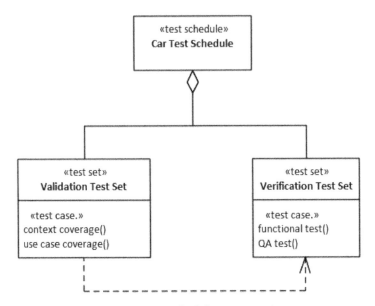

Figure 8.8 – Test schedule structure view

The diagram here shows a test schedule structure view for the car system that is visualized using a SysML block definition diagram.

The three levels of abstraction from the ontology definition view in *Figure 8.6* can be seen using the following stereotypes:

- <<**test schedule**>>, which is visualized by a SysML block and represents the highest level of the testing setup concepts, and comprises a collection of one (or more) <<**test set**>>.

- <<**test set**>>, which is visualized by a SysML block and forms part of the <<**test schedule**>> and itself comprises a collection of one (or more) <<**test case**>>.

- <<**test case**>>, which is visualized by a SysML operation and represents the actual test that will be executed.

This view is a neat way to show the entire hierarchy of the testing that needs to be carried out and, of course, may include many more test sets and, therefore, test cases, than those shown here.

Due to the fact that this is a structural view, the <<**test set**>> blocks show which test sets need to be executed but it does not show the order that the test sets need to be executed in. This may be specified using a behavioral view, as shown in the following diagram:

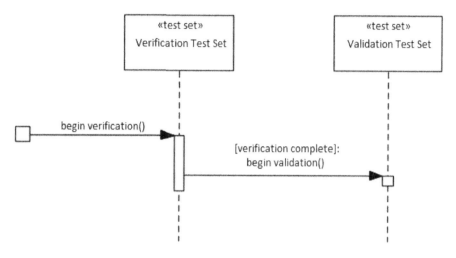

Figure 8.9 – Test set behavior view

The diagram here shows the test set behavior view for the car test schedule that was shown in *Figure 8.8*, and that is visualized using a SysML sequence diagram.

The SysML lifelines in this view represent instances of the test sets that were first identified in *Figure 8.8* but, because this is a behavioral diagram, we are seeing the actual sequences that the test sets must be executed in. There is an interesting modeling point here between the view in *Figure 8.8* and that in *Figure 8.9*. Notice that in *Figure 8.8*, there is a SysML dependency, represented by the dashed directed line between **Validation Test Set** and **Verification Test Set**. This dependency manifests itself in the sequence diagram in the order that the test sets are executed. Due to the fact that the **Validation Test Set** is dependent on the **Verification Test Set**, it is possible to infer the mandated ordered sequence between these test sets – the **Validation Test Set** must always follow the **Verification Test Set** due to the dependency between them.

From a modeling point of view, each of the test sets has a number of operations on them and, therefore, the behavior for each must be specified. This may be modeled as shown in the following diagram:

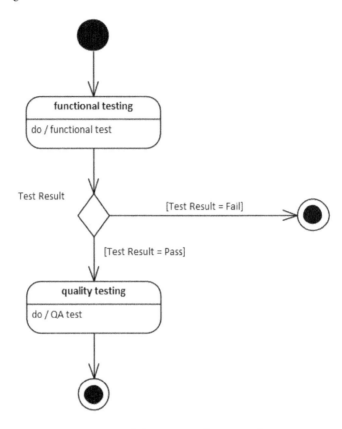

Figure 8.10 – Test case behavior view for the verification test set

The diagram here shows a test case behavior view for the **Verification Test Set** and is visualized using a SysML state machine diagram.

In this view, each of the SysML states represents a testing state. In the example shown here, there is only a single test case, shown by the SysML activities, in each state. It is possible to show more than one activity here, according to the standard SysML modeling guidelines that were discussed in *Chapter 2, Model-Based Systems Engineering*. Note that this state machine diagram not only shows the order of execution of the test cases, but also shows that if the first test case, **functional testing**, fails, then the testing activity stops and, only in the event that this test case is passed can the testing progress onto the **quality testing** test case.

The presence of these decision points and the relevant subsequent actions are very important from a testing point of view, as some test cases are dependent on the successful execution of another test case and, in the event that a previous one fails, there is no point continuing with the testing.

The views shown so far show the setup of the testing and the order that they must be executed, along with any conditions. It is also necessary to model the actual test cases, which will be discussed in the following section.

Modeling the testing configuration

Each test case relies on the different system elements in the element under test being connected together into a specific configuration. This may be based on the existing configuration views that were discussed in *Chapter 3*, *Systems and Interfaces*, and *Chapter 7*, *Modeling the Design*. An example of this is shown in the following diagram:

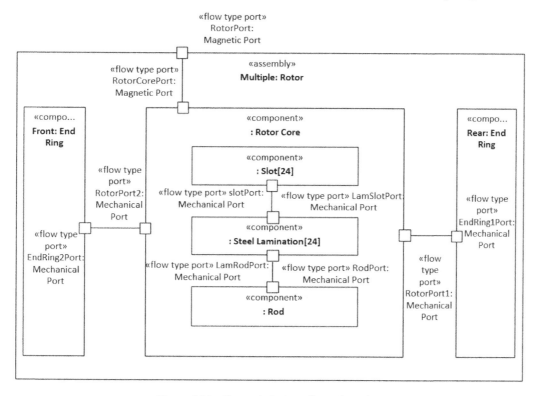

Figure 8.11 – Example test configuration view

The diagram here shows an example of a test configuration view that is visualized using a SysML internal block diagram.

This view shows how the system and its system elements must be connected together for a specific configuration. This may be used for a variety of testing purposes. Firstly, it will allow the connections between the physical system elements to be verified by ensuring that they exist and that they are connected to the appropriate system element. It will also allow the connections between these physical system elements to be checked in terms of the connector types, and so on. These views may also be used as part of the system setup views, in that they may be used to show specific system configurations for particular test cases. This contributes towards the *Ensure all design views are implemented* use case.

Using existing views for testing

The diagram in *Figure 8.7* showed the testing context for the car system, which laid out the basic needs for the testing activities. The use cases in this diagram represent a generic set of needs that will be applicable to most types of system. When considering these generic use cases, one of the great benefits of MBSE comes to light, which is the concept of reuse.

Whenever we create any view, it takes time and effort and consumes resources and, therefore, ultimately costs the project money. If it was possible to take one of the views that we had previously created and then to use it for some other activity during the life cycle, then clearly this would represent a saving of cost, time, and resources. Using something that already exists is known as reuse, and, when the modeling has been applied correctly, reuse should be common in any development.

Therefore, if it was possible to satisfy the use cases that were presented as the needs for the testing in *Figure 8.7* by using existing views, then this would offer a very attractive saving of valuable project resources. We shall revisit each of these use cases and consider whether any of the views that we have generated so far in this book may be used for testing.

Both the structural and behavioral views may be used for testing and, as a general rule, the behavioral views will be used directly as part of the test case descriptions for specific tests. The structural views will be used more for ensuring that the system is set up and configured correctly. It is also possible to automatically generate test cases, based directly on the model, but this is outside the scope of this book, but both the structural and behavioral views are an essential part of this automation.

Satisfying the Validate system use case

Validation, as has already been discussed, demonstrates that we are building the right system and is based on the initial needs of the system. It seems logical, therefore, to look at the needs views that were generated in *Chapter 6, Needs and Requirements*, and to see if any of them may be used as part of the validation activities. These views include the following:

- **Source Element View**: This view may be used in a number of ways that contribute towards the **Satisfy all use cases** validation use case. Firstly, it can be used to ensure that all of the use cases that must be satisfied have a valid source and, therefore, are valid use cases in their own right. Any use cases that cannot be traced back to a source element are immediately suspect and must be investigated to ensure that they have a valid source. If not, they must be removed. The source element view may also be used as part of the traceability of the whole model, as it represents the start point for all the information that will be contained in the set of views.

- **Needs Description View**: This view may be used to help satisfy the **Satisfy all use cases** validation use case. The **Need Description View** is often used as part of the contract and will form the legal basis for demonstrating that the system that is delivered is fit for purpose. This view is also very good for showing to non-technical stakeholders, as it will be text-based and, therefore, more accessible to any stakeholders that do not understand any of the technical notation, such as SysML.

- **Context Definition View**: This view contributes to the **Satisfy all contexts** use case, which is used to identify all of the relevant contexts that need to be considered to deliver the system. This is an essential part of any validation as it provides the start point for ensuring that all the relevant points of view of all the relevant stakeholders are being considered.

- **Need Context View**: This view forms the basis of the **Satisfy all contexts** use case as each view represents a single context. A combination of this **Need Context View** and the **Context Definition View** will ensure that all the relevant contexts have been both identified and defined.

- **Validation View**: It helps to satisfy the **Satisfy all contexts** and **Satisfy all use cases** use cases. This is the set of views that provides the criteria for demonstrating that any specific use case, or collection of use cases, in a context has been satisfied. These views may be used directly as testing scripts for the testing activities.

- **Need Rule Set View**: This view will contribute to all the **Validate System** use cases as it will ensure that the set of needs views are correct in themselves and comply with the needs framework.

- **Traceability Views**: These views are an important part of any testing activity as they allow impact and regression testing to be carried out. For example, if a specific test case fails, then it is possible to use the traceability paths that are inherent in the framework, through the ontology and viewpoint definitions, to identify which other system elements may be affected by the test case failure. This may be traced forwards, in terms of impact testing or, indeed, traced back to see which other test cases may need to be re-executed due to the original failure.

The needs views, therefore, may all be reused as part of the validation testing activities. This not only saves a lot of costs, time, and effort but also provides a single consistent set of information, a single source of truth, that is represented by the model.

Satisfying the Verify system use case

Verification allows us to demonstrate that we are building the system right. This means that the system has been developed according to the approach dictated and according to the development views that were generated during the development of the life cycle.

The **Verify system** use case includes two lower-level use cases, which we will consider in turn.

The first of these use cases is to *ensure all design views are implemented*, so the obvious place in the model to start looking for relevant views would be the design perspective, which was discussed in *Chapter 7, Modeling the Design*, and also the interface views that were discussed in *Chapter 3, Systems and Interfaces*. As part of the design perspective, the following views were discussed:

- **Logical System Structure Viewpoint**: This view allows logical system elements to be defined and, therefore, may be used to satisfy the **Ensure all design views are implemented** use case. It also satisfies three of the other use cases, which are: **Apply at system level**, **Apply at subsystem level**, and **Apply at assembly level**, as these are the levels that the logical system element was valid for. For example, there may be variations on the *Logical System Structure Viewpoint* (which is applied at the system level), such as the *Logical Subsystem Structure View* (applied at the subsystem level), and the *Logical Assembly Structure View* (applied at the assembly level). These views may then be used to test that the structure of the system under test matches that in the specified design perspective views.

- **Function Allocation Viewpoint**: This view allows the functions to be identified and then to be allocated to logical or physical system elements in the model, depending on the level of abstraction of the views. Again, this allows the system under test to be checked to ensure that all of the functions exist and that they are allocated to the correct corresponding system element in the design perspective views. This contributes towards the **Ensure all design views are implemented** use case.

- **Function Behavior Viewpoint**: This view specifies the behavior for an individual function. These are very powerful for testing and, like all of the behavior views, may be used directly as part of the testing scripts for test cases. The SysML activity diagram that is used to visualize this view provides the testing steps that must be carried out in order to execute the test case. This contributes towards the **Ensure all design views are implemented** use case.

- **Physical Structure Viewpoint**: This view identifies the physical system elements that comprise the overall system and its hierarchy. This view provides a check that all of the physical system elements are present in the system under test. This contributes towards the **Ensure all design views are implemented** use case.

- **Physical System Configuration Viewpoint**: This view shows how the system and its system elements must be connected together for a specific configuration. This may be used for a variety of testing purposes. Firstly, it will allow the connections between the physical system elements to be verified by ensuring that they exist and that they are connected to the appropriate system element. It will also allow the connections between these physical system elements to be checked in terms of the connector types, and so on. These views may also be used as part of the **System Setup Views**, in that they may be used to show specific system configurations for particular test cases. This contributes towards the **Ensure all design views are implemented** use case.

- **System Behavior Viewpoint**: These views specify the behavior of different configurations of system elements (both physical and logical) by defining scenarios. These scenarios, where they are operational scenarios (using SysML sequence diagrams) or performance scenarios (using SysML parametric diagrams), may also be directly as a part of the test scripts for each test case. These behavioral views contribute in a major way towards the **Ensure all design views are implemented** use case.

- **Interface Identification View**: These views allow the interfaces to be identified on specific system elements, whether they are logical or physical. These views are important as they allow each system element to be assessed as to whether each interface exists in the appropriate place. They may also be used to provide a specification for the acquisition (whether this is a commercial, off-the-shelf acquisition or bespoke acquisition) of specific system elements. In both cases, these views contribute towards the **Ensure all design views are implemented** use case.

- **Interface Definition View**: These views specify exactly what each interface looks like. They may also be used to provide a specification for the acquisition (whether this is a commercial, off-the-shelf acquisition or bespoke acquisition) of specific system elements. In both cases, these views contribute towards the **Ensure all design views are implemented** use case.

- **Interface Behaviour View**: These views allow an interface to be tested by treating each interface as a black box and testing the terminal inputs and outputs associated with each. Again, they may be used to provide a specification for the acquisition (whether this is a commercial, off-the-shelf acquisition or bespoke acquisition) of specific system elements. In both cases, these views contribute towards the **Ensure all design views are implemented** use case.

The second use case that made up the **Verify system** use case was to **Meet quality standards**. At first glance, it may appear that this has not yet been covered in this book, but it has been covered in great detail by demonstrating compliance of the MBSE approach with international best practice standards in two different places. The first example of this was shown at a high level in *Chapter 5, Systems Engineering Processes*, where it was shown how to use modeling to define a set of processes. The seven views approach that was used to model the MBSE process set (the **source process model**) is also used to model the standard (or set of standards) that must be complied with (the **target process model**), as was shown in the example of ISO 15288. The MBSE process set and the model of the chosen standard may then be mapped together to demonstrate compliance. This mapping is carried out using the seven views as follows:

- **Process Structure View**: This view forms the ontology for the chosen process or standard. As such, it is an excellent means to establish the basic mapping between the MBSE process set (the source process model) and the chosen standard (the target process model) that must be complied with as it maps the terminology used in each. This is an excellent example of using the ontology as the domain-specific language for the source and target process models. This mapping then forms the basis for all of the remaining compliance, as discussed in the next bullet points.

- **Process Content View**: This view allows the set of processes to be identified and summarized in terms of their artifacts and activities, and may be thought of as a process library. These process libraries for both the source and target process models may now be mapped together: between the actual processes; between the activities in each process; and between the artifacts in each process. It must be remembered that when mapping between the source and target process model, there will not necessarily be a one-to-one mapping between the processes, artifacts, or activities, which is perfectly normal and acceptable. Examples of specific process content views may be found in *Chapter 5*, *Systems Engineering Processes*; *Chapter 6*, *Needs and Requirements*; *Chapter 7*, *Modeling the Design*; and *Chapter 8*, *Verification and Validation*.

- **Process Context View**: This view provides the reason why each process model is needed and defines the scope of each. Mapping the process context view for the source and target process models provides a valuable insight into whether or not the two process models are compatible, by allowing the scope to be compared. This is also useful where non-compliance is identified between the process content views (as discussed in the previous bullet point), as the difference in scope may account for the non-compliance.

- **Information View**: This view provides an overview of the various artifacts associated with the source and target process models, along with the structure of each (this usually applies to the source process model, rather than the target process model) and the relationships between the artifacts. This is useful as a basic mapping but also provides a good source of traceability between the various artifacts. Again, there may not be a one-to-one mapping between the source and target artifacts, but this is quite normal.

- **Stakeholder View**: This view allows the stakeholders that are relevant to each process model to be identified. The mapping between these two is useful as it helps to identify any gaps in stakeholders that may be used to identify any skill gaps or lack of personnel.

- **Process Behavior View**: This provides the detailed behavior of a specific process. This will typically only exist for the source process model as most standards do not go into this level of detail. In these cases, these process behavior views are mapped to the process content views in both the source and target process models.

- **Process Instance View**: This view shows how executing processes in specific sequences may be carried out to demonstrate that the original use cases in the process context views can be validated. Again, these views will usually only be present in the source process model as it is very detailed information regarding specific processes. However, these may still be used to validate that the context of the target process model has been satisfied by the source process model.

When carrying out any of the mappings described here, it is possible to identify where the target and source process models comply and also any gaps in the compliance. These compliance gaps may be resolved in one of, typically, two ways. The first way is to provide a justification for why the non-compliance exists, such as a process in the target process model being out of scope. Where the compliance cannot be justified, then the source process model must be changed to reflect the non-compliance and updated, for example, by adding new processes, artifacts, or activities, to ensure that the gap is removed.

The second way that compliance of the MBSE approach may be demonstrated against relevant standards is by comparing the models of the framework itself. The MBSE framework that has been described throughout this book may be demonstrated to satisfy framework-based standards, such as **ISO 42010 – Systems and software engineering—Architecture description**, by considering the following framework views:

- **Framework Context View**: This view captures why the framework is needed and can be mapped onto the target framework's equivalent view. This may also provide a basis for mapping to the **Process Context View** for any process-based standard.

- **Ontology Definition View**: This view captures the main concepts and terminology used by the target standard. This may be used to map to the **Ontology Definition View** in a framework-based standard, or **the Process Structure View** in a process-based standard.

- **Viewpoint Relationship View**: This view identifies the various viewpoints and the relationships between them. This view may be mapped to its equivalent view in a framework-based standard or the **Information View** from a process-based standard.

- **Viewpoint Context View**: This view captures the basic need for each viewpoint. This may be mapped to the equivalent view in a framework-based standard or the **Process Context View** in a process-based standard.

- **Viewpoint Definition View**: This view identifies the ontology elements that will be present on each viewpoint. This may be mapped to the equivalent **Ontology Definition View** from the target standard or **the Process Structure View** from a process-based standard.

The two standards that are mentioned here form an excellent basis for compliance for any systems engineering endeavor.

Complying with best-practice processes

The techniques for applying model-based techniques to verification and validation that have been introduced and discussed so far in this chapter may be used to comply with international best practice – in this case, ISO 15288 – software and systems engineering life cycle processes.

The two processes that are of interest are both taken from the technical process group and, unsurprisingly, are the **Verification Process** and the **Validation Process**. Each of these will be discussed in the following two sections.

Complying with the ISO 15288 Verification Process

The ISO 15288 process that is relevant for verification is the **Verification Process**. This has been captured and modeled using the approach described in *Chapter 5, Systems Engineering Processes*. The process content view for this process is shown in the following figure:

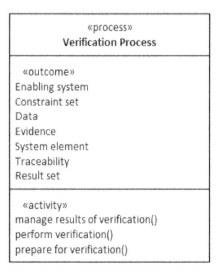

Figure 8.12 – Process content view for the ISO 15288 Verification Process

The figure here shows the process content view for the ISO 15288 **Verification Process**, and that is shown using a SysML block definition diagram.

The diagram uses standard SysML to represent the process perspective ontology concepts as follows:

- The block name shows the process name.

- The middle section shows the outcomes associated with the process, represented as stereotyped SysML properties.

- The bottom section shows the activities associated with the processes, represented as SysML operations.

The outcomes associated with the ISO process map to the views that have been discussed so far are as follows:

- **Enabling system**: This represents any other system that is necessary to perform the verification. This maps directly onto the **Enabling System** concept from the ontology definition view that was shown in *Figure 8.6*.

- **Constraint set**: This represents any limitations that are placed on the verification activities and are captured as part of the **Testing Context** from *Figure 8.6* and, specifically, the **Testing Need**.

- **Data**: This represents the information that is being used to directly perform the verification activity on the **Element Under Test**. This is represented in *Figure 8.6* by **Test Data**, which is between the **Test Case** and the **Testable Element**. In reality, this **Test Data** will take the form of the views that have been generated as part of the MBSE activities. Actual hard data, such as parameter values, will be present on these views as SysML property values and SysML parametric values.

- **Evidence**: This represents the information that is generated as part of the verification activity and that contributes towards the final result set. This is represented in *Figure 8.6* by the **Test Record**.

- **System element**: This represents the system or the system element that is the subject of the verification activity. This is represented in *Figure 8.6* by the **Testable Element** and, specifically, the **Element Under Test**.

- **Traceability**: This is a subject that is key to systems engineering, but one that is addressed implicitly when applying an MBSE approach, as all the traceability is established in the framework through both the ontology and the viewpoint definitions.

- **Result set**: This captures the final results that are generated by the verification activity. This is represented in *Figure 8.6* by the **Test Record**.

The activities that are identified on the process are mapped onto the modeling activities as follows:

- **manage results of verification**: This activity is associated with managing the test records that are generated as a result of the verification activity. All of this information must be carefully recorded and held under effective configuration management and control.

- **perform verification**: This activity is concerned with the actual execution of the verification activity. This is related to applying the test cases to the testable elements using the **Test Data**, as shown in *Figure 8.6*. From an MBSE point of view, this activity will use as many of the existing views as necessary from the model that will contribute towards verifying the system.

- **prepare for verification**: This activity is concerned with understanding why the verification activity is being carried out along with all the necessary enabling systems that are required to do this. This will also include setting up the test cases, test set, and **Test Schedule**. This is achieved by creating the views associated with **Testing Context** and **Test Case** in *Figure 8.6*.

The verification process is complemented by the validation process, which is discussed in the next section.

Complying with the ISO 15288 Validation Process

The ISO 15288 process that is relevant for validation is **Validation Process**. This has been captured and modeled using the approach described in *Chapter 5, Systems Engineering Processes*. The process content view for this process is shown in the following figure:

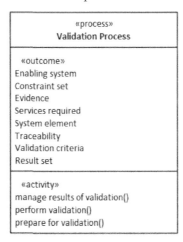

Figure 8.13 – Process content view for the ISO 15288 process Validation Process

The diagram here shows the process content view for the ISO 15288 process *Validation Process*, and that is shown using a SysML block definition diagram.

The outcomes associated with the ISO process map onto the views that have been discussed so far as follows:

- **Enabling system**: This represents any other system that is necessary to perform the validation. This maps directly onto the **Enabling System** concept from the ontology definition view that was shown in *Figure 8.6*.

- **Constraint set**: This represents any limitations that are placed on the validation activities and are captured as part of the **Testing Context** from *Figure 8.6* and, specifically, the **Testing Need**.

- **Evidence**: This represents the information that is generated as part of the validation activity and that contributes towards the final result set. This is represented in *Figure 8.6* by the **Test Record**.

- **Services required**: This represents any additional services that may be necessary in order to perform the validation activity. This is analogous to the **Enabling System** concept and is represented as such in *Figure 8.6*. In *Chapter 3, Systems and Interfaces*, we defined a service as a special type of system, so this mapping holds true here.

- **System element**: This represents the system or the system element that is the subject of the validation activity. This is represented in *Figure 8.6* by the **Testable Element** and, specifically, the **Element Under Test**.

- **Traceability**: This is a subject that is key to systems engineering but one that is addressed implicitly when applying an MBSE approach, as all the traceability is established in the framework through both the ontology and the viewpoint definitions.

- **Validation criteria**: This represents the information that is being used to directly perform the validation activity on the **Element Under Test**. This is partially represented in *Figure 8.6* by **Test Data** and will also directly refer to a subset of views that have been generated as part of the MBSE activities. Although the specific views that are used here may change, depending on the project, the mandatory views that will be used will be the two main types of validation views that were discussed in *Chapter 6, Needs and Requirements*. Actual hard data, such as parameter values, will be present on these views as SysML property values and SysML parametric values.

- **Result set**: This captures the final results that are generated by the validation activity. This is represented in *Figure 8.6* by the **Test Record**.

The activities that are identified on the process are mapped onto the modeling activities as follows:

- **manage results of validation**: This activity is associated with managing the test records that are generated as a result of the validation activity. All of this information must be carefully recorded and held under effective configuration management and control.

- **perform verification**: This activity is concerned with the actual execution of the validation activity. This is related to applying the test cases to the testable elements using the **Test Data**, as shown in *Figure 8.6*. From an MBSE point of view, this activity will use as many of the existing views as necessary from the model alongside the mandatory validation views that will contribute towards validating the system.

- **prepare for validation**: This activity is concerned with understanding why the validation activity is being carried out along with all the necessary enabling systems that are required to do this. This will also include setting up the test cases, test set, and test schedule. This is achieved by creating the views associated with the **Testing Context** and the **Test Case** from *Figure 8.6*.

Both the verification and validation processes are complementary and, indeed, very similar. This can be seen by directly comparing the two process content views shown in *Figure 8.11* and *Figure 8.12*. This is another advantage of carrying out the process modeling – it enables the similarities between the processes to be visualized very easily.

This similarity should not be too surprising as verification and validation activities relate to different aspects of testing. Again, this is something that is easily seen through the modeling, as verification and validation use the same ontology, as seen in *Figure 8.6*, which tells us that the concepts relating to each are the same.

The whole approach that has been introduced and discussed in this chapter has been shown to comply with current international best practice in the form of ISO 15288. The views that have been shown must be defined as part of the overall framework and the next section builds on the existing framework views by adding some of the verification and validation views to the framework.

Defining the framework

The views that have been created so far represent the center part of MBSE in a slide that was discussed in detail in *Chapter 2, Model-Based Systems Engineering*, and that was also revisited in the previous section. Each of the views has been visualized using SysML, which represents the right-hand side of MBSE in a slide. These views combine together to form the overall model, but it is essential that these views are all consistent otherwise they are not views but pictures! This is where the left-hand side of MBSE in a slide comes into play as it is important that the definition of all of the views is captured in the framework. The framework comprises the ontology and a set of viewpoints, therefore, it is now time to make sure that these viewpoints are defined thoroughly and correctly, which is the aim of this section.

Defining the viewpoints in the framework

It was discussed in *Chapter 2, Model-Based Systems Engineering*, that it is necessary to ask a number of questions for each view to ensure that it is a valid view. There is also a set of questions that must be asked of the whole framework, as well as the views, and the combination of these results in a set of questions that allow the whole framework to be defined.

When these questions are answered, then it can be said that a framework has been defined. Each of these questions can be answered using a special set of views that is collectively known as the **Framework for Architecture Frameworks** (**FAF**) (Holt and Perry 2019). At this point, simply think about creating a specific view to answer each question, as described in the following sections.

Defining the framework context view

The framework context view specifies why the whole framework is needed in the first instance. It will identify the relevant stakeholders that have an interest in the framework and also identify what benefits each of the stakeholders hopes to achieve from the framework. The framework context view for the verification and validation perspective is shown in the following diagram:

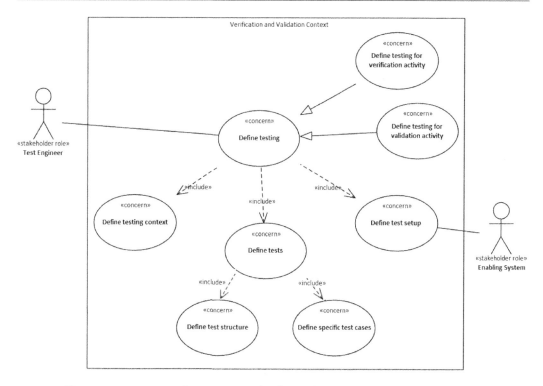

Figure 8.14 – Framework context view for the verification and validation framework

The diagram here shows the framework context view for the verification and validation framework that is visualized using a SysML use case diagram.

Note the application of the use case diagram here to capture the context, the approach of which was described in *Chapter 6, Needs and Requirements*.

This diagram may be read as follows:

- The main aim of the design framework is to **Define testing** in two ways: to **Define testing for verification activity** and to **Define testing for validation activity**. Due to the inheritance that is associated with the specialization relationship, the following three inclusions apply not only to the **Define testing** use case but also to its two specializations.

- **Define testing context**, which means that the reason for the testing, for both verification and validation, must be captured in the form of a testing context.

- **Define tests**, which requires that the actual tests must be defined in terms of their structure (**Define test structure**) and their test cases (**Define test cases**).

- **Define test setup**, which requires that the overall setup that is required in order for the test cases to be executed must be defined.

Notice that in this diagram, each of the SysML use cases is stereotyped as a <<**concern**>>. A concern is a need that relates specifically to a framework or one of its viewpoints.

Defining the ontology definition view

The ontology definition view captures all the concepts and associated terminology associated with the framework in the form of an ontology. This has already been done as the ontology for the design-related views was defined in *Figure 8.6*. The ontology elements shown on this view provide all of the stereotypes that have been used for the actual views that have been created so far in this chapter.

Ontology elements that are related will often be collected into a **perspective**, as was discussed in other chapters. In this chapter, a new perspective has been created that relates to verification and validation.

Defining the viewpoint relationship view

The viewpoint relationship view identifies which views are needed and, for each set of views, identifies a viewpoint that will contain its definition. Remember that a viewpoint may be thought of as a type of template for a view. These viewpoints may be collected together into a perspective, that is, simply a collection of viewpoints with a common theme. In this chapter, the emphasis has been on defining a set of views relations to design, therefore it is appropriate to create the **Verification and Validation Perspective**. The basic set of views that has been discussed so far is shown in the following view:

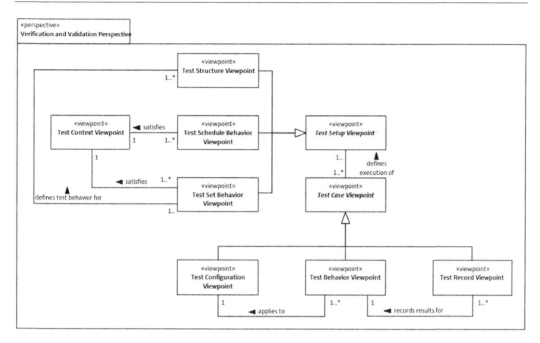

Figure 8.15 – Viewpoint relationship view for the Verification and Validation Perspective

The diagram here shows the **Viewpoint Relationship View** for the **Verification and Validation Perspective** using a SysML block definition diagram.

The **Verification and Validation Perspective** is shown using a SysML package, stereotyped as <<**perspective**>>, that simply collects together a number of viewpoints. There are nine viewpoints shown here, but it should be noted that two of these viewpoints are actually *abstract* viewpoints. When a SysML block is identified as being abstract, it means that it has no direct instances and, therefore, is typically used to show the situation where a block is being used as a generic type that is not instantiated directly. Abstract blocks are shown visually by italicizing the block name, therefore the two abstract blocks here are **Test Setup Viewpoint** and **Test Case Viewpoint**.

These two viewpoints, therefore, will not have any views associated with them; they are being used as generic categorizations for their specialized viewpoint. The non-abstract viewpoints are as follows:

- **Test Context Viewpoint**, which defines the reason why the testing is needed in the first place.

- **Test Structure Viewpoint**, which is a type of the abstract **Test Setup Viewpoint**, and it defines the structure of the testing, in terms of test cases, test sets, and the test schedules.

- **Test Schedule Behavior Viewpoint**, which is a type of the abstract **Test Setup Viewpoint**, and it describes the order that the test sets must be executed in for each test schedule.

- **Test Set Behavior Viewpoint**, which is a type of the abstract **Test Setup Viewpoint**, and it describes the order that the test cases must be executed in for each test set.

- **Test Configuration Viewpoint**, which is a type of the abstract **Test Case Viewpoint**, and it defines the configuration of the testable elements and any enabling systems that are necessary in order to carry out the test cases.

- **Test Behavior Viewpoint**, which is a type of the abstract **Test Case Viewpoint**, and it describes the behavior for each test case that describes the order that the specific testing steps must be carried out in. This may be thought of as a kind of script for the test case.

- **Test Record Viewpoint**, which is a type of abstract **Test Case Viewpoint**, and records the results of each test case and any other relevant information that is generated as a result of executing the test case.

This set of viewpoints is focused on the verification and validation activities and they are concerned with defining, setting up, and running the test cases. The information that is used in the execution of each test case, referred to as the **Test Data** on the ontology definition view in *Figure 8.6*, will take the form of existing views and associated parametric values.

Each of the viewpoints that has been identified here may now be described by its own viewpoint context view and its viewpoint definition view.

Defining the viewpoint context view

The viewpoint context view specifies why a particular viewpoint and, therefore, its set of views, is needed in the first instance. It will identify the relevant stakeholders that have an interest in the viewpoint and also identify what benefits each of the stakeholders hopes to achieve from the framework. The following diagram shows the viewpoint context view for the **Testing Context Viewpoint**:

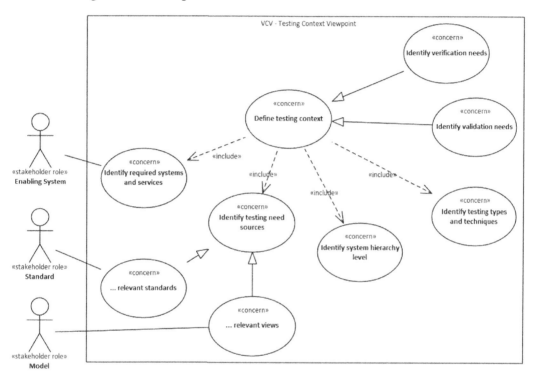

Figure 8.16 – Viewpoint context view for the Testing Context Viewpoint

The diagram here shows the viewpoint context view for the **Testing Context Viewpoint**, which is visualized using a SysML use case diagram.

This diagram may be read as follows:

- The main aim of the logical system structure viewpoint is to **Define testing context**. Note that this has been identified as the highest-level use case due to the fact that it has four <<**include**>> dependencies coming out of it and two specializations that emerge from it. These two specializations represent the two main types of testing, which are to **Identify verification needs** and **Identify validation needs**.

- **Identify required systems and services** is important as it identifies any enabling systems, such as other systems or services, that may be needed as part of the test configuration.

- **Identify testing need sources** identifies anything that is required in terms of testing data that is necessary to carry out the test cases. This may be specific views that are used as a part of the testing (**…relevant views**) when verifying that the system under test meets its design or a **Standard** (**… relevant standards**) that may be needed when verifying that the **Model** satisfies a particular best-practice reference, such as a **Standard**.

- **Identify system hierarchy level** relates to identifying exactly which part of the system under test will be tested, from the various testable elements.

- **Identify testing types and techniques** allows any specific testing requirements to be addressed and any constraints to be identified. For example, there may be a need for regression testing to be applied (a type of testing) using state-based views (a specific technique).

Now that the reason why the viewpoint must exist has been established, the viewpoint definition view may be considered.

Defining the viewpoint definition view

The viewpoint definition view defines the ontology elements that are included in the viewpoint. It shows the following:

- Which ontology elements are allowed in the viewpoint

- Which ontology elements are optional in the viewpoint

- Which ontology elements are not allowed in the viewpoint

The viewpoint definition view focuses on a single viewpoint and particular care and attention must be paid to not just the ontology elements that are selected, but also to the relationships that exist between these ontology elements.

An example of a viewpoint definition view for the **Need Description Viewpoint** is shown in the following diagram:

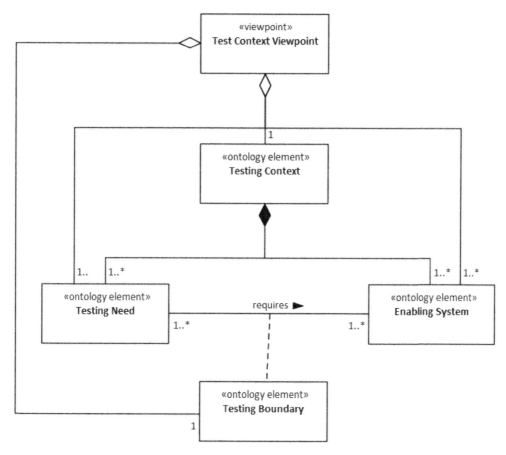

Figure 8.17 – Viewpoint definition view for the Test Context Viewpoint

The diagram here shows the viewpoint definition view for the **Test Context Viewpoint**, using a SysML block definition diagram.

This view defines the exact content of what is allowed in all the views that are described by the viewpoint. The ontology elements that are legal on the views associated with this viewpoint are as follows:

- **Testing Context**: It is the focal point of the viewpoint. Each **Test Context Viewpoint** is concerned with a single **Testing Context**.

- **Testing Need**: This allows all the needs and also the constraints associated with the **Testing Context** to be captured. As these needs are contextual, they will be represented by use cases.

- **Enabling System**: This represents other systems or services that are needed in order to execute the test cases.

- **Testing Boundary**: This helps to define the scope of exactly what is included in the **Testing Context**.

The viewpoints and the ontology elements that are permitted in each viewpoint are constrained by a number of rules, which will be described in the **Ruleset Definition View** for the needs perspective.

Defining the Ruleset Definition View

The Ruleset Definition View identifies and defines a number of rules that may be applied to the model to ensure that it is consistent with the framework.

The rules are based primarily on the **Ontology Definition View** and the **Viewpoint Relationships View**. In each case, the rules are defined by identifying the key relationships and the associated multiplicities that exist:

- Between viewpoints on the **Viewpoint Definition View**

- Between ontology elements on the **Ontology Definition View**

Some examples of these rules are shown in the following diagram:

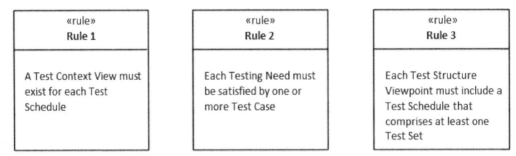

Figure 8.18 – Example Ruleset Definition View

The diagram here shows an example of a Ruleset Definition View using a SysML block definition diagram. Each block in the diagram represents a rule that is derived from either the Ontology Definition View or the Viewpoint Relationship View.

These rules are defined as follows:

- **Rule 1: A Test Context View must exist for each Test Schedule**: This rule is taken from the Viewpoint Relationship View that was shown in *Figure 8.14* and states that a Test Context is required for each Test Schedule that exists.

- **Rule 2: Each Testing Need must be satisfied by one or more Test Case**: This rule is taken from the Ontology Definition View that was shown in *Figure 8.6*.

- **Rule 3: Each Test Structure Viewpoint must include a Test Schedule that comprises at least one Test Set**: This rule is also taken from the Viewpoint Relationship View that was shown in *Figure 8.14*.

Notice how the rules are derived from the Viewpoint Relationship View and, therefore, the viewpoints and the Ontology Definition View, and therefore, the ontology elements. The actual rule descriptions themselves apply to the instances of the viewpoints (views) and instances of the ontology elements.

Of course, any number of other rules may be defined here, but not every relationship will lead to a rule, as this is at the discretion of the modeler.

Summary

In this chapter, the fundamental issues of verification and validation were discussed, both of which relate to testing activities. The key difference between the two is that verification shows that we have built the system right whereas validation shows that we have built the right system.

Verification and validation are particularly interesting from an MBSE point of view as the structure, content, and behavior of the testing activities are defined using our standard MBSE techniques for processes (see *Chapter 5*, *Systems Engineering Processes*) and frameworks, however, we are able to reuse many of the views that we have generated as a part of our MBSE activities.

This is a very important aspect of MBSE, as the more that we can reuse views from any part of the model, then the more time and effort we will save.

Finally, we looked at how the techniques used in this chapter comply with international best practice, in the form of ISO 15288, and we looked at the partial framework for the verification and validation perspective.

The next chapter deals with some of the management concerns that relate to systems engineering, and how these may be modeled using our MBSE techniques.

Self-assessment tasks

1. Revisit the Ontology Definition View in *Figure 8.6* and consider how this applies to your organization. Wherever necessary, change the different types of system elements to reflect your organizational needs.

2. Think about the different types of testing that are important for your organization. Which views from which perspectives that we have discussed so far in this book may be reused as part of this testing?

3. Define a test behavior view for any system element using a SysML activity diagram.

4. Define the **Viewpoint Context View** and **Viewpoint Definition View** for at least one other viewpoint that was shown in *Figure 8.14*.

References

- (Holt & Perry 2019) Holt, JD and Perry, SA. *SysML for Systems Engineering – a model-based approach*. Third edition. IET Publishing, Stevenage, UK. 2019

- (Holt *et al* 2016) Holt, JD, Perry, SA and Brownsword, MJ. *Foundations of Model-based Systems Engineering*. IET Publishing, Stevenage, UK. 2016

9
Methodologies

This chapter describes two widely used methodologies that may be applied in systems engineering and are used in modern industry.

Industry methodologies adopt standard, established life cycle approaches, such as linear, incremental, and iterative, which were discussed in *Chapter 4, Life Cycles*. In this chapter, we shall consider two of these methodologies: the **Scaled Agile Framework** (**SAFe**) and the **Object-Oriented Systems Engineering Methodology** (**OOSEM**). Each was selected based on its different yet complementary approaches and the different practices that they advocate.

In this chapter, we will cover the following topics:

- Methodologies, where we will briefly discuss methodologies and how they apply to systems engineering

- SAFe, which is an agile, iterative, and incremental framework

- OOSEM, which may be applied to traditional linear approaches but also agile, linear, incremental, and iterative approaches

- Methodologies and MBSE, where we will discuss how the methodologies covered may be used as part of a broader MBSE activity

This will give you a good overview of two prominent methodologies and show you how the knowledge and skills that we have provided so far in this book can be applied to existing methodologies.

Introducing methodologies

Methodologies are an important part of any systems engineering endeavor. Methodologies sit firmly in the *Approach* section of the *MBSE in a slide* diagram that has been referred to throughout this book.

Methodologies may include aspects of both frameworks and process sets but differ from frameworks and process sets in that they will define more details regarding actual techniques that may be used at specific points in a process, or they will define specific views in a framework. For example, a process will define the activities that need to be executed and the artifacts that must be created by such activities. However, a typical process does not go into detail about how each activity should be realized, as there may be many ways to do so. It may be, for instance, that a specific methodology uses a particular notation and toolset, whereas another methodology may realize the same activity using a different notation and toolset.

There are two main methodologies that will be discussed in this chapter:

- **SAFe**: The agile approach is one that is of much interest in the systems engineering community.

- **OOSEM**: This methodology has been chosen as it is widely used in industry and is also mentioned in the INCOSE systems engineering handbook as good practice.

Of course, there are many more methodologies, but the purpose of this chapter is to provide an overview of just two. Also, we will see how we can apply MBSE techniques to understand and explain the methodologies, and then we will conclude by considering how these methodologies may contribute to MBSE.

Introducing SAFe

SAFe is an approach that supports both Lean and Agile approaches to development. The difference between the aforementioned concepts is the following:

- A **lean** approach is one where the emphasis is on making delivery more efficient by managing and controlling the workflow. Lean was initially developed and deployed in the manufacturing sector by Toyota.

- An **agile** approach is one where the emphasis is on working in collaborative teams in order to develop and deliver a product in an incremental manner. An agile approach is intended to allow businesses to quickly adapt and respond to emerging competitive threats. Agile was initially developed as a way to develop software-based systems, although this has now been broadened to include business- and system-oriented applications.

The SAFe approach embraces both of these concepts and is aimed at improving the way that businesses operate; it is claimed that SAFe helps to sustain and also drive faster time-to-market rates, has good upward scaling in productivity and quality, and improves employee engagement.

Defining the SAFe concepts

SAFe was first published in the wider community in 2011 where it was focused firmly on software, but it has since had its scope extended to cover systems and enterprises. The basic philosophy of SAFe is captured in the following diagram:

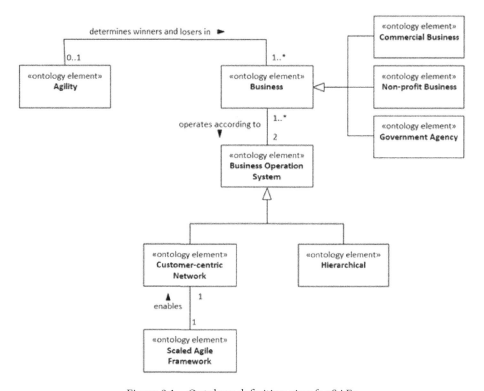

Figure 9.1 – Ontology definition view for SAFe

The diagram here shows a high-level ontology definition view for the SAFe approach, visualized using a SysML block definition diagram.

The starting point for SAFe is the assumption that due to the ever-changing face of business and its increased dependency on software-based systems, the presence of agility will determine the winners and losers in business. When referring to business, there are three main types, as follows: **Commercial Business**, **Non-profit Business**, and **Government Agency**.

All types of business operate according to two business operation systems, which are as follows:

- The **Hierarchical** business operation system is found in most businesses already. This is a more traditional approach that provides the necessary capability, in terms of processes, services, and so on, to meet the current business needs.

- The **Customer-centric Network** business operation system aims to efficiently identify and deliver customer needs and maintain quality for a variety of products that may form part of a higher-level portfolio.

The SAFe approach targets enabling this customer-centric network business operation model.

At first glance, it may not be immediately apparent how such an approach may be applied to systems engineering, but by analyzing the structure of SAFe, some parallels will emerge. The structure of SAFe is shown in the following diagram:

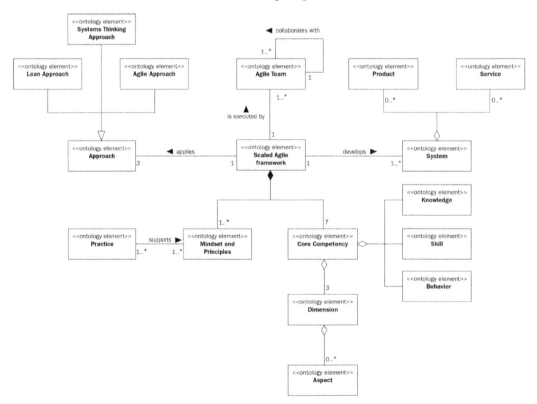

Figure 9.2 – Ontology definition view for SAFe, focusing on the structure

The diagram here shows an ontology definition view for SAFe with an emphasis on the structure and its main concepts, visualized using a SysML block definition diagram.

The diagram shows that SAFe is used to develop one or more systems, each of which comprises products and/or services. There is an immediate similarity to systems engineering here and the MBSE ontology that we have been developing throughout the book. Indeed, way back in *Chapter 1, Introduction to Systems Engineering*, one of the first concepts that we looked at was how systems engineering is used to develop successful systems.

The next really interesting point from this diagram is that SAFe applies three types of approach, which are the **Lean Approach**, the **Agile Approach**, and the **Systems Thinking Approach**. The first two of these yield no surprises, as they are embedded in the very core of the whole SAFe philosophy. The third approach, however, that of systems thinking, has not been mentioned so far in the overall description of SAFe, yet it makes an appearance here as a fundamental part of SAFe. The whole area of systems thinking is touted as a key approach, but it is not covered in much detail in the literature. Systems thinking is a very important aspect of SAFe, though, and it is held at the same level as lean and agile; plus, there is a clear link back to the world of systems engineering.

SAFe comprises seven core competencies and a number of mindsets and principles.

Each core competency is made up of and described by knowledge, skills, and behaviors. Each core competency is also made up of three dimensions, each of which may comprise a number of aspects.

As an example of this, there is a core competency identified as *continuous learning culture*, which has three dimensions: *learning organization*, *innovation culture*, and *relentless improvement*. The relentless improvement dimension is made up of five aspects, which are *constant sense of competitive danger*, *optimize the whole*, *problem-solving culture*, *reflect at key milestones*, and *fact-based improvement*. These core competencies relate to some of the processes, particularly the customer, organizational, and management process groups, from ISO 15288. It should be stressed, however, that the nature of some of these processes will change as SAFe employs Lean and Agile, which is often not the case with traditional systems engineering processes.

The mindsets and principles are supported by a number of practices. These practices include examples such as specify, architect, design, implement, test, deploy, and operate. Clearly, there are parallels between the technical processes in ISO 15288 and what are identified as practices here. Again, the nature of these processes may differ to take the Lean and Agile processes into account.

The concepts of mindsets and principles are explored in more detail in the following diagram:

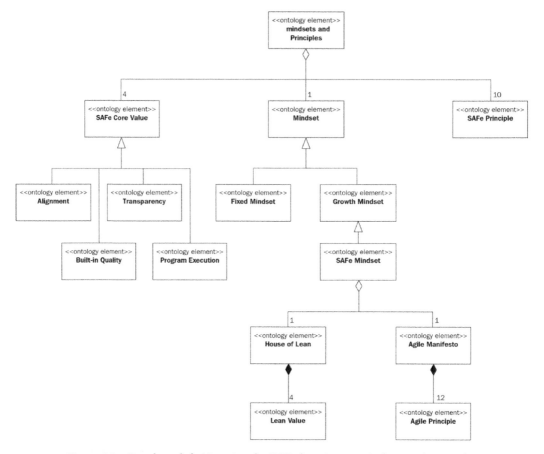

Figure 9.3 – Ontology definition view for SAFe focusing on mindsets and principles

The diagram here shows the ontology definition view for SAFe with an emphasis on the structure of mindsets and principles, visualized using a SysML block definition diagram.

The mindsets and principles comprise 2 mindsets and 10 principles.

The two types of mindset are as follows:

- **Fixed mindset**, which is based on a traditional, linear way of thinking about things.
- **Growth mindset**, one type of which is the SAFe mindset. Here, we see a combination of traditional approaches with the more agile SAFe mindset.

The SAFe mindset comprises the following:

- The **House of Lean**, which has four Lean values
- The **Agile Manifesto**, which comprises 12 Agile principles

So, here we see examples of explicit references to the Agile and Lean approaches that were mentioned in *Figure 9.2*. Interestingly, there is no mention at this point of the third approach, systems thinking.

Alongside the 2 mindsets and 12 principles, there are also 4 SAFe core values: **Alignment**, **Built-in Quality**, **Transparency**, and **Program Execution**.

So far, we can see a good relationship between SAFe and a systems engineering approach, as defined in this book. This can be achieved by comparing the ontologies and identifying relationships between them.

SAFe also defines additional information concerning how the system is developed, and this is shown in the following diagram:

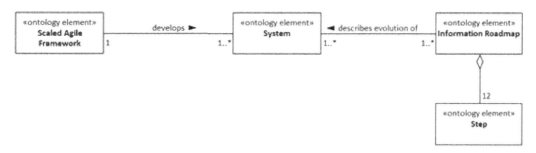

Figure 9.4 – Ontology definition view for SAFe focusing on system evolution

The diagram here shows an ontology definition view for SAFe that emphasizes the evolution of the system, visualized using a SysML block definition diagram.

SAFe develops one or more systems, and these systems have associated information roadmaps that describe their evolution. The roadmap evolution comprises 12 steps.

Previously, when we have discussed the evolution of systems, we have used life cycles, life cycle models (as described in *Chapter 4, Life Cycles*), and their associated processes (as described in *Chapter 5, Systems Engineering Processes*). This is directly analogous to the information roadmap and its associated steps. Again, this is another strong parallel to systems engineering.

Defining the SAFe core concepts

The core competencies form a major part of SAFe and are elaborated upon in the following diagram:

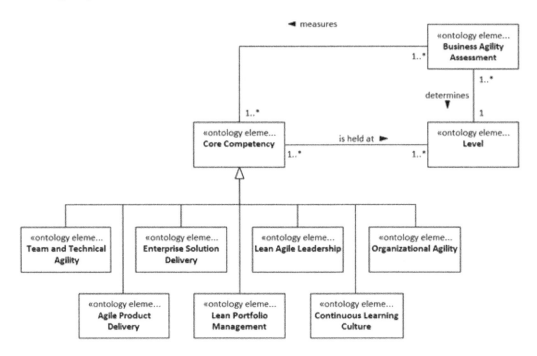

Figure 9.5 – Ontology definition view for SAFe focusing on core competencies

The diagram here shows an ontology definition view for SAFe that emphasizes the core competencies, visualized using a SysML block definition diagram.

We know from *Figure 9.2* that SAFe comprises seven core competencies, which are expanded upon in this diagram:

- **Team and Technical Agility** describes the Lean-Agile skills, principles, and practices that agile teams use to create successful systems for stakeholders. The three dimensions associated with this core competency are *agile teams*, *teams of agile teams*, and *built-in quality*.

- **Agile Product Delivery** utilizes a customer-centric approach that can help to define, build, and then release a continuous flow of valuable products and services to customers and users. This incremental delivery of the system in discrete releases is key to the whole philosophy of Agile. The three dimensions associated with this core competency are *customer-centric and design thinking*, *develop on cadence*, *release on demand*, and *DevOps and the continuous delivery pipeline*.

- **Enterprise Solution Delivery** is to do with how to apply Lean-Agile principles and practices (such as specify, develop, deploy, operate, and evolve) to the largest and most complex systems. The three dimensions associated with this core competency are *lean system and solution engineering*, *coordinating trains and suppliers*, and *continually evolving live systems*.

- **Lean Portfolio Management** is concerned with addressing the fundamental issue of what solutions should be built and why. This involves addressing portfolio concerns specifically. The three dimensions associated with this core competency are *strategy and investment funding*, *Agile portfolio operations*, and *Lean governance*.

- **Lean Agile Leadership** is concerned with ensuring that key stakeholders, such as business leaders, are responsible for the adoption and success of a lean and agile approach and the competencies that enable business agility. Such stakeholders must have an appropriate level of responsibility to be able to effect business change by creating agile teams. The three dimensions associated with this core competency are *mindset and principles*, *leading by example*, and *leading change*.

- **Continuous Learning Culture** describes values and practices that encourage individuals, and the entire business, to continually improve all of their activities. The three dimensions associated with this core competency are *learning organization*, *innovation culture*, and *relentless improvement*.

- **Organizational Agility** is concerned with ensuring that an organization is able to respond quickly to cope with any challenges and opportunities that arise that relate to the system. The three dimensions associated with this core competency are *lean-thinking people and agile teams*, *Lean business operations*, and *strategic agility*.

A key theme that runs throughout these core competencies is that of agile teams, and this is elaborated upon in the following diagram:

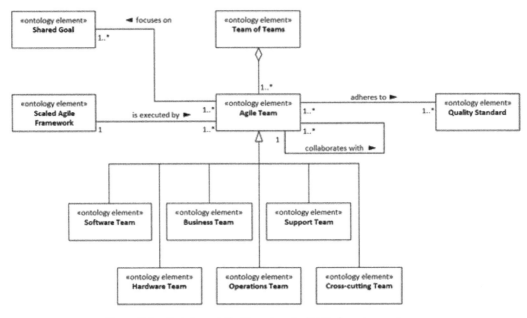

Figure 9.6 – Ontology definition view for SAFe focusing on teams

The diagram here shows the ontology definition view for SAFe with an emphasis on teams, visualized using a SysML block definition diagram.

It can be seen that SAFe is executed by one or more collaborating agile teams. These agile teams focus on shared goals and adhere to quality standards. There are six types of agile teams identified, which are **Software Team**, **Hardware Team**, **Business Team**, **Operations Team**, **Support Team**, and **Cross-cutting Team**.

The main emphasis in SAFe is on the fact that none of these agile teams exist or work in isolation, and hence collaboration is the key to success. To this end, these agile teams may be grouped into higher-level teams of teams.

Deploying SAFe

Another feature of SAFe, which is not too surprising, is that it is scalable for different sizes and types of projects. This scalability is realized in practical terms by tailoring the base framework and configuring it in different ways. The following diagram shows four possible configurations of SAFe:

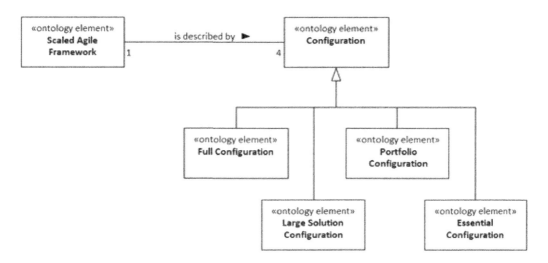

Figure 9.7 – Ontology definition view for SAFe focusing on configurations

The diagram here shows the ontology definition view for SAFe that focuses on configurations, visualized again using a SysML block definition diagram.

It can be seen here that SAFe is described by four configurations, which are as follows:

- **Full Configuration** includes all seven core competencies and is aimed at organizations that develop portfolios of large, integrated, and complex systems.

- **Portfolio Configuration** is aimed at businesses where the portfolio must be aligned to the overall business needs and strategy.

- **Large Solution Configuration** is aimed at enabling organizations to develop large, complex systems.

- **Essential Configuration** is the simplest of the configurations and is the starting point for implementing an agile and lean approach.

Remember from *Figure 9.2* that SAFe comprises, among other things, seven core competencies as described in *Figure 9.5*; it is the inclusion or exclusion of these core competencies that determines the configurations.

Summarizing the SAFe method

SAFe provides a powerful and widely used approach for developing successful systems, often referred to as **solutions**, that employs both the Lean and Agile approaches.

It also states that a systems thinking approach is also provided, but this is not focused on in much of the literature.

In terms of MBSE, SAFe sits firmly in the *Approach* section of the *MBSE in a slide* diagram and, in particular, it sits with the process set rather than with the framework part of the MBSE approach. This may seem counter-intuitive at first, but remember that when we define a framework in MBSE, we are referring to a blueprint for the model, and the emphasis is on the information. The use of the term framework in SAFe is subtly different and the emphasis is more on changing how we do things, which is more related to the process set than the framework.

In the next section, we shall look at another popular methodology that has a different emphasis, OOSEM.

Introducing OOSEM

OOSEM was originally developed by systems engineers from Lockheed Martin and the Systems and Software Consortium. OOSEM is a systems-level development method that combines object-oriented concepts with traditional systems engineering practices.

OOSEM was originally based on the **Object Management Group (OMG) Unified Modeling Language (UML)**, but since SysML was developed, it has been revisited to use SysML to capture the system model. Because of this, there are explicit mappings between the artifacts in OOSEM and specific SysML diagrams that may be used to visualize them.

Defining OOSEM concepts

The basic structure of OOSEM is shown in the following diagram:

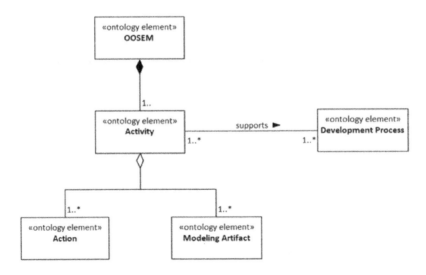

Figure 9.8 – Ontology definition view for OOSEM

The diagram here shows the ontology definition view for the structure of OOSEM, visualized using a SysML block definition diagram.

The OOSEM comprises one or more activities, each of which is made up of one or more modeling artifacts and one or more actions (please note that there is no explicit term for this concept, so the term **Action** will be used for the purposes of this explanation). So far, this part of the ontology looks very similar to the MBSE ontology for process modeling that was introduced in *Chapter 5, Systems Engineering Processes*, with **Activity** mapping to *Process* in the MBSE ontology, **Modeling Artifact** mapping to *Artifact* in the MBSE ontology, and **Action** mapping to *Activity* in the MBSE ontology.

As a slight aside, this is an excellent example of exactly why we need to have a good ontology in place. We have the same term, *Activity*, being used here and in the MBSE ontology, but each time it represents a different concept.

The activities in OOSEM do map to the processes in the MBSE ontology and they do have the same structure; however, they are applied at different levels of abstraction. As can be seen in the diagram, activities support one or more development processes, and this is a point of equivalence between the two ontologies. As OOSEM is a methodology as opposed to a process, it goes into more detail regarding specific techniques that can be used to develop the modeling artifacts. Processes generally state what needs to be done but not how to do it, whereas methodologies state how to do something.

OOSEM is not intended to be used in isolation but to support any number of different development processes. This means that it is not trying to represent the whole process set from *MBSE in a slide*, but is instead providing valuable additional information on exactly how to carry out the processes in the process set.

OOSEM can be used to model different types of systems, as shown in the following diagram:

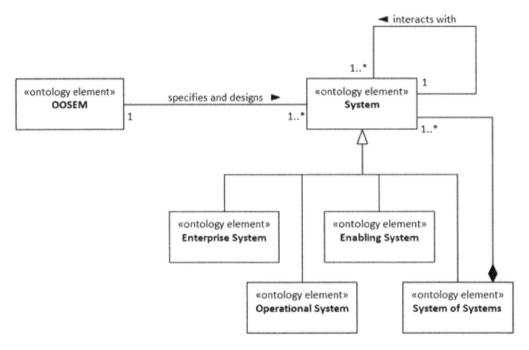

Figure 9.9 – Ontology definition view for OOSEM focusing on systems

The diagram here shows an ontology definition view for OOSEM that puts an emphasis on systems, visualized using a SysML block definition diagram.

An important part of OOSEM is this relationship: **OOSEM** specifies and designs one or more systems. This is quite subtle, but OOSEM is intended to be used only for specification and design and does not cover the implementation, support, or retirement of the system. This is important as it sets the scope for the OOSEM activities.

OOSEM has been designed to be used at a high level and, indeed, it advocates a traditional, top-down, functional decomposition approach to system development. As such, it can be applied to many types of systems, including the following:

- **Enterprise System** means a system that can be used to specify and design entire organizations and their associated businesses.

- **Operational System** means a system that is used and operated by customer stakeholders, such as trains, planes, and automobiles.

- **Enabling System** means a system that may be used to help with systems engineering activities, such as processes, frameworks, and so on. Please note that this is a different definition of the term *Enabling System* than was used in *Chapter 1*, *Introduction to Systems Engineering*.

- **System of Systems** means an interacting set of systems that delivers some emergent behavior that may not be realized by any single one of its constituent systems.

All of these different systems may interact with one another to form a higher-level system or, indeed, a system of systems.

Defining the OOSEM approach

The preceding point reflects one of the most powerful aspects of OOSEM, which is that it is designed to be flexible; this is further elaborated upon in the following diagram:

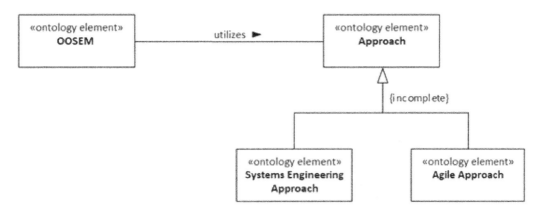

Figure 9.10 – Ontology definition view for OOSEM focusing on approaches

The diagram here shows an ontology definition view for OOSEM that emphasizes approaches, visualized using a SysML block definition diagram.

This diagram really emphasizes that OOSEM is not intended to be used as a standalone methodology, but that it should be used in conjunction with other approaches. There are many such approaches, but the two main ones that are mentioned in the literature are as follows:

- **Systems Engineering Approach**, which is hardly surprising

- **Agile Approach**, which is interesting as it provides a link between what is defined as part of OOSEM and its potential use with an Agile approach, such as SAFe

Now that the main structure of OOSEM has been discussed, it is time to look at the activities that form the focus of OOSEM. The OOSEM activities are shown in the following diagram:

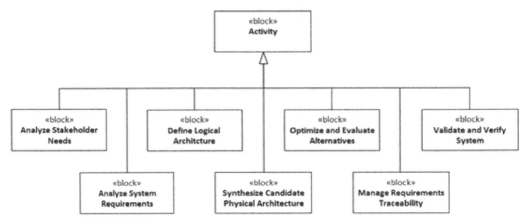

Figure 9.11 – Process content view for OOSEM

The diagram here shows a high-level process content view for OOSEM that is visualized using a SysML block definition diagram. The process content view is one of the views that was discussed in *Chapter 5*, *Systems Engineering Processes*, and is part of the *seven views* approach to process modeling.

The activities defined in OOSEM are as follows:

- **Analyze Stakeholder Needs**, which captures both the as-is and to-be stakeholder needs that describe the system of interest. This is all captured by use cases and scenarios, and measures of effectiveness are also defined.

- **Analyze System Requirements**, which allows the stakeholder needs to be refined into systems requirements; the interactions between the system and its stakeholders are analyzed.

- **Define Logical Architecture**, where a conceptual solution is captured that satisfies the original needs but is independent of any specific solution.

- **Synthesize Candidate Physical Architecture**, which develops a number of specific solutions to the generic one that was generated in the previous activity.

- **Optimize and Evaluate Alternatives**, where trade-offs are assessed and the different solutions are evaluated for effectiveness.

- **Manage Requirements Traceability**, which ensures that all the information generated by the modeling artifacts is traceable back to the original needs.

- **Validate and Verify System**, where it is demonstrated that the right system was built and that the system was built right.

These activities are intended to be carried out in a linear fashion; however, the approach allows for a high degree of iteration between these activities. Therefore, the overall execution of these activities may be linear, but there is not a single path of flow between them all.

These activities may also be used in an incremental fashion; it is possible to execute many sweeps through the activities, each of which results in an increment of the final system delivery. Again, this is another example of how flexible OOSEM can be when applied using different approaches, as described in *Figure 9.10*.

We shall take the description of the activities one step further by focusing on a single activity, as shown in the following diagram:

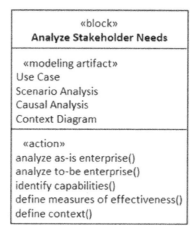

Figure 9.12 – Process content view for OOSEM focusing on the Analyze Stakeholder Needs activity

The diagram here shows the process content view for OOSEM with an emphasis on the **Analyze Stakeholder Needs** activity, visualized using a SysML block definition diagram. Again, the process content view forms part of the overall *seven views* approach, but this time we are emphasizing the modeling artifacts and the actions that comprise the activity.

We can see here that the **Analyze Stakeholder Needs** activity comprises the following modeling artifacts:

- **Use Case**, which represents the needs and capabilities of the system from the contexts of different stakeholders.

- **Scenario Analysis**, which captures different *what if* situations to be explored using sunny-day and rainy-day scenarios. These are used to help to identify measures of effectiveness for the system.

- **Causal Analysis**, which captures the impact of the interactions between different stakeholders and the system to be explored. The limitations of the current as-is system form part of this modeling artifact.
- **Context Diagram**, which captures overall contexts, based on both stakeholders and the system to be defined.

The **Analyze Stakeholder Needs** activity comprises the following actions:

- **analyze as-is enterprise**, which captures the current needs of the system
- **analyze to-be enterprise**, which captures the desired needs of the system
- **identify capabilities**, which identifies the desired capabilities of the system, based on the higher-level needs
- **define measures of effectiveness**, which may be based on the scenarios that were generated as part of the scenario and causal analyses
- **define context**, where the various contexts are captured based on the previous analyses

The other activities in OOSEM may also be captured in the same way as illustrated here. Now, let's revise what we have learned in this section.

Summarizing the OOSEM method

OOSEM provides a flexible methodology that may be used to help to specify and design a number of different types of systems. It is important to remember that OOSEM is not a full life cycle methodology and focuses on the specification and design of the system rather than implementation, support, or retirement.

OOSEM is also designed to work specifically with SysML (originally UML), which may be attractive to many systems engineers.

Also, OOSEM has been designed to be used in conjunction with other approaches, which makes it a potentially valuable addition to any MBSE toolkit.

Methodologies and MBSE

This section looks at how the two different methodologies discussed in this chapter fit into the big picture of MBSE. This discussion is limited to these two methodologies, but the concepts and discussion points may be applied to any methodology.

One of the fundamental mechanisms used to explain and understand MBSE throughout this book has been the use of *MBSE in a slide*, which was introduced back in *Chapter 2, Model-Based Systems Engineering*. As a refresher, this diagram is shown again in the following figure:

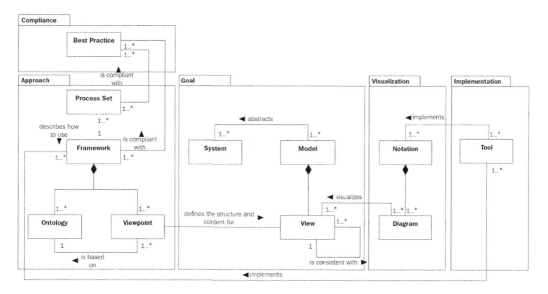

Figure 9.13 – MBSE in a slide (and a bit) – recap

The diagram here shows the now-classic *MBSE in a slide* that was used to identify the key aspects of MBSE that must be understood in order to implement MBSE effectively. This is visualized using a SysML block definition diagram.

One of the uses for *MBSE in a slide* is to be able to not only understand the main five concepts of MBSE but also map existing abilities onto this diagram.

The next sections, therefore, will relate the two methodologies that we have discussed so far to *MBSE in a slide*.

Methodologies and approach

The *Approach* section of *MBSE in a slide* is concerned with process sets and frameworks. We shall start the discussion by considering the process sets, or their equivalents, in *MBSE in a slide*.

The two methodologies that were chosen here to be discussed were selected because, between them, they exhibit properties of linear, incremental, and iterative approaches. This was discussed in *Chapter 4, Life Cycles*, where we used modeling to illustrate the difference between these different approaches using different life cycle models. Remember that a life cycle simply identifies the stages that describe the evolution of a system, whereas a life cycle model shows how these stages are executed in different sequences. It is the execution of these sequences of stages, and the process executions that are contained within them, that allows these different approaches to be visualized.

A very important aspect of life cycle modeling is the interactions between the different types of life cycles, for example, between the procurement and development life cycles. The way that these different types of life cycles are executed may differ; for example, linear, incremental, or iterative approaches may be used.

The emphasis of the SAFe methodology is on improving the effectiveness of a business by changing its overall approach to business, ensuring that it can react to change. It may also be applied at all different levels of abstraction, from portfolios down to individual systems. The SAFe methodology uses both Agile and Lean approaches, which themselves utilize incremental and iterative execution of their processes. The equivalent of a life cycle is the information roadmap, which describes the evolution of the system. The equivalent of a process in SAFe is the concept of a practice, which maps closely to the technical processes in ISO 15288. The rest of the SAFe approach focuses on the various management and organizational activities, captured in the core competencies, that need to be put into place.

The emphasis of the OOSEM methodology is on specifying and designing different types of systems. It may also be used at different levels of abstraction, ranging from systems of systems to specific-system development. The OOSEM methodology uses more of a classic linear approach that uses much iteration, and it may also be used as part of an overall incremental development system. The equivalent of a process is an activity, but these exist at a lower level of abstraction and, as such, are intended to support the implementation of traditional systems engineering processes.

There are, therefore, strong similarities between the ways that these two methodologies may be executed with regards to the process set part of *MBSE in a slide*.

The second part of *Approach* in *MBSE in a slide* is the framework, which focuses on the blueprint and the structure of the model.

In SAFe, the information that is to be produced is described as part of the core competencies that relate to **Agile Release Trains** (**ARTs**) and solution trains.

In SAFe, the emphasis is on changing the way that organizations work by changing mindsets, creating and empowering effective teams, and reacting effectively to business change. SAFe advocates enterprise architecture and the role of the enterprise architect but does not specify any specific architecture framework.

In OOSEM, there is a distinct structure to the model, which is based on the modeling artifacts that are generated as part of the activity execution. Although there is no specific framework defined for OOSEM, the number of views and, therefore, viewpoints is relatively low, and it would be a straightforward task to capture the framework for OOSEM.

Methodologies and goals

The *Goal* section of *MBSE in a slide* focuses on the model and its views, and how they relate to the system.

In SAFe, the emphasis is on the enterprise and how to make it work effectively. SAFe does consider portfolios of systems and individual systems as part of the core competencies. Modeling is referred to in the contexts of mental models, operation models, exaction models, and so on. Again, these relate to aspects of the enterprise.

In OOSEM, the model is central to everything that is done and, therefore, is truly an abstraction of the system, regardless of the type of system.

Methodologies and visualization

The *Visualization* section of *MBSE in a slide* focuses on the notations that are used to visualize the views.

In SAFe, there are no explicit nor mandatory notations that must be used. Having said that, SAFe may be implemented using any appropriate notation, so this leads to a flexible implementation.

In OOSEM, the notation that is used is explicitly SysML. Originally, this was UML, but as SysML is a profile of UML, this is a straightforward and intuitive transition between the notations.

Methodologies and implementation

The *Implementation* section of *MBSE in a slide* focuses on the tools that may be used to visualize views.

There are a number of commercial tools available that implement SAFe from a number of different vendors.

For OOSEM, there are no dedicated commercial tools available. However, there are a number of generic MBSE tools that have profiles available, typically for free, that allow OOSEM to be implemented as part of the tool.

Methodologies and compliance

The *Compliance* section of *MBSE in a slide* is concerned with standards and other best-practice sources.

The SAFe methodology formally states that agile teams adhere to quality standards. Notice again that the emphasis is on the people aspect and the compliance relates to the teams.

In OOSEM, compliance with certain best-practice sources, including ISO 15288, has been mapped out and is freely available. It should be noted that it is the activities in OOSEM that map to the standards.

We have now seen, therefore, how the methodologies form part of the bigger picture of MBSE that was described in *MBSE in a slide*. This provides an important frame of reference for methodologies and also validates just how important the overarching concepts contained in *MBSE in a slide* are to any systems engineering initiative.

Summary

This chapter has introduced two example methodologies: SAFe and OOSEM. Both of them may be used as part of a wider systems engineering endeavor, but they have quite different purposes.

Each methodology was modeled using ontologies.

Finally, each methodology was mapped to the *MBSE in a slide* diagram that has been referred to throughout this book. It should be clear that both methodologies fit in with MBSE and can be used to satisfy the different aspects of *MBSE in a slide*.

By relating these existing methodologies to what we have learned so far in this book, it has been illustrated how we can use MBSE to incorporate any approach into a wider systems engineering initiative.

In the next chapter, we will understand the management processes and associated techniques to be considered and implemented.

Self-assessment tasks

1. Create a framework context view for both of the methodologies discussed in this chapter. Now analyze each of them with regards to how they fit into the MBSE approach that has been introduced in this book.

2. Create a process content view for SAFe, based on its practices. Now relate this to the process content view that was discussed for OOSEM in *Figure 9.11*.

3. Map the process content views for SAFe and OOSEM to the process content view for ISO 15288 that was introduced in *Chapter 5, Systems Engineering Processes*.

4. Finally, come to your own conclusion as to whether these two methodologies could be used together. Use the ontology definition views and process content view to back up your conclusion.

References

- *A Practical Guide to SysML: The Systems Modeling Language*, Third Edition, S Friedenthal, A Moore, and R Steiner. Morgan Kaufmann Publishers, 2014.

- *Achieving Business Agility with SAFe® 5.0*, a Scaled Agile, Inc. whitepaper, December 2019. Available from `scaledagileframework.com`.

- *SAFe 5.0 Distilled; Achieving Business Agility with the Scaled Agile Framework*, R Knaster and D Leffingwiell. Addison-Wesley Publishing, 2020.

10
Systems Engineering Management

This chapter provides an overview of some of the key management processes and associated techniques that need to be taken into account and how they can be implemented. The relationship between management techniques and technical techniques is also discussed. We will then have a discussion of how designs fit into the systems life cycle and which processes are relevant and how to comply with them.

This chapter covers the following topics:

- Introducing management
- The project planning process
- The decision management process
- The project assessment and control process
- The risk management process
- The information management process
- The configuration management process
- The measurement process
- The quality assurance process

This chapter provides us with an overview of how the basic management-related processes in ISO 15288 can be realized using the MBSE techniques that have been described so far in this book. Each process references other relevant chapters where example views may be found.

This demonstrates that MBSE activities are not just limited to technical processes but may be used for any aspect of systems engineering.

Introducing management

A key part of any systems engineering endeavor is ensuring that the system is delivered successfully, which includes not only the technical aspects of the system but also the management aspects.

It is essential that the system satisfies its basic needs, which has been a theme running throughout this book, but remember that these needs are captured according to a number of different contexts. These contexts include looking at the needs from different points of view, and one of these points of view must consider the management aspects.

For example, it is not good enough to deliver a system that satisfies the technical needs if it is delivered late, is over budget, or consumes too many resources. The best practice standard, ISO 15288, which we have been using as the main source for compliance throughout this book, has a process group that is dedicated to technical management processes, and this will form the basis for our discussion on management.

The processes that are contained in the technical management process group are shown in the following diagram:

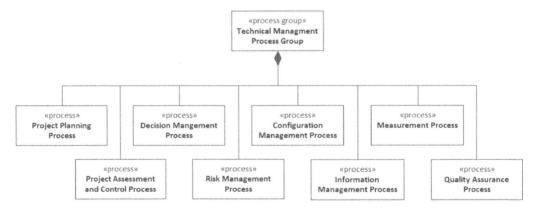

Figure 10.1 – Process content view showing the processes in the technical management process group from ISO 15288

The process content view here is visualized using a SysML block definition diagram.

The process content view is one of the views that comprise the **seven views approach** to process modeling that was described in *Chapter 5*, Systems Engineering Processes. By way of a recap, the process content view allows the library of processes to be defined at a high level by showing which processes are contained in which process group, as shown in *Figure 10.1*. It may also show the specific outcomes and activities associated with each process, which will be used in the more-detailed discussion for each specific process in the following sections.

The processes that comprise the technical management process group are as follows:

- **Project Planning Process**: The aim of this process is to produce effective plans for the project.

- **Project Assessment and Control Process**: The aim of this process is to assess the suitability of the plans that are generated for the project and to control the execution of these plans to ensure that they satisfy the original needs.

- **Decision Management Process**: The aim of this process is to provide a set of structured techniques that will allow the project's progress to be assessed at key points and, where necessary, for alternative action to be taken.

- **Risk Management Process**: The aim of this process is to identify, understand, and control any risk that occurs throughout the project.

- **Configuration Management Process**: The purpose of this process is to control the evolution of the information produced as part of the system development throughout the project.

- **Information Management Process**: The aim of this process is to ensure that all the information concerning the project is managed and maintained throughout the project, and to ensure that the appropriate stakeholders have access to relevant information.

- **Measurement Process**: The aim of this process is to provide techniques that will allow objective information concerning the project to be captured in order to manage the project effectively.

- **Quality Assurance Process**: The aim of this process is to ensure that the systems engineering processes are applied effectively to the project.

Each of these processes will now be introduced in turn and the use of the modeling and views that have been presented in this book will be discussed.

One of the themes that has been discussed throughout this book is that whenever we need to understand something, we can model it to gain a thorough and complete analysis. Therefore, we will present the process content views introduced to *Chapter 5, Systems Engineering Processes*, which will provide a simple overview of what outcomes need to be generated and what activities need to be executed for each process.

The project planning process

The project planning process is concerned with defining the project, planning the project, and activating the project, as shown in the following diagram:

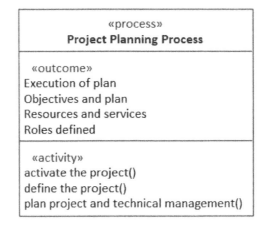

Figure 10.2 – Process content view for the project planning process

A SysML block definition diagram is used to show the process itself and the following outcomes, represented by SysML properties, which are identified for this process, described as follows:

- **Execution of plan**: This outcome ensures that the plans for the execution of the project are activated.

- **Objectives and plan**: This outcome ensures that the objectives and plans for the project have been defined.

- **Resources and services**: This outcome ensures that the resources and services that are necessary for the achievement of the aims and objectives that were previously defined are identified and acquired.

- **Roles defined**: This outcome ensures that the roles, responsibilities, accountabilities, and authorities are defined.

These outcomes are achieved by executing a number of activities, each of which comprises a number of tasks. These activities will now be discussed in more detail and reference will be made to the various modeling views that have been discussed in the book.

Applying modeling to the activate the project activity

The *activate the project* activity comprises the following three tasks:

1. Implement project plans.

2. Obtain authorization for the project.

3. Submit requests and obtain commitments for necessary resources to perform the project.

All of these tasks are concerned with initiating the project based on the information that was generated by executing the last two activities: define the project and plan the project and technical management. All of the views that were discussed as part of these activities may now also be used to activate the project. For example, the *obtain authorization for the project* task can be realized by using the life cycle and process views, combined into the schedule view, to obtain the authorization.

Applying modeling to the define the project activity

The *define the project* activity comprises the following five tasks:

1. Define and maintain a life cycle model that comprises stages using the defined life cycle.

2. Define and maintain the processes that will be applied to the project.

3. Define the project scope as established in the agreement.

4. Establish a work breakdown structure based on the evolving system architecture.

5. Identify project objectives and constraints.

At first glance, there may seem to be a lot of action required to achieve these tasks, but the good news is that all of these tasks have already been addressed by the modeling that we have carried out so far in this book.

Consider now *Task 1*, which is concerned with defining the life cycle that will be used for the project. This has already been covered completely in *Chapter 4, Life Cycles*. In particular, the following viewpoints and their associated views are of direct relevance:

- The *Life Cycle* view, which defines the stages that comprise the life cycle

- The *Interaction Identification Viewpoint*, which identifies points where the system development life cycle may interact with other life cycles

Next, consider *Task 2* and *Task 4*, which are both concerned with the processes and their associated work breakdown structure. Again, all of these have been covered in the modeling in *Chapter 4, Life Cycles*, and *Chapter 5, Systems Engineering Processes*, as follows:

- The *Process Content Viewpoint* from *Chapter 5, Systems Engineering Processes*, identifies the processes that are available to be executed on the project. Either all of these processes or a subset of these processes may be selected for any specific project.

- The *Life Cycle Model Viewpoint* from *Chapter 4, Life Cycles*, may be used to provide the highest level of project behavior. Remember that processes are executed in process execution groups that live within each life cycle stage. This viewpoint, therefore, provides an excellent overview of the life cycle stages and which processes are realized in each, which may be used for the highest level of the work breakdown structure.

- The *Process Behavior Viewpoint* from *Chapter 5, Systems Engineering Processes*, is used primarily, at this point, for the work breakdown structure, as it shows how each of the activities associated with each process is executed.

Finally, consider *Task 3* and *Task 5* from the list. Both of these tasks are associated with identifying and defining the overall scope, in terms of its objectives, of the project, along with the constraints that are associated with these objectives.

This was the topic of *Chapter 6, Needs and Requirements*, and the whole modeling approach that was described in that chapter can be applied here. In particular, the following viewpoint and its associated views are of direct interest:

- The *Need Context Viewpoint*, where the overall aims are identified and are defined using use cases. These aims are defined from different points of view, or contexts, and form the heart of the whole system development. As part of this view, the constraints are also defined using use cases and the relationships to their relevant aims-based use cases are identified.

The next activity that will be considered is planning the project and technical management.

Applying modeling to the plan project and technical management activity

The *plan project and technical management* activity comprises the following seven tasks:

1. Define achievement criteria for the life cycle stage decision gates and delivery gates.

2. Define and maintain a project schedule based on management and technical objectives.

3. Define roles, responsibilities, accountabilities, and authorities.

4. Define the costs and plan a budget.

5. Define the infrastructure and services required.

6. Generate and communicate a plan for the project and technical management as well as the execution.

7. Plan the acquisition of materials and enable system services supplied from outside the project.

Again, all of these tasks can be addressed by existing views that have been discussed previously in this book.

Consider *Task 1*, which is associated with the gates for each of the stages, and the following viewpoints are relevant to this:

- The *Life Cycle* view, which defines the stages that comprise the life cycle

- The *Interaction Identification Viewpoint*, which identifies points where the system development life cycle may interact with other life cycles

Consider *Task 2*, *Task 4*, *Task 5*, and *Task 7*, all of which are concerned with creating and maintaining the project plan. The following viewpoints and their associated views may be used as a basis for these tasks:

- The *Life Cycle Model Viewpoint* from *Chapter 4, Life Cycles*, may be used to provide the highest level of project behavior. This viewpoint provides an excellent overview of the life cycle stages that are used as the highest-level entities in the project schedule. The life cycle itself applies across the entire project, and each stage within the life cycle represents the next level of abstraction down.

- The *Process Instance Viewpoint* from *Chapter 5, Systems Engineering Processes*, identifies the processes that are executed in each process execution group on the project. Each process execution group collects together a set of processes that are executed in a specific sequence inside a gate. It is possible for more than one of these process execution groups, visualized by a process instance view, to be executed inside a single gate. This provides the next level of abstraction down for the behavior of the schedule.

- The *Process Behavior Viewpoint* from *Chapter 5, Systems Engineering Processes*. This is used to describe how each process behaves internally by showing the detailed order of execution of the activities within each process. This provides the fine detail of behavior for each process that is used to define the project schedule.

These three viewpoints and their associated views are interesting as they all have a direct impact on an overall project schedule, which is not too surprising as they are all behavioral views. The diagram that is used predominantly in the project management world to visualize a project schedule is the Gantt chart, which shows the planned behavior of a project, along with its milestones, resources, and so on. The Gantt chart is, of course, not a SysML diagram but this certainly does not mean that it should not be used as part of the systems engineering management. Consider the classic MBSE in a slide that was first introduced in *Chapter 2, Model-Based Systems Engineering*, and that has been used throughout this book. The right-hand side of this diagram shows the visualization of the views that comprise the model and, very importantly, it has been discussed at some length how the notation that is used for this visualization is largely irrelevant, providing, of course, that it is consistent with the underlying viewpoint that defines the set of views.

Indeed, the information that is required to create a Gantt chart has already been defined as part of our MBSE approach and is readily available in the views that were described in the previous bullet list. In order to illustrate this, consider the following generic Gantt chart:

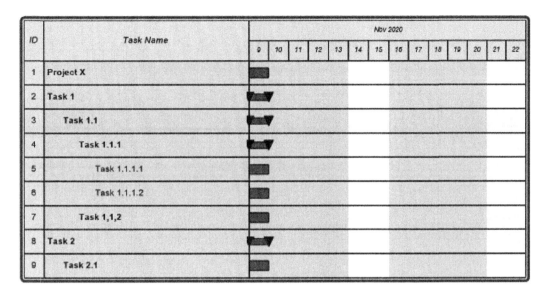

Figure 10.3 – Generic project schedule showing the different levels of a task

The diagram here shows a generic project schedule in a Gantt chart that traditionally emphasizes the various levels of a task in a project schedule, and then shows the timings associated with each (such as the start date, end date, duration, and so on), along with any major project gates, milestones, and resources. For the purposes of this discussion, we will be focusing purely on the levels of task information and, therefore, all the other information has been omitted from the diagram for reasons of clarity.

The Gantt chart is basically a structured table with a number of columns and rows that describe the properties of the project. Note the second column, titled **Task Name**, which is a typical way to describe the actions that are taken on a Gantt chart. If we now go down this column and consider each row, it can be seen that the tasks actually exist at a number of levels of abstraction or detail, as shown by the numbering system and the indentations that are applied. In fact, despite the main column stating **Task Name** here, it is quite clear that there are several levels here, which are as follows:

- **Row ID: 1 – Project X**, which shows the highest level of task that is applied to the project as a whole

- **Row ID: 2 – Task 1**, which shows the next highest level of task and starts the main numbering system as **1**

- **Row ID: 3 – Task 1.1**, which shows the next level down of task and continues the breakdown indicated by the numbering system as **1.1**

- **Row ID: 4 – Task 1.1.1**, which shows the next level down, again as level **1.1.1**
- **Row ID: 5 – Task 1.1.1.1** and **Row ID: 6 – Task 1.1.1.2**, which each show the lowest level on this diagram and are indicated using **1.1.1.x**
- **Row ID: 7 – Task 1.1.2**, which goes back up a level
- **Row ID: 8 – Task 2**, which goes up again another level
- **Row ID: 9 – Task 2.1**, which starts to descend through the levels again

Note how each of these task levels is still referred to as **Task**, which makes the numbering systems and indentations essential to the understanding of the chart. Also, because of the same term, **Task**, being used, it can easily lead to potential confusion when referring to different types of tasks. Indeed, this type of confusion was discussed at length in *Chapter 2, Model-Based Systems Engineering*, and is one of the reasons why having a good, solid, unambiguous ontology in place is so important. Another problem with this is that there is potentially no end to the level at which it is possible to descend, so it would be possible, for example, to have a task `1.2.3.4.5.6.7.8.9.20.1.2.4.5` as there is no bounding on the level of abstraction.

All of these potential problems can be solved easily and effectively by applying an ontology to the levels. To illustrate this, consider the following revised schedule:

ID	Task Name	Nov 2020													
		9	10	11	12	13	14	15	16	17	18	19	20	21	22
1	Life Cycle: Project X														
2	**Stage 1: Concept**														
3	**Project Needs**														
4	Stakeholder Needs and Requirements Definition Process														
5	Define stakeholder needs														
6	Analyze stakeholder requirements														
7	System Requirements Definition Process														
8	**Stage 2: Development**														
9	**Candidate design development**														

Figure 10.4 – Generic project schedule using ontology elements for levels of task

The diagram here shows the same generic schedule as in *Figure 10.3* with tasks defined by the ontology and is visualized by a Gantt chart.

The information in this diagram is the same, and it has the same number of levels of abstraction of task, but this time, the levels are based on the concepts from the MBSE ontology that we have been developing throughout this book. Using these ontology elements as a basis for the task levels, the following may be observed:

- **Row: ID 1 – Life Cycle: Project X**, which shows the highest level of the task that is represented as *Life Cycle* on the ontology.

- **Row ID: 2 – Stage 1: Concept**, which shows the next highest level of the task and is representing a *stage* from the ontology; in this case, this stage is **Concept** from ISO 15288.

- **Row ID: 3 – Project Needs**, which shows the next level down of the task and is representing a *process execution group*, in this case, named **Project Needs**.

- **Row ID: 4 – Stakeholder Needs and Requirements Definition Process**, which shows the next level down again and is representing the concept of a *process* from the ontology, in this case, **Stakeholder Needs and Requirements Definition Process**.

- **Row ID: 5 – Define stakeholder needs** and **Row ID: 6 – Analyze stakeholder requirements**, which each show the lowest level on this diagram and are representing the *Activity* concept from the ontology.

- **Row ID: 7 – System Requirements Definition Process**, which goes back up a level and is representing another *process* from the ontology.

- **Row ID: 8 – Stage 2: Development**, which goes up again another level to represent another *stage* from the ontology, in this case, the **Development** stage from ISO 15288.

- **Row ID: 9 – Candidate Design Development**, which starts to descend through the levels again, and represents another *process execution group*.

The use of these views from the model to create the schedule is very important and very powerful. By ensuring that all the information in the schedule comes directly from the ontology, it means that the schedule is a proper view in the model. The use of a Gantt chart, therefore, just becomes a matter of the visualization for the schedule view.

All of the other information that is required for the schedule, such as the stakeholders, resources, and gates, is also part of the overall ontology and can, therefore, also be derived directly from the model. This is crucial as the schedule is not directly based on the overall MBSE approach, rather than just being fabricated with no real basis by a project manager.

Summary of the project planning process

It can be seen that all of the activities related to this process and all of the outcomes that are necessary for the successful completion of the process can be achieved by using existing views from the model.

Notice that the views that have been utilized are primarily from the life cycle perspective and the process perspective, which is to be expected as they both deal with the running of projects.

The next section will discuss the next process from ISO 15288, which is the decision management process.

The decision management process

The main aim of the decision management process is to provide mechanisms for exploring alternative options for making decisions at any point in the life cycle, and is shown in the following diagram:

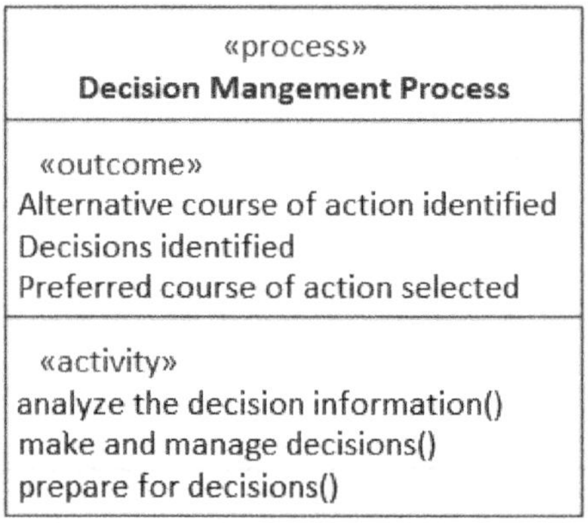

«process»
Decision Mangement Process
«outcome» Alternative course of action identified Decisions identified Preferred course of action selected
«activity» analyze the decision information() make and manage decisions() prepare for decisions()

Figure 10.5 – Process content view for the decision management process

The outcomes, represented by SysML properties, that are identified for this process are described as follows:

- **Alternative course of action identified** identifies the options that are available at the key decision points that were identified in the previous outcome.

- **Decisions identified** identifies the key decision points that are available at any point in the life cycle.

- **Preferred course of action selected**, where based on the previous outcomes, the most appropriate course of action is selected.

These outcomes are achieved by executing a number of activities, each of which comprises a number of tasks. These activities will now be discussed in more detail and reference will be made back to the various modeling views that have been discussed in the book.

Applying modeling to the prepare for decisions activity

The *prepare for decisions* activity comprises the following tasks:

1. Define a decision management strategy.

2. Identify the circumstances and the need for a decision.

3. Involve relevant stakeholders in decision making.

The first of these tasks is a general one that the other two can contribute to. The main task here is the second one, *Identify the circumstances and the need for a decision*. These decision points can be easily identified based on the following viewpoints and their associated views from the model:

- *Life Cycle Model Viewpoint*: This behavioral viewpoint from *Chapter 4, Life Cycles*, may be used to identify the main decision points and, by considering any different life cycle scenarios that have been modeled, allow different options to be explored.

- *Process Instance Viewpoint*: This behavioral viewpoint from *Chapter 5, Systems Engineering Processes*, may be used in a similar way to the previous viewpoint, by identifying decision points and different scenarios.

- *Process Behavior Viewpoint*: This behavioral viewpoint, also from *Chapter 5, Systems Engineering Processes*, describes the internal behavior of specific processes. As part of this, there are explicit decision points that are identified as part of the view.

The next activity that will be discussed is analyzing the decision information.

Applying modeling to the analyze the decision information activity

The *analyze the decision information* activity comprises the following four tasks:

1. Determine desired outcomes and measurable selection criteria.

2. Evaluate each alternative against the criteria.

3. Identify the trade space and alternatives.

4. Select and declare the decision management strategy for each decision.

Each of these four tasks uses the same three sets of viewpoints – *Life Cycle Model Viewpoints*, *Process Instance Viewpoints*, and *Process Behavior Viewpoints* – that were described for the previous activity. While the previous activity was more concerned with identifying the decision points and criteria, this activity uses the same information to execute the activity. In some cases, additional information may be recorded and associated with the different views. For example, the reasoning behind why one alternative was chosen over another may be captured as a SysML note and stored as part of the overall view.

This is very closely related to the third activity of making and managing decisions, which is discussed next.

Applying modeling to the make and manage decisions activity

The *make and manage decisions* activity comprises the following tasks:

1.   Determine the preferred alternative for each decision.

2.   Record the resolution, decision rationale, and assumptions.

3.   Record, track, evaluate, and report decisions.

Again, these three tasks are so closely related to the tasks in the previous two activities that the same set of viewpoints, *Life Cycle Model Viewpoints*, *Process Instance Viewpoints*, and *Process Behavior Viewpoints*, may be used to address these tasks.

The emphasis in this activity is on capturing and recording the results, the rationale behind them, and any other information. All of this information, and any other information that may be required, may be annotated onto any view by adding SysML notes to the view. If necessary, the relevant views may be copied and saved as marked-up versions based on the decisions that have been made.

Summary of the decision management process

This process may, again, be largely met by reusing the existing views that form part of the overall MBSE approach. This is, of course, good news as it minimizes the new work that needs to be carried out but, very importantly, it ensures that all of the decision making is based on the same set of consistent information. This is another excellent example of how the single source of truth, the model, is used time and again to provide the basis for running the project.

This process also relies on the fact that additional information, such as the rationale, results, and so on, for the decision making can be added to the original information. Fortunately, SysML has a built-in mechanism for this in the form of SysML notes that may be added to any diagram.

The next process that will be discussed is the project assessment and control process.

The project assessment and control process

The main aim of the project assessment and control process is to assess the management plans that have been put in place and to monitor the progress of the project against these plans. This process is very closely related to the project planning process as it is concerned with ensuring that all the outcomes of that process are fit for purpose and are executed appropriately. The project assessment and control process is shown in the following diagram:

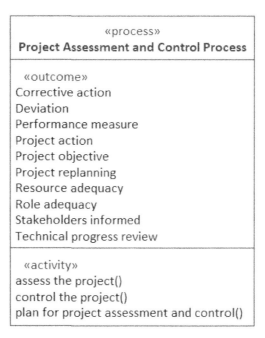

Figure 10.6 – Process content view for the project assessment and control process

The outcomes, represented by SysML properties, that are identified for this process are described as follows:

- **Corrective action** ensures that the decision management process is applied effectively.
- **Deviation** also ensures that the decision management process is applied effectively.
- **Performance measure** ensures that the measurement process is applied effectively.
- **Project action** ensures that the gate reviews are carried out effectively.
- **Project objective** ensures that the outcomes of the project planning process are implemented effectively.
- **Project replanning** ensures that the decision management process is applied effectively.
- **Resource adequacy** relates to the resources that are needed to execute the problem and ensures that they are available and valid.
- **Role adequacy** relates to the stakeholders and how they are defined in terms of their responsibilities and so on.
- **Stakeholders informed** relates to ensuring that each stakeholder has the information that is relevant to them.
- **Technical progress review** ensures that technical reviews are carried out effectively.

These outcomes are achieved by executing a number of activities, each of which comprises a number of tasks. These activities will now be discussed in more detail and reference will be made to the various modeling views that have been discussed in the book.

Applying modeling to the plan for project assessment and control activity

The *plan for project assessment and control* activity comprises the following single task:

- Define the project assessment and control strategy

This activity will be covered by the processes that are defined as part of the overall MBSE process set. This was covered in *Chapter 5, Systems Engineering Processes*, and will specifically relate to the following views from the process perspective:

- The *Process Content Viewpoint*, which identifies all the processes in the form of a process library.

- The *Process Behavior Viewpoint*, where the specific processes are defined. The processes that relate to project assessment and control are relevant here.

- The *Information Viewpoint*, where the artifacts from each process are identified, related together, and defined.

The next activity that will be discussed is assessing the project.

Applying modeling to the assess the project activity

The *assess the project* activity comprises the following 11 tasks:

1. Assess the alignment of the project objectives and plans with the project context.

2. Assess the management and technical plans against the objectives to determine adequacy and feasibility.

3. Assess the project and technical status against appropriate plans to determine the actual and projected cost, schedule, and performance variances.

4. Assess the adequacy of roles, responsibilities, accountabilities, and authorities.

5. Assess the adequacy and availability of resources.

6. Assess progress using measured achievement and milestone completion.

7. Conduct required management and technical reviews, audits, and inspections.

8. Monitor critical processes and new technologies.

9. Analyze measurement results and make recommendations.

10. Record and provide the status and findings from assessment tasks.

11. Monitor process execution within the project.

Several tasks in this list, *Task 1*, *Task 2*, *Task 3*, *Task 6*, *Task 7*, *Task 8*, and *Task 11*, are all covered by ensuring that the project schedule is being followed and implemented correctly. The viewpoints and associated views that are relevant for this are as follows:

- The *Need Context Viewpoint*, which defines the aims of the overall project, as described in *Chapter 6*, *Needs and Requirements*.

- The *Life Cycle Viewpoint* and the *Life Cycle Model Viewpoint*, which describe the life cycle and how it is to be followed, as described in *Chapter 4*, *Life Cycles*.

- The *Process Behavior Viewpoint*, which describes how each process is executed, as described in *Chapter 5*, *Systems Engineering Processes*.

These viewpoints and their associated views are the ones that were identified as being relevant for the project planning process.

The next two tasks that will be considered are *Task 4* and *Task 5*. The aim of *Task 4* is to ensure that stakeholders are identified and their involvement in the execution of the project schedule is defined, whereas *Task 5* is related to resources. These may be achieved by considering the following viewpoints from the process perspective that were described in *Chapter 5, Systems Engineering Processes*:

- The *Stakeholder Viewpoint*, which identifies the stakeholders in the form of a classification hierarchy
- The *Process Behavior Viewpoint*, which allows the stakeholder and resource involvements for each process to be defined

The next task is *Task 9*, which relates to the measurement of the project and then making recommendations based on these measurements. The measurement aspect of this task will be covered by the *measurement process*, which will be covered in the *The measurement process* section. The recommendations and further actions that are required are covered by the *decision management process*, which was discussed in the previous section.

The final task that must be considered is *Task 10*, which is concerned with recording information about the execution of the project. This will be covered by the *information management process*, which will be discussed later in this chapter.

The final activity is control the project, which is the subject of the next section.

Applying modeling to the control the project activity

The *control the project* activity comprises the following four tasks:

1. Initiate necessary actions needed to address identified issues.
2. Initiate necessary project replanning.
3. Initiate change actions when there is a contractual change to cost, time, or quality due to the impact of an acquirer or supplier request.
4. Authorize the project to proceed toward the next milestone or event, if justified.

All these tasks are covered by existing views and processes.

The first three tasks are all covered by the *decision management process* and are concerned with ensuring that this process is applied effectively.

The fourth task is concerned with the gate reviews, which are covered by the usual set of viewpoints from the process perspective, which are as follows:

- The *Process Content Viewpoint*, which identifies all the processes in the form of a process library.

- The *Process Behavior Viewpoint*, where the specific processes are defined. The processes that relate to project assessment and control are relevant here.

- The *Information Viewpoint*, where the artifacts from each process are identified, related together, and defined.

Summary of the project assessment and control process

This process is particularly interesting as it is really concerned with ensuring that the other technical management processes are applied effectively. Notice that all of the viewpoints and associated views that are mentioned here have already been discussed, or will be discussed later in this chapter, in relation to other processes from the technical management process group in ISO 15288.

The next process that will be discussed is the risk management process.

The risk management process

The main aim of the risk management process is to identify, analyze, and, where necessary, treat the risks that relate to executing the project. This risk management must also be planned and managed throughout the entire life cycle of the project.

A high-level representation of the risk management process is shown in the following diagram:

```
┌──────────────────────────────────────┐
│              «process»               │
│       Risk Management Process        │
├──────────────────────────────────────┤
│              «outcome»               │
│ Risk treatment identified            │
│ Risks analyzed                       │
│ Risks evaluated                      │
│ Risks identified                     │
│ Treatment implemented                │
├──────────────────────────────────────┤
│              «activity»              │
│ analyze risks()                      │
│ manage the risk profile()            │
│ monitor risks()                      │
│ plan risk management()               │
│ treat risks()                        │
└──────────────────────────────────────┘
```

Figure 10.7 – Process content view for the risk assessment process

The diagram here shows the process content view for the risk assessment process from ISO 15288 and is visualized using a SysML block definition diagram.

The outcomes, represented by SysML properties, that are identified for this process are described as follows:

- **Risk treatment identified**: This ensures that there is an effective strategy for risk management in place.

- **Risks analyzed**: This outcome ensures that the risks are fully understood.

- **Risks evaluated**: This monitors the progress of risks and where they are with regards to their treatment.

- **Risks identified**: This ensures that risks are able to be identified whenever they occur.

- **Treatment implemented**: This outcome ensures that identified risks are treated appropriately.

These outcomes are achieved by executing a number of activities, each of which comprises a number of tasks. These activities will now be discussed in more detail and reference will be made to the various modeling views that have been discussed in the book.

Applying modeling to the plan risk management activity

The *plan risk management* activity comprises the following two tasks:

1. Define and record the context of the risk management process.

2. Define the risk management strategy.

This activity is really key to everything that needs to be done for effective risk management. One of the themes that has run throughout this book has been to always question why something is being done and, as part of this, to always consider the context of what we are doing. Context, as has been pointed out many times, is key to successful MBSE. Notice that *Task 1* explicitly calls for the context of the risk management process to be defined. Only when this has been done can the strategy be defined, which is the subject of *Task 2*.

The whole subject of risk covers every aspect of MBSE and there are many applications of risk, including technical risk, financial risk, safety risk, security risk, and so on. Depending on which types of risk are identified, this list will differ. It is beyond the scope of this book to go into great detail concerning the different types of risk, but the modeling that we have considered so far may be applied to identify these types. The following viewpoints and their associated views are relevant for this activity:

*   The viewpoints contained in the *process perspective* in *Chapter 5, Systems Engineering Processes*. By applying the modeling approach to the risk management process, it is possible to identify the context of the risk.

*   The viewpoints contained in the *needs perspective* in *Chapter 6, Needs and Requirements*. If further investigation is required to define the context of the risks, then the *Process Context Viewpoint* from the process perspective may be enhanced by applying more viewpoints from the needs perspective.

The whole area of risk management is a prime example of where a new risk perspective could be defined. This will not be covered in any detail in this book, but some viewpoints will be identified that may form a starting point for any of you who wish to take this further.

Following on from this, the analyze risks activity is considered next.

Applying modeling to the analyze risks activity

The *analyze risks* activity comprises the following four tasks:

1. Identify risks in the categories described in the risk management context.

2. Estimate the likelihood of occurrence and the consequences of each identified risk.

3. Evaluate each risk against its risk thresholds.

4. For each risk that does not meet its risk threshold, define and record recommended treatment strategies and measures.

All of these tasks rely on the fact that an ontology must be in place that has appropriate properties for the different types of risk to be calculated. The basic formula for generic risk is as follows:

risk = likelihood of occurrence x severity of outcome

This formula, however, will vary depending on the type of risk. The formula will be captured as part of the measurement process and the associated measurement strategy.

The modeling viewpoints and their associated views that may be used as part of this analysis include the following:

*   The *Need Context Viewpoint* from the needs perspective. This provides the reason why the risks may exist and provides the context for the different types.

*   The *Validation Viewpoint* from the needs perspective. This is a crucial set of views as it captures the scenarios associated with each use case from the contexts. These scenarios may be used to identify the likelihood of occurrences and the severity of the outcomes by considering the rainy-day scenarios to explore these outcomes.

*   The *Ontology Definition Viewpoint*, which will need to be defined to cover the risk concepts.

Notice again how a combination of viewpoints and therefore views are used to achieve our desired outcomes. It is also interesting to note how we are able to use the same sets of views that we have discussed previously to address new problems.

The next activity that will be discussed is manage the risk profile.

Applying modeling to the manage the risk profile activity

The *manage the risk profile* activity comprises the following three tasks:

1. Define and record the risk thresholds and conditions under which a level of risk may be accepted.

2. Establish and maintain a risk profile.

3. Periodically provide the relevant risk profile to stakeholders based upon their needs.

The *risk profile* is concerned with allocating threshold values to the risks that have been identified. This has not been covered explicitly in this book, but it is an area where a risk ontology would be required, to define concepts and terminology associated with risk for a given organization. A key part of this ontology would be to explicitly define the different types of risk, as identified in the previous activity. Based on this ontology, it is then possible to allocate properties to ontology elements that will allow thresholds to be defined. This will also relate to the *measurement process*, which is discussed later in this chapter, and the *information management process*.

Applying modeling to the monitor risks activity

The *monitor risks* activity comprises the following three tasks:

1. Continually monitor all risks and the risk management context for changes and evaluate the risks when their state has changed.

2. Implement and monitor measures to evaluate the effectiveness of risk treatments.

3. Continually monitor for the emergence of new risks and sources throughout the life cycle.

These tasks are concerned with monitoring the risks throughout the project life cycle. Both *Task 1* and *Task 3* are related to the *analyze risks* activity, where they are to be continually monitored for the occurrence of risks.

Task 1 also relates back to the *plan risk management* activity, which defined the original context for risk. In this task, this context is monitored for any changes that may have occurred.

The evaluation of risks is also covered here by *Task 2*, which will relate closely to the measurement process.

Applying modeling to the treat risks activity

The *treat risks* activity comprises the following four tasks:

1. Identify the recommended alternatives for risk treatment.

2. Implement risk treatment alternatives for which the stakeholders determine that actions should be taken to make a risk acceptable.

3. When the stakeholders accept a risk that does not meet its threshold, consider it a high priority and monitor it continually to determine whether any future risk treatment actions are necessary.

4. Once a risk treatment is selected, coordinate management action.

All of these tasks relate to how risks are treated once they have been identified. The viewpoints and views that may be used to contribute toward this are similar to the previous activity, specifically as follows:

*   The *Need Context Viewpoint* from the needs perspective. This provides a reason why the risks may exist and provides context for the different types. This is useful here as it identifies the core use cases and, very importantly, the extensions to these core use cases that allow alternative actions to be explored.

*   The *Validation Viewpoint* from the needs perspective. This is a crucial set of views as it captures the scenarios associated with each use case from the contexts. These scenarios may be used here to explore and define alternative sets of actions that may be followed in order to treat the different types of risk.

Again, notice how we are reusing views that we have used for previous activities. This reuse is a very powerful aspect of MBSE as not only does it allow savings in terms of time and effort but it also ensures that all the information used or created is consistent as it is from a single source of truth – the model.

Summary of the risk management process

The risk management process is a very interesting one, as it justifies a whole perspective for itself, including an ontology for risk. The whole topic of risk is one that has a vast scope and multiple meanings, so it is a good candidate for its own perspective that would be bespoke for a specific organization. The core of risk management, in terms of how the risks are identified, measured, analyzed, and treated, will be different for many organizations and, therefore, will depend on the specific risk ontology for that organization.

Having stated this, however, it has also been discussed that many of the viewpoints that we have already seen in this book can be reused for the control and management of risk and many benefits can be gained from doing this. In particular, the context of risk can be modeled and defined using use cases, and then the scenarios associated with these use cases can be used for many aspects of the identification, analysis, measurement, and treatment of these risks.

The next process that will be discussed is the information management process.

The information management process

The main aim of the information management process is to capture, control, and disseminate all the knowledge, information, and data associated with the system and its development. This is of particular interest to MBSE as all the relevant knowledge, information, and data associated with a system is contained in the model as the single source of truth. In the context of MBSE, the information management process is primarily concerned with the management of the model. Indeed, all of the information management outcomes, activities, and tasks can be related directly back to *MBSE in a slide*, which was introduced in *Chapter 2, Model-Based Systems Engineering*, and has been referenced throughout this book. Refer to the following diagram:

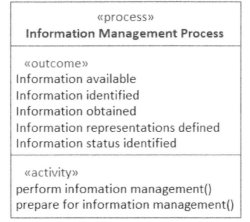

Figure 10.8 – Process content view for the information management process

The diagram here shows the process content view for the information management process from ISO 15288 and is visualized using a SysML block definition diagram.

The outcomes, represented by SysML properties, that are identified for this process are described as follows:

- **Information available**: This outcome is concerned with specific information related to particular stakeholders, which is captured as part of the viewpoint definition in MBSE in a slide.

- **Information identified**: This outcome applies to the process set and framework from MBSE in a slide, which defines the information that needs to be identified.

- **Information obtained**: This outcome relates to the control of all the information that is referred to in MBSE in a slide.

- **Information representations defined**: This outcome applies directly to the notation identified in MBSE in a slide.

- **Information status identified**: This outcome relates to the configuration of the information contained in MBSE in a slide.

These outcomes are achieved by executing a number of activities, each of which comprises a number of tasks. These activities will now be discussed in more detail and we will then reference the various modeling views that have been discussed in the book.

Applying modeling to the prepare for information management activity

The *prepare for information management* activity comprises the following five tasks:

1. Define the strategy for information management.
2. Define the items of information that will be managed.
3. Designate authority and responsibilities for information management.
4. Define the content, formats, and structure of an information item.
5. Define information maintenance actions.

All of these tasks may be related back to MBSE in a slide. The first task, *Task 1*, is concerned with defining the context and, therefore, the strategy for the information management process, which will be captured using the viewpoints from the process perspective that were defined in *Chapter 5, Systems Engineering Processes*.

The information items that are referenced in *Task 2* and their structure and content referred to in *Task 4* are all defined in the process set and framework that form the approach for MBSE. All of these are, therefore, already defined by the process perspective for the *process set* and then all of the other perspectives that comprise the MBSE framework.

The authorities that are responsible for the information management in *Task 3* and the maintenance in *Task 5* will be defined as part of the process set definition that is contained in the process perspective.

The next activity that will be discussed is the perform information management activity.

Applying modeling to the perform information management activity

The *perform information management* activity comprises the following five tasks:

1. Obtain, develop, or transform the identified items of information.

2. Maintain information items and their storage records, and record the status of information.

3. Publish, distribute, or provide access to information and information items to designated stakeholders.

4. Archive designated information.

5. Dispose of unwanted, invalid, or unvalidated information.

All of these tasks relate to model management and can be defined and captured as part of the overall process set. These tasks are also closely related to those that form part of the configuration management process that is discussed later in this chapter.

Summary of the information management process

Information management for MBSE is concerned with managing the model, as all of the information that is pertinent to developing the system is contained in the model. This can be achieved relatively easily by defining a model management process. As all of the information, knowledge, and data that is required to develop the system is contained in one conceptual place – the model – the management of the model is relatively simple compared to managing many disparate types of documents. Of course, there will still be documents that exist and the same issues will apply to those as would exist in any document-based systems engineering approach.

However, in a true MBSE approach, these documents become visualizations of views and are, therefore, part of the model. It is when documents exist that live outside the model and that contain and own information that is not contained in the model that the information management process becomes very complex. In this situation, it is not a true MBSE approach but is more likely to be model-centric or model-enhanced, as discussed in *Chapter 2, Model-Based Systems Engineering.*

The configuration management process

The main aim of the configuration management process is to identify and control configuration items that exist as part of the system development across the life cycle.

Configuration items may be directly related to particular aspects of the model and, as a consequence of this, the whole configuration management process for an MBSE approach is typically far simpler than one that is applied to a document-based systems engineering approach. Refer to the following diagram:

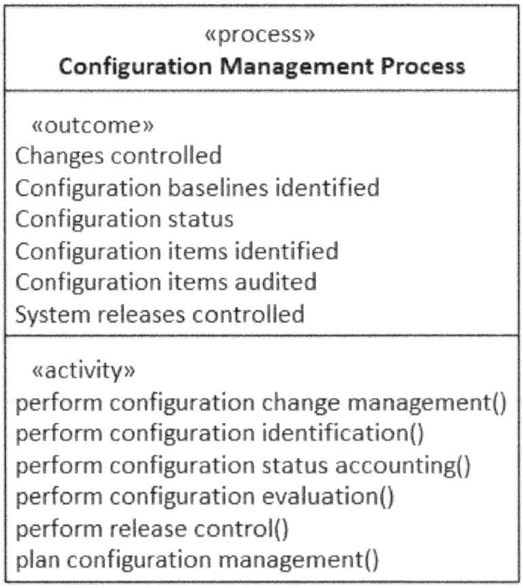

«process»
Configuration Management Process
«outcome»
Changes controlled
Configuration baselines identified
Configuration status
Configuration items identified
Configuration items audited
System releases controlled
«activity»
perform configuration change management()
perform configuration identification()
perform configuration status accounting()
perform configuration evaluation()
perform release control()
plan configuration management()

Figure 10.9 – Process content view for the configuration management process

The diagram here shows the process content view for the configuration management process from ISO 15288 and is visualized using a SysML block definition diagram.

The outcomes, represented by SysML properties, that are identified for this process are described as follows:

- **Configuration items identified**: This outcome identifies which elements in the model are classed as configuration items and will, therefore, be held under configuration control.

- **Configuration baselines identified**: This outcome allows different sets of configuration items to be grouped together into specific baselines.

- **Changes controlled**: This outcome ensures that changes made to the configuration items in the model are controlled.

- **Configuration status**: This outcome uses a configuration naming system to allow the specific status of any configuration item to be established.

- **Configuration items audited**: This outcome ensures that all configuration items and baselines can be assessed in terms of their structure and content or in terms of the processes that apply to them. Basically, this audit ensures that the MBSE approach is being applied effectively to the configuration items.

- **System releases controlled**: This outcome ensures that the system releases, themselves configuration items, are controlled, along with the other configuration items.

These outcomes are achieved by executing a number of activities, each of which comprises a number of tasks. These activities will now be discussed in more detail and reference will be made to the various modeling views that have been discussed in the book.

Applying modeling to the plan configuration management activity

The *plan configuration management* activity comprises the following two tasks:

1. Define a configuration management strategy.
2. Define the archive and retrieval approach for configuration items, configuration management artifacts, and data.

Both *Task 1* and *Task 2* here may be achieved by defining the context and defining the process effectively. This will be done by developing the views described in the viewpoints in the process perspectives that were described in *Chapter 5, Systems Engineering Processes*.

The next activity that will be discussed is closely related to this one and is the perform configuration identification activity.

Applying modeling to the perform configuration identification activity

The *perform configuration identification* activity comprises the following five tasks:

1. Identify the system elements and information items that are configuration items.

2. Identify the hierarchy and structure of system information.

3. Establish system, system element, and information item identifiers.

4. Define baselines through the life cycle.

5. Obtain an acquirer and supplier agreement to establish a baseline.

The first four of these tasks can be carried out by considering the framework that forms part of the overall MBSE approach. In *Chapter 8, Verification and Validation*, we discussed the idea of a cross-cutting concept that could be applied at the meta-model level and would allow any ontology elements to be further classified. In the examples in *Chapter 8, Verification and Validation*, the concept of a **testable element** was defined and then applied as a second stereotype to specific ontology elements from the ontology definition view in order to identify them as such. The same principle may be applied here to identify a configuration item, as shown in the following diagram:

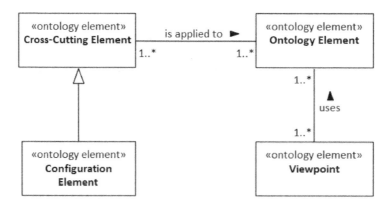

Figure 10.10 – Ontology definition view showing a configuration item

The diagram here shows an ontology definition view that identifies a configuration item as a type of cross-cutting element and is visualized using a SysML block definition diagram.

The concept of the cross-cutting element applies at the meta-model level, which is to say that it applies to conceptual model elements. In this case, these model elements are the ontology element and the viewpoint. This means that any ontology element or any viewpoint may be held as configuration items. Remember that the diagram here is generic and should be applied to the ontology and the viewpoints. This is carried out by applying the configuration item stereotype to the following two viewpoints and their associated views from the MBSE framework definition:

- The *Viewpoint Relationships Viewpoint*, which will allow specific viewpoints to be identified as configuration items. In reality, this will apply to every viewpoint that forms part of the framework and, therefore, will apply to every view that comprises the actual model.

- The *Ontology Definition Viewpoint*, which will allow specific ontology elements to be classified as configuration items. Technically, all ontology elements may be identified as configuration items but, in reality, only a subset of the ontology elements will be identified as such. This becomes important for purposes of change control, as the configuration item identifies the level of granularity that change control will be applied.

Once the configuration items have been identified (*Task 1*), the structure of these will also be known through the following:

- The *Ontology Definition Views*, in the case of the configuration items applying to ontology elements

- The *Viewpoint Relationship Views* and the *Viewpoint Definition Views*, in the case of the configuration items applying to the viewpoints

These two items also fulfill *Task 2*, which is concerned with the structure of the configuration items. Indeed, the same approach may be taken to identify the specific baselines, as required to satisfy *Task 4*.

As all of the configuration items relate to different elements in the model, they may be automatically identified by their instance classifiers in the model. Remember that all model elements are actually instances of ontology elements, which provides the basis for model consistency, therefore each model element has its own identifier that is contained as part of the model. Following on from this, each configuration item is also part of the model and will, therefore, have its own unique identifier within the model. This satisfies *Task 3* in the list.

The final task, *Task 5*, relates to the information management process, in that it identifies which stakeholders are interested in the specific information in the model (viewpoints and ontology elements) that forms the baselines that were defined as part of *Task 4*.

The next activity that will be discussed is closely related to this one and is the perform configuration change management activity.

Applying modeling to the perform configuration change management activity

The *perform configuration change management* activity comprises the following four tasks:

1. Identify and record requests for change and requests for variance.
2. Coordinate, evaluate, and disposition requests for change and requests for variance.
3. Submit requests for review and approval.
4. Track and manage approved changes to the baseline, requests for change, and requests for variance.

All of these tasks relate to the change control of the configuration items. Again, because all of the configuration items form part of the overall model, the process becomes simpler as everything is contained in the model.

In order to achieve these tasks, therefore, a change management process for the model must be put into place. This will involve defining the process, as described in *Chapter 5, Systems Engineering Processes*, where the context for the process is defined and then the process is described using the other views described in the process perspective.

Applying modeling to the perform configuration status accounting activity

The *perform configuration status accounting* activity comprises the following two tasks:

1. Develop and maintain the configuration management status information for system elements, baselines, and releases.
2. Capture, store, and report configuration management data.

These two tasks may be easily achieved when using an MBSE approach, but it will depend heavily on the use of a modeling tool. The status information for any and all of the configuration items may be held and recorded easily in the tool by defining the status as part of the model element definition in the tool, satisfying *Task 1*. Many tools will allow a configuration status to be assigned to a model element, and even tools that don't have this specific capability will allow information to be recorded against any element anyway.

Once this information is in the model, it has been captured and stored and may be retrieved easily by running a report that is part of any modeling tool, satisfying *Task 2*. Of course, the exact nature of how this is achieved will depend on the specific tool.

Applying modeling to the perform configuration evaluation activity

The *perform configuration evaluation* activity comprises the following six tasks:

1. Identify the need for configuration management audits and schedule the events.

2. Verify that the product configuration meets the configuration requirements.

3. Monitor the incorporation of approved configuration changes.

4. Assess whether the system meets baseline functional and performance capabilities.

5. Assess whether the system conforms to the operational and configuration information items.

6. Record the CM audit results and disposition action items.

This activity is primarily concerned with ensuring that the configuration items are fit for their purpose and meet their original needs. The key to this is defining the context for the configuration management process and establishing the use cases that represent the needs. This may be achieved by creating the views based on the viewpoints in the needs perspective that were described in *Chapter 6, Needs and Requirements*. This contributes to satisfying *Task 1* and *Task 2*.

Following directly on from this, the needs perspective may also be used to create a number of scenarios using validation views. These will be the two types that were discussed in *Chapter 6, Needs and Requirements*: operational scenarios that are used to establish the functional capabilities of the configuration items, and performance scenarios that are used to capture the performance capabilities. This contributes to satisfying *Task 4* and *Task 5*.

In terms of *Task 3*, which is concerned with managing changes to the configuration items, this is covered by a previously discussed activity: perform configuration change management.

The final task, *Task 6*, is covered by the information management process.

The final activity that will be discussed is the perform release control activity.

Applying modeling to the perform release control activity

The perform release control activity comprises the following two tasks:

1. Approve system releases and deliveries.

2. Track and manage system releases and deliveries.

The releases of the system will be based on a specific configuration that may be described using the viewpoints that were discussed in the *systems perspective*, which was described in *Chapter 3, Systems and Interfaces*. These views will form the basis for the approval process that is required by *Task 1* and the system may be tracked by creating instances of the configuration items, using the views described in the systems perspective, as required by *Task 2*.

Summary of the configuration management process

The configuration management process is crucial to successful MBSE as the model is a living entity that will evolve as time goes on, and this evolution must be controlled by applying effective configuration management. In a true model-based approach, the actual management is easier than in a document-based approach as all of the information is contained in a single place, which is the model. Therefore, if the model can be controlled, then so can all of the information that we intend to use to develop and deliver the system.

Also, configuration items, whether these are model elements, views, or baselines (based on configurations of the system), can all be identified and defined using the ontology, which provides the basis for consistency across the whole model.

Almost every organization will already have a configuration management process in place, so, in most cases, it will be a matter of tailoring that existing process to cope with models, rather than creating the process from scratch. Of course, all of this should be done using modeling as described in *Chapter 5, Systems Engineering Processes*.

The measurement process

The aim of the measurement process is to define how different attributes of the project will be identified and measured. The process content view for the measurement process is shown in the following diagram:

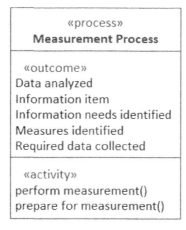

Figure 10.11 – Process content view for the measurement process

The diagram here shows the process content view for the measurement process from ISO 15288 and is visualized using a SysML block definition diagram.

The outcomes, represented by SysML properties, that are identified for this process are described as follows:

- **Data analyzed**: This outcome is concerned with ensuring that the data from the measurements is understood.

- **Information item**: This outcome is concerned with ensuring that all relevant information items that are to be measured are identified.

- **Information needs identified**: This outcome is concerned with ensuring that the context for the measurement process is adequately captured and understood.

- **Measures identified**: This outcome ensures that relevant measures are identified, based on the context.

- **Required data collected**: This outcome makes sure that the data created as a result of the measurement is managed effectively.

These outcomes are achieved by executing a number of activities, each of which comprises a number of tasks. These activities will now be discussed in more detail and reference will be made back to the various modeling views that have been discussed in the book.

Applying modeling to the prepare for measurement activity

The *prepare for measurement* activity comprises the following seven tasks:

1. Define the measurement strategy.

2. Describe the characteristics of the organization that are relevant to the measurement.

3. Identify and prioritize the information needs.

4. Select and specify measures that satisfy the information needs.

5. Define data collection, analysis, access, and reporting procedures.

6. Define the criteria for evaluating the information items and the measurement process.

7. Identify and plan for the necessary enabling systems or services to be used.

This activity relies on an effective understanding of the underlying needs of the measurement process, which can be captured by creating need views based on the viewpoints described in the needs perspective that were described in *Chapter 6, Needs and Requirements*. This satisfies *Task 1*, *Task 2*, and *Task 3*.

The needs perspective may also be used to achieve *Task 4*, as the performance scenarios that are created as part of the validation views may be used to define what these actual measures are using SysML constraint blocks for. Also, and very importantly, as these measures are captured in validation views, they may then be related directly back to the original use cases from the context, which satisfies *Task 4* and *Task 6*.

Task 5 is covered by the information management process, which was discussed previously in this chapter. The final task, *Task 7*, may be satisfied by considering the configurations of the system that were described in the systems perspective, where other enabling systems and services were identified.

Applying modeling to the perform measurement activity

The *perform measurement* activity comprises the following four tasks:

1. Integrate procedures for data generation, collection, analysis, and reporting into the relevant processes.

2. Collect, store, and verify data.

3. Analyze data and develop information items.

4. Record results and inform the measurement users.

All of the tasks for this activity rely heavily on the information management process.

The first task, *Task 1*, may again be achieved by applying the approach described in *Chapter 5*, *Systems Engineering Processes*, where the process perspective was described.

The remaining tasks, *Task 2*, *Task 3*, and *Task 4*, are all covered by applying the information management process effectively. These will also use the views that were created as part of the previous activity to define the actual measures.

Summary of the measurement process

The measurement process is concerned with defining a number of measures that can be applied to different pieces of information. As a result of this, the measurement process relies heavily on the information management process.

As with all of the processes that have been described, there is a strong need to establish the context of exactly what needs to be done for the process to achieve its ends. Again, this can be achieved successfully by applying the process perspective that was described in *Chapter 5*, *Systems Engineering Processes*.

The quality assurance process

The main aim of the quality assurance process is to ensure that all the processes, products, and services that are associated with the system are fit for their purpose. Refer to the following diagram:

```
┌─────────────────────────────────────────────┐
│                 «process»                     │
│          Quality Assurance Process            │
├─────────────────────────────────────────────┤
│  «outcome»                                    │
│  Evaluation results provided                  │
│  Incidents resolved                           │
│  Problems treated                             │
│  Project products evaluated                   │
│  QA criteria identified                       │
│  QA procedures defined                        │
├─────────────────────────────────────────────┤
│  «activity»                                   │
│  manage quality assurance records and reports()│
│  perform process evaluations()                │
│  perform product or service evaluations()     │
│  prepare for quality assurance()              │
│  treat incidents and problems()               │
└─────────────────────────────────────────────┘
```

Figure 10.12 – Process content view for the quality assurance process

The diagram here shows the process content view for the quality assurance process from ISO 15288 and is visualized using a SysML block definition diagram.

The outcomes, represented by SysML properties, that are identified for this process are described as follows:

- **Evaluation results provided**: This outcome ensures good communication with the stakeholders.

- **Incidents resolved**: This outcome covers what needs to happen if any non-conformances are discovered.

- **Problems treated**: This outcome also relates to resolving issues.

- **Project products evaluated**: Consistent with quality management policies, procedures, and requirements, this relates to evaluating the actual processes for quality assurance.

- **QA criteria identified**: This ensures that the quality attributes can be measured.

- **QA procedures defined**: This outcome ensures that processes are defined for quality assurance.

These outcomes are achieved by executing a number of activities, each of which comprises a number of tasks. These activities will now be discussed in more detail and reference will be made to the various modeling views that have been discussed in the book.

Applying modeling to the prepare for quality assurance activity

The *prepare for quality assurance* activity comprises the following two tasks:

1. Define a quality assurance strategy.

2. Establish independence of quality assurance from other life cycle processes.

Both of these tasks are covered by creating an effective process context view for the quality assurance process set and framework.

Applying modeling to the perform product or service evaluations activity

The *perform product or service evaluations* activity comprises the following two tasks:

1. Evaluate products and services for conformance to established criteria, contracts, standards, and regulations.

2. Perform verification and validation of the outputs of the life cycle processes to determine conformance to specified requirements.

Both of these tasks are satisfied by validating the context. This includes ensuring that the constraints are satisfied, *Task 1*, and ensuring that all the other needs are satisfied, *Task 2*.

Applying modeling to the perform process evaluations activity

The *perform process evaluations* activity comprises the following three tasks:

1. Evaluate project life cycle processes for conformance.

2. Evaluate tools and environments that support or automate the process for conformance.

3. Evaluate supplier processes for conformance to process requirements.

All of these tasks may be achieved by mapping the process perspective views to the source tools or supplier processes. This is another good use of the process perspective that was described in *Chapter 5, Systems Engineering Processes*.

Applying modeling to the treat incidents and problems activity

The *treat incidents and problems* activity comprises the following seven tasks:

1. Incidents are recorded, analyzed, and classified.

2. Incidents are resolved or elevated to problems.

3. Problems are recorded, analyzed, and classified.

4. Treatments for problems are prioritized and implementation is tracked.

5. Trends in incidents and problems are noted and analyzed.

6. Stakeholders are informed of the status of incidents and problems.

7. Incidents and problems are tracked to closure.

All of these tasks relate to the correct execution of the quality assurance processes. As these processes will be fully modeled, it is relatively easy to identify any non-conformances or any other issues by considering two of the views in the process perspective:

*   The *Process Behavior Views*: These views will show any deviation from the intended flow of the processes.

*   The *Information Views*: These views will show any deviation from the defined structure and content of any artifacts associated with the processes.

Also, as the stakeholders have already been identified in the stakeholder view, and their responsible activities are defined in the *Process Behavior Views* as described in *Chapter 5, Systems Engineering Processes*, then communication with stakeholders has already been established.

Applying modeling to the manage quality assurance records and reports activity

The *manage quality assurance records and reports* activity comprises the following three tasks:

1. Create records and reports related to quality assurance activities.

2. Maintain, store, and distribute records and reports.

3. Identify incidents and problems associated with product, service, and process evaluations.

Again, these tasks will be achieved by using the views defined in the process perspective, which covers the information management processes.

Summary of the quality assurance process

The quality assurance process is relatively straightforward as, once more, almost all of the information called for by the standard is contained in existing views in the model.

At the heart of any quality assurance process lies a well-defined set of processes, and we have already seen in *Chapter 5, Systems Engineering Processes*, how this is an excellent application for modeling. It is no surprise, therefore, that the process perspective is used extensively for quality assurance.

Summary

This chapter has considered, at a very high level, the management processes that are demanded by the ISO 15288 standard. It should be very clear by now that almost all of the information required to satisfy ISO 15288 is already contained in the model.

The main aim here is to show how the model views that we have been creating and discussing throughout this book may be used to help define the approach for MBSE in terms of the processes that are specified in the standard. The more that we can reuse these views, the more value we can demonstrate from each view.

Remember that MBSE is an approach, and the heart of this approach comprises the process set and the framework. Both of these have already been defined in a rigorous fashion by modeling, as has been demonstrated throughout this book.

The next chapter looks at some specific examples of methodologies that may be useful for MBSE activities.

Self-assessment tasks

1. Create a high-level process content view, based on the one in *Figure 10.1*, but add dependencies between the processes.

2. Now, tailor the process content view created in *Task 1* for your own organization.

3. Select one of the management processes and define it for your organization.

Section 4:
Next steps

This final section of the book provides direction on where you can go next in order to continue with Systems Engineering.

This section has the following chapter:

- *Chapter 11, Best Practices*

11
Best Practices

This short chapter provides information that can be used by you to continue your systems engineering work in your own organization. This includes the following:

- A brief look at modern standards, specifically ISO 15288, which has been used as a reference throughout this book

- Best practice sources such as guidelines, specifically the INCOSE Competency Framework, which provides a valuable insight into the people side of systems engineering

- A short list of organizations that actively promote systems engineering and provide valuable resources

Finally, as with all the other chapters, we shall conclude with a brief summary.

At this point in the book, we shall leave it to you to read the diagrams and understand them in order to test the modeling knowledge that you have gained from this book.

At the end of this chapter, you will have a good idea of what best practice sources exist and where to find more information about the different aspects of systems engineering.

Introducing key standards

Standards form an important part of any systems engineering endeavor and allow us to demonstrate that the approach we have taken complies with some established norm. Standards are typically mandatory in projects.

The main standard that has been used throughout this book is ISO 15288 – Systems and software engineering life cycle processes, and that will be discussed in the next section.

ISO 15288 – Systems and software engineering life cycle processes

By applying the techniques that we have introduced and discussed in this book, in particular in *Chapter 5, Systems Engineering Processes*, it is possible to capture and present some of the key views associated with the standard. The emphasis has previously been on looking at specific processes and relating MBSE techniques to them in order to demonstrate compliance. Rather than repeating these views, in particular the process content view, we shall look at some of the higher-level views for the standard, starting with the process context view:

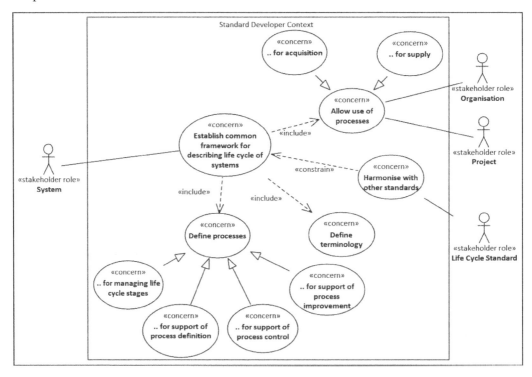

Figure 11.1 – Process context view for ISO 15288

The diagram here shows a process context view for ISO 15288, visualized using a SysML use case diagram.

There are a few key points that are worth considering:

- One of the main use cases is **Define terminology**. This is a central part of the standard and may be realized by creating an effective ontology.

- Notice how there is an explicit need to **Harmonize with other standards**, which reinforces the mapping between standards that has been covered in this book in *Chapter 5*, *Systems Engineering Processes*.

- All four types of **Define processes** that are identified here have also been covered in both *Chapter 4*, *Life Cycles*, and *Chapter 5*, *Systems Engineering Processes*.

- Again, the two types of **Allow use of processes** have also been discussed in this book.

Notice how all of the use cases for the standard have been covered by the MBSE activities described in this book. This makes the whole development of a systems engineering approach using MBSE very effective. Indeed, this in itself is an excellent example of applying MBSE.

The next diagram addresses one of these points explicitly by looking at the ontology for ISO 15288:

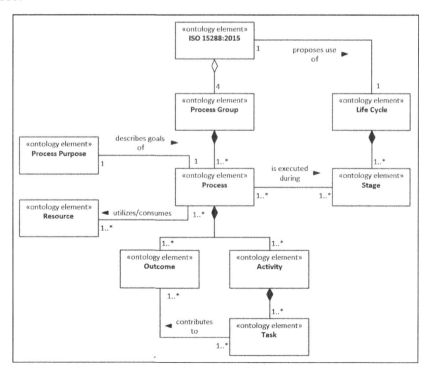

Figure 11.2 – Ontology definition view for ISO 15288

The diagram here shows the ontology definition view for ISO 15288 and is visualized using a SysML block definition diagram.

Again, the reading of this diagram is left to you, but notice how the ontology for ISO 15288 compares to the generic MBSE ontology that has been developed during this book.

The final view that we shall be considering here is the high-level process content view, as shown in the following diagram:

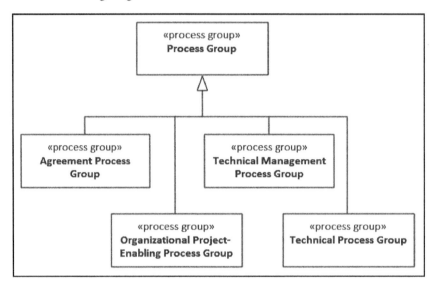

Figure 11.3 – High-level process content view for ISO 15288

The diagram here shows a high-level process content view that has been visualized using a SysML block definition diagram.

Notice how the four types of process groups have been defined and how they relate to the processes that have been used throughout this book.

Other standards

Some other standards that are worth looking at in more detail include the following:

- **CMMI for Development**: By the Carnegie Mellon University Software Engineering Institute. Available at `https://resources.sei.cmu.edu/library/asset-view.cfm?assetid=9661`. This covers process maturity and its assessment.

- **Systems and Software Engineering – Architecture Description ISO/IEC/IEEE 42010**: This is the main international standard for architecture and architecture framework descriptions.

Another topic that is strongly related to standards and also covers best practice sources is that of guidelines, which are discussed in the next section.

Introducing key guidelines

Guidelines are another very useful resource that can be used for best practice compliance. Guidelines, unlike standards, are typically not recognized at such a high level and are not typically mandated but just recommended. Having said that, they are a very powerful resource and the techniques that we can apply to modeling standards may also be used to model guidelines.

The main guideline that we shall be focusing on is the INCOSE Competency Framework, which will be discussed in the next section.

The INCOSE Competency Framework

The ISO 15288 standard focuses on the processes and life cycles associated with systems engineering, but it is also important to consider the people aspect, which can be done by looking at a competency framework. The competency framework that is most relevant for our purposes is the one that has been developed by INCOSE and is known as the **INCOSE Competency Framework**, and this is presented in this section. We shall start by looking at the context for the INCOSE Competency Framework:

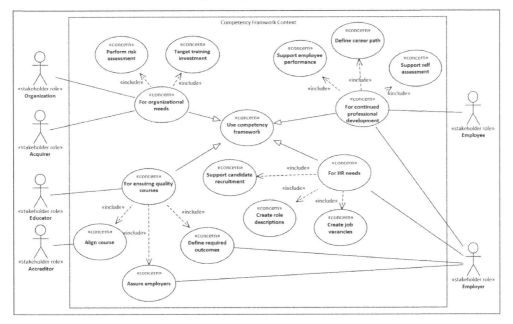

Figure 11.4 – Framework context view for the INCOSE Competency Framework

The diagram here shows the framework context view for the INCOSE Competency Framework, visualized using a SysML use case diagram.

Notice how the emphasis here is on the uses of the competency framework and the stakeholders that may be interested in each use.

The next few diagrams will focus on the main concepts that are used in the framework by considering a number of ontology definition views:

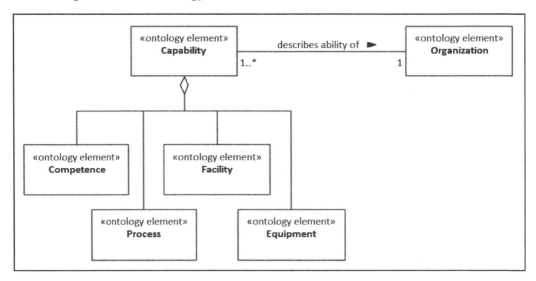

Figure 11.5 – Ontology definition view showing Capability

The diagram here shows an ontology definition view that focuses on the concept of **Capability**, visualized using a SysML block definition diagram.

Notice how **Capability** here describes the ability of an organization, which has been discussed previously in *Chapter 5*, *Systems Engineering Processes*. Notice here, however, the addition of new concepts that contribute to defining **Capability**: **Competence**, **Facility**, and **Equipment**.

The next diagram focuses on the concept of **Competence**:

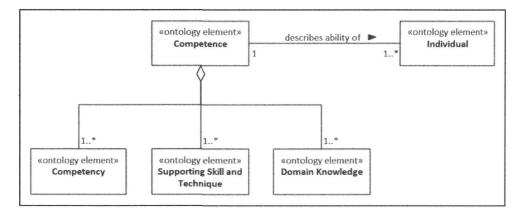

Figure 11.6 – Ontology definition view focusing on Competence

The diagram here shows an ontology definition view that focuses on **Competence** and, again, is visualized using a SysML block definition diagram.

Notice how we are evolving the ontology by focusing on a different element in each view. This is typically how an ontology will be presented, rather than trying to fit all of the concepts onto a single view. With this in mind, we'll now take a look at the structure of the framework in the following diagram:

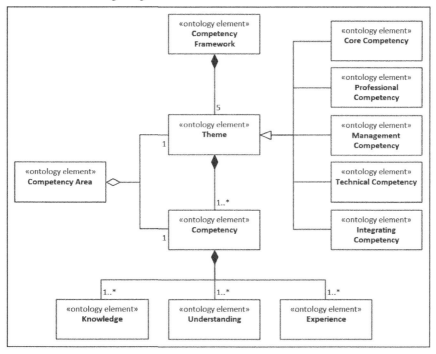

Figure 11.7 – Ontology definition view showing the structure of the framework

The diagram here shows an ontology definition view that shows the structure of the framework.

Notice how the term **Competency** relates back to *Figure 11.6*, providing consistency between the ontology definition views:

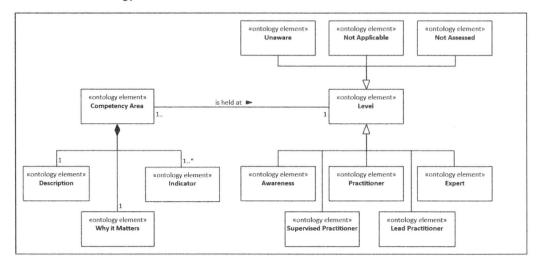

Figure 11.8 – Ontology definition view focusing on Level

The diagram here shows an ontology definition view that focuses on **Level** and is, once more, visualized using a SysML block definition diagram.

The combination of these ontology definition views provides a good overview of the framework itself, and you are encouraged to take a look at the framework and identify a set of competencies that relate to your systems engineering activities.

It is also interesting to note that there is a *Core: Systems Modelling and Analysis* competency area that covers MBSE. Notice how this is included in the *Core* theme for systems engineering, which reinforces just what an essential skill modeling, and, therefore, MBSE, is for all systems engineers.

Other guidelines

Other guidelines that are worth looking into include the following:

- *INCOSE Systems Engineering Handbook – A Guide for System Life Cycle Processes and Activities.* Version 4. INCOSE; 2016. This provides an in-depth description of the life cycle and processes that are described in ISO 15288 in the form of general guidance.

- *The UK Standard for Professional Engineering Competence (UK-SPEC)*. Available from `https://www.engc.org.uk/standards-guidance/standards/uk-spec/`. This provides the benchmark for all UK professional bodies for competence and competency frameworks.

- *Skills Framework for the Information Age (SFIA)*. Available from `https://sfia-online.org/en`. This provides a competency framework that is aimed primarily at the IT sector but has much crossover with systems engineering.

- *APM Competence Framework*. Available from `http://www.apm.org.uk/`. This provides a competency framework that is aimed primarily at the project management sector but has much crossover with systems engineering.

- *APMP Competency Framework*. Available from `http://www.apmp.org/`. This provides a competency framework that is aimed primarily at the proposal management sector but has much crossover with systems engineering.

- *OMG Systems Modeling Language (OMG SysMLTM)*. Version 1.5. Object Management Group. Available from `http://www.omg.org/spec/SysML/1.5`. This provides the original specification for the Systems Modeling Language, version 1.5.

- *A Guide to the Project Management Body of Knowledge (PMBOK® Guide)*, 4th edition. Newtown Square, PA: **Project Management Institute (PMI)**; 2008. This is the official body of knowledge concerning project management.

One other valuable set of resources alongside standards and guidelines is organizations that provide systems engineering-related resources.

Organizations

This section identifies just a few of the organizations that provide information or resources associated with systems engineering.

INCOSE is the premier global systems engineering organization. INCOSE is a not-for-profit membership organization founded to *"develop and disseminate the transdisciplinary principles and practices that enable the realization of successful systems."* At the time of writing, INCOSE has over 18,000 members worldwide across three main sectors, which are the Americas; Europe, the Middle East, and Africa; and Asia and Oceania. Each sector comprises a number of chapters and there are a total of 74 chapters spread across 35 countries.

Chapters are typically set up based on geography and are responsible for "*organizing a multitude of professional and social programs; attracting new members from industry, government and academia; supporting technical activities striving to advance the state and art of systems engineering; and, showcasing INCOSE as the international authoritative body on systems engineering that it is.*"

In real terms, INCOSE runs a number of events at the organizational, sector, and chapter levels, such as workshops, symposia, and conferences. It also produces technical services and publications (such as books, papers, posters, and journals) and provides routes to professional recognition through certification and accreditation.

INCOSE also has a number of working groups, which function within individual chapters as well as on the organizational level and are one of the main drivers behind the technical products, services, and events that are produced.

It is this combination of activities at the local chapter level, as well as at the organizational international level, that makes INCOSE stand out in the world of systems engineering.

There are several other organizations that promote systems engineering or are related to systems engineering in some way, and these include the following:

- **Institute of Electrical and Electronic Engineering** (**IEEE**): The IEEE is "*the world's largest technical professional organization dedicated to advancing technology for the benefit of humanity.*" The IEEE hosts an annual international symposium on systems engineering and has a number of systems engineering-related groups that are active in promoting the overall field of systems engineering.

- **Institution of Engineering and Technology** (**IET**): The IET has been involved in systems engineering for many years and used to run several systems engineering-related groups and professional networks. Their contribution is currently limited to publishing books and providing training courses, both live and virtually through the IET Academy. It should be noted that the IET was formerly known as the **IEE** (short for **Institution for Electrical Engineering**), which should not be confused with the IEEE!

- **Object Management Group** (**OMG**): The OMG owns, manages, and configures industry standards that relate to object technology. For the purposes of systems engineering, they are responsible for both the **Unified Modelling Language** (**UML**) and its systems engineering-related spin-off language, SysML. Interestingly, both of these standards are now full ISO standards, such is the recognition that they have achieved.

Of course, there are many more such organizations throughout the world, and this list presents just a few of them.

Summary

This chapter has completed the book by providing a good starting point for you to go and find out more about the fascinating world of systems engineering. This chapter has included some standards, guidelines, and organizations that will be of interest to those who want to continue their study of systems engineering.

Other Books You May Enjoy

If you enjoyed this book, you may be interested in these other books by Packt:

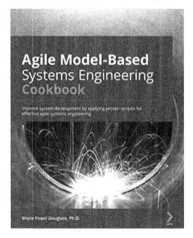

Agile Model-Based Systems Engineering Cookbook

Dr. Bruce Powel Douglass, Ph.D.

ISBN: 978-1-83898-583-7

- Apply agile methods to develop systems engineering specifications
- Perform functional analysis with SysML
- Derive and model systems architectures from key requirements
- Model crucial engineering data to clarify systems requirements
- Communicate decisions with downstream subsystem implementation teams
- Verify specifications with model reviews and simulations
- Ensure the accuracy of systems models through model-based testing

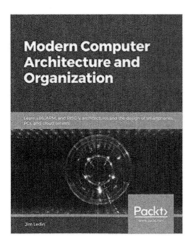

Modern Computer Architecture and Organization

Jim Ledin

ISBN: 978-1-83898-439-7

- Get to grips with transistor technology and digital circuit principles
- Discover the functional elements of computer processors
- Understand pipelining and superscalar execution
- Work with floating-point data formats
- Understand the purpose and operation of the supervisor mode
- Implement a complete RISC-V processor in a low-cost FPGA
- Explore the techniques used in virtual machine implementation
- Write a quantum computing program and run it on a quantum computer

Leave a review - let other readers know what you think

Please share your thoughts on this book with others by leaving a review on the site that you bought it from. If you purchased the book from Amazon, please leave us an honest review on this book's Amazon page. This is vital so that other potential readers can see and use your unbiased opinion to make purchasing decisions, we can understand what our customers think about our products, and our authors can see your feedback on the title that they have worked with Packt to create. It will only take a few minutes of your time, but is valuable to other potential customers, our authors, and Packt. Thank you!

Index

D

decision management process
  about 375, 384
  modeling, applying to analyze the
    decision information activity 385
  modeling, applying to make and
    manage decisions activity 386
  modeling, applying to prepare
    for decisions activity 385
  summary 386
define the project activity
  tasks 377
dependency 178
design definition process 291
designed abstract systems 6
designed physical systems 5
designs
  architectural design 266, 267
  defining 266
  detailed design 268
diagrams 40
discriminators 270
document-based systems engineering 51
document-centric systems
    engineering 52, 53
domain-specific language 84

E

enabling system 7
enterprise process group 173
evolutionary life cycle models 150
example behavioral modeling
  about 76
  behavior, modeling between
    elements 82, 83

interactions, modeling within
    system element 77-81
example structural modeling
  about 64
  blocks, describing 68-71
  blocks, identifying 64-68
  relationships, describing 71-75
  relationships, identifying 64-68
external stakeholder
  standard 193

F

flow charts 63
flow port 114
flow type definition view, properties
  name 118
  symbol 118
  type 118
  unit 118
framework 42
framework, designs
  defining 298
  framework context view,
    defining 299-301
  ontology definition view, defining 301
  ruleset definition view, defining 307
  viewpoint context view,
    defining 304, 305
  viewpoint definition view,
    defining 305-307
  viewpoint relationship view,
    defining 301-303
  viewpoints, defining 298
Framework for Architecture Frameworks
    (FAF) 127, 156, 201, 299, 338

G

S

Printed in Great Britain
by Amazon